The Rapaport–Holt Correspondence

1948–1960

Edited by

Robert R. Holt

With a Foreword by
ARTHUR A. LYNCH

Associate Editor
DANIEL W. E. HOLT

IPBOOKS.net
International Psychoanalytic Books

The Rapaport–Holt Correspondence: 1948– 1960
Copyright © 2017 by Robert R. Holt, Ph.D.

International Psychoanalytic Books (IPBooks),
25–79 31st Street Astoria, NY 11102
Online at: www.IPBooks.net

Interior book design by Maureen Cutajar
www.gopublished.com

ISBN: 978-0-9980833-5-3

Acknowledgments

So many years have passed since my discovery of a forgotten cache of old letters that it is difficult for me to recall all the people who should be thanked for helping me turn these letters into a book. I must add that the present words are being written shortly after my 99th birthday, and I am far from being exempt from the normal geriatric losses of memory and other cognitive functions and skills. The circumstance that I can still write a decent sentence, plus many readers' probable wish to indulge an old man to whom they may feel gratitude and/or loyalty, may stand in the way of giving adequate weight to the above caveat lector.

First, I must credit my dear wife Joan for having done so much to keep me not only out of the grave but also in good enough shape to do a little more work. Our sons, Daniel and Michael, continue to make my life worth living, while quietly taking over much of what I can no longer do for myself. Michael, a musician, lovingly and empathically supports and enables me in many ways.

I feel deeply grateful to my elder son, Daniel Holt, Associate Editor of the book, without whose help I could not have completed this endeavor. When the going got tough for me, he assisted with pretty much everything. In the initial phase of this project, he prepared selected letters and posted them on InternationalPsychoanalysis.net. He went through the entire manuscript several times, suggesting revisions, correcting errors, improving clarity, ensuring consistency of formatting, improving visual design, incorporating all my revisions and additions, and copy editing. He researched copyright issues and located Rapaport's grandchildren so we could obtain their permission to publish his letters. Lastly, he facilitated communications between me, Arnold Richards, Tamar Schwartz, and Arthur Lynch.

I am indebted to Arnold Richards and his excellent staff, especially Tamar Schwartz and Lawrence L. Schwartz. They were deeply involved in this project: assisting in the compilation of letters, scanning, typing and formatting, organizing the sections, helping to design and format this document, and publicizing its publication. Thanks also to Arthur A. Lynch for his foreword and for his help in the later stages of the project.

Besides David Rapaport, I am indebted to my teacher, Hadley Cantril, who was responsible for my becoming not just a psychologist, but one with a wider than usual conception of that role. As my first important mentor, he inspired a broad and humanistic as well as scientific outlook, making it possible for me to follow my own bents. He directed me to Harvard for my graduate work with a fine faculty, notably Gordon Allport, Garry Boring, Bob White, and especially my thesis supervisor and inspiring role model, Harry Murray. Also a major influence in numerous ways was a roster of gifted fellow students—too many to acknowledge individually in this small space, but see my autobiography, in Walker, 1993. A curious reader can learn a lot from that source.

I should not fail to acknowledge and thank my sources of financial and institutional support, notably the Ford Foundation and the National Institutes of Health. The former awarded a program grant to support the new-born Research Center for Mental Health, 1953–1958, while the latter supplied two multiyear program grants and several project grants, as well as an annual Research Career Award to me from 1962 until 1988. New York University also supported my work throughout those years.

With more specific relevance to this book, I am indebted to Arnold Richards and his excellent staff, especially Tamar Schwartz and Lawrence L. Schwartz. They have supported and assisted me in countless ways, including gentle but persistent prodding, over a period of some years. I owe them apologies, as well, for my special kinds of fussiness and demandingness. If roles had been reversed, I doubt that I would have been as uncomplainingly helpful. Thanks also to Arthur A. Lynch for his foreword and for his help in the later stages of the project.

This book would not have been possible without generous funding provided by the American Psychoanalytic Foundation through the American Psychoanalytic Association.

Contents

CHAPTER 3

II. NEW YORK AND STOCKBRIDGE

CHAPTER 4

CHAPTER 5

CHAPTER 6

III. FINAL PROJECTS AND ENDINGS

CHAPTER 7

CHAPTER 8

FOREWORD

By Arthur A. Lynch

THE HISTORY AND SCOPE OF THE CORRESPONDENCE

The historical context of this correspondence reflects one of the summits of Ego Psychology in North America. It occurs at a time when David Rapaport was in the most productive years of his demanding and inspiring career. It must be noted that Rapaport owed much of this culmination to a movement begun by Karl A. Menninger and Robert P. Knight. Menninger found Rapaport in the Osawatomie State Hospital and brought him to the Menninger Foundation. Knight took him from Topeka to Stockbridge and nurtured his research efforts at the Austen Riggs Center.

Rapaport's prolific contributions offer the reader an invaluable sense of the breadth and depth of his thinking. Rapaport took a systematic approach to the study of psychoanalytic theory, especially with regard to the ego functions of affects, memory, thought, and learning. To these contributions he added the translations of separate works by Heinz Hartmann, Erik Erikson, and Otto Fenichel. When one considers the output of many of the students he attracted, like Robert R. Holt, George S. Klein, Roy Schafer, Merton M. Gill, Lester Luborsky, Philip Holtzman, and Benjamin Rubinstein, the aggregate contribution to theory is huge. Rapaport's influence continues to be evident in the work of the students of the next generation of psychoanalytic scholars, such as Leo Goldberger, Irving Paul, Fred Pine, Donald Spence, Morris Eagle, Nancy Goldberger, and Robert J. Langs. Then there are the staff members of the Research Center for Mental Health at NYU: Judith Antrobus, Harriet Linton Barr, Hartvig Dahl, Harry Fiss, Sydney Segal, and David Wolitzky. Also influenced were graduate students at the Research Center, who worked on a range of projects. These include Sheldon Bach, Phebe Cramer, Yael Danieli, Carol Eagle, Rita Eagle, Darlene Ehrenberg, Steven Ellman, David Fitzgibbons, Stanley Grand, Ricardo Hofer, Helene Kafka, John Kerr, Leah B. Lapidus, Paul Lippmann, Frances Lippmann, Judith Rabkin, John Munder Ross, George Silberschatz, Doris K. Silverman, Harriette Weintraub Kaley, and Carl Zlatchin. Finally, on the periphery of this effort, three figures must be added who helped hold the Menninger Foundation together throughout the years after Rapaport left: Robert Wallerstein, Otto F. Kernberg, and Glen Gabbard.

When one looks at the cumulative effects of this overall alliance, it is easy to recognize that their contributions essentially defined the new directions of psychoanalysis in North America, taking it well beyond the Ego Psychology they began with. What is important here is not just the quantity of work produced but the quality of that work. Rapaport sent his students into the world with a mission that he taught by example: "A fierce *devotion to the search for truth,* through science" (Holt, 2012, p.2). In that spirit, this group jointly and separately challenged many of the main beliefs of the day, including the place of reified psychic structures and agencies, drives and energetic mental functions, and many other cherished beliefs within psychoanalytic metapsychology.

Rapaport and his first generation of students remained outside of the mainstream primarily because another line of American psychoanalytic theorists had taken on many of the same issues. That line, also, chose Freud's work as its main focus and followed the developments through their teachers, who were Hartmann, Ernst Kris, and Rudolph Loewenstein. That group consisted of Charles Brenner, Leo Rangell, Jacob Arlow, David Beres, Martin Wangh, and their colleagues and associates. It is striking that Klein, Holt, Gill, and Schafer, on one side, and Brenner and his colleagues, on the other, failed to recognize the convergence of their approaches to psychoanalytic theory without any collaboration and often in conflict with one another. Or perhaps this was just another example of the politics of exclusion (Richards, 1999). The letters of the present correspondence interestingly enough represent the same theoretical lineage and ultimately a similar outcome of theoretical change.

David Rapaport left the Menninger Foundation, and at the invitation of Robert Knight, moved to the Austen Riggs Center, in 1948. He kept in touch with former students and colleagues in Topeka, most frequently with Robert R. Holt. Holt had been recruited by Rapaport and had been at the Menninger Foundation from 1947 until 1953, when he moved to NYU to co-direct the Research Center for Mental Health with George Klein.

In his introduction to this volume, Holt points out that, in the letters, the reader will observe how Rapaport functioned as a teacher and mentor, at the same time treating his younger colleague as an equal whose critique of his own work was to be welcomed and respected. The reader will watch how Rapaport developed and reworked his greatest theoretical contributions, especially the critical and synthetic review of major problem areas in psychoanalysis. One can appreciate how he made good use of sympathetic if unsparing criticism, which was modeled on his own critiques of Holt's efforts. Always working to reveal and secure Freud's best and most lasting work, Rapaport shows his willingness, in these letters, to take seriously some fundamental problems in the basic structure of metapsychology, which Holt was beginning to formulate at the time and which he developed more fully in the years after Rapaport's death.

If we glance ahead, we see a good example of this theoretical change in the October 28 and November 11, 1954, minutes of the staff seminars at the NYU Research Center for Mental Health. The staff members of the Research Center, Holt, Klein, Rubinstein, Spence, and Linton, were then in frequent correspondence with Rapaport at Austen Riggs. At the time they were carefully reviewing Freud's *Interpretation of Dreams*, Chapter VII of the recently published Volumes 4 & 5 of the *Standard Edition*. There was a problem: In their review of Chapter VII, questions emerged about consistency in defining primary and secondary thought processes. Holt had already had some doubts about the theory's consistency and other problems before he left the Foundation but he had struggled quietly with Rapaport over them. Rapaport had done a masterful job explaining his point of view on the theory.

But let's return to the staff seminars of October and November 1954. In the minutes of the first meeting we find in attendance George S.

Klein, Harriet Linton, and Robert R. Holt. The focus of the discussion was on primary and secondary process, in Chapter VII of *The Interpretation of Dreams*. Drawing from two paragraphs on page 597, Holt quotes Freud's discussion of the two fundamentally different kinds of thought processes. These occur in dreams, symptom formation, and waking life. "One of these produces perfectly rational dream-thoughts, closer to normal thinking; while the other treats these thoughts in a manner which is in the highest degree bewildering and irrational" (Freud, 1900, p. 597). In the next passage, Freud seems to be saying that the primary process is involved only in a defensive way in the production of dreams and neurotic symptoms, while the thought process producing the latent thoughts underlying a hysterical symptom or the dream is "perfectly rational and valid," just like "normal thinking," about which Holt noted that it sounds as if he means secondary process. After some discussion the group concluded that Freud was attempting to convince his reader that under the chaos and seemingly surreal impulses of dreams and symptoms, there is something "intelligible and determined." Under the manifest dream, childhood wishes and worries come to foreground. Likewise, the ungovernable emotional excess masking the hysteric's suffering is mainly from "reminiscences." But the group felt that Freud had overstated his case. This meeting turned to further considerations of primary and secondary processes, and the structures and transactions involved in displacement, condensation, and symbolic formation. This topic continued into the next seminar meeting and the group was joined by Rubinstein and Spence. Their conclusions were reinforced and they sent the minutes of the meetings with their considerations off to Rapaport.

Rapaport read the minutes carefully and agreed: Freud overstated his case. But he offered another way to look at it. "Let us add to this that I agree fully . . . that 'Freud overstated his case.' The latent dream thought which is perfectly rational is nothing else but what would happen if the latent dream thought would become fully systematized without censorship intervening in secondary-process terms. *The primary process manifestations in the dream are there because the secondary process is not working.*"[1]

The "not working" is due to the censorship. Merton Gill speaks about regression in these terms: "the higher mental processes are countercathected." That is to say, "a barrier is set up against the thought processes taking their usual course and being translated into secondary process terms."

In this sense, the primary process is not a "defensively organized stratagem of thinking" but rather the manifestations of the primary process in dreams and psychoses are a result of certain defensive processes.

In a letter to Holt, Rapaport wrote, "[try to see it as an effort to link what you are concerned with, with a number of issues that I have been concerned with and tried to work out. Assume for the moment that I was trying to be helpful by indicating in what terms I have tried to struggle with the same problems. If I would have more leisure it would have come out less peculiarly."

When this illustration is put into context we realize that, at the time, critique of psychoanalytic theory was not an option in most places. One could not dissent easily. Looking at the period (1940–1960) using an altered version of Martin Bergmann's (1993) taxonomy of psychoanalytic innovators we can see that the "heretics" had long since left the psychoanalytic landscape. Some of the "modifiers" were in a pitched battle to open the critique of theory up to consideration in a broader context, but they (e.g., Karen Horney, Harry Stack Sullivan, Sandor Rado, Melanie Klein, Wilfred Bion) remained in disparate discrete groups outside of the mainstream. Other "modifiers" (e.g., Sándor Ferenczi; Hartmann, Kris, and Loewenstein; Anna Freud, Leo Stone, and Phyllis Greenacre) altered the theory, practice, or both, but stayed within the boundaries of the mainstream profession. They were making changes within the existing theory to correct for obvious problems. Finally, there were those in the mainstream who acted to preserve and stultify the homeostasis of the conservative stance. This group was in certain ways like its predecessors but in other ways it was quite unique, more zealous and possessed.

---

[1] Italics added.

Robert Prince (2009) discusses these phenomena quite clearly.[2]

There was a persistent nagging doubt that took different forms in the correspondence and in the larger group itself. Rapaport was perhaps the most dedicated to keeping Freud's broad theory intact. But his first generation of students (i.e., Holt, Gill, Klein, Schafer) were less satisfied with the existing theory and sought to make their own contributions. They stood between the two different groups of modifiers. They let the data guide their assumptions and worked to empirically verify their hypotheses. But, as mentioned, at the time a coercive and immutable undercurrent discouraged disagreement.

The case of Benjamin Rubinstein is a good example of this intolerance. Rubinstein had his psychoanalytic training at the Topeka Institute and paid heavily for writing a thesis critiquing Freud's psychoanalytic theory of sexuality. To the training analysts at his oral exam it was a scandal, and his graduation was postponed. Holt (1997) notes that "in the end he was allowed to substitute a conventional case history," and was graduated in March 1953. This episode was not an incentive for curiosity.

The Story Begins

The story of the book opens with a descriptive encounter of the first meeting between Robert Holt and David Rapaport, in the early 1940s at the Harvard Psychological Clinic. Rapaport was delivering a paper on diagnostic testing. Holt was finishing his graduate work and on the clinic's staff. The clinic was run by Henry Murray. After this brief encounter, Holt graduated and went to work for the Department of Agriculture doing survey research. After the war, he told Murray he wanted to get back to

---

[2] Psychoanalytic refugees, who endured persecution and exile during World War II, were essential in reviving and maintaining the psychoanalytic movement in the US. Prince (2009) puts forth the premise that the traumatic nature of their life-threatening transition made it impossible to mourn the multiple losses they incurred. Prince believed the trauma was often "represented in psychoanalytic ideas and enacted in institutions within the context of delayed or incomplete mourning." Their psychoanalytic identity was held together by their theory and practice. In the case of Paul Federn and Fritz Wittels we see a zealot's attachment to psychoanalytic ideology.

working on clinical issues. Unbeknownst to him, Rapaport contacted Murray looking for staff for the Topeka VA hospital where Karl Menninger had the aim of creating the "world's largest psychiatric residency program." Murray recommended Holt. It was 1946; Holt got two calls while at work. One was from a Dr. David Rapaport, who set up a meeting in which he conducted a formal interview with Holt. He asked about Holt's experience at the Harvard Clinic, his interest in psychoanalysis and in diagnostic testing; Holt was comfortable with the TAT but only slightly familiar with the Rorschach. Rapaport seemed pleased and told him about Menninger's vision.[3] Next, the other phone call: "Dr. Karl Menninger wants to talk to you!" someone shouted. No one in that shop had heard of Rapaport, but everyone knew Dr. Karl A. Menninger and they were impressed. Holt recalls: "Karl spoke with his usual expansive seductiveness: both Olympian and welcoming, telling me about the great new enterprise they were beginning: a *Menninger School of Psychiatry* now (biggest in the world); and a *School of Clinical Psychology* later. He was offering me not just a job but the opportunity to enlist in this historic endeavor on the ground floor, as if it were a great privilege (which it was)." Holt packed up his belongings, his wife Louisa, and their newborn daughter, and moved to Topeka in 1946 to live in the VA barracks and learn diagnostic testing. Louisa joined Rapaport's research department. Holt worked half-time for the VA hospital, half for Menninger.[4]

In 1947, the funding for the Selection Project[5] allowed Rapaport to hire Holt to work with Lester Luborsky half-time in the research department; William Morrow and other part-time staff for the project were added later. After a few months of intensive training in diagnostic

---

[3] From Holt's "Notes for Reminiscence of David Rapaport" on the 40th anniversary of the Rapaport Klein Study Group.

[4] Other members of the newly reorganized department were Robert Challman, the head of the department, and Michael Dunn, Milton Wexler, and Martin Mayman.

[5] The Selection Project was conceived of by Rapaport, Karl Menninger, and Robert Knight and started at the same time as the School of Psychiatry to take advantage of the size of the new operation. Its aim was to provide data to rethink the traditional local methods of selecting young physicians for training in psychiatry, testing and interviewing them in essentially the same way as patients.

psychological testing, supervised by Rapaport, the group was promoted to supervise the newly arriving students in the Menninger Foundation School of Clinical Psychology ("MFSCP").

The next year, however, brought dramatic changes. Rapaport, who had been with the Menninger program since 1939, had decided to join the group who left the Foundation for Austen Riggs, the year before. This group included Knight, Gill, Brenman, Schafer, and Allen Wheelis. Erik Erikson also soon joined them. This, it could be argued, was the new A-Team.

The correspondence begins on November 2, 1948, with the just-transplanted Rapaport asking Holt for some help in to finding a psychologist, Babette Whipple. He took the opportunity to ask about the work on the Selection Project and how Louisa's thesis was progressing. Rapaport was also keeping track of his Selection Project and his staff, and ended asking, "won't you write?" Holt responded on November 8 with much of the history cited above. He had been inspired by Rapaport and carefully saved the correspondence. He remembers, "Somehow, he and I hit it off personally and professionally. . . I felt an enormous boost in my self esteem when he offered friendship by asking me to call him 'David.'" Holt notes that the early letters were neither intimate nor plentiful but, as the years passed and their lives changed in complex ways, the letters reveal a growing friendship and a deepening intellectual partnership, with lots of room for critique and disagreement.

In the December 15th letter, Rapaport writes as the Secretary of the new Division of Clinical and Abnormal Psychology of the APA to inform Holt that the Executive Committee has appointed him Chairman of the Committee on Examinations. Holt thanks him and asks for a copy of his draft of "Organization and Pathology of Thought." The collaboration is now taking shape. By 1949, Holt is responding to letters from Rapaport and reports that the research department is running well under Sibylle Escalona's leadership; George Klein, who had joined the department shortly after Holt was back from vacation, and had afforded some relief to Holt; and the MFSCP had its growing pains. Philip Holzman and Herbert Schlesinger, students in the first class, both completed their dissertations under George Klein's direction. 'These were on diagnostically dependent newly defined distinctive perceptual and cognitive patterns which could be seen on psychological tests revealed distinctive patterns (hysterical vs. obsessional) indicating differences in perceptual and other cognitive functions."

In a letter dated June 23, 1950, Rapaport comments on a draft Holt wrote for presentation at the Topeka Psychoanalytic Society in 1949. Rapaport notes that Holt's discussion of criteria for the stimulus barrier had manifold dynamic roots and spoke to the issue of autonomy. Rapaport says that the "problem" lay in "choosing the conceptual level for description." By choosing the lens used by Adorno et al., Rapaport suggests, Holt may have missed the opportunity to study the hierarchy of motivations, as they had missed it. Illumination of such a hierarchy may well be "an avenue to dynamic expression of traits, character-pictures, ego-attitudes, etc.," clearing up a great deal of conceptual confusion among Murray, Allport, Eduard Spranger and Wilhelm Dilthey, Ernst Kretschmer and Stanley Smith Stevens with an additional comparison between them and ego psychology. Rapaport encourages Holt by calling this the most needed contribution in the barely defined field of personality and character. On June 29th another letter comes offering at first constrained praise and then critiquing Holt's chapter on the TAT. While good in many ways it "displays . . . far less your theoretical, integrative capacity than the other. . . I do not think that you 'ran true to form.'"[6]

Holt replies in a July 31, 1950, letter that he has sent a copy of his "Sheldon review" and is curious about Rapaport's treatment of Norbert Wiener and Clyde Kluckhohn-Henry A. Murray. Holt soon turns to the issue of hierarchy and autonomy and his concern that Rapaport may be heading down the road to "nominalism" with his assumption that the emergence of a "hierarchically higher order of generalization" is actually

---

[6] Rapaport reveals that he is compelled to be sharp because Holt has told him that he wanted to do theory. He praises Holt's gathering and systematization of abstractions; the next step, however, is to further generalize and establish the common background. In a note to the reader, Holt points out that he never transformed that chapter into a book but the idea stayed with him. In Chapter 3 of his book on *Primary Process Thinking* (2009), he offers his final attempt at a theory of thinking.

autonomous.[7] What troubles Holt here is the issue of structure in ego. This causes him confusion (of concretistic origins), since the parts of the structure [i.e., of ego] are themselves abstracted functions of the total organism. Holt's way out of this problem is his realization that substance and process are indistinguishable: what is function or process on one level (e.g., biochemical) is structure on another (e.g., the cytological); constancies of function produce some kind of steady state that concretely gives rise to an appreciable structure. And with this last monumental struggle (which Ronald Fairbairn and Harry Stack Sullivan were struggling with separately) the topic is switched to who will review Rapaport's book.

By August 8, 1950, Rapaport responds to Holt's doubts about autonomy, the ego, and other concerns, all the while wondering "What's next?" In connection with Holt's review of Sheldon, Rapaport discusses *Blessed is the Match* by Marie Syrkin (1948), an account of the history of the extermination of Jewry and Jewish culture. Rapaport reports on reading about the horrors of the Warsaw ghetto, feeling overwhelmed but still reading. He tells Holt, "I can't tear myself away from the topic: neither my feelings about my people, nor the impotent curiosity to understand what happened here psychologically let me off easy." He comes away with the conviction that "hope can be our worst enemy and ally of our destroyer; how rebellious distrust only can grasp and envisage the fate in store for us; how situations can rob man of all dignity and yet how belief in ideas can retain and raise, above all carnage and filth, human dignity." With regard to Holt's review, Rapaport explains, hesitantly at first, that he finds a maturity in Holt's writing of this review. "It has an authority and inner validity only given by [personal] maturity." This kind of writing is not something that once possessed endures but must be struggled for continuously. The hesitancy, he notes, was tied to his impression of Holt's response to him, which sometimes felt as accepting and sometimes rejecting. The rejection seemed to Rapaport based on an image of him rather than

---

[7] "If concept A is on a higher level of abstraction than concepts a & b, it is in a formal sense only autonomous of them; empirically, it may be quite dependent on the lower-level existents and thus genetically and prognostically have no autonomy."

on the argument. So his fear of speaking to him about maturity is his fear of Holt's object-related response: not one of "the admiration of an equal but a condescension of a pretentious 'old one.'"

Next Rapaport turns to the discussion of *autonomy*. He agrees with Holt that many of the facets forming his concept of autonomy are based on observations on concept-formation. Likewise, to confuse an abstraction-system, which is autonomous from the concrete ideas that are its referents, cannot (i.e., must not) be confused with the genetic formations (which are both the referents of the concrete ideas and the abstraction-system). Autonomy in the abstraction-system does not imply autonomy in the genetic formations "which are its referents—but it requires a proof that there is such a relationship between these referents." He agrees with Holt that autonomy is always relative and has spoken about "relative autonomy," indicating that "the 'controlling organizations' are in a sense 'controlled organizations.'"

Now there appears a gap in the correspondence of about six months. During this time Holt was going through a personal crisis: his marriage ended and he reentered analysis, and he was unaware of what was going on in Rapaport's life. Rapaport had come to Topeka early in 1951 to lecture, but Holt had not felt up for a private talk. Rapaport wrote on March 3, 1951, but Holt was unable to respond. Even though they were close he could not burden Rapaport with his personal problems. Rapaport had written again on April 25 to let Holt know his book was out and Holt responded (April 27), with evident annoyance, "keep your pants on."[8] Rapaport responded satirically on April 30, "My pants were not in danger of falling off." He went on to say more caringly, "Pants or no pants, I want you to know that I would like to know whatever you feel like letting me know about what goes on with you." And once again on May 17, after reading Holt's review of Erikson's *Childhood and Society* (1951e) he wrote to congratulate Holt

---

[8] Holt's impatience was admittedly that he had a lot to say and it would take him the better part of a full evening to write it down, an evening that at that time he could not spare. He nonetheless thanked Rapaport for inquiring and sent his great satisfaction that Rapaport's latest book (*Organization and Pathology of Thought*) was finally out.

and told him that Erikson's material has the kernels of the direction in which Holt's development may lie.

The next day (May 21, 1951), Rapaport received the heartwarming letter from Holt of May 17. His mood shifted. Holt spoke of how much Rapaport's friendship and appreciation mean to him. The book (Rapaport, 1951a) arrived on May 22, 1951, and Holt had not expected to find such a formidable work. He ended the letter with some of the good and bad news at MFSCP. The first two graduates would be Nathan Greenbaum, and then Milton Horowitz. Then, Bille (Sibylle Escalona) would be leaving and they were currently looking for a successor. The prospects of the research department were uncertain. The brothers Karl and Will, among other senior physicians, had a different conception about the kind of research undertaking that should be built. Holt told Rapaport that "we are losing our 'big guns' and may not have the inherent group cohesion and driving purpose without them that may be needed to withstand pressures which I feel may be directed against us in the coming months." In two years' time the Selection Project would be complete; Holt wondered, what then?

These vignettes highlight some of the many stories in the correspondence. But the correspondence was not just a story of the people of the day. It was an historical methodological handbook on the way this group approached psychoanalysis as a general psychology always in need of validation.

TOPICS OF THE BOOK

Threads of diverse topics weave themselves through this correspondence. In the first period 1948 to 1953 (Chapters 1, 2, and 3), the themes include the stimulus barrier, Adorno's theory of the authoritarian personality, the ego and ego autonomy, regression in the service of the ego, states of consciousness, the hierarchy of motivations, psychoanalytic application to the TAT and the Rorschach, projection and projective techniques, the underlying mechanistic versus organismic assumptions (Kant versus Whitehead), channels of communication, and problems with the structural theory. To these we can add Rapaport's memories from his formidable arrival in the US, his first job, and his first years at Menninger's; the beginning work on the Holt-Luborsky book (*Personality Patterns of Psychiatrists*), and problems of selecting persons for training in psychiatry and psychoanalysis.

The period between 1954 and 1956 are the beginning years for Holt at the Research Center for Mental Health at NYU. The themes of this period (Chapters 4, 5, and 6) include work on immediate memory and reminiscence, the theory of thinking (primary and secondary processes) and its relation to metapsychology and clinical measurement, the tension reduction and the reflex arc, and problems of research on psychoanalysis.

The period also covers Rapaport's struggle over whether or not to accept an invitation to write a chapter on psychoanalysis in Sigmund Koch's book on theories of psychology.[9] This chapter, "Project A," was prepared between 1954 and 1957. The decision of whether to do the chapter was manifold. Two primary difficulties stood out: Could the material be adequately expressed in the outline Koch was using for all contributors? And could the magnitude of the topic be contained to a single chapter? Participation in "Project A" was accepted by Rapaport but involved the heavy collaboration of Holt who read every new draft, as did Gill, Klein, and Schafer. This chapter was later expanded into a monograph,[10] which continued to rely on Holt's critiques of Rapaport's drafts as well as Rapaport's responses.

Another theme of the period covered the methodology of psychoanalysis. Chapter 6 (1956) focuses on the Selection Study and the enormous work in the interpretation of the findings and the writing of the manuscript, as well as plans for isolation research. The chapter also looks closely at a study proposed by Leo Berman and a critique of Kenneth Colby's paper on metapsychology.

---

[9] Koch, S. (Ed.) (1959). Psychology: A study of a science. Study I: Conceptual and systematic. Volume 3: Formulations of the person and the social context. New York: McGraw-Hill, pp. 55–183.

[10] Rapaport, D. (1960). The structure of psychoanalytic theory: A systematizing attempt. Psychological Issues, Vol. II, No.2 Monograph 6. New York: International Universities Press.

In the final section, the letters cover the period from 1957 until 1960. The topics cover perceptual isolation research, autonomy from the drives and from the environment, developmental psychology, and conflicts over the dissemination of copies of personal letters without clear personal consent. The letters of 1958 to 1960 deal with the Rapaport-Gill paper on Metapsychology and the Holt review of Ernest Jones's Freud biography. They delve deeper into the ego, self, and identity; neutralization and binding, regression in the service of the ego; activity and passivity; motivation, repression and subliminal registration; sensory deprivation, isolation; states of consciousness and dreams; among other issues.

The Rapaport-Holt Correspondence:
A Master-Apprentice Collaboration on
Psychoanalytic Theory

Late in July 2011, I had an unexpected call from Arnold D. Richards, an old acquaintance. He asked if I happened to have any unpublished papers on psychoanalysis; if so, he offered to make them available to their most likely audience through International Psychoanalysis. It happened that, for about a year, I had been trying to find a publisher for a collection of letters between David Rapaport and me during his final 12 years (1948–1960). When I mentioned that to Dr. Richards, he at once expressed interest, and at last here we are.

MY RELATIONSHIP WITH RAPAPORT

When I was a graduate-student member of Henry A. Murray's staff at the Harvard Psychological Clinic in the early 1940s, David Rapaport, as one of many stellar visitors, gave a talk about his approach to testing. (Despite its name, Murray's "clinic" saw no patients but was devoted to psychoanalytically oriented research on personality with Harvard students as subjects.) Several years later, Rapaport asked Murray to recommend people to be trained by him for the psychological staff of the VA hospital, and Prof. Murray gave him my name. My memory of Rapaport's presentation was vivid enough for me to be eager to accept an invitation to an interview, though my hopes were not high in light of my total lack of experience with patients. As I soon saw in my job interview, however, Rapaport paid little attention to the prior training and practice of his recruits, some of whom had had years of experience—all of us had to learn diagnostic testing of psychiatric patients in *his* way.

That interview took place in 1946, when I was working in my first post-PhD job, at Rensis Likert's ground-breaking public opinion research enterprise in the US Department of Agriculture. Rapaport was then looking for staff members for the Winter Veterans Administration (VA) Hospital in Topeka, which was being taken over by Karl A. Menninger (universally called "Dr. Karl") to house the world's largest psychiatric residency program. It was a time of grandiose projects conceived and run by charismatic, gifted leaders. Part of Dr. Karl's big scheme was to complement the Menninger Foundation School of Psychiatry with Menninger Foundation Schools of psychiatric social work, adjunctive therapies, and clinical psychology. The last was led by Rapaport but, like the others, centered at Winter Hospital and affiliated with the nearby University of Kansas.

After a few months of intensive training and supervised testing of patients, I and other recruits were pressed into service as supervisors of the newly arrived students in the Menninger Foundation School of Clinical Psychology. They were getting their clinical training in the VA hospital. In 1947, Rapaport invited me to join the staff of his Research Department at Menninger's, as we all called the Clinic/Hospital/Foundation, to take the leadership of the Selection Project (see Holt & Luborsky, 1958). He and Dr. Karl had started that research at the same time as the School of Psychiatry, at Rapaport's urging, to take advantage of the size of the new operation by rethinking the traditional local method of selecting young physicians for training in psychiatry: testing and interviewing them in essentially the same way as patients. Soon Lester Luborsky joined us, later William R. Morrow and a couple of other part-timers. Rapaport met with our little team frequently, not telling us what we were to do but facilitating discussions of how to proceed. That was typical of his way of leading the Research Department: immersing himself in each project so that he could give advice, but doing his best to train autonomous researchers.

Somehow, he and I hit it off personally as well as professionally. I of course looked up to him (as did virtually everyone else on both staffs) as if he were of my father's generation though he was only six years my senior, and was in awe of his astonishing and varied gifts. I felt an enormous boost in my self esteem when he offered friendship by asking me to call him "David." (I have described that episode and its significance for me in my Memoir [Holt, 1967].)

And then, in 1948, David Rapaport left Topeka, KS, for Stockbridge, MA. He joined a select group who had made the same exodus from the Menninger Foundation the year before with Robert P. Knight, at that time Chief of Staff. Knight took with him some of Menninger's most brilliant staff members: the team of clinical researchers Merton M. Gill and Margaret Brenman, with their families (notably including Brenman's husband, the writer William Gibson); Roy Schafer; and Allen Wheelis. Knight had been offered the leadership of the sagging Austen Riggs Center, a once-famous private psychiatric clinic and hospital, and set out to make it an even more outstanding, now psychoanalytically oriented institution. At about the time Rapaport joined them, Erik H. Erikson did so too, completing a dazzling team.

Meanwhile, Rapaport kept in touch with former students and colleagues in Topeka. As the one who had been most inspired to try to follow in his footsteps, I was among his most regular correspondents during this period of his life. At first, the letters were scanty and not very intimate. But as you will see, as the years passed, the letters show the growing depth of our friendship as well as intellectual collaboration and mutual aid. These years also saw major changes in our personal lives. Though these aspects of the letters are downplayed, some readers may be interested in what is revealed of the human side of our lives and its effects on our joint work.

WHY READ THESE OLD LETTERS?

In this collection, one can follow the interlocked final and most productive years of a master of psychoanalytic theory, and the early-mature developmental phase of a follower who sought to continue and even transcend the master's work. In them, readers can observe how Rapaport functioned as a teacher and mentor, at the same time treating his younger colleague as an equal whose critique of his own work was to be welcomed and respected.

The reader can see here how Rapaport developed and reworked his greatest theoretical contributions, the critical and synthetic review of major problem areas in psychoanalysis, and how he made good use of sympathetic but unsparing criticism, modeled on his own critiques of my early writings. Always with a primary concern to discern and preserve the best and most lasting parts of Freud's work, Rapaport was willing to take seriously some fundamental challenges to the basic tenets of metapsychology, which I was beginning to formulate at the time and which I developed in the years after my mentor's death.

I hope it is obvious that *historians* of several kinds may find these letters interesting, not only those who focus on the history of psychoanalytic theory in particular but those involved in various other branches of the history of science: that of clinical psychology, of psychiatry, of medicine more generally, even of the history of ideas. For both correspondents were well aware of the fact that they were touching, from time to time, on a broad range of historical literatures and aware of the ways that the development of psychoanalytic theory resonated to recurrent themes in those histories.

Perhaps the largest group of possible readers are *psychoanalysts* by profession, or other mental health professionals with a strong interest in the discipline Freud began. If that description fits you, you probably know of David Rapaport and associate him with ego psychology and metapsychology, two largely outmoded endeavors in the psychoanalysis of a good many years ago. Yet in your reading of Freud, you will have discovered that a good deal of what he wrote dealt with just these matters, and that those are among the most difficult parts of his works. You may have not felt wholly satisfied by some teachers' dismissal of them as outmoded and not worth the effort required to make an independent judgment. Rapaport was notable precisely for his deep interest in elucidating the meanings of Freud's ego-psychological and metapsychological works, and showing their relevance to clinical realities. Moreover, Rapaport is famous for his mighty effort to organize Freud's theories, integrate them, compare them with other contemporary sciences, and lay out the result with clarity and a keen architectonic sense. He was able to do that because of an un-surpassed mastery of Freud's entire output and of the rest of the psychoanalytic literature of his time. My efforts to follow the work of my mentor, applying to the latter's drafts the same searching critical methods and standards he had taught me, led me to raise questions that helped the older man to think through and clarify his writing. Questions Rapaport could not answer and those on which we two agreed to disagree continued to motivate me in my subsequent contribution to the overthrow of meta-psychology generally and ego psychology in particular.

Following our conversation and arguments may therefore help you understand how and why those branches of psychoanalysis have been generally abandoned. It may also stimulate adherents of contemporary schools to ask how far the variant of psychoanalysis they prefer satisfies the standards to which the correspondents held the theory of their day. Presently, psychoanalysis looks to the interested outsider like a loose grouping of more or less competing schools of thought and practice. I find it hard to believe that it has a bright future unless they can be rein-tegrated in the fashion Rapaport undertook in *The Structure of Psychoanalytic Theory*.

Since both of us correspondents were deeply interested in and com-mitted to *empirical research* on psychoanalytic propositions, the letters should be of value to anyone with a similar interest today. One sees here how Rapaport stimulated the formation of the Research Center for Men-tal Health at New York University by me and George S. Klein, and nurtured its growth, even though he never succeeded in gratifying his own wish to develop an experimental program. The origins of lines of work at the NYU center may be clearly seen in these letters, work that continues to develop in a variety of settings today.

Finally, both of us were concerned with *philosophy* and its implica-tions for what we were trying to do. We knew that our efforts must be grounded on methodology and related aspects of the philosophy of sci-ence, but we were aware, also, of fundamental, metaphysical implications. Freud could not be fully understood, we realized, without searching out his implicit basic assumptions and his relation to developments in philo-sophical thinking of his time. For example, it becomes evident to any close student of his works that he was bedeviled by the mind-body problem and never developed a satisfactory stance on it.

THE REDISCOVERY AND COMPILATION OF THESE LETTERS

When Rapaport died of a sudden fibrillation on December 14, 1960, I was in Palo Alto (on sabbatical from my professorship of psychology and directorship of the Research Center for Mental Health) for a year's fellowship at the Center for Advanced Study in the Behavioral Sciences, freed from my usual administrative, investigative, and teaching obligations at NYU. It was therefore easy for me to go at once to Stockbridge, to give some emotional support to Elvira, his widow, and their daughters Hanna and Juliet. I was also able to plunge into helping David's remarkable assistant, Suzette K. Annin, with the task of dealing with the accumulation of files, books, correspondence, multiple drafts of papers, and fragments of a considerable variety of projects. (More than just a secretary, Sue had quietly corrected her boss's idiosyncratic English and made valuable substantive suggestions when typing up his letters and papers.) With Elvira's consent, much of what he would have called his *Nachlass* went to the Library of Congress, his personal collection of books and journals being donated to the Riggs library.

Several decades later, in 1989–1990, I had to face a similar task in disposing of my own collections when I retired from NYU and, with my wife Joan, moved to our final home on Cape Cod, in Truro. In the process, I had to decide what to do with many years of correspondence, since my tiny basement office was far smaller than my NYU quarters had been. When I winnowed the letters down, I took especial care of two fat file folders of exchanges with Rapaport. Two more decades passed, however, before I took the time to read through their contents. How vividly these letters helped me relive twelve years of some of the most intellectually stimulating experiences of my life! I felt the obligation to share them with any interested colleagues, especially because Rapaport had been in the most productive years of his psychoanalytic scholarship. Many of our exchanges give an insight into his way of working, of thinking through difficult issues by discussion. Those who knew him well were aware of the many drafts his papers would go through, but few of us were privy to his ways of working ideas out, making them at once more subtle and clearer.

The letters also display Rapaport as a critic, a mentor and teacher, as he sent me his critiques of my various attempts, often to follow in his footsteps and at times to branch out on my own. He set the example of close reading, responding empathically as well as unsparingly in pointing out difficulties, lapses in reasoning, omissions of relevant data or of treatments of apposite points in the literature. Though he never succeeded in writing English like one born to it, he was a fine critic of grammatical and rhetorical lapses—as the reader will soon see. I did my best not only to meet his criticism but to learn from it his style and technique of editing and advising, and to apply that learning to the drafts that he sent me.

My two old file folders contained 232 items, mostly letters, plus a few manuscripts and copies of letters to and from other scholars. When I was in the process of consulting two friends and colleagues, Morris Eagle and David Wolitzky, about the possibility of making the collection into a monograph, I happened to hear from another researcher, Dr. Nellie Thompson. She was looking for letters between Rapaport and another scholar in whose work she was interested. She told me that she had discovered several in the Library of Congress, and kindly sent me a copy of its holdings of Rapaport materials. I was amazed to learn that his correspondence not only filled 90 boxes, but that the only one devoted to exchanges with another single person was labeled "Holt." Through Dr. Thompson's good offices I got in touch with Dr. Leonard C. Bruno, on the Library of Congress staff, and wrote him about my project and what I had. He was extraordinarily helpful. Dr. Bruno offered to go through the "Holt box," check its contents against my listing of my own holdings, and personally make photocopies for me of the unduplicated letters. I owe him more thanks for his unusual generosity and helpfulness than I can easily express.

There was of course extensive overlap between the two collections, but I now had photocopies of 59 additional items, making a total of 291. Of these, 138 are from Rapaport and 133 from me, leaving 20 not written by either of us—mostly notes from secretaries conveying manuscripts or letters from third parties concerning David and Elvira Rapaport's sabbatical at NYU in 1959–1960. We of course had no need to exchange letters during that academic year. David and I continued to consult intensively about what we were then working on, but there are no written records of those conversations.

I have omitted 126 of the total of 271 letters by the two of us, because they dealt only with personal rather than intellectual matters, or because they discussed institutional or professional topics. I have, however, summarized the contents of all and have quoted passages of interest from some that seemed not worthy of including in toto. Some of the 126—plus a few from or to Rapaport from other professionals, mostly psychoanalysts—may be of possible interest to a future biographer or historian, and will remain available at the Library of Congress, to which I have sent all items not previously in their collection. Another complete set will be donated to the Rapaport collection at the Austen Riggs library.

A note about format: I have made very few and minor unnoted corrections of the letters (mostly typographical errors). David was overly fond of dashes between sentences, for no apparent reason; I have eliminated most of them. Both of us used underlining for emphasis; I have retained it without change. Where entire letters were handwritten, that is noted at the beginning. Dissimilar typefaces are used to distinguish the original text of the letters, and other documents, from commentary and other added material. Brief editorial interpolations in texts, however, are in brackets [thus]. Notice that there is a list of Persons Mentioned (more than once) with brief identifying paragraphs which do not, usually, include their accomplishments after 1960.

Readers interested in further background about the two of us may find such materials at psychomedia.it/rapaport-klein. See also the following items from the attached References: re Rapaport—Gill & Klein (1967), Holt (1967); re Holt—Holt (1993); re Research Center for Mental Health—Holt (in press).

I am the only surviving member of Rapaport's Research Department at the time of his departure except Herbert J. Schlesinger, whose name and work will doubtless be known to many readers. Also still with us, of course, and currently being honored is Roy Schafer (who was not in the Research Department in 1948). I have therefore not been able to obtain permission from any of the persons about whom personal details are mentioned or evaluative comments are made in these letters, except Drs. Schafer and Schlesinger, whose gracious cooperation I am happy to acknowledge.

CHAPTER 1

Getting Started—The First Letters, 1948

Sometime in the late summer of 1948, after farewell parties, David and Elvira Rapaport with their two young daughters Hanna and Juliet left Topeka for Stockbridge. The first letter in this collection came from David, on November 2.

Its immediate stimulus was his need to get in touch with a psychologist friend of mine, Babette Whipple. But he also added some questions indicating a continuing interest in the work of Louisa (then my wife) and myself—a natural enough outgrowth of the fact that we had both been members of his Research Department. For his practice was to meet with each member regularly and discuss the progress of our various projects, about which he kept himself well informed and helpful: "I am wondering how your wife's thesis is getting along and how the work of selection is going? When will we see either or both of you around these parts? Won't you or Louisa drop a brief note how things are going?"

I met Louisa Pinkham (later, Howe) when we were both graduate students at Harvard, about 1940. I was working under Gordon W. Allport in psychology, she in sociology under Talcott Parsons, with whom I was taking a course. We married one week in February 1944, during which I had my final analytic session (with Felix Deutsch) and passed my doctor's oral. Shortly thereafter, I moved to Washington to accept a job at the Division of Program Surveys, United States Department of Agriculture. Louisa stayed in Cambridge to try to finish her dissertation and her analysis with Edward Bibring; she had accepted a Freud Memorial Fellowship for analytic training of social scientists at the Boston Institute. That summer, she joined me in DC, having been awarded a fellowship to train social scientists in the actual work of government. (Through that, we once had tea with Eleanor Roosevelt in the White House.)

When I accepted the Topeka job, Louisa joined Rapaport's Research Department. He was attracted by her new dissertation topic, an ambitious and original attempt to integrate psychoanalytic and sociological theory. A highly gifted person, she somehow never got much of her excellent work published, though she did finish the dissertation in Topeka while bearing us two daughters.

The "work of selection" mentioned in that first letter was a reference to the Selection Project, as we called the big undertaking for which Rapaport had hired me away from the Winter General VA Hospital staff. He had also brought Lester Luborsky to the new project's staff, followed by another young PhD, William R. Morrow.

On November 8, I replied (in part):

> It was good to hear from you, even so briefly. [. . .] Louisa has been working away slowly—more slowly than I had wished, but the end draws even nearer. [After a reference to "domestic delays," an implicit reference to the fact that we had two baby girls:] For a month she was on ¼ time for the education department, trying an interesting experiment in teaching group relations in situ. Dr. Karl has raised objections, however, which enables her to [. . .] devote nearly full time to finishing her thesis. There are some very nice things in the latest parts, which I think you'll enjoy.
>
> The more that time goes on, the more I enjoy working with Bille.[11] She gives us the kind of leadership that we need. [. . .] [Recently] we have been involved in preparing our Progress Report. [. . .] It is a big and difficult job, requiring a lot of thinking through of plans and rounding out of results—all of which is very good for us. We are beginning to know [. . .] just what we have been doing and a reason for every step. The main difficulty is the time pressure. Each of us sees each candidate [for a residency] for nearly

---

[11] Sibylle Korsch Escalona, who took over Rapaport's roles as head of the Research Department and supervisor of the Selection Project.

two hours [administering tests or an interview in a final predictive study, after much preparatory work]. [. . .] But we're going to pull something pretty good out of it, yet.

George [S. Klein] has just returned to work [after an illness contracted on a vacation in Mexico], which has enabled me to cut my VA hours to 9/week, six hours now being devoted to MFSCP [the Menninger Foundation School of Clinical Psychology, a joint enterprise with the University of Kansas, Lawrence]. My course [in theories of personality] is going rather well; I'm learning a good deal, and at least some of the interns [i.e., students] like it. Helen Sargent [the new Chief of the VA hospital's Psychological Staff] has just arrived, and it seems that she is going to work out all right. Personally I find her very pleasant and easy to deal with.

George's illness kept him near enough at hand [in the VA hospital, a short walk from our house] so that either Louisa or I could get over nearly every day. [. . .] We greatly enjoyed the opportunity to get to know him better—and Bess [Bessie Boris, his wife, a painter] too, for we saw a lot of her; I even taught her to drive. Kindly tell Margaret [Brenman Gibson, a close friend of Bessie's] that she does fairly well, now.

There followed a section on the difficulties of the students in the second class of the MFSCP in doing well on their preliminary exams for the doctorate, in which Rapaport took considerable interest, having directed and taught in the school. Two members of its first class are well known to contemporary psychoanalysts: Philip S. Holzman and Herbert J. Schlesinger. Each did his doctoral dissertation under the direction of George Klein on a specific new cognitive style, in a research program directly stimulated by Rapaport's discovery that psychiatric patients with different diagnoses (e.g., hysterical vs. obsessional neuroses) had distinctive patterns of results on psychological tests indicating differences in perceptual and other cognitive functions.

No doubt you heard about the excellent policy adopted by the [Topeka] psa. institute about training for psychologists. They are now on the same plane as psychiatrists. Incidentally, I may immodestly report also that they are running away with the ball at the [psychoanalytic] literature seminar. Topic: Chapter VII [of Freud's *Interpretation of Dreams*, as Rapaport always referred to its final chapter]. Dr. [Jan] Frank[12] commended us after one evening, saying that the reason all of the best contributions came from the psychologists was probably to be sought in the medical training of the doctors, who had been schooled in so much neurologizing that they had difficulty in thinking psychologically. [. . .]

The Luborskys finally found a house to buy with which they are pleased, and moved in just about 10 days ago. Ruth is expecting her child imminently. [. . .] Bill [Morrow] continues to work smoothly with us [on the Selection Project]; there has been no recurrence of the old friction. I think he and I have a new respect for each other, and he is certainly pulling his share of the load. [. . .]

This is enough for one time. [. . .] Do pay me back in kind—I am most interested to hear how your work goes, how things are with the family and the other ex-Topekans, and Louisa is too, just as much. She joins me in warmest regards.

On December 15, 1948, Rapaport sent an official note as Secretary of the new Division of Clinical and Abnormal Psychology of the American Psychological Association, informing me that the Executive Committee had appointed me Chairman of the Committee on Examinations, and listing six other members. It ends, however: "The official businesses are so extensive right now that I cannot yet answer your good letter. I hope soon to get around to it." Apparently he did so, though his reply is regrettably missing.

A few days later, I responded with "thanks for writing such a good, news-filled letter," but mostly about the Committee on Examinations, accompanied by a draft first committee report. It echoes some of my earlier concerns about "prelims"; in particular, hopes for exchange of questions across all clinical doctoral programs. It ends:

---

[12] Training analyst, Topeka Psychoanalytic Institute.

I should like very much to have a look at your translations and commentary [apparently being prepared for Rapaport, 1951] and will indeed promise to write detailed criticisms and English corrections. [. . .] After Louisa's ideas have crystallized a little more, she will write to you herself. [. . .] Harry Murray wrote me that he had been to see you at the same time that he said he was coming here.

A letter of April 20, 1949, comes after another gap in the record. I express regrets for not having been able to find him at a recent professional meeting in Chicago, and make some comments about exam committee matters. There follows the good news about renewed funding of the Selection Project, a brief update on the work, and chat about our move to another house in Topeka.

I sent a brief note on June 13, concerned with similar matters, ending: "I'm hoping that you may find time for a personal note early this summer. At any rate we shall have chances for some good long talks at Estes Park." (See below.)

Next is a note from me, of July 11, more about committee work. On August 15, Rapaport responded: "I notice your place on the program and I am looking forward with great interest to listening to you. I do hope that you and I will have a good long chat."

In other (vanished) letters, we had learned that both families were going to vacation in Colorado, and attend a gathering of students and associates of the recently (1947) deceased, distinguished social psychologist, Kurt Lewin. I have only vague memories of the meeting and am surprised to learn that I presented some kind of paper. Nor do I recollect any conversations with Rapaport there. We both thought highly of Lewin as a person and a contributor to action research in social psychology, though neither was enthusiastic about his "topological" theory. I had taken a course with him in my Harvard days.

On September 29, Rapaport commented on a little story in the just-published *TAT Newsletter* (3, No. 1), which at Harry Murray's suggestion in 1946 I had begun issuing a few times a year to interested users of his most famous projective technique. A Dutch psychologist, David van

Lennep, author of the Four Picture Test (which I had reviewed there), had become a good friend of mine, first by correspondence and then during and after a brief visit to Topeka. I published in the newsletter some extended remarks from his letters about the concept of projection. Dissatisfied with the way it was used by many American diagnostic testers, he had begun by complaining about the "inadmissible watering-down of the concept of projection in American writings [. . .] projection is put almost on a level with 'to express oneself, to lay oneself open' (Rapaport, [L. K.] Frank, [H. A.] Anderson)." Rapaport wrote:

> I don't believe that I ever did this. My paper "Principles Underlying Non-Projective Tests" [Rapaport, 1946] showed this. In fact, I discussed this issue in detail in my course at the MFSCP. I wonder whether one of the boys would be interested in consulting the notes and writing a clarifying note on the concept of projection. (Mind you, not a clarifying note concerning my stand or Lennep's mistake).

A nice, if minor, illustration of Rapaport's overriding concern with the theory itself, not with his own correctness or another's erroneous statement.

Then begins the more extended, substantive exchange of ideas.

Rapaport to Holt—June 23, 1950

Dear Bob,

Your letter and the two enclosures just arrived. I read the psa. soc. paper[13] and can't resist writing to you about it.

I found that it sustained my interest throughout: a feat when concrete material is not fully presentable and theory not yet fully encompassing.

The part of the discussion related to the stimulus barrier interested me particularly. I wonder whether George read it and whether some definite differences in "schematization"[14] could be found that parallel your results. I found your discussion to have "span" and ability to [i.e., for] flexible modulation and tolerance for weight—it was good to see that—though I can't say that it came as a surprise from you.

The discussion of criteria which have manifold dynamic roots was very illuminating. I am sure that this is related in your mind also to the issue of "autonomy." I am not sure but that your point is amenable to generalization and that many concepts applicable

---

[13] A paper I presented to the Topeka Psychoanalytic Society sometime in 1949. I can find no trace of it and know the content only from Rapaport's comments, which imply that I presented some findings from the Selection Project with possible relevance to admission to psychoanalytic training.

[14] The first of what Klein was later to call cognitive styles, Leveling and Sharpening, was measured by means of a "schematizing" test, in which a person estimated the sizes of projected squares in a series gradually but not regularly increasing in size (Klein, G. S., & Holzman, P. S., 1950; Holzman, P. S., 1954).

to the description and "first removed abstraction" of behavior will prove to be of such character. Indeed the theoretical and experimental demonstration of this point is a huge job ahead of us. If I am not sufficiently clear on this point, please let me know and I'll try again.

The matter of "authoritarian personality": (1) You feel a need to justify it; (2) your justification is not on all fours. The fact that even though Morrow brought it, you nevertheless found it [useful?] proves to me nothing—well hardly anything. This is a problem of choosing the conceptual level for description. On one level you may find the same as [they did in] California; on the other you may find drives which are hardly differentiable interindividually with our tools of observation; on a third you find sensitivity and differentiation referable to two different levels of integration (in final analysis). The danger with the "authoritarian personality" and the whole California study—to my mind—is that they missed the opportunity to study the hierarchy of motivations into which the attitudes that they summarily describe as "authoritarian" and other "personalities," fit and arise from. You seem to have a beginning of such penetration into such hierarchies—so at least I gather from your discussion to which I referred in the previous paragraph.

More generally, you give me the impression that you have an avenue to dynamic expression of traits, character-pictures, ego-attitudes, etc. If you have such a beginning which will clear up the conceptual mess existing between [H. A.] Murray and [G. W.] Allport, [E.] Spranger and [W.] Dilthey, [H.] Kretschmer and [S. S.] Stevens, and all of them vs. ego-psychology—you may be preparing for one of the most needed contributions in the field of the more narrowly defined study of personality and character. Surely besides speculation, testing, case history, it will take some systematic study of various groups of normals also. But I imagine this may sound pretty hazy.

My best to Louisa and the children,

      yours

        David

This letter is chiefly notable for Rapaport's ability to find in the gropings of a student much more than I had suspected I was saying, and thus to encourage a deepening and broadening of what I thought myself capable of. I hope that I managed to make some progress on a few of the issues he raised in a much later paper (Holt, 1962), written after his death: "Individuality and Generalization in the Psychology of Personality." A recently revised version may be found at publinet.it/pol/ital/docum6-i.htm.

Rapaport to Holt—June 29, 1950

Dear Bob,

I have read your TAT chapter.[15] I am sure you will take my comments on it exactly as they are meant though you may not find it entirely easy to do so on first reading.

First of all: it is an excellently written piece which—considering its scope and limited extent—is by far the most <u>instructive</u> piece written on the TAT. Both its stress on rationale and its concrete illustrativeness are pitched to a higher level than the stuff before.

Now as to critique: while in concrete and instructive aspects it is by far superior to your other paper [see previous letter], it displays (to my mind) far less your theoretical, integrative capacity than the other. True, the job was more complex and you were not in a virgin field where your imagination was unfettered by cluttering prior statements, facts, and assumptions—yet I do not think that you "ran true to form." This does not intend to minimize the service you did by stress on rationale. In trying to weigh my feelings and ideas about the chapter, I—in all fairness to you this should be stated explicitly—considered scrupulously whether you're underplaying Roy's and my views and their influence on your ideas. I believe that my criticism does stand up even though I—and this human frailty is understandable even if not forgivable—did

---

[15] Holt, R. R. (1951a). I had sent my draft to him on June 17 with a note saying (*inter alia*) "I am more or less seriously thinking of expanding it, with some other material, into a handbook." That never happened.

feel that you did not do justice to our contribution and did take a critical attitude about that, too.

But enough of the preliminaries and to the core of the matter (as I see it).

(1) The strict need determination of thought and the limitation of that by structural considerations is the core hypothesis for the interpretation of any ideational product. This <u>axiom</u> remains only implicit in your presentation, or comes (it does come in one place) to expression in a subordinate partial position. If and when you will make it explicit <u>as an axiom</u> (indeed, two axioms) your rationale will gain hugely in clarity and impact, because this will force you to relate your nine points of rationale to each other.[16]

(2) As your nine points[17] stand now, they are a congeries rather than a systematic presentation. Each one by itself stands and is useful, but their inter-relations remain weak even though the dream analogy helps (but not enough). After all, the sentimentive content of the associative elaboration is not unrelated to the personal style. What is the common basis of both? How do they differ? Are not both closely related to the "internal milieu"? And so one could go down the line.

I fully realize that you may have thought all this out but for this paper chose not to go into these so as to make it <u>practically</u> useful. I imagine I would have concurred. But this shouldn't blind us to the fact that further generalization and abstraction may become a real contribution to the theory of thinking and may also prove a rationale less close to the empirical data (less ad hoc) and more powerful and decisive.

---

[16] I did not deal with this criticism because I did not understand its logic, in part because I was uncertain what definition of "axiom" Rapaport had in mind. Unfortunately, we never discussed it. In retrospect, it sounds to me as if he wanted me to produce a theoretical rationale beginning with a limited number of assumed basic truths, from which propositions would be rigorously derived. Neither of us ever followed that model, which seems inappropriate to the modest theoretical status of psychoanalysis.

[17] See comment following this letter.

The main reason—I believe—that this critique of the good, practical, and thoughtful job you did turns out this sharp is the comment you made to me in walking to the Lozoffs: "I want to do theory." Well, if so then there is further and really theoretical work to be done: you started it with thoughtful gathering and systematization of abstractions "once removed." The next step is to generalize further and establish the common background out of which these nine descriptive (relatively descriptive) concepts issue.

May I keep your manuscript for my files? May I say that I do not know the answers to the questions I raised here? I see (cf. Part VII of my new book [Rapaport, 1951]) a possibility for a new theory of thinking. But even if that should prove a useful theory, I don't have the transition from your systematization of phenomenal (once removed) determinants to its concepts. Whether you arrive to a theory like mine by seeking for further removed abstractions from your nine categories of determinants or to another, is unimportant. Important is to generalize.

I hope this is the kind of comment you expected and that I communicated and not just soliloquized above.

My best to you and the family,

       Yours,

         David

Comment

My letter of transmittal accompanying the chapter draft mentions my hope (never realized) of writing a book-length treatise on the interpretation of the TAT, though I gave a course on it afterwards for several years at NYU. In one sense, Chapter 3 of my 2009 book on *Primary Process Thinking* was my own final attempt at a theory of thinking as ambitious as the one Rapaport was urging.

Here is a summary of the nine categories of determinants of TAT stories:

1. The situational context (e.g., treatment, research; including the physical setting and the nature of the administering person)
2. The directing sets (anticipations, guiding ideas, or mental sets)
3. The perceptual impact (of the TAT card)
4. The arousing of needs and affects (by all 3 preceding determinants)
5. The arousing of defenses against and controls of needs and affects
6. The associative elaboration
   A. Personal-historical (autobiographical) content
   B. Sentimentive content (attitudes both cognitive and emotional)
   C. General informational content
7. The enabling and limiting effects of abilities
8. The internal milieu (prevalent emotional climate, e.g., optimism, zest, anxiety, fatigue)
9. The personal style (e.g., tempo, rhythm, colorfulness)

Holt to Rapaport—July 3, 1950

Dear David,

The second of your two thoughtful and most welcome letters of reaction to my MSS just arrived, catching me in the middle of writing a review of Sheldon's latest piece of scientific effrontery and pretense, Varieties of Delinquent Youth [see letter of August 8, 1950], but I must stop to answer you. Both letters have been heartening and stimulating, and especially rewarding because you have the gift of seeing so clearly what I was trying to do in each case. More than that, what you say shows me leads, sign-posts to new paths of which I was only dimly aware in my own work.

The point you stressed most, the one about emergent higher-order abstractions or concepts in personality, was one about which I had some doubt when I wrote the psa. paper [see letter of June 23, 1950], and I by no means had thought it through clearly. Not having read your [1951] book nor recently any of the ego-psychological contributions that lead up to or are included in it, I did not relate my considerations to the issue of autonomy, and I must confess that I don't really follow you entirely in what you said about this whole matter in your letter. Indeed, your discussion of hierarchies is one of the most difficult parts (for me) of your chapter [VII. "Toward a Theory of Thinking"], one that I vainly raised for clarification in the meeting we had last Tuesday. (Did you know that the Research Department spent an evening discussing and criticizing the chapter? Afterwards we regretted very much that we didn't record it for you, but when I write you at greater length about it I hope that I'll be able to recall most of the points made.) Part of my difficulty lies in my inability to understand your conception that the counter-cathecting forces derive their energy from that which they oppose (remember your analogy of the river damming itself with its own silt—really a very loose parallel). But I am straying from the point; I agree that it is an important issue in personality theory to straighten out levels of abstraction and to explore relationships between concepts on neighboring levels. Beyond that I haven't thought much.

I feel a little embarrassed to discuss my psa. paper, because the fact is that it was written in a great hurry, without time to think out the issues at all clearly. Mostly the ideas are set down just as they first occurred to me during the day or so before the meeting (though of course after considerable soaking of myself in the data), and I haven't attempted to follow the trains of thought out any further since, being absorbed in many other things. This Sheldon review is taking an inordinate amount of time, but I think that it's important that he get slapped down properly in the Journal of Abnormal and Social [Psychology]. But before the APA [annual meeting] I intend to get back to the stimulus barrier speculations and try to think that all through some more for my paper in Bruno's [Klopfer's] round-table.

You were really too apologetic in your criticisms of my TAT chapter; actually my impression is that you ended up by being more complimentary than "sharp," as you put it, though it is clear enough that you felt quite critical. But without such criticisms as yours I would receive no help in developing my thinking, so I value very highly your pointing out the weaknesses in my discussion. The whole thing suffers (as does most of my output) from too much haste, from having to be written during off hours and to meet a deadline. It is easy for me to feel that the ambivalence I felt toward it was similar to yours: that it was pretty good on a concrete instructional level, but left a lot to be desired as a theory. Of course it was a chapter in an introductory book and wasn't supposed to contain any original theorizing, but I do want to go on with it someday and work out the problems into something that can stand on its own feet as theory. It is quite true that the nine classes of determinants are not coordinate and to very differing degrees conceptually unitary or complex; they overlap, too, as you correctly point out. I am not even positive that they are very helpful empirically, after just having finished teaching a group of students the TAT. They seemed to grasp the ideas readily enough but their actual interpretations remained almost completely unaffected by any of this!

An obvious flaw of the chapter is that I knew too little about the psychoanalytic theory of thinking; at the time I wrote it, I had not even read The poet and daydreaming [Freud (1908), SE 9, 143–153]. Having [now] read your MS,[18] one of the first thoughts I had was to try to apply some of your ideas to this problem of TAT rationale and see what happened—both to your formulations and to mine. I haven't yet done so, and maybe that particular idea isn't quite the way to go about it, but I do want to get a better grasp of ego psychology before I tackle the task of reworking my own thoughts again.

I am sorry that I hurt your feelings in the way I treated your contribution to the TAT. The fact is that I do not find your concepts of cliché and compliance helpful; I do not know how to salvage much out of them, beyond what is already there implicitly. Nor is the idea of the TAT as a test of ideational content very meaningful to me. All of these concepts are so different from the way I most naturally think about the TAT, after my Harvard beginnings, that I doubtless was unaware of the extent of my debt to you in my thinking about it. Of course, the trail is plain to see of the basic conception that I learned from you (and George [Klein] agrees that this is one of the few most important contributions you made to his thinking): the importance of the ego-structure in which dynamic interactions take place. It sounds simple enough

---

[18] He had sent me a manuscript copy of the final chapter VII of *Organization and Pathology of Thought*, which is what the Research Department had read.

and after one has been around here long enough it is so much a part of what is universally taken for granted that it is easy to forget how completely unaware many other clinicians are of this crucially important point of view. As I see it, an insistence on considering the particular kind of defensive structure in which perception goes on [embedded in the concept of "cognitive style"] is the main hallmark of George's research, the one really fruitful idea that he has that the others seem to lack. But I think we are all likely to overlook and to forget the debt we owe you for this crucial emphasis.

All of which leads up to your point, that the core of the matter is the twin ideas of "the strict need determination of thought and the limitations of that by structural considerations." I certainly agree, even though I have a feeling that some third most generalized element is missing; it would have to do with the cultural setting and the individual's experiential background as the source of particular contents, driven into new combinations by the needs, and expressed & transmuted within the framework of the "structural considerations." But this is just something that strikes me at the moment; I will want to think it over more carefully.

I don't feel that I can take any more time with this now; as always the pressure of time is heavily upon me. One of my dreams is to have a research job in which there is the possibility to take out a day to think about something quite apart from the ongoing principal activity, without guilt. Perhaps it will yet work out that way here when we finish the predictive study [the final phase of the Selection Project].

Warm regards from Louisa and myself, and as for the girls, they now look on you as some sort of wonderful fairy godfather!

Bob

Rapaport to Holt—July 6, 1950

Dear Bob:

I want to answer your letter point by point.

I am glad that you take Sheldon over the grill. As long as you have a chance to do such, you may want to consider how much of the restless pace is due to yourself and not to the job; I am finding out something like this for myself. Review writing is an important public obligation. I prefer to use it as a conveyer not only of critique, but also of ideas in the making. I have written a review of the Murray-Kluckhohn book [Rapaport, 1949], and recently one of Wiener's Cybernetics [Rapaport, 1950b]. Would you care to see them?

As to the higher-order abstractions: all I meant to say in the fourth paragraph of my first letter is that you did make such a step. The less reading went into it, the more original it was. I doubt whether reading first would have done too much good, and there is little to read anyway. On this point I have expressed merely pleasure and interest to hear more: the question is whether you can marshal empirical evidence to show that criteria[19]

---

[19] I believe that he and I were referring to criteria for selecting people for training in psychoanalysis or psychotherapy; i.e., necessary qualities of personality. My lost paper no doubt contributed to Chapters 15 and 16 of Holt & Luborsky (1958), Vol. 1 and the appendices to those chapters in Vol. 2. It is impossible to say how much each author contributed to this part of the work. Many readers may not know that Lester B. Luborsky (1920–2009) has been called "one of the founders of scientific research in psychotherapy," to which he devoted most of his subsequent career at the University of

which have manifold dynamic roots do, in effect, appear as autonomous entities, neither requiring nor allowing for reduction.

The conception of hierarchy does not depend on the loose parallel (you are right in calling it loose) of the river. Already in Emotions & Memory [Rapaport, 1942], the material collected was such that it forced me to indicate that there seems to be a "whole hierarchy" of "emotional" organizing forces working in memory. In an attempt to understand how various motivations work in thought-organization, I came again upon this problem. The motivations which find symbolic pictorial expression, and those which find expression in the form of realistic logic, and those which find expression in wishful thinking, differ in character. There are three main hypotheses that one could set up about them: 1) that this appearance is fallacious and there are no differences between these motivations; 2) that these differences indeed exist but have no genetic connections; 3) that these motivations indeed differ from each other, yet they are genetically connected. These three hypotheses have a relation to the TAT rationale, but I shall not pursue that here. The third hypothesis is the one which, to my mind, necessitates a postulation of a hierarchy. The issue of this hierarchy is related to the issues I discussed in my "States of Consciousness" [Rapaport, 1951b] paper in Topeka. (By the way, could you inquire for me how I could get hold of the recording of that lecture?) The assumption of this hierarchy is consonant with the findings of Piaget concerning socialization, consonant with Lewin's conception, "Intention, Will, and Need" [pp. 95–153 in Rapaport, 1951] of automatization, with Hartmann's similar conceptions, with the whole problem of sets and attitudes, and a lot of other similar things which I again cannot enter [into now].

Pennsylvania, where he went after leaving Topeka. In 1973–1974, he was president of the Society for Psychotherapy Research. His contributions to psychoanalysis were acknowledged by two major tributes from the American Psychoanalytic Association, the Sigourney award and one for Distinguished Psychoanalytic Theory and Research.

My parallel is loose, that is true, but that is due to the fact that self-regulating systems are not sufficiently well understood, particularly not where the institution of self-regulation is created by the very energy distribution which arises to regulate it. We know such events, however, from our experience when we ourselves create a concept. The concept arises from the individual data, but when it arose it regulated those data and further ones. This too is a vague analogy, but the point where we can get out of vague analogies is the whole problem of the emergence of feed-back systems.[20]

I do not think you need to feel embarrassed at all about your Psychoanalytic Society paper.

As to the TAT chapter, I hoped it would be obvious that I would [i.e., meant to] recognize in my letter the limitations imposed by the purpose and publication channel of the paper. This recognition was one of the reasons for my hesitancy to criticize. I would not depreciate the nine classes of determinants; they are good material to go on from. The comparison with dreams also contains an important and fortunate point of departure.

"To take a critical attitude" and to have "hurt feelings" are two different things. I do not think you propose to equate them and thereby make it impossible for me to be fair and square in my communications. "Cliché and compliance" are not the points I had in mind, though they have far more to do with what you call "some third generalized element having to do with the cultural

---

[20] This paragraph and the one preceding remain obscure and difficult for me to follow today. The basic difficulty, I believe, lies in Rapaport's constant reliance on what he called economic concepts such as "energy distribution." He was in the habit of using that concept as if it was common in physics where, he implied, it had the meanings he attributed to it. My own later forays into the development of the concept of energy in physics did not turn up any behavior of energies and their distributions that had the hierarchical and structural properties he assumed except with the aid of structural elements like wires (for electricity) or pipes (for liquids), which plainly do not emerge from "distributions" of the same energies (Holt, 1989, Chaps. 4–6 and 13). Nevertheless, his use of the concept of self-organizing systems was in advance of his time.

setting" than you seem to assume. What I would have in mind (just to be explicit) were matters like <u>rationale</u> in general, <u>tune of the record</u>, and similar conceptions. I was critical of this because the literature is barren in these respects and reference focuses the attention. It is a grave misunderstanding if you talk about "indebtedness." The ego-structure issue, for instance, is right now spreading in the literature, and thus whether or not you or George happen to have come in contact with it through me is quite irrelevant. It is my impression that that does not hold for <u>rationale</u>, <u>tune of the record</u>, etc.

I am interested in hearing about your further ideas about the third generalized impression. With best regards to you, Louisa, and the children,

      Yours,

        David

Rapaport to Holt—July 29, 1950

Dear Bob:

This is about the "TAT Newsletter," the last two issues of which I just read. First of all, it is a really good and friendly job, one which can be accomplished only when it is a "labor of love."

On the fourth page there is a quotation which refers to "a hypothesis" advanced by me. I think it would be worthwhile to call attention to the misunderstanding implied. I think many of us will consider it a commonplace that a group of patients who suicided, or are rife with suicidal ideas, may give as many [i.e., no more] outright suicidal responses to a topic implying suicide as any other group of patients, or even normals. I believe it is also assumed that this happens because: a) the fundamental impulses which underlie suicide are present—though in different constellations and intensities—in all of us; b) the controls prompting to dissimulate, suppress, repress, deny, make reaction-formations to such dynamic factors and corresponding ideas, are also present in all of us.

A second misunderstanding seems to lie in the conception of what constitutes "revealing [a] preoccupation." If somebody, for instance, blocks on the suicidal picture, that is as revealing for the analysis of an individual case as a direct self-reference, and both of them are far more revealing than a story with suicidal content—provided that the self-reference and the blocking (I could add here conceptual [I think he meant "perceptual"] misrecognition, extreme elaboration of the story, etc., in other words, interpersonal deviations) are clearly inconsistent with the patient's handling of the rest of his own stories.

I believe that the responsibility for these misunderstandings can be apportioned 50-50 to the deficiencies of our writing, and to the still prevailing "experimental" thinking in clinical psychology. All we meant when describing to what topic a card—in our experience—refers, was to point out what the examiner should look out for, where he should begin to make a hypothesis which he is to verify or falsify thereafter from the rest of the TAT protocol and the other available data.

I feel like making these comments particularly since in your last letter you expressed your doubts about some of the concepts which I consider indispensable in this connection.[21] Let me add that I consider them indispensable, not merely on the grounds of TAT experience, but on the grounds of experience with thought-formations and particularly communications. I also feel that the reference of these concepts is steadily present in the therapist's choice of significant topics of discussion, and interpretation in the course of the therapeutic process.[22]

---

[21] This is the beginning of what turned out to be a misunderstanding between us. In the letter referred to (of July 3, 1950) I said that "I do not find your concepts of cliché and compliance helpful" in understanding and interpreting TAT stories. In his major work, *Diagnostic Psychological Testing* (1945–1946), he uses these terms frequently; in the revision and abridgment I undertook at his request shortly before his death, I left the sections on theoretical rationale of each test virtually untouched except for minor matters of unclear or unidiomatic wording. Rereading his chapter on the TAT now, I continue to have trouble with these concepts. Rapaport did not give a direct definition of "cliché": he contrasted it with "essential ideational content," by which it is evident that he meant verbal expressions about matters that are important to the person, consciously or unconsciously. See, however, his comments about our differences in the letter of August 8, 1950, when he accidentally substituted the concept of *consistency* for *cliché*. Of course, I completely agreed on the importance of consistency.

[22] I also see now what he meant when, his letter of July 6, he made a passing allusion to the idea that cliché and compliance imply what I alluded to (vaguely) as a "generalized element having to do with the cultural setting." If a theme strikes the tester as a cliché it can have that status only in a particular culture or even subculture. For example, an expression uttered by a teenager from a middle-class suburb of a northeastern US city

I do not think of going to the meetings. Any chance that you would come to New York or Stockbridge after them? My best to all of you.

> Yours,
>> David

---

might be well so described, even though it might strike a peer living on a southern farm as odd. And compliance surely implies an understanding of the implicit structure of the testing situation grounded in various cultural norms, even though the ones assumed operative at the moment by the patient and by the tester may be quite different in revealing ways. My understanding of such matters was greatly advanced by discussions of them by Roy Schafer (1954).

Holt to Rapaport—July 31, 1950

Dear David:

Thanks for your good letter of the sixth, with all its food for thought. [omitted: problems about transcribing the lecture Rapaport gave on his recent visit to Topeka.]

Since I had an extra copy of my Sheldon review, I'm sending you one, and would like very much to see what you said about Wiener and Kluckhohn-Murray.

Coming to the issue of hierarchy and autonomy, I want to report an impression that I have received from your letters as well as from your manuscript: that you seem to assume that the emergence of a hierarchically higher order of generalization means ipso facto that the emergent is autonomous. The danger I see in this line of thinking is that of nominalism[23] (unless I misuse terms). If I am able to set up a concept on a higher level of generalization than "obsessive defenses" or "hysterical defenses" are on, I cannot see that such a fact in any way implies that there is any actually existent structure in the concrete personality corresponding to

---

[23] Nominalism is the philosophical position that only concrete terms referring directly to perceptible objects are real, abstract and general terms being only bits of language and not part of reality. At the time of the correspondence, the principal nominalists with whom we were familiar were logical positivists, whose doctrine both Rapaport and I rejected. As I develop my point, however, the position I take could sound pro-nominalist, partly because autonomy does not mean reality. Issues of ontology and of freedom are involved in a way too complex to summarize here. See Holt (1984; 1989, Chap. 9).

my generalization. If concept A is on a higher level of abstraction than concepts a & b, it is <u>in a formal sense only</u> autonomous of them; empirically, it may be quite dependent on the lower-level existents and thus genetically and prognostically have no autonomy. Conscious processes cannot be <u>reduced</u> to physiological ones; the respective concepts are on different abstractive levels, which must be respected. But that is not to say at all that conscious processes are therefore <u>autonomous</u> of their physiological substrates, as I understand the meaning of autonomy (in relation to ego-theory); purely physiological means of affecting the nervous processes can knock consciousness right out.[24] This is obvious, and I feel sure that you will agree; but I wonder if you are aware of the extent to which you seem to ignore this kind of distinction in your discussions of autonomy.

Reading over again what you said in your chapter [the final one of Rapaport, 1961] about autonomy, I came to the impression that you had followed very closely the conceptual model of the development of concept formation in your theory of the ego-hierarchy. This is something that gives me pause, because I cannot see that there is any <u>necessary</u> connection between them. But I must confess that the issue of structure in ego causes me great confusion (of concretistic origins), since the parts of the structure [i.e., of ego] are in themselves abstracted functions of the total organism. Perhaps there is something that you could suggest that I read to help me in this issue; I feel that it is a rather basic one for my penetration any further into ego psychology. I read in Sheldon that structure and function are continuous, not to be dichotomized, but that only makes me feel that it is probably not true. It's easy for me to see <u>social</u> structure or morphological structure as separate from functions that take place in each, because the elements are tangible and concrete (well, I know that the unit of social structure is the role, which is <u>not</u> concrete, but it is easy to

---

[24] Again, this philosophical issue, the mind-body problem, is a good deal more complex and subtle than I seemed to assume here, as I later found.

think of it as the actual person occupying that role). Now I realize that in the last analysis substance and process are indistinguishable, but it seems to me that what is function or process on one level (e.g., the biochemical) is structure on another (e.g., the cytological), when constancies of function produce some kind of steady state (cf. a flame—a steady state of processes giving rise to a concretely appreciable structure). But now when we come to steady state processes such as those of the ego, the result is not something you can see or visualize in any way, and I'm apparently so bound to visual imagery that I start losing my moorings. Clearly, one issue on which I need further instruction is that of the existential status of structure in relation to levels of abstraction. Perhaps even the question is asked wrongly, but that is as far as I can carry it now.[25]

Before I forget it, I want to tell you that both Fritz [Heider] and Eugenia [Hanfmann] have agreed, with some enthusiasm, to review your book. Do you remember which was to do it for which journal? I remembered Genia for the JASP [*Journal of Abnormal and Social Psychology*] and Fritz for the [*Psychological*] Bulletin, and put it that way in asking, but she anticipated a little difficulty in getting [Wm. K.] Estes'[s] consent on the grounds that she is at Harvard and he wants to keep from having too many local people do the reviews [he was professor of psychology there then]. So maybe it would be better to switch them. Does that seem all right?

The occasion on which I finally was able to ask was just after an evening in Lawrence at which the faculty seminar discussed your chapter [VII in Rapaport, 1951], or attempted it. I had rather mixed feelings about the result, which was very muddled indeed at times. Genia and Fritz spoke rather little, though thoughtfully and with indications of having grasped quite well what you were trying to say.

---

[25] This seems to be the first time (except perhaps in conversation) that I voiced critical doubts that David never rebutted to my satisfaction, and which were the beginnings of my later (e.g., Holt, 1989) judgment that similar problems beset metapsychology as a whole and destroy its usefulness.

Both spoke their conviction at the end that you had made an important contribution, even though more rigor would have been desirable. Most of the ideas were produced by Al Baldwin, who took in general a line of disagreement, attempting as it were to explore various means of finding <u>other</u> concepts to handle some of the problems, particularly in order to avoid the use of energetics. There was criticism of the concept of a fixed amount of libido (though Louisa and I mentioned that that was not presupposed nor necessary to the theory), and criticism of an economic point of view about non-measurable energies. Al wanted to see how far one could go with general concepts of valence, force, and tension unrelated to any energetic source or economics, and with the notion of equivalence of stimuli. At the moment I don't recall others of his ideas, but they were rather thoughtful and in some cases freshly enough conceived to require a re-thinking of (to me) seldom challenged assumptions—probably the reason I don't recall them! Perhaps he would be willing to write you about them; I'm seeing him tomorrow and will suggest that he do so.

Your latest letter came just as I was writing this—thank you for your appreciation of the [TAT] Newsletter. It has indeed been a labor of love, but at this point I'm tempted to quote Bettelheim.[26] I have just made arrangements with Bille to take care of it on research department time from now on; it was eating into my precious off-time to far too great an extent.

Would you be willing for me to quote from this last letter in the next issue of the Newsletter that I write? I think it would be constructive for this naive piece of work on suicide to be examined as carefully and as objectively as you did. If you are willing, I'd like to reword a couple of sentences and send it to you just as I want to print it for your prior approval. Here's how it might go:

"The account of D. C. Broida's investigation of suicidal themes given to Card 3BM in the Summer 1950 Newsletter prompted David Rapaport to write the following comments. He takes note of a

---

[26] Probably a reference to Bruno Bettelheim's book, *Love Is Not Enough*.

couple of misunderstandings of his work that were involved in the study. First, he says,

'I think many of us will consider it a commonplace that a group of patients who later commit suicide, or patients who are rife with suicidal ideas, may give as many and no more outright suicidal responses to a stimulus implying suicide as any other group of patients, or even normal persons. I believe that we generally assume that this happens because: a) the fundamental impulses which underlie suicide are present—though in different constellations and intensities—in all of us; b) the controls prompting dissimilation, suppression, repression, denial, or reaction formation to such dynamic factors and corresponding ideas are also present in all of us.

'A second misunderstanding seems to lie in the conception of what constitutes "revealing a preoccupation." If somebody, for instance, blocks on the suicidal picture, that is as revealing for the analysis of an individual case as a direct self-reference, and both of them are far more revealing than a story with suicidal content—providing that the self-reference and the blocking (I could add here perceptual misrecognition, extreme elaboration of the story, etc., in other words, interpersonal deviations) are clearly inconsistent with the patient's handling of the rest of his own stories. [. . .] All we [i.e., Rapaport, Gill, and Schafer] meant when describing to what topic a card—in our experience—refers, was to point out what the examiner should look out for, where he should begin to make a hypothesis which he is to verify or falsify thereafter from the rest of the TAT protocol and the other available data.'"

I hope that I have not changed the sense of anything; the revisions I am suggesting are chiefly in the service of clarity. Discussions of this kind are just the kind of material that to my mind make a Newsletter most vital and interesting, so I hope you will let me carry it.

You say that I expressed doubts about some of the concepts you consider indispensable in the above connection, and go on to give the reasons for your prizing these concepts so highly. It is my impression that I do not differ with you at all in estimating the importance of the phenomena and the distinctions that you make, but that I prefer a slightly different way of conceptualizing them. Do I omit anything important in slicing the cake my way? Please let me know if you can see that I do. [. . .]

       With warm regards,

         Bob

Rapaport to Holt—August 8, 1950

Dear Bob,

Thank you for your letter of July 31. The information and ideas were real food for thought and I need that sorely these days. I am struggling to decide what next and that is not easy. One could pretend that such a struggle doesn't exist, but I chose not to. I am mentioning this also because I remember the similar problem you are faced with underneath the preoccupation with present work.

Enclosed please find copies of my Wiener and Kluckhohn-Murray reviews. Your and Louisa's comments will be most appreciated. Your Sheldon review[27] excited me for various reasons. I have been just reading the "Blessed is the Match"—the history of the extermination of Jewry and Jewish resistance.[28] It is a book all of us interested in human nature must read—I believe. It shows where Sheldon—as you describe him—must end. It shows how hope can be our worst enemy and ally of our destroyer; how rebellious distrust only can grasp and envisage the fate in store for us; how situations can rob man of all dignity and yet how belief in ideas can retain and raise, above all carnage and filth, human dignity. In the Warsaw ghetto, while it was being slowly liquated and [Jews] quickly murdered, the people at the danger of their life were educating the children and each other, while preparing to take a last armed stand. But I cannot give a picture of this, nor of the experience of becoming numbed by

---

[27] Holt, R. R. (1950).
[28] Syrkin, M. (1948).

all the horrors read, so that slowly no more violent feelings were aroused as I went on reading—just a few tears but even those rarely—reading about mothers and children and teachers: mothers who killed themselves when it was believed that orphans will be spared, teachers who went voluntarily with their wards into the trucks taking them to extermination to give a few more hours of support, and to die with them.—As you see, I can't tear myself away from the topic: neither my feelings about my people, nor the impotent curiosity to understand what happened here psychologically let me off easy.

Yet there is something else about this review of yours that struck me. I am somewhat unsure how to put it. Well, let me say first it first and explain it after. This writing seemed to me mature. I do not mean that others of yours were immature—I mean that it is easy to write blandly, or with an ageless sprite witticism, or with a cool detached objectivity, etc. so that the writing has nothing to do with the category of "personal maturity." Well, this one had to do with it, and it has an authority and inner validity only given by maturity of this sort. (I mean to distinguish here mature writing and writing displaying the authority of personal maturity.) I think this is again something (like "what to do next") which is not "possessed" after once had, but rather striven for in continuous struggle.—Now about my hesitancy to write this; well, I am hesitant to write even about that hesitancy. At times I am sure that you accept what I say, and at others you reject what I say on an image of me and not on my argument. I mean something I can not further here express. I feared that my speaking of "maturity" may similarly rub you the wrong way: I feared you might not take it for the admiration of an equal, but a condescension of a pretentious "old one."—But I want to come back to this later in another context.

As for the quotation from my letter: I wrote it to you because in a former letter you said something to the effect that you have "no use for concepts like <u>consistency</u>, etc.".—Well, I thought to demonstrate that even [the] "standard reaction" has [i.e., makes] no sense without such concepts. The idea is developed more in detail in my paper on "Principles Underlying Non Projective Tests" (N.Y. Academy of Science Symposium) [Rapaport, 1946]. In this letter you raise the question whether your "slightly different conceptualization" loses anything. I am certainly not prepared to judge this lightly or quickly—but neither do I expect you to do that. There seems to be a discrepancy between "no use for" and "slightly different." Off hand my impression is that to my mind consistency and compliance are central concepts of all clinical investigating methods, because they somehow express that the material studied is a product of progressive socialization (I mean now in Piaget's sense and in that of my VIIth Part), while in your treatment of TAT they are not explicit concepts but implications. But I may have misjudged the situation and therefore I'll re-study it as soon as Merton, to whom I sent your 2 papers (I hope you don't mind!), returns them. As for quoting the letter: I have no objection. But I do not want you to give the impression that I wrote it to the Newsletter, because I didn't. So the preamble should change! If you care to indicate that this came up in our correspondence concerning the merits of the concepts consistency and compliance, that would be fine with me.

Now as to autonomy: First of all, it is so little clarified a concept that all doubts about it are surely justified. Secondly, your questions imply really serious problems. Thirdly, I feel that your letter implies answers to them which I'd at present accept. Let me put it this way: (a) you are right that many facets of my conception of autonomy are modeled on observations on concept-formation; indeed, at one point I said so explicitly (the conceptual simile for "hypercathetic organizations"). (b) You are right that to mix up an abstraction-system which has autonomy in relation to the concrete ideas which are the referents of its individual abstractions can and must not be mixed up with the genetic formations which are the referents of the concrete ideas on the one hand, and the abstraction-system on the other. The autonomy of the latter does not necessarily imply an autonomy in the genetic formations which are its referents—but requires a proof that there is such a relationship between these referents. The abstraction-system is valid only if either it implies such an autonomy of referents and that is proven, or if it disclaims such if it is not proven, but the autonomy of such abstractions <u>qua thoughts</u> does not imply or disclaim anything about the referents. This is an instance of the Russell-Wittgenstein type-problem.[29] (c) You are right in saying that autonomy is always relative—at least to my mind you are right, and I did speak of "relative autonomy," pointing out that the "controlling organizations" are in a sense "controlled organizations." Actually your point of the relativity of structure and function does state this point. (d) I am [i.e., was] not aware that I ignored this point in my discussion of autonomy—you were correct in saying so. I still have the feeling that I just did not dwell on it explicitly (not even as much as above)—but I thought that implicitly I did avoid these pitfalls. Could you help me by pointing out where I disregarded the necessary caution?—Let me say that I am especially grateful for this discussion; the areas it forces me to think over seem to me especially foggy. (This is, by the way, the point where you accuse yourself of limitations and attribute to me either arbitrariness or consummate knowledge. Actually, however, we are both a bit stunned by the complexity of the matter.)

Thanks for the disks. We have not yet contacted a transcriber. I may yet have to ask for the wire-record. Since the Menninger Bulletin asked for the papers I thought they could have transcribed it for courtesy's sake. Thanks for the information on the faculty seminar. Could you tell Baldwin that I'd be most grateful for his writing to me his criticism? I'd love to correspond with him. What were points of "lack of rigor" Heider and Hanfmann criticized? You know, I feel that even so it had more phony rigor than actual

---

[29] A reference to the famous first encounter between Russell and Wittgenstein who argued at cross purposes about the truth of Russell's assertion, "there is no rhinoceros in this room." An important part of the resulting confusion was the failure to agree on terminology to distinguish statements about concepts from statements about empirical realities.

knowledge would permit. More of it would have seemed to be "rigor mortis." Thanks for the "review" help. Either way it would go, between Heider and Hanfmann, would be just fine with me.[30]

My best to all four of you. Write if you feel like it. I hope you will.

> Yours,
> David

---

[30] He had asked advice on possible reviewers of his book, *Organization and Pathology of Thought* (1951). So far, I have been unable to find a review by either author.

Summary—Letters from June 17, 1950, to May 17, 1951

On June 17, I wrote that "it was heart-warming to see you again," thanking Rapaport for a brief note (not found), and enclosing two drafts: the paper I had presented to the Topeka Psychoanalytic Society shortly before, and my chapter on the TAT. (See his responses in letters of June 23 and 29).

There followed a gap of almost six months in the correspondence, with a possible exception: an undated, handwritten note of David's delighted thanks for a book, probably a Christmas present: *The Thirteen Clocks*, by James Thurber. I am not aware of what may have been going on in Rapaport's life during those months, but I myself was going through a personal crisis: my marriage to Louisa broke up and I went back into analysis with a highly regarded Topeka psychoanalyst, William Pious. Early in 1951, David came to give a lecture at Menninger's, but I didn't feel up to a private talk with him.

He wrote on March 3, regretting but respecting its lack. He added: "I would be glad to hear from you in general, about your reactions to my lectures, particularly your criticisms. [. . .] Won't you write to me?"

I was not able to do it. Close though we had become, I had not yet felt I could burden him with my personal problems—which I was in any event fully venting in my analysis. On April 25, he wrote in some embarrassment, not having heard from me, but to let me know that his (1951) book was out.

With evident annoyance, I responded on April 27:

Keep your pants on; when I have time I'll write. All I could have written for months was a note such as this. [. . .] You know very well that there is so much I want to say to you that it will take me at least a full evening to write it, and I <u>just haven't had such an evening</u>.

But thanks for your note; I'm delighted that your book [*Organization and Pathology of Thought*] is at last out, and that you're sending me a copy. No notice to Heider and Hanfmann [about their reviews] is necessary. [. . .]

These have been exceptional times for me in every way. I just returned from a conference with Dr. Will in which I tentatively accepted the directorship of the psychology staff when Bob [Chalmers] leaves.

David's response (April 30, "With warm regards") follows:

My pants were not in danger of falling off. My first note meant to indicate that if we didn't talk in Topeka it was either a misunderstanding or a wish of yours which I respected. My second note meant to indicate that I needed some information which I did not seem to have. Thank you for giving it.

Pants or no pants, I want you to know that I would like to know whatever you feel like letting me know about what goes on with you.

Again, the next letter (of May 17) was from him:

I have just read your review of Erik's book [Erikson's *Childhood and Society;* Holt 1951e). I found it excellent. Let me say simply two things about it: a) I have understood a number of things about Erik's stuff better from reading it, than from the book (though I thought to begin with that I did understand it, as I read proof for him); b) it had, to my delight, kernels of the directions in which— as I told you once, I thought—your development may lie.

With warmest regards,
David

I hardly need add how enormously supportive he could be in hard times.

Holt to Rapaport—May 18–22, 1951

Dear David,

If, as appears likely, I'm never going to have enough <u>consecutive</u> time to write you some of the things I've been thinking about, at least I can make a start at doing it piecemeal. I have just been reading a thoughtful little article in the American Scientist, to which I'd like to call your attention; it's only nine pages long. (Birch, L. C. Concept of nature. *Amer. Scientist*, 1951, *39*, 294–302). I'm not sure that I agree with a lot of the author's ideas, but I think that his historical presentation has merit, and is worth thinking about. He traces the development of a mechanistic view of nature and an organismic view, as well some other offshoots, but these are the most important. I was interested to note that he puts Kant in the mechanistic tradition, while Whitehead is the principal philosopher of organism—[I was] interested because when you gave your paper to the psychology forum on Kant [Rapaport, 1947c] I got a glimpse of some of the basic philosophic ideas that separate our thinking, and I planned to write a detailed rejoinder to you from the position of Whitehead. I never got around to it, and don't know that I actually would be able to do it as well as I thought at the time, but I have thought about that difference a number of times.

Freud, it seems to me, was educated in the tradition of mechanistic science, and strove mightily to create a mechanistic psychology with frankly reductionistic aims. But fortunately he was not doctrinaire enough to disregard facts and was such a good observer that he incorporated important organismic elements into his theory. Yet since he never gave up his allegiance to a way of thinking that is basically foreign to the trend of modern ego-psychology, psychoanalysis remains a confused science. I regret to say that, in your admirable attempts to systematize and clarify psychoanalytic theory, I have a feeling that you are sticking with Freud's fealty to Helmholtz and are creating a more orderly mechanistic view. Rather, I should say that this is a <u>tendency</u> I sense in much of your work; I'm not prepared to document it very well. Partly it comes from the impression I have that you are willing to accept a great deal of the Seventh Chapter of the Interpretation of Dreams, with its attempt at a thorough-going mechanism. Now, I by no means reject all of that; much of it can be incorporated into the kind of ego-psychology that you bring together in your book, but there seem to me to be very important parts which are not tenable today.

[May 21]

Unfortunately I have lost the thread of what I wanted to continue here, and it strikes me that perhaps I was only trying to provoke you. After the heartwarming letter [of May 17] I got from you this morning, my mood is different. When and if I can cite chapter & verse, I'll come back to the above argument; meanwhile I want to take the few minutes I have before Bill Brown comes and he and I go over to Lawrence for his final oral, to tell you again how much your friendship and your appreciation mean to me. I don't speak of praise, because you have the rare gift of recognizing worth in a way that does not sound like flattery, does not evoke embarrassment nor the desire to put up a show of modesty, but invites a perfect mutuality and focus on the issues themselves.

[May 22]

And now the book itself [Rapaport, 1951a] has arrived! I have spent the last two and a half hours reading the introductory parts, glancing it all over and sampling bits here and there. I am extremely well pleased with it. The organization seems admirable, the selections well chosen, and the system of commentary one that performs many functions very well. Frankly, I hadn't expected to find the book so inviting in appearance and so readable; rather than seeming formidable, it impresses me as a huge feast for the mind, one that will nourish me over months to come. I have read enough of several papers to admire the rendering into English and to be grateful for your helps to the reader's understanding of difficult points through the commentary. Not only does one feel respect for an enormous labor of scholarship, but he gets the pleasant sense also of an invitation to share personal experiences of intellectual excitement and discovery. You have succeeded in putting into print some of your enviable capacity to inspire others with your enthusiasm for ideas, which has so great a part in making you the teacher that you are.

Though it will be a poor counterpoise to this handsome gift, I am going to have the pleasure of sending you a book this summer in which I have had some part [Holt, 1951e]: "Thematic Test Analysis," edited by Ed Shneidman. I hope there will be others to follow which will be meatier.

My feelings are in turmoil at present for [personal] reasons which, alas, I don't feel I can yet discuss with you. This is one of the reasons it is difficult to write even when there is time. At present I feel oppressed by the burden of an obligation I undertook to give a talk to a lay study group on international relations—some remarks on the problems of group fear in this country today [Holt, 1951f]. The topic interests me, but I feel very inexpert, and have difficulty driving myself to work on it. A week from Saturday it will be over, and then the next day will bring another small culmination: a performance of Brahms'[s] Requiem given by the Washburn chorus, which I have joined for the occasion. I am also beginning to take singing lessons again, after at least 12 years' lapse, something that is giving me a good deal of gratification.

You will be glad, I think, to hear that Bill Brown acquitted himself well, and has become the first of our "MFSCP" [Menninger Foundation School of Clinical Psychology] group to get to the Ph.D. Nat Greenbaum's thesis has been accepted, and he will be examined Friday to make the second. [Milton J.] Horowitz will be the third, it now looks, since he has submitted a completed draft of his thesis; apparently it won't be finished in acceptable form in time for a formal award of the degree this spring, but he'll have it in substance. And [Gerald A.] Ehrenreich is still faltering at the prelim hurdle! while [Herbert J.] Schlesinger and [Philip S.] Holzman grind away on their theses. I should never have predicted such an outcome; would you? Herb, incidentally, is getting married to Elizabeth Griffin, an excellent girl, on June 6; tomorrow night we're having a stag party for him. I'm going to read the enclosed bit of doggerel [omitted], and there will be other horseplay which we were hoping George [Klein] could share, but he told Bille at the last moment that he'd had to defer coming a week; Bessie is apparently not in the best of health.

Bille's leaving, though it is still far in the future, troubles me and other members of the research group too. She has been looking for a successor as Director [of the Research Department] for some time, even before her decision, and we are trying to think of someone for the job. We are at the moment looking over a sociologist friend of Louisa's who is interested in it; his name is Richard Williams.[31] He has not made a good impression on the group, and his research interests do not fall close enough to ours to make him look like a real candidate, even in a situation of desperation. Which we do not have as yet! I wonder if Bille has asked you your opinion of Bob Harris[32] as a possibility? I feel a little guarded about him personally, not knowing him very well, but he seems to me like someone who might turn out pretty well. It's really the kind of position that should be filled from

---

[31] Clearly a mistake, for Robin M. Williams (1914–2006), a leading sociologist of the century.

[32] Robert E. Harris, founded and directed the Clinical Psychology Training Program at the Department of Psychiatry, UCSF, with a strong emphasis on research.

within the group, I think, but with Milt [Wexler] leaving I don't really see any of us as up to it.

I'm a little disturbed about the prospects of the Research Department, anyway. As you know, Karl and Will and a good many others among the senior physicians (prominently Lew[is L.] Robbins) are not very happy about having the kind of research undertaking that you built up here. As I get it, their conception is that research is something that should not be the exclusive occupation of a "privileged" few, but a part-time activity of the majority of the working clinicians. I doubt that they really want to spend part of their time in research, and I'm even more dubious that the same amount of money spent on this kind of research program would amount to nearly as much [as if spent] on our present program. Yet you, Margaret [Brenman], Merton [Gill] have left, Milt and Mary [Leitch, MD, Escalona's collaborator] on their way and Bille to bow out after only one more year—we are losing our "big guns" and may not have the inherent group cohesion and driving purpose without them that may be needed to withstand pressures which I feel may be directed against us in the coming months. George's problematic status makes things worse; and when the final two years of the Selection project are up, what then?

A bright spot is Paul [Bergman]'s success in continuing to nurse Ben[jamin B.] Rubinstein and Don[ald J.] Watterson along in their interest in psychotherapy research. Maybe I do them an injustice, but the facts have been that their interest seems to have been not a very hardy flower, one that needed a good deal of careful handling not to get completely crowded out by the many demands on their time for clinical work and teaching. But right now—in large part, thanks to Lester [Luborsky]!—things are looking up. Les and Paul worked out a method of summarizing key data about cases which I am sure Paul must have written about to you; this has served to catalyze some new interest and drive on Ben's part. (To make an even half-dozen, our group [I was an active participant] includes Jerry [Gerald J.] Aronson, who is joining the staff in six weeks—one of our ablest residents, clear-thinking and really interested in research.) It's Paul's hope to get these fellows into the research group, eventually, and I'm pulling with him, though not really very confident of success.

These are not well-organized thoughts, and I don't know where they lead, except to bring me back to the (perhaps infantile?) wish for a new leader for the Research Department, one with a lot of drive and infectious enthusiasm. But even if we knew of just the person we wanted, I don't feel very confident that we have a great deal to offer him. With George back, I think our group would have some of its old verve, but the losses we're sustaining have hit our group morale—which I think was (and could be again) an important something to offer a director.

I have made some notes to myself, trying to remember what our difference was on channels of communication, but since I unfortunately didn't do so at the time they are rather amorphous. I don't remember very well just what you said nor what I said, but I shall try to think it out for my next letter. Meanwhile, this formless potpourri had probably better go on out, with my deep affection and gratitude.

      Bob

Rapaport to Holt—June 14, 1951

[handwritten]

Dear Bob:

I am sorry that this answer is so delayed, but I was all swamped and since I don't typewrite, I had to wait to get a leisurely frame of mind for a long, long-hand letter. I enjoyed your writing and hope to see more of it in the future. Did I write to you that I understood Erik better after reading your review of his book? Send me please a copy of your review.

Let me take your letter point by point: <u>Kant vs. Whitehead</u>. I did not read any Whitehead carefully—tell me what to read. I have read all of Kant, and to my mind he was the only one who understood how to make a transition between solipsism and naïve empiricism: the categories of reason and the space-time dimensions of our sensibility are at the core of his solution. To my mind all Werner's, Piaget's, Freud's, etc. work bear out the fruitfulness of Kant's general conception. This doesn't make Kant necessarily a thinker free of "mechanistic" thought. He has been called transcendentalist, idealist, nativist, mechanist—and all other things. Essentially he defies classification like all the great ones: you actually refused to classify Freud in your letter.—But let me meet you on a personal level: you are right, I am intrigued by order and specificity and therefore averse to "organismic thought" (e.g., of the Goldstein sort) which replaces understanding with non-specific, vague, catching [catchy] formulations. But (and you seemed in your letter to allow me something like this—and I think charitably so, because you could have been harsher on me too) I also <u>feel</u> for the free interplay of forces forming organic self-regulating unities and therefore distrust any and all mechanistic simplicity, order and specificity. Well, I imagine you have your own similar pet paradox and squirm on the horns of that pet dilemma. Not a comfortable role, but a relatively honest one. I am having no programme, but how to see the facts so that I avoid falling into either camp. If I do fall—it's my shortcoming of means and talent, but not of intention. In other worlds: "Don't shoot the piano player, he is doing the best he can." I hope to be able to once produce something which will be perfectly balanced between these—if I die before I did it I hope my intent will be clear from what I tried.[33]—I'd like for you to see my new paper on "The Psychoanalytic Model" [Rapaport, 1951c]—written for George's book [Krech & Klein (eds.), 1952]. I tried there something further on this score, though it might look to some very mechanistic. The VIIth chapter: you see, I see in it the least mechanistic of Freud, something that leads beyond sole rule of libido theory. I'll be glad to send you a copy of my Kant paper and see your rejoinder. Maybe I rejoin again and perhaps something worthwhile and of public use may come of it?! Let me know if you want me to send it.

Then about your good words: you can not know how they warmed me. I know you have your own struggles right now and that you can warm a hard-boiled fighter like me even then, is a promise for calmer days!—Your reaction to the book naturally pleased me immensely; but I am also expectant to hear your criticisms and I know you will not spare me: you know I do not like to be spared. I am curious how my mechanistic-organismic balance

---

[33] I shared his feelings about the vagueness of much "organismic" writing, along with my rejection of mechanism. I don't recall just when I met Ludwig van Bertalanffy and had a conversation that moved me to learn about General Systems Theory, but it was in Topeka. I found in that theory a resolution: room for mechanistic laws on one level of abstraction, a more rigorous holism at higher levels. My old friend Jim Miller's 1975 book, *Living Systems*, helped me understand the synthesis, as did (in another way) Douglas Hofstadter's (1979) wonderful *Gödel, Escher, Bach* some years later, well after David's death.

turned out in this book.—I am looking forward to see your "TT Analysis." [TAT? or perhaps he was reaching for "ESP Analysis," my satirical beginning (Holt, 1952a).]

I know how difficult it is with personally intense and hurtful matters, and particularly for those of us who will keep our own counsels about them. But you do manage to keep a catholicity of interests alive and that is—to my own experience—the best safeguard.

The doggerel was witty and pleasing. You will love to hear—when you come to visit here—when will you?! the two skits Miller and Co. wrote for the last two Christmas parties.

The position in Topeka does seem complex and the clouds do gather heavy. I still hope that you and the others remaining will create their own form and tradition of research. But if that would not work out—the world is wide and you have many prospects and possibilities. I hope it will not come to that, but if it would I am sure you will not hesitate to let your friends know in time. I do not know enough about Harris.

What you say about Paul delighted me particularly. You know I think much of him and feel very strongly about him.

I have finished this year a paper on Schilder [Rapaport, 1951c], one on Autonomy of the Ego [Rapaport, 1951b], one on Projective Techniques [Rapaport, 1952b], one on States of Consciousness [Rapaport, 1951d], and one on the Psa Model of Psych. Theory [Rapaport, 1951e]. Did you see any of these? The last one I will send along soon, for the rest—please indicate which you wish to see. I am now preparing to put into order eight lectures I gave on Ego Psychology here, and two of my lectures (on Theory of Affects and Communications) of the six I gave at Yale. By the time I have cleaned these up I'll be done with some side jobs, Fall will be here, and I will have cleared decks for action.

In the meanwhile I have interesting stuff from the two patients I treat. I may be soon dismissing the first one.

Otherwise the new California turn, the Supreme Court decision, the world events, all cast a pall on the world for me and I too am in a haze. But work keeps one's head over the water, the group-work development here in the patient group is cheering and we are still kicking.

Please forgive the delay and scribbling and write.

Yours,

David

Holt to Rapaport—July 15, 1951

Dear David:

These are extraordinary times to be in Topeka![34] All kinds of casual heroism are going on all around, and a great deal of rather casually-taken suffering. The plight of many people whose homes have been ruined is desperate, yet there are no surface indications of it. Everyone is calm, friendly, and either doing his best to help in the crisis somehow or acting exactly like usual (which isn't necessarily all good).

The focal point of the whole disaster has been the waterworks, for the last few days. Along with a number of other citizens, I didn't wake up to the reality of the crisis until it became clear Friday that the water supply might go out at any minute. Then I got me down to help work on the dikes, where I was all night also. As a result, I don't feel like much of anything except talking to a friend, so that's what I'm doing! The waterworks, incidentally, are pretty safe, despite very extensive damage and a continuing threat.

The Kaw never looked more powerful and ugly as on those still-rainy days when the dikes broke flooding North Topeka, and most of the bridges were knocked off their moorings. (Not the big Topeka avenue bridge, of course, and the one on Kansas avenue may be reparable; we'll know better when it emerges from the water that is covering most of it now.) Very extensive sections of

---

[34] Referring to the flood of the Kansas/Kaw river.

49

the residential district where you used to live were under water for awhile, from the backing up of little streams.

I guess I just can't give you the feel of it, largely because my own perspective is such a peculiar one. [One of my daughters] has been having a pre-therapeutic evaluation at Southard, which involves going over many painful matters, and my own analysis will terminate in two more weeks. It's a strange personal world from which to look out on suffering cheerfully borne. (Not all of it, of course; there are a number of psychoses which were precipitated, and perhaps a number of others which were uncovered by the disaster; they're at the State Hospital together with other, less disturbed refugees.) None of our friends has been hard hit, however. Things have been at a virtual standstill here at the Foundation for the few climactic days, while most people have been doing various kinds of emergency work.

But let's turn to our delayed-action, remote-control conversation. You asked in your last letter for a copy of my review of Childhood and Society, which you praised—did Erikson show you the copy I sent him? (He never acknowledged it and the letter I sent with it, and I have been uncertain whether or not it reached him, but I can think of no other way you could have read it.) At the moment I have no copies, but I think I can send you one under separate cover in a few days. I don't yet know whether or not the journal will print it in full, though I think so.

About the philosophers: I'm badly read in philosophy generally, and in Kant particularly. I haven't even read much of Whitehead, but what I did get a good deal from was Science and the Modern World [1925] (now available in a "pocket" paperbound edition), and I believe that I have heard that The Idea of Nature is a basic statement of his outlook. I can tell you some of my objections to Kant's ideas as I have heard them from others, however. I get the impression that he trusts the human intellect too much as an instrument for the direct revelation of basic truths, through a sort of phenomenological approach. The categories of space and time, for example: as he saw them, are they not abstracted from direct experience, and subject to the errors of that frail instrument? I am thinking of what I read in Infeld's delightful little book on [with] Einstein [1938], which made a lot of things clearer to me. I didn't realize, for example, that Einstein's ability to free himself from the prejudice or preconceptions about <u>time</u> was basic to his first relativity theory. Not knowing Kant well, I don't know for sure that the category that he discerned was couched in terms that Einstein had to reject, though I suspect that his kind of thinking was a real obstacle here. If, however, he meant time only in the most generalized sense, (and space likewise, so that he is not embarrassed by non-Euclidean geometries and curved space), then I am off base. Anyway, I'd be glad to see that paper of yours and try to grapple with the issues more directly; if "something worthwhile and of public use" does come out, fine; otherwise, fine too. Only I can make no promises about when I will do things. (I must mention here that I have not read any further in your book since I first wrote; mostly it has been out on loan, since some of it's being assigned in an [Psychoanalytic] Institute course, the Hartmann article.)

About Paul [Bergman] and the psychotherapy research: the latest good news is that Don Watterson has decided to try to get some research time and to work actively on it. Though administratively he will still be in DAP [Department of Adult Psychiatry], if all goes well he will de facto be a part of the research group, which pleases me very much. I think that he and Ben [Rubinstein] are two of the very best minds in the psychiatric group—as well as being people whose friendship I value. I head this as being "about Paul" since I think it's his doing, very largely. I like him better all the time, and am beginning to feel rather close to him.

Which brings up a very interesting topic! He tells me that there is a good likelihood that he may drive to Stockbridge to give a lecture or something, after the APA meetings. If so, we plan to drive together, take George back with us, and get a chance to visit the Klein family and our Stockbridge friends! I hope very much that it will come off; I'd like so much to see you and the Schafers and Margaret [Brenman] on your home grounds.

Please do send me your paper on the conceptual model of psychoanalysis [Rapaport, 1951c]. George spoke of it in the highest terms when he was here. I found his visit one of the most stimulating and buoying events of the year; we had some good discussions, which we're going to try to keep up by correspondence through the year. Of course George is upset by his uncomfortable situation [at Harvard], but I don't see how he could really do otherwise. He is thinking hard and well on the important issues, I think, and is beginning to turn out fine work. I think he may well be a <u>significant</u> contributor to science.—I'm enclosing a copy of a letter I wrote Krech recently about his series of three articles; it's really a continuation of some of the conversation between George and me, in part. I thought you might be interested in some of the points, though I get pretty picayune at times.

I tried to think over my reactions to your paper on channels of communication [Rapaport, 1951f], and here is what I could recover. I felt that you ignored the essentially interpersonal nature of communication, treating as equivalent and sort of mixing up two problems: how does individual thought emerge despite <u>intra</u>psychic barriers? and, how do people communicate from one to another despite <u>inter</u>psychic barriers? There may be a good deal that we can learn from one that bears on the other, but they must be studied separately, I think. Then, I felt that you used the concept of <u>channel</u> too variously. At one time, a channel seemed to be a <u>topic</u>, something we two could talk about (if we were the subjects). But then again, it seemed to be a mood or a state of mind, as when alcohol "opens channels," or an atmosphere of intimacy does. I should prefer a definition that said something like this (only more clearly): a channel of communication is the used possibility of interpersonal exchange of information and feeling. Thus, if I repress something, that doesn't block a channel between us; rather, it would dry up the source of what might be flowing through the channel that exists.—Well, I don't think that takes us very far, but may give you an idea of what I was trying to say that day which now seems so very long ago.[35]

I have seen the other papers you mention—you have sent reprints of some, others have been circulated—except for the one on states of consciousness [Rapaport, 1951d] . That's essentially what you presented here, isn't it? I'd like to get a chance to read it, if you won't feel bad about the delay that will probably ensue between your sending and my discussing it.

If we have a few days this fall, perhaps we can get some things really talked over. Will you be at Chicago? I hope you will come to the Topological group and hear Bille present the infancy material—the piece de resistance of the program.

　　　　　　Affectionately,
　　　　　　Bob

---

[35] I now feel that, behind these not very persuasive criticisms—in particular, my charge that he equated channels with moods—lay my growing dissatisfaction with most of Rapaport's formulations concerning psychic *structures*.

Rapaport to Holt—July 23, 1951

Dear Bob:

I hasten to answer your letter and so this time I will dictate it. First of all, I am looking forward to seeing both Paul and you here. I may even come to Chicago and then we will have a lot of time, both there and here. If Chicago won't make me absolutely depressed, I may even try to bum a ride. I am glad you and Paul get nearer to each other. I know that you have much to offer each other. Paul has a freedom from tradition which permits him things few of us dare, while in turn you have anchorages which permit you continuity and systematic thinking of an original sort. Needless to say, both these freedoms have their own severe limitations. I hope I am not presuming when I say so: I feel I suffer under both.

In a way I envy you for the extraordinary times in Topeka. I have experienced such quite a few times and have always felt driven far closer to people, with far less fear, than under any other conditions, and often dreamt that perpetual danger may make the human animal less shelled in. But just like a perpetual holiday is poorly tolerated by us, the perpetual danger, or revolution, or enthusiasm, too corrodes us. There seems to be no single recipe and no perpetual optimal condition for human living. A "community of brethren" is as corroding as is a "splendid isolation." The difference is that the corrosion processes have different qualities, and their pleasures and pains make a different configuration, though they are made of the same kind of basic stuff.

It was Erik who showed me the review. Please don't be surprised that he doesn't answer. I gathered he felt understood and thus happy with it. He too has to make an adjustment, and though he does it with unusual grace, it cannot help but be absorbing, and anyway he belongs to the group of poorest damned letter-writers I have had the fortune to encounter in my wanderings.

Whitehead is placed on my reading list herewith, but I wish you would have Kant on yours. I mean particularly the <u>Prolegomena to All Future Metaphysics</u> [Kant, 1783]. I don't think I can make it clear here how you misunderstand Kant, getting him second-hand, particularly not since Kant has been and can be interpreted variously. My understanding of him (which in many ways is similar to that of Cassirer in his History of Newer Epistemology[36]) is only one of the possible ones. It is by no means embarrassed by Einstein or by any non-Euclidean space, whether it is Hilbert's, Rieman's, or phase space. Let me try to put it succinctly: stripped of all the frills, Kant denied a mechanical empiricism, as well as a nativistic idealism. Knowledge about the outside world is neither pre-given nor totally acquired by experience. He denied the justification both of solipsism and of a naive realism: the world of objects is not what is naively perceived, nor is it a phantom world of shadows of ideas. The human being has categories and perception-forms through which it integrates sense experiences into ideas.[37] The "thing by itself" must be assumed as existing, but is never cognized directly but only through the integration by categories and perception-forms. He does not raise the question how man came by these categories and perception-forms. Or more correctly, he does not raise any genetic question about this. Dynamic psychology attempts to give the genetic answer to the question how such categories and perception-forms come about when it investigates the genetics of the

---

[36] Probably Cassirer (1950).

[37] These concepts are rather amazingly prescient in light of recent neuroscience (Meyer, 2012).

secondary process. It is quite irrelevant whether Kant's categories and perception-forms were fortunately chosen. Piaget's studies and my own studies in thinking show the necessity for such. In fact, your demand to Krech on the third page of your letter implies the demand for the investigation of specific forms in this area also. You will note Piaget's second paper in my volume [Rapaport, 1951] where he too sets up categories, but in fact memory, concept-formation, and the triad—attention, concentration and anticipation—are such attempts; and historically motivation, cognition, and affection have also been such attempts. It is in the Kantian spirit to ask: what are the ways in which a human being can look upon his experiences at large, and upon his psychological experiences in particular?

I was delighted with your letter to Krech and can subscribe to every point of it, though I felt that the last paragraphs on pages five and six were weaker than the previous ones.[38] I would strongly recommend that you publish it in just this form, either in The Psychological Review or The Journal of Personality. Enclosed please find my paper on "Communication" [Rapaport, 1951f]. I feel that your comment was justified and I learned something real from it. I have a new paper since, but it is not yet in clean form. Enclosed also please find the paper on "States of Consciousness" and the final form of the paper I wrote for George's book [Rapaport, 1951e]. Please do write to me soon again.

                    Yours,
                    David

---

[38] Never published; lost.

Summary—Letters from July 24 to December 18, 1951

The July letters ended with an exchange about a Hungarian woman's possible suitability for a job in Topeka, which put David on the spot, hoping to help an acquaintance in need of a position but aware that she was probably not suitable. In a postscript came the first mention of his translating Schilder's *Medical Psychology*, the English being smoothed (as often in the past) by Bill Gibson. He wanted my advice about matters like places where explanatory footnotes were needed and where his terminology was not sufficiently American. The response in which I agreed is lost.

Three months later came another exchange triggered by my visit to Stockbridge with Paul Bergman but delayed by the fact that David's wife, Elvira, had had "a very tough time" with a back ailment. He also hoped that I could fill in for him and write a paper on diagnostic testing in psychosomatic illnesses. I declined at once because I had no time, not even to write a decent letter, even though "there's much I want to talk to you about."

A couple of days later (October 19), unable to do most work because my eyes had been dilated, I dictated a report on what I had been up to: our divorce, Louisa's plans, my ulcer's flare-up. Gossip follows about staff coming to and going from the Menninger Foundation, with first mention of Gardner and Lois Murphy as possible newcomers, who "may do a lot to offset the sense of loss that I have from this continual losing of all these other people, but it certainly does stir up in my thoughts about possibly leaving, myself." I complained that both Les Luborsky and I suffer

57

"from a chronic inability to get deeply involved in and excited by" the Selection research project. I promised reflections on some papers of his when I can read my own notes, and confessed that I have not started on Schilder. And then I mentioned agreeing to write a chapter on theory for Bruno Klopfer's new Rorschach book (Holt, 1954).

My letter of November 2 deals mostly with personal family matters, but ends with a report on a visit by the Murphys, who made "an excellent impression on everyone." After a couple of further exchanges about finding a therapist in the Bay area for one of my children, David sent me, for comments, his review of Mowrer's book, *Learning Theory and Personality Dynamics* [Rapaport, 1952a].

On December 12, I wrote about the pleasure of being able to send him books in which I have a chapter (Holt, 1951a, 1951b), and was "fully in mid-stream in your own book [Rapaport, 1951] [. . .] finding it a most exciting and rewarding experience." In his response of December 18, after saying that he had similar feelings about giving me his books, Rapaport added (a propos book reviews he has sent and is writing), "Don't scorn them because they are just reviews: I put more work into them than into most papers." Merton Gill (ed., 1967) wisely concurred about the meatiness of those and a good many other book reviews by including them in Rapaport's *Collected Papers*.

CHAPTER 2

Holt to Rapaport—March 1, 1952

Dear David,

What an age it has been since I wrote you last! Many things have happened, in both my personal and professional lives, really too many to get started on in this brief letter, for I am writing mainly to make a request of you; I will write soon, at greater length and leisure about other things.

A couple of weeks ago, we had as a guest here at the Foundation, Dr. D. J. van Lennep, director of the Netherlands Institute for Industrial Psychology in Utrecht. You probably know of him mainly because of the Four Picture Test, but this is only one of an astonishing variety of interests. If anything, Dr. van Lennep probably has too many interests, and yet he has managed to turn out work of impressive quantity and quality in many areas—not just dilettante stuff. Personally, I found him one of the most interesting and stimulating people I've met in a long time, and a man whose friendship I value highly. I think you'll like his independence and originality of mind, his humor and a kind of sturdy self-sufficiency that he has. I use the future tense because I hope that you will see him. It's partly on my advice that he wants to visit Stockbridge, about March 29th; he's particularly eager to have a chance to talk with you and with Erik.

Dr. van Lennep has a number of new tests and reports of unpublished research, a discussion of which might make a very interesting staff seminar evening for your group as it did for ours here. I suppose part of the impression of originality and freshness that I get from hearing his ideas comes from the fact that he has been trained in a European idealistic tradition of philosophy and psychology that is quite different from my own background. He is an existentialist and phenomenologist, and at the same time a man who appreciates the importance of good research design and of statistical treatment of data.

I don't want to overdo this by drawing a picture of too re-markable a person;[39] I think I have said enough to let you know whether he is the kind of person you would like to have some talks with or not. In either event, would you be good enough to write to him directly at the Hotel Durant, Berkeley 4, California? He will be there for approximately another week.

Just a few words of news: Louisa and the children left for Berkeley on February the 8th. She has now remarried and they are settled down comfortably. I have just come back from an execu-tive committee meeting [of Division 12, American Psychological Association] at the Ortho[psychiatric] convention. I must confess that it seems to me that the affairs of the Division are now in the hands of youngsters and second raters. Sam Beck is a likeable enough fellow, but he is so confused in his thinking and inarticu-late in what he says that I wonder how he has attained the position that he holds in clinical psychology today. I suppose a great deal depends on his having had the good luck to be one of the first people here with the Rorschach. I had a chance to be-come quite friendly with Stark Hathaway on the trip, and to exchange quite a lot of ideas with him. I have a lot more respect for the [Minnesota] Multiphasic [Personality Inventory] now, and I like the man. My main other impression from this meeting was surprise at the way in which this bumbling, oafish-appearing person Harry

---

[39] Let me just quote the independent opinion of Edwin S. Shneidman: "He is an amazing person. He has a breadth of interests, a catholicity of taste, and a lack of fear of uncon-ventional psychological ideas not often seen. [. . .] One day he lectured to Bruno Klopfer's class at UCLA about some intriguing, but esoteric concepts of projective phe-nomena, and the next day he talked to J. P. Guilford [. . .] about factor loadings, stanine scores, and pilot selection." (*TAT Newsletter*, 1952, 6, 1).

McNeil kept coming up time and again with very sensible, sound ideas. Fortunately, Ann Magaret is doing a very capable job as secretary-treasurer. I saw various old friends at the meetings, and heard the astonishing report that J. F. Brown has started up a "psychoanalytic institute" in Southern California, where he is giving a Ph.D. in psychoanalysis in a couple of years! I wonder if you know anything about this.

Please give my affectionate regards to the Schafers, Margaret and Bill, and all the Rapaports.

Yours,

Bob

Rapaport to Holt—Early March 1952

[handwritten]

Dear Bob,

A belated and brief answer to your letter and to your sharp and thoughtful review [1952b]. I liked it altogether, but what I envy is the apparent ease with which you just refer to salient points which are devastating without further exploiting them: I am always tempted and too often yield to the urge to use the sledgehammer. Though clearly: your elegance about it might have its dangers too—they did not seem to trap you in this review nor in the Sheldon one.

I was just beginning to convalesce after an operation when your letter came. I am quite on the way to being well, but it left me weakish. The years tell on one—and the not taking vacations even more.

I gave the letter to our Seminar Committee and I understand that—barring unforeseen difficulties—we will see van Lennep here. This reminds me of Hathaway: it is humbling to read that you find him a nice person. Many years ago on one casual meeting I had filed him away as an insecure guy who makes up to you, salivates around you and might backbite you. Isn't it a shame to do this on one casual meeting? The fly in the ointment is only the Multiphasic: what the hell do you see in it? Would anyone with dynamic thinking be committed to it as Hathaway is? What do you see in it? But Hathaway or anyone might be a nice person even if a poor psychologist, though such extreme commitments to something primitive are rare in nice people.

This must suffice for today. I am tired. Please write. I am glad you liked the Mowrer piece. My Miller-Dollard piece is in birth-pains for 7 months and does not seem to come off.

Yours

David

Holt to Rapaport—March 19, 1952

Dear David:

I can't resist taking a few minutes to answer your recent note, though I feel the pressure of undone work weighing heavily on me. I am glad you liked my review [Holt, 1952b]; it was particularly gratifying to have you recognize that there were a number of points where I could have hit McClelland much harder than I did. I refrained largely because of limitations of space, not because of any nicety of disposition.

It's a little saddening to hear you in low spirits and weak from your recent ordeal. I am sorry that you had to undergo it, and hope that by now you will have fully recovered. I wish that I had known sooner, so that I might at least have written you when you perhaps would have most welcomed communications from friends.

What a unitary world view you must have! It seems to me that I have known many nice people who were more heavily committed to things much more primitive than the MMPI. What do I see in it? I see only a complex instrument with some proved empirical value, the complexity of which lies mainly in our failure to understand the processes in people that bring about this empirical validity, and in its rather atomistic multifariousness. Certainly I prefer not to work with tools of that kind, but I feel humble enough about our ability to understand the processes that mediate the effectiveness of projective tests, and impressed enough with the proved ability of tests like the multiphasic and the Strong

[Interest Inventory] to get at something—even though we don't know what—important in personality so that I'm not willing to rule them out of court as "something primitive." I don't think that we can advance psychology by this kind of blind empiricism, but I believe that it has important contributions to make to psychotechnology. Have you read the Kelly-Fiske [Kelly, E. L., & Fiske, D. W., 1951] report? If you have, I wonder if you don't share with me the feeling of surprise that they actually got quite a lot of good results in spite of Lowell Kelly's calamity howling, and with the fact that many of these results were based on objective test scores. It makes me regret that we didn't use Multiphasic and perhaps another test or so of that kind in our project—purely for the chance that they might have given us better predictive results, of course.

I can appreciate your labor pains over the Dollard-Miller book; it seems to me that I'm having just as intense difficulties in getting written this Rorschach piece for which I had at one time such great hopes. I am almost beginning to be persuaded that I ought to give up the attempt to do this kind of creative work during off hours until I get my personal life straightened out satisfactorily. I don't want to write something that I would be ashamed of a few years hence, and yet I have just a few more days in which to finish! It would be a great help to me if I could have your advice and guidance in this undertaking, but there's hardly time for it.

I was surprised to hear that Roy is going to Yale; I imagine that this will be quite a loss to you, though of course he won't be so far away. Are you seeing anything of George these days? I have owed him a letter for a shamefully long time, too, but that's the old dilemma of writing to one's friends: having so much to say that there never seems to be time enough to write the kind of letter one wants to write. So I am ending this one now, though there are many personal matters I long to discuss with you. There'll be time for it after the paper is in, however.

Affectionately,

Bob

Note on George Klein and His Contributions

Since there is no readily available online biography of George S. Klein (1917–1971), it might be helpful to provide some background on him. First, let me say that there is a pretty good biographical piece in Gill & Holzman (1976), which is subtitled "Psychoanalytic Essays in Memory of George S. Klein." That work also includes a complete listing of his 66 publications, many of which are gathered into two books (Klein, 1970, 1975). He was the founding editor-in-chief of the monograph series, *Psychological Issues*, a position he held until his death. A brief obituary appears in the *Bulletin of the Menninger Clinic*, 35, 207–208.

George came to Topeka in 1946, directly after his discharge from the US Army Air Force. He had enlisted after getting his doctorate from Columbia in experimental psychology, 1942. By 1947, George had become my good friend, fellow member of Rapaport's Research Department at Menninger's, and someone I wanted to work with when and if we both left Topeka. He had attracted some first-rate graduate students in his role, like mine, of adjunct member of the Department of Psychology at Kansas University, located nearby in Lawrence. With Herbert Schlesinger and Philip Holzman, and under Rapaport's general guidance, he launched a program of research on individual differences in ways of perceiving and conceiving the world and their grounding in what Rapaport called ego structures. In diagnostic testing as Rapaport taught it, we learned to recognize several clinically relevant types of such structures: notably hysterical, obsessive-compulsive, paranoid, and schizoid ego-organizations. Using the same basic conceptual approach but experimental designs and methods, George and his group began to isolate what they at various times called cognitive system principles, cognitive controls, and finally cognitive styles. The program was well under way in 1948 when Rapaport transferred to Stockbridge, and its first publication appeared the next year (Klein, 1949).

It also happened to be a time of ferment in American perceptual research, known as the New Look movement. The central theme of much of the new work was showing the effect of personality, especially motivation, on perceptual phenomena. It seems to have been launched by two papers: "Value and Need as Organizing Factors in Perception" (Bruner & Goodman, 1947) and "Symbolic Value as an Organizing Factor in Perception" (Bruner & Postman, 1948). The theories and facts conveyed under those titles seemed revolutionary in the staid world of sensation and perception, conceived the way the founding father of experimental psychology, G. T. Fechner, had formulated it in his psychophysics. Building on the work of a predecessor, E. H. Weber, he had made psychology into a quantitative science of testable hypotheses by postulating that a sensation was proportional to the logarithm of the stimulus intensity, the physical energy (e.g., of light or sound) causing it. Any deviation from the predicted results was treated as mere experimental error. Now, however, people were beginning to realize that such "errors" were not random but were caused (in part) by determinants within the person.

George and his group, who were among the first to start a program of such research, felt that the claim of some that this work was a belated recognition of Freud's insights was a bit glib, and that cognitive processes were far from the passive plaything of needs, emotions, and the like. Indeed, that was one of the main reasons for calling the determinants they were discovering "cognitive controls." The first of these to be published (Holzman and Klein, 1954), "Leveling-Sharpening" was measured by a classical procedure of getting people to judge the size of projected squares of light, a series of them gradually getting bigger but in random order. People who were slowest to notice the small increments were called Levelers; others who seized on slight changes, even exaggerating them, were called Sharpeners. Levelers were clearly making heavy use of what Piaget called "assimilation" (to a prior memory), as opposed to "accommodation" (of memory to the new information), which characterized the Sharpeners. Moreover, this cognitive control proved to be related, as predicted, to the repressive defensive style of hysterical personalities as measured by independent assessment of their responses to Rorschach ink blots.

In a personal communication (December 28, 2011), Herb Schlesinger recalls the time when Klein left Topeka in 1950:

> I believe George was in [had just begun training] analysis with Hans Jokl, whose command of English was nominal at best; not one of KAM [Dr. Karl]'s best recruits. It would have been in 1947 or 1948 that George got in touch with Jerry. I joined George in late 1946, delighted to discover that he too had the notion that people see the world differently and that we ought to be able to find systematic variation in what researchers dismissed as error. We set up the perception lab in North Office basement and began our experimental program. Phil joined us shortly after. [. . .] Our research program began with a replication and critique of Jerry's article on the effect of personal values on perception: a swastika, etc. on a hand-held disc affected its perceived size. We showed that individual differences among subjects, the subject variability that averaging could wash out, were partly a function of what we called their perceptual style. In the course of this work, George arranged to meet with Jerry (Bruner) at Harvard to discuss our findings, [. . .] and took me along; a very heady experience. I recall that Jerry wasn't much impressed.

Nevertheless, not very long afterwards, Bruner invited George to join his own informal research group at Harvard for a year in the spring of 1950. Recently, Jerry commented:

> He was certainly an amazing guy intellectually, and a lovely human being. And, believe me, he gave me courage to go more deeply into the more psychodynamic aspects of the perceptual process—and of cognition generally.
>
> What I particularly loved in George was his ability to infuse the

so-called scientific process with an imaginative playfulness. I never knew him to be "heavy-handed" in his thinking about psychological research. And what a relief that was there at heavy-handed old Harvard!!! What a great companion he was!

He returned to Topeka periodically to supervise the work of his own team: Holzman, Schlesinger, and in 1951 Riley Gardner. The initial Harvard fellowship was for only one year, but he had transferred to the Boston Institute for Psychoanalysis, entering training analysis with Grete Bibring, which was so much more successful that he felt he could not go back to Jokl. Most likely,[40] Jerry helped him get some sort of grant or adjunct appointment from year to year, through the first semester of 1953, to continue their research collaboration. He joined me to share the leadership of the Research Center for Mental Health that September, then completed his analytic training in the New York Institute. He seemed to have come to a satisfactory conclusion of his psychoanalytic treatment; he did not enter another in the rest of his regrettably short life. He died suddenly from heart failure on April 11, 1971, at the age of 53, in Stockbridge, MA, where he, Bessie, and their daughter Rachel had a summer home.

Nothing above gives a hint of the personality of this unique, charismatic, magnetic figure. He was very sociable, a warm, funny, and caring friend, with a strong interest and some talent in graphic art. He could get so intensely absorbed in some new idea that he might hardly notice people around him. Graduate students greatly prized him as a dissertation sponsor. He had one great asset which Rapaport and I both envied, recognizing that despite our strong wishes we lacked it: the kind of creativity plus lab know-how that generated many feasible experiments— practical ways of putting theoretical propositions and hunches to test against the reality of hard data. Klein was so fertile of such productive ideas that I often had to argue for finishing what we had already begun

---

[40] None of the survivors of that era recalls precisely how it was managed. I am indebted to Jerry Bruner, Herb Schlesinger, and Leo Goldberger for their help in assembling the above information.

before launching off into another, exciting direction. His enthusiasm for new "studies" had an infectiousness that made the atmosphere of the Research Center for Mental Health electric with excitement—one of the Center's most memorable attributes. He brought some of that spark along with him to the meetings of the Rapaport Study Group. The organization's name was appropriately changed after his death, becoming the Rapaport-Klein Study Group.

A letter of July 17, 2012, from Robert S. Wallerstein provides a nice finale:

> George [. . .] is the one who started my whole research career. Gardner Murphy had just arrived in Topeka as Director of Research and looking for a research-minded psychiatrist who would fill the same kind of role that Merton Gill played under Rapaport in the Research Department. George enthusiastically proposed my name to Gardner on the basis of a research program I had engineered at the VA Hospital studying the treatment of chronic alcoholism. Gardner had not known me, but on George's advice interviewed me and offered me the job with him at the Menninger Clinic, half-time in the Research Department. (The other half being clinical work.) For me that was the start of everything [notably Wallerstein's work directing the Psychotherapy Research Project] and I owed it all to George's sponsorship.

Rapaport to Holt—April 4, 1952

Dear Bob:

Thank you for your letter and for the first draft [of Holt, 1954]. It is difficult to react to an incomplete first draft. I liked its general idea and tone, and I am not sure that the comments I have to make will be helpful or not, because the scope of it remains unclear.

1) To the four points covered on pages 2–3, I would add one which you may consider simply an amplification of Point #4: without a theory, the Rorschach cannot contribute to the development of psychology (general knowledge and theory)—with it, it can. It has contributions to make to perception, thought, association, organization, and their pathology.

2) In the paragraph, pages 4–5, you could have well castigated not only Schachtel[41] but me also. I think you actually should. But I wish you would counter balance it by referring to what seems to me to be a fact: neither Schachtel's nor my theories have been subjected by others to empirical or experimental test in a sensible way. Scores of papers followed up our monographs (true, most of them were on the Bellevue), but most of them took the narrowest classificatory view, checking whether the "signs" we derived can, or cannot, be verified. The theory itself was not applied in these studies. Some-

---

[41] Ernst G. Schachtel (1903–1975) was my first real teacher about the Rorschach in a course at the Washington School of Psychiatry, about 1942. Most remembered for his 1959 book, *Metamorphosis*, he wrote a series of influential papers on the theory of Rorschach responding, which were later collected in a book (Schachtel, 1966).

body in New Orleans tried to follow up with eye movement studies our Rorschach conceptions, but it proved too complex to him and he skipped it. Somebody else tried it in Buffalo (there is actually a <u>Psychological Monograph</u> on that), but did not go too far. Stein, Bruner and Hanfmann[42] [each] did a tachistoscopic study, but that remained an isolated piece. There is something wrong in the relationship of experimenters and theoreticians. I suspect that the trouble lies in the teachers, who are not really clinicians, besides the trouble you point out in your big paragraph on page 5. In the last line of that paragraph you write, "so many excellent clinical testers"—I think part of the trouble is there are not so many.

3) Now a few points concerning the personality theory requisites: a) It is to be primarily an ego theory which treats of it not as "ego involvement" but as a structure. Roy is trying to do this in terms of defensive operations. b) It must be a theory which explains the relation between acute momentary functions (motivations) and quasi stationary functions, attitudes, sets, etc. c) It must be a theory which clarifies the relation between apparatuses (perception, memory, thought, etc.) on the one hand, and structure and motivation on the other. You could argue that I tailor-made these so that they can be satisfied only by psychoanalytic theory. I do not think that this would be just. One could start out with Lewin's theory to show that he was forced (before he threw up his hands) to feel his way toward such features for his theory. Indeed, one could argue that psychoanalytic theory fulfills these criteria only <u>in spe</u> [hopefully] and is only trying toward such.

Just the same, it was stimulating to read your paper, even if these comments will prove of no use to you.

Yours,

David

---

[42] All three did write about similar research, but there is no available record of a joint experiment. The much quoted doctoral dissertation, *Personality Factors Involved in the Temporal Development of Rorschach Responses* (Harvard, 1949) of Morris I. Stein seems not to have been published. See also Hanfmann (1956).

Holt to Rapaport—April 21, 1952

Dear David,

I was very grateful for your comments on that small part of my first draft that I was able to send. I incorporated several of them in the draft that I sent off to Bruno [Klopfer] on Saturday. It isn't exactly a first draft any more, having been read by several people and some parts of it retyped a number of times; nevertheless, I think that there will probably a further edition before the thing goes to print, so I would be very happy if you could take up where you left off and give me the benefit of your comments.

I didn't think that you deserved the kind of castigation I gave Schachtel (incidentally, I didn't think that I was really very harsh with him) because I got much more the feeling in re-reading your sections on rationale that they were oriented toward research. Actually, you recall, they are almost always linked up directly with certain tests of your hypotheses on the control group. I didn't use your ideas about personality theory requisites, because they involved a number of complicated arguments to make the terms clear and the implication self-explanatory. Nevertheless, I am mostly in agreement with you. I think the only point that gives me pause is your use of the term "apparatuses" for perception, memory, thought, etc. I don't know what you mean by that. You contrast it to structure, but the term apparatus itself has very strong structural connotations. I think of perception and the others as phenomenologically derived abstractions pertaining to functions or kinds of behavior that [it] is occasionally convenient to single out, but I'm not convinced that it is theoretically crucial to try to make any hard and fast distinction between [among] them.

I am tempted to discuss with you already before you read them, some of the ideas about psychoanalysis that I have put into this chapter, but on second thought, I think that it would be best if you read it without any more introduction than any other reader gets, to see if I succeeded in communicating what I was trying to do. As you see, I don't feel certain that I have.

I hope that you are feeling stronger and better these days. When you have time and inclination, I'd like very much to hear about your ideas about communication that you are planning to put to experimental test. About myself, I might say that I am feeling very good these days, considerably happier than I've been in quite some time. I am succeeding at last in unloading from my shoulders many more burdens than I thought I was going to be able to make myself do. Being essentially finished with this chapter is of course a big one. An even larger one is my decision to resign my position as Director of the Psychological Staff. I was very glad that Bille backed me up quite strongly in this, and felt that it was quite essential for me to clear the deck as much as possible for full time work on the [Selection] Project in the coming final year. I am trying to get Walter Kass to accept the position for the coming year; we are changing it to a rotating chairmanship. I hope that George will do it the year after. As I have written Roy, I was much tempted by the offer of a job there with you, but I don't really think it's the kind of thing for me. I also mentioned to him that I hoped you would share this copy of my manuscript with him, since I am very eager to hear how his views compare with mine.

My warmest regards to all my friends there, especially your-self—

> Bob

Rapaport to Holt—May 20, 1952

Dear Bob:

Only now am I in the position to answer your letter of April 21, and write about your big paper [Holt, 1954]. I hope my note reached you indicating that when it arrived I was involved in a breakneck effort to complete my paper for the Psychoanalytic meetings [probably "On the Psychoanalytic Theory of Affects" [Rapaport, 1953a], which was delayed by my sickness and lingering weakness. I completed the paper, and I think it is a fair one. I am sending you a copy with the request that you circulate it to Paul and Bille. For the time being I have no more copies, so it is meant for all three of you.

As to the second paragraph of your letter the distinction "apparatus" vs. "structure" comes from Hartmann. Apparatuses have primary autonomy and enter structure as relatively independent units; though they become integrated with the rest of the structure and become involved in conflict also. The rest of structure is of secondary autonomy. What all must be included under apparatuses is not very clear. There is probably more than the sensory-perceptual, threshold, memory, etc., apparatuses. Surely they are structures, and I did not mean to contrast them with structures, but only with psychic structure at large.

I wish I would have a chance to come to Topeka, to discuss with you experimental plans. I am very glad that you will have an opportunity to give full time to the Project, and to clear the decks for work of your own. This, however, already leads into the very middle of my comments on your paper. I have shown it to Roy—I do not know whether or not he wrote to you about it.

Bob, I have two major comments on the paper:

1) I feel that you spoke out on personology as well as on its relation to Rorschach, in a clear and authoritative way. I don't mean that this is the final word necessarily—I do not know what the final word is. I feel the authoritative certainty (this is quite independent from certainty in details) and the secure grasp in it. Once we had a conversation on a car ride, where I tried, in a very unsatisfactory way, to express my hope that you will do something like this once. I was delighted to see it. I feel that few people are in the position to do just this. You are. I hope that your next step will be (I mean that sometime you will make a step which will be) to move toward a synthesis of these theories. You held them up [i.e., for inspection], but you know very well that there is more to be done. Allport has things to say, and so do the others, which psychoanalysis has not been able to say as yet, and if it could be said, it would be a definite contribution to particularly the ego psychology of psychoanalysis, and to many other things also. I don't think I can be clearer on this at this moment. I would fully agree if you would call it very vague—but if so we can have a chance some time to discuss it further.

2) I can't put this point simply. Last time I wrote to you about your review. You rejected my compliment. I want to repeat it. To characterize by expression instead of hammering something into the ground, is a gift on the border of art and science. You seem to have the flair for doing just that. I admired it in this paper. It reminded me again and again of what The New Statesman and Nation can do in literature, politics, art, writing, criticism, etc. It is probably the only cultured journal left in the world. I want to send you a gift subscription of it—only let me know that you do not have one yet. I have phrases in mind like on page 6, "Some command respect because of their rigor, some because of their vigor; and at times it seems that formal elegance varies inversely with explanatory and predictive power." Or on page 8, "doughty universalists;" or on the same page, "Self-contradiction and incon-

sistency are at least as characteristic of human beings as their opposites." [. . .] I could amass many further examples. I believe that this is not only a matter of nicety and humor of presentation, but a veritable avenue to clarifying and appropriately assessing states of affairs in psychology. I hope you will have the possibility to develop this deliberately without taking away its spontaneous flair and without making it forced and artificial.

There are many, many ideas which would be worth discussing. I can not do that in a letter. (Not even in a long one, as this one will prove to be.) Thus I will restrict myself to a few comments. In the middle paragraph (the definition of personology) on page 9, and in the big paragraph on page 10, you are not making explicit that you are talking about interpersonal interaction also.[43] Particularly on the points you make on page 10, Roy has been insistent and successful in demonstrating that these things are, to a great extent, the matter of observations of interaction in a little-controlled situation.

On page 17, in the first paragraph, you are discussing issues to which you come back later in Murphy's "stable needs." In both cases, my discussion in "Principles Underlying Non-projective Tests" [Rapaport, 1946] seems to me to be relevant. Your treatment of Lewin seemed to me to be too harsh. I believe that this results from your disregarding the very specific contributions to "micro-dynamics" which are implied in Lewin's early work with Zeigarnik, Ovsiankina, Karsten, etc.

On page 23 I find the only place where your mouth remained open and you didn't articulate. In the second paragraph, second sentence, you fail really to characterize your author, in "genuinely organismic standpoint." Couldn't you spell this out somehow? Or rather, characterize it adjectivally as you usually do?

---

[43] The letter bears pencil marks by each of the criticisms and suggestions, indicating that I tried to alter the text accordingly. Knowing how much care and thought went into his critiques, I always gave them corresponding consideration. Only occasionally, however (e.g., the footnote on p. 518) is it apparent how the published text was changed.

Page 38: I wondered whether you considered my points on the topic discussed in the passage to which the footnote refers.

On page 39, what you attribute to me I have indeed done, but it was started by Binder on the chiaroscuro, and I only continued it.

Your discussion of psychoanalysis: I really found no bones to pick with it. I shall make some comments below. I regretted that you allowed my contribution to prevent you from presenting a not extremely detailed, but as yet self-contained section on this. I do not believe, however, that your solution is inappropriate for this paper. I believe later on you will want to present your own statement of it, and I am sure it will go far beyond what I could say.

Now a few comments: around the end of the second paragraph on page 40, you say "Freud was always ... restlessly discarding . . . ." I don't believe that these phrases are anywhere near as true or as fortunate descriptions as you were able to give of the other people.

At the bottom of page 41, your sentence seems to suggest a much more close and much more profitable collaboration than I have seen anywhere in these years in this country.

Now for pages 43 and 44. I actually agree in essence with what you have to say here. I think that "Principles Underlying Projective Techniques" [Rapaport, 1942b] and my recent paper on projection [probably Rapaport, 1952b]—which I am sending enclosed—do indicate this, though not quite directly. I have discussed with van Lennep in detail his idea. The difference between him and me is that I indeed think that there is a hierarchy of projections or externalizations which are apparently linked to each other by some intrinsic "system connection." I feel that he tries to sever things maybe too sharply and somewhat arbitrarily in his threefold division. But his intent and yours I concur with, as I hope my paper will also show.

Now as to the bottom of page 44: I think here you are absolutely right in criticizing me, and Roy has done so too. My stand was extreme, and I could bring up only one thing in my self-defense: I took "content" in the most literally extreme sense. That is, content which is directly symbolic. I did not mean content in the broad sense, as my stress on "analysis of verbalization" and "the tune of the record" shows. I believe, however, that these refer much less to direct unconscious content than to defense mechanisms, attitudes, values, quasi-stable affective states, etc. I believe that on the top of page 47, you somehow refer to that very point. Indeed, in the last paragraph of page 51, I again seem to see you returning to that.

Bob, I am afraid this is all I can write at this moment. I have taken on two and a half patients to take care of while others are on vacation. My daughter Hanna is leaving for England next week, and I am taking her to embark in Montreal. An old friend (of 26 years standing) from the youth movement, who lives in England, came to this country, and got the idea to invite her to England and France for the summer. A Palestine friend is here with us for the whole week, and I have to do a great many things before the week is over and I don't want to delay this any longer.

Did you see my review of Mowrer's book [Rapaport, 1952a]? What of my reprints did you get recently: "Mass Communications" Seminar [Rapaport, 1953b]; "Paul Schilder's Contribution to the Theory of Thought-Processes" [Rapaport, 1951c]; "The Theoretical Implications of Diagnostic Testing Procedures" [Rapaport, 1950b]; Mowrer review [Rapaport, 1952a]—so that I can send you the rest.

Yours,

David

P.S. Once more, I enjoyed this paper.

Holt to Rapaport—May 23, 1952

Dear David:

To say that I was pleased to get your big letter of the 20th would be putting it very mildly indeed. You outdid yourself in the generosity of your praise, and I appreciate every bit of it. If before I gave you the impression that I "rejected your compliment" I am sorry; it is only my awkwardness in knowing how to accept commendation. It means a great deal to me, coming from you, and it gave me a great lift. The comparison with <u>The New Statesman and Nation</u> was very flattering; I have long been an admirer of that journal, though I am not subscribing presently.

Fortunately, the delays that seem to be inevitable in all publishing are just as much with us in this book, so there is plenty of time to incorporate changes suggested by your comments. By the way, if you have a reprint of your "Principles underlying non-projective tests" [Rapaport, 1946a] I'd love to have one—I can easily believe that I have not been fair to Lewin. The fact is that I have never read that special series in the Psychologische Forschung, and I can well believe that there is a great deal that is valuable in those articles but unavailable to me. It's a slow enough task for me to read difficult material in English or French, and I have given up the thought of ever mastering German sufficiently to dispense with translation.

The fact that you did not cover pages with many fine points is, if anything, a relief to me. I have plenty of other friends who are doing that kind of thing for me to just about the extent that I can stand. What I wanted from you, and what you gave me so well, was a consideration of the main lines of the argument, and an assurance that I was not distorting psychoanalytic ideas in my discussion of them, or specifically [of] your own contributions.

I am grateful that you sent your little paper on projective techniques and the theory of thinking [Rapaport, 1952b]. I call it a little paper only because of its brevity; the ideas expressed are, I think, quite important. You have done a great service to clinical psychology in the past by your insistence on attention to rationale, and though I think it has had some effect (the fact that Klopfer asked me to write this chapter is one such effect, I believe) there is still a need for a lot more hammering at this point. You put it very cogently, especially in the last sentence on page 2. This formulation had a clarity and convincingness that makes one say, "of course—it's so plain, why didn't anyone ever say it so distinctly before?"

As far as the content of the paper is concerned, I like best the section on projection. We certainly are a great deal closer on this issue than I had supposed. I guess it really just comes down to a question of preference about words; I'd prefer not to use the term projection in these more extended senses. Incidentally, you might want to use that quotation from Totem and Taboo which I lifted from [Leopold] Bellak, to help make the point that Freud used the term quite flexibly himself. I'm not altogether happy as yet about applying the concept of externalization in [i.e., to] structural organizing principles. Such principles do organize behavior and thought, and we see the results of such organization in our test findings. But how is this externalization any more than any other expression of a person? I can easily see Lennep's Projection I (the "pathetic fallacy" of the older literary critics) as externalization, and I can see the attribution of egosyntonic personal characteristics to a Rorschach percept or to a TAT story character as externalization, too, because in these cases [there] is some kind of direct re-creation on the outside of something that exists on the inside. I was about to go on and say that I think there is a principle difference between these externalizations and the sort of thing that we find in Bellevue scatter, when I noticed that you make the same point on pages 5 and 6, yet still retaining both kinds under the common heading of externalization or projection. Perhaps you can make it clearer to me why you think these very different processes belong under the same heading.

In the next section, your discussion of hierarchy and autonomy of motivations suggested to me what might be a very useful study for someone to undertake: the fate of previously "autonomous" motivations in a psychosis. I have the hunch that a careful personality study of a pre-psychotic person might reveal a number of systems of motivation which appear to be functionally autonomous, and that later study of the same person might reveal that the ravages of the psychosis had undone apparently successful sublimations, had turned back into developmentally older, more primitive channels certain placid streams of interest that seemed to be securely mature and adult. I also believe, however, that such an investigation would show in the same person the preservation of a number of pre-psychotic sublimations or higher-level motivations relatively unchanged. Perhaps these are commonplaces of clinical observation, but I think they need to be observed and set down systematically for their theoretical relevance.

One reason that I want to review that paper of yours on non-projective tests is that it isn't clear to me why "the more structured the test, the more . . . quasi-stationary processes will play a role in it." I agree that this seems to be true to a large extent, but it certainly isn't self evident <u>why</u> it should be true. Perhaps in that article you define the crucial concept of structuredness of tests. I suppose you define it in some way like the degrees of freedom in response that a person has. Here I think of the Minnesota Multiphasic, where of course the degrees of freedom are most limited. Yet I believe that a person's personality may find its expression in the pattern of his responses, even though the validity of specific items taken at face value may be quite low. Incidentally, Marty Mayman is going to be developing ideas of this sort in his Ph.D. thesis, in which he uses a highly structured self-report questionnaire, and gets out of it quite a number of interesting things about personality that are revealed in patterns of the scores that are not subject to conscious control.

Your last section, on the varieties of conscious experience, I found least satisfactory. In these few pages, you really only hint at your point. It isn't at all clear how the recognition of different states of consciousness can be useful in diagnostic testing, nor is it very convincing (in the second paragraph on page 12) when you generalize about the concept of "distance." It seems to me that the loss of distance that we see in the Rorschach and in TAT self-references is quite different from anything having to do with close or distant responses in the Word Association test. I don't really follow the connection that you seem to see here. But I must confess that I have not yet had a chance to read your paper on States of Consciousness [Rapaport, 1951c], though I am looking forward to reading it. I did of course see your review of Mowrer's book [Rapaport, 1952a]; I thought that I had written to you about it. I don't think that I had too much to contribute, since I hadn't read the book. The only other reprint that you mention that I don't have is the "Mass Communications" seminar [Rapaport, 1953b].

I hope very much that you will come to Topeka soon. I'd love to discuss your experimental plans with you, as well as many other things. What is the hitch? Do you need to get your expenses out here paid? Or would an invitation that didn't carry any implications of remuneration do the trick? I'm afraid the latter is the only thing that is within my power, but I'll certainly extend it and make it as formal as you like if you'll just say the word. It's been too long since I saw you.

> With gratitude and affection—
> Bob

P.S. I don't know if you've heard about Bille [Escalona]'s illness. She came down with labyrinthitis on the plane coming back from Europe—just before getting to Chicago. She had to lay over there for a while, but is here finally, having arrived last night. She doesn't feel very good for long as yet, but thinks she'll be able to work in bed. This is about all I can tell you about it as yet; I'm going over to see her today for the first time.

Holt to Rapaport—June 6, 1952

Dear David:

Thank you for your note of June 2nd; I realize that these are extremely busy days for you, and I can certainly wait for a longer answer. Meanwhile, there are a few things that I want to communicate to you.

First, thanks very much for the reprint of the symposium on non-projective tests [Rapaport, 1946a]. I read your article attentively, but I was not thoroughly convinced by the point that you referred to in your notes on my paper. It seems to me that you overstate the differences between the different kinds of tests. I believe that there are indeed differences in emphasis of the kind that you mention—that more structured types of tasks where there are fewer degrees of freedom for the subject call more on the quasi-stationary functions, and that projective or less structured tests give more of an opportunity for the more dynamic aspects of personality to manifest themselves. But I don't think that this is more than a matter of relative emphasis. Certainly you yourself have pointed out ways in which the quasi-stationary functions of anticipation, concentration, concept formation, and most of the rest of them enter into the Rorschach performance, and I think that the same thing can be done for the TAT. As a matter of fact, I tried to do just that in my Anderson chapter, to show how a complex performance of this kind calls on many, perhaps most of the organism's levels of psychic functioning. Looking at the other side of it, we certainly see multitudinous expressions of mood, need, ideology, and the like in the most structured sub-tests of the Wechsler-Bellevue. It's true, they have a harder time expressing themselves and are seen less frequently and less blatantly than in other kinds of tests, but they certainly operate when a person is taking a non-projective test. Well, I guess I don't need to labor this point any more, since I am sure you agree with it. As a matter of fact, I probably learned it from you!

The other evening, in Don Watterson's Ego Psychology psychoanalytic seminar, I had the pleasure of reporting on three of the chapters from your [1951a] book, the ones on experimental dreams. At the same time, Dr. Seymour Friedman presented an excellent summary of your paper, "On the psychoanalytic theory of thinking" [Rapaport, 1950a]. In doing so, he remarked that this was the clearest and most comprehensible paper of its kind that he had ever read, and thought it a model of metapsychological writing. During the discussion, a point was raised, I think by Phil Holzman, that you might like to comment on, and I can relay it back to the seminar. The question is, do you see an inconsistency between Kris' concept of regression in the service of the ego, and Hartmann's concept of secondary autonomy? If so, what is this inconsistency? I didn't recall having seen anything in which you had written on this question, and I don't see the inconsistency, myself. Can you elucidate?

I'm glad that you brought up the question of my review of Erik's book. It has never been published, and in fact I have never heard definitely whether [Karl] Zener decided to accept it for the Journal of Personality or not. I have just written a letter to George Lehner, the book review editor of the journal, asking what its status is. If Zener is going to say no or if he is going to be continuously unable to say either yes or no, I'm going to withdraw it and try to publish it somewhere else. I had thought maybe of selling it to Murchison, but I find that it's not one of the books currently listed for which he will buy reviews. Do you have any suggestions?

I was pleased to hear that Hanna is having a summer in Europe. Alas, it looks now that Bille may not have one, though I

don't think I'd raise the question in writing to her. She continues
not to be much better. I just talked to her on the phone, and she
was in the middle of a rather bad spell. She did say, however, that
she got your note and appreciated it very much, and will write
you when she feels better. She sends her love.

       Yours,

          Bob

Rapaport to Holt—June 20, 1952

Dear Bob:

Finally I come around to answering your two good letters, though still not in as peaceful a frame of mind as I would like to do them. Bille's illness, some troubles with my parents, who are getting quite old and for whom life becomes quite difficult, and a few other odds and ends make this a crowded time, particularly since I want to take my first real vacation on the 24th of July, and I have very much to do before I can feel that this vacation will be one with peace of mind also.

Let me first go to the point on projection, in your letter of May 23, the paragraph going from page 1 to page 2. I had the feeling that you, Van Lennep, and I share one conviction. Namely, that there are many processes subsumed under the concept projection, and that the concept itself is not sharply divided from other concepts either. Van Lennep was inclined to delineate the different concepts and be more interested in the phenomenological differences than in the systematic and dynamic commonalities. I in turn am more interested in discovering the commonalities and studying the conditions under which different phenotypes arise from them. It is my impression that you have been wavering between the two points of view. It is my impression that I have not been sufficiently articulate about my point. I am particularly interested in keeping all the phenomena usually subsumed under the concept projection under one concept lest their commonality be forgotten, and also because I have the suspicion, and some indirect evidence, that there is something factual to this suspicion too, namely that we are dealing here with a hierarchic representation of form changes of one fundamental process. Most broadly, I could put it this way. Tensions tend to be discharged. If they cannot be discharged they are either projected or tied up in structure. Once a tie up in structure is possible, the original full projections become "tamed" and take various hierarchic forms of externalizations. But even the very tensions which are tied up in structures retain the tendency to externalize themselves in those broad terms in which they externalize themselves in scattergrams. I believe that what we call "expressions" differs from externalization in that another process, namely somatic auxiliary discharge, takes place in them. The pure expressions are those which are executed on the body itself. The overlap is made more confusing and is bolstered by the fact that somatic expression becomes just as much a structure partially and is used then for externalization as any other tension. I know this is not very clear, but I can't do any better at this moment.

Concerning your second paragraph on page 2: I concur with you completely. The fact that the clinician considers this a commonplace (for that matter, only clinicians who are concerned with the issue of autonomy do so) does not change the situation. Systematic studies are needed and imperative.

Concerning your third paragraph on page 2: the definition of the structure of the test can always be only relative. It is relative to the person who takes the test. It is only an abstract concept of structuredness, an idealized one, that one can talk about. Even in tests which are most structured in this sense certain people find segments or broad areas which are not structured for them at all, because either of ignorance or because it touches on least structuralized parts of themselves. The converse is true for the most unstructured tests and test situations. Actually, every test elicits structured and unstructured responses. Think only of the populars in the Rorschach. But the unstructured test is prone to bring out more content aspects of the personality, and the structured test more formal aspects of it. But then content and formal aspects shade also imperceptibly into each other.

As for the last paragraph, I think that the paper on "States of Consciousness" will shed some light on this. I won't undertake to elaborate on it now, but rather only after you have commented on the paper on "States of Consciousness." [Rapaport, 1951c]

I am afraid that the problem of a trip to Topeka is primarily a financial one.

Now I come to your letter of June 6. The issues in the first big paragraph I have discussed above, though I am sure that a personal conversation on it would do better. We seem to be working on two sides of the same issue and a bit of leisurely talking could probably show where the difficulty of transition from one side to another is.

To my mind there is no contradiction between the concept of "secondary autonomy" and "regression in the service of the ego." First of all, it must be remembered that any autonomy per se must be considered relative. That is, any autonomous structure may become involved in conflict and may come to serve id strivings. I have tried to make that clear in my paper which is published in the Bulletin [of the Menninger Clinic; Rapaport, 1951a]. That does not totally dispense with the autonomy of that function; it indicates that that autonomy is only relative, and can be again re-cathected libidinously and serve libidinous purposes. In autonomy there are two problems: a) Can this function be used again by id forces; b) Can it be reduced to an interaction of id forces. In all people there are functions well enough entrenched that they cannot be reduced in the sense of this second point. This seems to be rather certain. Whether there are ever functions which cannot be re-invaded by id forces and remain always autonomous in a complete sense of the word is still questionable.[44] If the ego is in a sufficiently good command and social approval attends to it too, then the very fact of libidinization of thought structures, as in experiences of discovery,

---

[44] In the margin is a (not wholly apposite) note in my handwriting: "We see this in fluctuations of psychosis in psychological tests."

becomes in a sense a function which is autonomous. That is, the ego autonomously can waive its control over id forces and allow some representatives control of thought or motility.

Zener's procedures are altogether irresponsible. I can't get an answer out of him for 8 or 9 months by now. The Murchison journal is a good idea. It would be much the best to send it to him; even if he doesn't buy it he will publish it just the same. You could try it also with the <u>Psychological Bulletin</u> if you prefer that. At any rate, it would be worth then to buy enough reprints of it and circulate it.

I talked to Bille on the phone a week ago, then I visited her on Monday in New York, and I talked to her yesterday again. It seems that she is much better, though by no means well, and that the gloomy diagnosis in Topeka is not confirmed. But nobody seems to know what the situation actually is. All we can do is to hope for the best.

Yours,

David

Holt to Rapaport—June 25, 1952

Dear David:

Thank you for your good long letter of the 20th. You cleared up a number of points for me. You are quite right that I waver on the question of projection, largely because I feel that I lack sound methodological moorings. We get so far from operations in discussions of this kind that I get to have the feeling that it doesn't really matter very much what we decide, whether we keep a broad concept because we can find conceptual similarities between different processes, or whether we use only separate concepts. So, until we can get a little clearer on what processes are actually involved, I can't get too excited about how we conceptualize them. I must confess, though, that I still find it hard to think of scattergrams as expressions of externalized tensions, in the sense that I understand externalization. That is, I can't see any purposeful externalization at work here; I don't see how it profits the tensions anything to get externalized, or as I should prefer to say it, to be expressed in this way. What you mean by "somatic auxiliary discharge" is quite unclear to me. Are you referring to the somatic elements of the emotional experience? Surely all behavior, or nearly all, has some accompaniment of somatic discharge.[45]

---

[45] It was not until after David's death that I began to see how odd and misleading it was to use the term "discharge" in this way. It never occurred to me that in physics, discharge is a rare phenomenon and in the ordinary use of energy, it is instead degraded via work.

I agree with your general idea about structuredness, though I'm not quite clear on what you mean by structured and unstructured responses. Would you be referring here to the difference between a distinct response say, for example, and a descriptive remark about the color of the Rorschach? You reiterate that "the unstructured test is prone to bring out more content aspects of the personality and the structured test more formal aspects of it." But it doesn't become any clearer to me. I never felt very happy about this idea of "content aspects of the personality" anyway. It seems to me that this looks suspiciously like attributing to the personality, for convenience's sake, the distinctions that are easy to make in our tests. Certainly it is very difficult to draw up a good definition of formal aspects, or to differentiate them clearly from contentual aspects of tests. I tried to do that some time ago for the TAT, and gave it up as a bad job.

I have read your paper on States of Consciousness [Rapaport, 1951c] now, and I do feel a good deal clearer on the issue that I raised earlier. I liked the paper very much indeed, particularly for the part in which you report on your own experiments on self-observation; I think it should become a classic reference for people who are interested in ego-psychology and the problems of thinking. The other sections in which you discuss psychopathology were very interesting and convincing also, but somewhat loosely knit. Somehow your points don't come through with quite the directness and clarity that I think you could achieve with a careful re-working of the paper, though I consider this far from necessary. The theoretical section disappointed me a little bit, though I thought you did push the Freudian theory of thinking a little further and get from it some points that were distinctly relevant to the phenomena you had described. I suppose I am too impatient for a more detailed process theory that would come a good deal closer to explaining in detail the many subtle differences in conscious states that you have described. But then I guess it's almost always easier to write clinical description than theory!

Your explanation about secondary autonomy and regression in the service of the ego was very helpful in classifying.

It seems to be a universal experience that an answer cannot be got from Zener. I have heard from George Lehner,[46] who tells me, however, that Zener is not slow to return manuscripts that he does not wish to print. He thinks, therefore, that it is Zener's intention to publish my review [of Erikson, 1950; Holt, 1951d] as soon as he can find space for it. I'd much rather have it in the Journal of Personality [of which Zener was editor] than in one of Murchison's journals. My impression is that a review has already appeared in the Psychological Bulletin, but I'll look into that.

I'm enclosing an extra copy that I happened to have of my contribution to the [APA] Diagnostic Case Symposium for this fall.[47] I thought you might like to see it because of the fact that in it I am trying to use the TAT as a way of getting at ego-identity. Actually this is my second attempt to analyze the TAT in this way, the first being a re-test study I am currently in the middle of on one of our psychiatrists [not published]. It struck me forcibly in going over his first TAT that he was struggling with an identity problem of the sort that Erik describes, which was very clearly perceptible in his stories.

As far as my "ESP interpretation" is concerned, I'm not sure that I will actually go through with it in the seminar. For one thing, I have to repeat so many of the same banal statements in my TAT report! But I think that there is a real lesson contained in this stunt, one that I would like to put across at the symposium.[48]

I imagine that you are in at least as close touch with Bille as we are here, and have heard the latest good news about her being

---

[46] George F. J. Lerner, a frequent contributor to the *Journal of Personality*, may have been a member of the editorial board.

[47] Later published as Holt, R. R. (1952).

[48] As a way of satirizing the tendency of some testers to write too generally about a generic person, I preceded my real "blind" interpretation of the stories by a cliché-filled one that, in a transparent joke, was allegedly generated by extrasensory perception (ESP).

out of the hospital. It is a great relief to know that the illness is so much more benign than had been thought and particularly that she is over the worst of it and no longer suffering. I only hope that she will still be able to get to Europe.

A little card came today informing me about Roy and Sarah's little girl. I'm pleased to see that they did not break the feminine tradition that so many of us have been at such pains to establish. Incidentally, I hear only good things from Louisa about Dorothy and Cathy. [. . .] But in about six weeks I will be seeing them my-self, so I can give you a first hand report. Louisa is still working away at her book, and is doing quite a bit of psychotherapy now, at the University Psychiatric Clinic. I hope that your family worries have cleared up by now, and that you have completely regained your strength. My ulcer continues not to heal, and not to give me any appreciable amount of trouble—not a satisfactory, but not a too unsatisfactory state of affairs. I'm sorry that the prospects for a Topeka visit [by him] sometime soon don't look too good, but we'll keep working on it.

        Your

         Bob

Rapaport to Holt—July 24, 1952

Dear Bob:

Finally I get around to your letter of June 25.

We are far from the operations [i.e., needed to measure our concepts]. You are right. But there are other criteria besides operations. Hughlings Jackson[49] used his intuition, taste, and sense of parsimony to describe phenomena and conjecture relationships. He was in many ways wrong, in many ways right. But Sherrington,[50] who used operational criteria, would not be conceivable without the thinking of Jackson. My taste in this case dictates keeping together as much as our synthetic functions permit, what seems to belong together.

As to externalization. I am not sure what you mean by purposeful. If you mean by purposeful "tension-relieving," I agree with you fully, but if you mean by purposeful the internal balance of the weight each of the functions represented by the scattergram can carry, then I do not. The positions of the scattergram, to my mind,

---

[49] J. Hughlings Jackson, FRS (1835–1911) practiced neurology in London hospitals from 1862 until his death. He is best known for his major studies of epilepsy and for his evolutionary conception of the nervous system. He conceived of it in three levels, the later controlling the more primitive, introducing the concept of regression. Major figures from Freud to Oliver Sacks have acknowledged his influence.

[50] Sir Charles Scott Sherrington, OM, GBE, PRS (1857–1952) was an English neurophysiologist, histologist, bacteriologist, and pathologist, president of the Royal Society in the early 1920s. He received the Nobel Prize in Physiology (shared with Edgar Adrian) in 1932.

represent quasi-stationary functions, that is, structuralized functions. Their distribution of strength corresponds to distribution of tensions tied up in structures. Now as to the economic problem: if you think that I am not unhappy about it also, you are wrong. I used not to be while I was preoccupied in systematizing. Now when I got over it, I am beginning to see many pitfalls of it, and many difficulties. For the moment, however, I am trying to do everything about clearing it up, or so to say, rescue it for myself. It is in this spirit that I am making the following comments. Let us think about motivation in general. Let us, however, draw a sharp line (such does not exist; we have to draw it just for the experiment's sake) between what [Gordon W.] Allport called motivating attitudes and instrumental attitudes. Nowadays, many things are called motivations that should be considered rather instrumental sets than motivations proper. I think this is why Hebb tries to relegate all motivation to such instrumental settings. When a motivation arises, I would want to conceive of that as a force. Wherever there is a force, there is always an energy distribution behind that [which] the force represents. There are no forces otherwise conceivable. When this force ceases to operate, and there is no perceivable or conjecturable counterforce or barrier in sight, then I would consider that a discharge took place.[51] (As you see, for the moment I am avoiding the issue of binding and structuralization here.) I myself used energy distribution usually in connection with counter-cathectic energy distributions. I did so primarily because once a counter-cathexis is established, it tends to spread to motivations other than the one which was established to defend against it, or which was established to control it.

---

[51] In the margin, I had jotted a note to myself: "But this arouses confusing concrete imagery and puts an undue temptation in our way to misplaced concreteness." I think what I meant was that concepts such as "barrier" tend to bring up images of walls or roadblocks, easily making us forget that the intent is quite abstract and makes us fall into the fallacy of misplaced concreteness. Behind that, I now think, was my growing discomfort with the implicitly reductionistic replacement of psychological concepts (like purpose) by physicalistic ones (like *force* and *energy-distribution*) with no physically measurable properties.

That is, it isn't an energy which manifests itself as a force representable by a single vector, but rather as a broad distribution of energy, to [I think he meant "in"] which a whole force field [is] directed toward various motivations.

When I speak about structured and unstructured response[s], I have in mind mainly the distinction between Bellevue responses on the one hand, and Rorschach responses on the other, with the exception of popular responses and their penumbra. As far as the content aspect of personality is concerned, I agree with you that it is a most unfortunate expression. Indeed, it carries the danger that you indicate. But don't forget that this is not merely a business deriving out of tests, but also a business deriving out of [the] psychoanalytic interview. The old-fashioned psychoanalyst vented [he probably meant "vetted"] the content of the patient's material, and interpreted that. We are more prone to interpret the resistances, the defenses, etc., at least at first. A more correct distinction would be that between the ideational representations of forces and structures of the personality versus the formal characteristics of any level of behavior through which these forces and structures manifest themselves. The difficulty of making [a] distinction between formal and content aspects is that what is on one level content is form on another, and vice versa. There is an ascending hierarchy of increasing formalizations.

As far as the "States of Consciousness" paper is concerned, I think your critique is cogent, well taken, so much so that I in a way regret that you soften it down for me. I must admit that I didn't realize the real inherent weaknesses of the paper, which you point out, until quite recently. The major reason for the weakness was that my laziness was aided and abetted by the need to present it to the Macy people, who are anything but worth the metapsychological theory. So I tried to pull my punches. I am planning to write a new paper on this, and to present it somewhere, sometime in the fall or winter.

Your contribution to the Symposium [on blind analysis of a TAT] I will have to postpone writing about until next time. I want to give thought to the point you make about "ego identity." The stunt itself, however, is impressive. If you would read all the tripe that comes here as psychological test reports from some of the "best-known people," you would certainly go through with it.

Bille's going to Europe is over and done. I feel happy and relieved that she is as far [recovered] as she is.

I am delighted with the good news about your children. I hope that will continue. When do you go to see them? I am still exhausted, and the heat doesn't help. I am about to take off for a three weeks vacation, traveling all around, mainly Stockbridge.

Yours,

David

Holt to Rapaport—September 22, 1952

Dear David,

Thanks very much for your prompt reply to my letter of inquiry about Suzanne Reichard. I have also written to Else Frenkel-Burnswik, who has known her since her analysis, and I have asked her to tell me candidly if she thinks that the analysis has made much change in her personality. I certainly agree with you that the kind of person you describe would not be suitable for the job, and as you may know, I don't believe that an analysis accomplishes miracles. Nevertheless, I want to give her careful consideration. I think it's interesting, in view of the resistance that you remarked in her accepting our way of doing things, that she speaks of the year and a half that she had here as "one of the most stimulating experiences of my whole professional life." I'll let you know how it all turns out.

I got back last night from the Institute in Montana. It was a rather exhausting week in some ways, although extremely pleasant and quite diverting; I feel as if I've been away from Topeka for a month. It was a rather humbling experience in some way to see these earnest people, many of them practicing in remote mountain areas where the nearest psychologist or psychiatrist colleague is 400 or more miles away—to see how they struggle with and probably are pretty effective in dealing with a tremendous variety of psychological problems, unaided. What a specialist I am, I thought, and how narrow my working experience has been! I think it's because of that very narrowness that I have been able to make some contributions that have brought me the attention of my colleagues, yet it has certainly been at the expense of the kind of intense and extensive clinical experiential background that I wish I had. Another striking thing to me was the frequency with which people referred to Roy, and the unanimity of everyone who had been at last year's Institute, students and faculty alike, that Roy was far and away the most effective and stimulating teacher they had.

This year our faculty included, besides Ija Korner and Bill Brown (the Deans), Joe Zubin, Art Combs, a very nice and thoughtful young San Francisco analyst named Vic Calef, Hardin Branch, and Fred Wyatt.[52] The experience was very much worthwhile to me if only to have given me a chance to get well acquainted with this variegated bunch of mostly pretty thoughtful people. I found Joe Zubin to have an astonishingly warm human side, despite the icy-sadistic quality that I have so often felt in him; you should have seen him fathering the three little kids of the woman who ran the dude ranch where we were located. I learned to have a good deal more respect for Combs, and hit it off exceptionally well with him personally, even though I have a number of theoretical disagreements with him. I had enough of a chance to discuss his phenomenological system with him to attain a little more respect for it than I had had. Hardin Branch and Ija Korner are two delightful and entirely different characters, whom I think a great deal of—and I could go on this way giving a lot of impressions though I don't quite know how interesting it would be to you. Another person I enjoyed getting to know was Hans Huessy, the regional consultant for USPHS, operating out of Denver, a very friendly and thoughtful young German-born psychiatrist.

What we accomplished, I think, was worthwhile though rather nebulous: I believe the main thing we did was to stir up a lot of ideas and generate a good deal of cerebration among a good many psychologists who have very little professional stimulation

---

[52] For identification of the named persons, see Addendum below. Pious was a Menninger psychiatrist, somewhat later my analyst.

normally and who very rarely get to professional meetings. I was rather surprised at their eager thirst for discussions on a theoretical level in preference to practical discussion of some of the everyday working problems with which they are faced. In a way, I suppose the best one can do in a week of this kind of intensive and informal contact is to give the students an opportunity to develop some identification with persons whom they consider leaders and contributors in the field. And this I believe we did. The setting was very pleasant: a group of log buildings on the shore of a beautiful lake which is so teeming with fish that I understand Bill Pious went there last year and is returning next for his vacation. It is big game hunting country, too, and as a result we had a few meals of roast elk and buffalo steaks. Kind of a thrill for a city boy like me.

I do hope you have recovered from whatever it is that has been restricting your mobility, and that you will let me know sometime what you are going to be working on primarily this year. Perhaps you know that Lois Murphy has just joined Gardner, and they had the good luck to find an adequate house into which they moved yesterday, I believe. That's about all the news I know, since I just got back to town and haven't seen anybody yet.

My best to all my friends there,

Yours,

Bob

Addendum—Other Faculty of the Institute

C. H. Hardin Branch received his MD at Tulane in 1935. He was Professor and Head of the Department of Psychiatry at the University of Utah College of Medicine from 1948–1970. He then became Chief of the Department of Psychiatry, Salt Lake General Hospital and University Hospital, 1948–1970, and President of the American Board of Psychiatry and Neurology, 1962–1963.

William H. Brown was the first of my graduate students to get his doctorate (from the University of Kansas). He taught at the medical school at the University of Utah, was president of the Utah Psychological Association and then of the Rocky Mountain Psychological Association.

Victor Calef lived most of his life in San Francisco, where he practiced and taught psychoanalysis. The San Francisco Psychoanalytic Institute established an honorary lectureship in his memory after his death. He published many papers on psychoanalysis and became one of the editors of the *Journal of the American Psychoanalytic Association*.

Arthur W. Combs is best remembered for his joint work with Donald Snygg on "Phenomenal Field Theory" (Snygg, D., & Combs, A. W., Individual behaviour: Harper, 1949; revised ed. 1959), but he published 10 other books.

Ija N. Korner was best known for his well-received book, *Experimental Investigation of Some Aspects of the Problem of Repression* (1950). A Swiss by birth, he published articles and book reviews on a number of topics in clinical psychology, plus two papers on community psychology with Bill Brown.

Frederick Wyatt was born in Vienna, got his PhD from the University of Vienna, and began his psychoanalytic training there, finishing it in Boston. He was a staff member at the Harvard Psychological Clinic in the early 1940s, where I worked with him. After a stint as Chief Psychologist at McLean Hospital, he went to the University of Michigan, where he directed the Psychological Clinic and became Professor of Psychology.

Joseph Zubin in 1956 founded the Biometrics Research Unit for the New York State Department of Mental Hygiene to apply objective measurement procedures (biometrics) to evaluating psychiatric disorders. Diagnostic criteria in the *Diagnostic and Statistical Manual-III* were based on the unit's work. Zubin moved to the University of Pittsburgh School of Medicine, where he established a new Biometrics Research Program focusing on schizophrenia, becoming Distinguished Research Professor of Psychiatry.

Rapaport to Holt—September 25, 1952

Dear Bob:

Thank you for your letter.

I am glad that you are looking further into the Reichard business. She needs an institutional setting and belongs to the few who know how we used to do things. She must also have mellowed with the years, and the setting we had at the time was prone to exacerbate people's bad reactions: it was not a collaboration of peers: I was a heavy-handed boss (I guess I, too, mellowed in the years or so I hope). You may wonder about the contradiction between the previous letter and this one. But I think both carry factual truth.

In a way your letter about the Montana experience made me aware how harshly I judged her, and what I wrote is certainly not all I think about her. It is humbling to know that Zubin, whom I regarded much like you did and, in addition, somewhat of a "wooden Indian" in face and mind, is actually a warm, paternal person; and Combs, whom I encountered only as a glib and arrogant fellow, proves on a closer look-see a thoughtful man. I wished I would hear more often about these people, because the public appearances and writings of this "fraternity" dismays and exasperates me in the extreme.

I thought you know about the trouble I am having: my rheumatic heart caught up with me and I am beginning to watch my step. As for work: I am about done with the leg-work on the Fenichel "Collected Papers" [Fenichel & Rapaport, 1953]. I am finished with the translation of Schilder's <u>Medical Psychology</u> and should, within the next four to six weeks, complete the introduction and footnotes to it. For over a year I have been involved in trying to write a review of the Dollard-Miller book, and I hope I will get that out of the way. I am supposed to write a review of Kris's new book. I will have to put the finishing touches on my paper on "The Psychoanalytic Theory of Affects" [Rapaport, 1953a]; it will be published in the International-al Journal [of Psychoanalysis]. I may transcribe the other seven lectures of my "Ego-Psychology" seminar (the first one you have). But when all this is done, and I hope it will be done sometime early in November, I will quit desk work and theorizing and will do some experiments. I just came back from Boston, from a long talk with George, which helped me considerably to put together just what I want to do. I do not mean to say that I know as yet what I will do. It will be probably first a lot of preliminary exploratory stuff. But I do know that I want to fool around with an attack on the problem of learning, and while I do not know how to ask the right question about learning (I am under the impression that the question has been wrongly asked by most people—but this again sounds haughty and arrogant to me), I do think that the way I will have to ask it will be on the pattern of the sequence attention-anticipation-automatization. The reading of the Hebb [1949] book had influ-enced me considerably in this and I am much indebted to George, who had sold me on this book. Did you read it?

I would like to know what you are doing.

> Yours,
>
> David

Rapaport to Holt—November 1, 1952

Dear Bob:

First of all, thanks for your letter you asked Roy to show me. Your way of writing, again—as always—was most enjoyable to me, and the subtlety of nuances was particularly pleasing. That you found so much good to say about so many I partly envied, partly slightly suspected. But let me assure you that the envy, [in] manifold, outweighed that which seemed to me suspect.

This is an inquiry and a request. I do want you to refuse it flatly if you are either not sufficiently interested in just this thing, or if it would be at this moment not possible for you. I have translated a Schilder book—it is about 421 pages of translation, corrected by Bill Gibson. I have written footnotes to it which, if they would be condensed into pages, would not amount to more than about 60–70 pages. It is planned to reprint my Schilder "Memorial Lecture" as an Appendix. I wrote an Introduction of some 15 pages. The Introduction and the footnotes are not as yet corrected for the English. I need a balanced distant view whether I executed fairly what I promised in my Introduction. I am particularly worried that I did too much in the footnotes. I didn't intend to. Do you think you could read this material for me and give me your criticism? The material could reach you about a week from this Friday, for about two weeks (if some additional time would make the difference, that could be done, but usually what we cannot do in two weeks we cannot do in three either). Let me say that the perceptual stuff was looked over by George, and the neurological stuff was looked over by Norm Reider. Lauretta Bender has seen the translation and will look it over once more. What I need is a synoptic, sufficiently distant view, and I would not know anybody who could do that for me as well as you could, if you possibly could manage it. As you know, the title is <u>Medical Psychology</u>, and it is an attempted integration of Brentano's act-psychology, Husserl's phenomenology, neurology, aphasias and other brain-injured experience, psychoanalysis, psychoses-experience. I consider the book an important predecessor of psychoanalytic ego psychology, though his understanding of contemporary psychoanalysis, when he wrote it, was quite poor. It is a loose, irresponsible, ingenious, insightful, arbitrary piece.

I feel that you could do me a great favor by doing it, but I would in a way consider it a token of your real confidence in me if you would at this point flatly state that you cannot do it. Looking forward to an immediate answer,

        Yours,

          David

Holt to Rapaport—November 5, 1952

Dear David:

I'll do it. I won't pretend that this is the one book of all others that I would most like to read just now, but I do want to get some familiarity with [Paul] Schilder's thought sooner or later, and this seems like a good way to do it. This is above and beyond what I'm sure you know exists anyway: my pleasure that I can do a favor for you, and the gratification that I feel because of your selecting me to undertake just this task. I'm quite intrigued to see the book after your tantalizing summary description of it. I imagine that I'll be able to manage it in the two weeks; if I see that I am not going to be able to, I'll let you know how things stand as soon as I can see.

I'm glad that you enjoyed my letter to Roy, and I must confess that I am amused by your reaction to the nice things that I said about some people. You know, I used to have a reputation as a terribly sarcastic, bitingly critical person, who could always be depended on to find the weak chink in somebody's armor. Obviously I have changed over the years, perhaps as a result of some kind of reaction formation, perhaps (I'd rather see it this way) as a result of some kind of mellowing, but I still retain in my self-concept enough of that kind of picture of myself so that I am constantly surprised when people say things to me like what you said in your letter.

Let me just bring you up to date briefly on the question of Suzanne Reichard. Lew Robbins decided, wisely, I think, that it would be better to promote somebody from within the group rather than to bring someone in from the outside, so we gave up considering Reichard and Sargent any further for this position. So far, no leader has "emerged" yet from the group, but I feel fairly confident that one will fairly soon. Meanwhile, Helen Sargent is being hired as a kind of special assistant to Dr. Karl for the next six months, during which time we are going to see if there isn't some organic place for her in the Foundation.

I am grateful for your account in your letter of September 25th of the work you have been doing and are expecting to undertake in the near future. That's a formidable writing schedule you have for yourself; by contrast, I feel as if I had been doing nothing. I suppose in a small way I am beginning to feel something the way that you once did here, that so much of your time went in conferring with other people about their work that not enough of your own work got done. Of course, I don't actually spend a great deal of time that way, and yet it seems constantly to increase. The latest thing is that I am meeting regularly with Gardner [Murphy] to discuss his plans for experimental work—something that I enjoy very much, and yet I am beset by my old doubts, my feelings that I ought to be more productive myself before I presume to advise others. Yet despite this kind of feeling (which is by no means always with me) Lester and I are managing to get some work done on our book. We have several chapters roughed out, and should be able to get the final quantitative analysis of the data, the validation of our predictions, done by IBM [card-sorting machine, pre-computer] methods rather soon. Meanwhile, I am a part of the Admissions Committee, by a whim of Dr. Karl's, and am finding it interesting work. I am sure that my membership on this committee is the only way in which a significant part of our research will ever get used by the School!

That's about all that I think I can tell you at the moment about my own activities. About yours, I can tell you that you have too many of them, even from this distance I can see that. For a man with a bad heart, you act remarkably like someone who thought he had plenty of physical resources to abuse. When I think about my own physical condition, I feel proud of myself for managing to do so little, though I more generally take the opposite view of it! I guess we have some of the same problems, and it's a great deal easier to preach to the other fellow than it is to pluck out the beam from one's own eye. Well, anyway, take care of yourself, and send me that manuscript at once.

        Affectionately,
        Bob

Rapaport to Holt—December 5, 1952

Dear Bob:

Thank you for your letter of December 3. [. . .] The two batches of manuscript arrived in good order and your comments, criticisms and suggestions are a great help. Your feeling that the stuff is worth while allays a continuous uneasiness that has been besetting me: I do get worried that my historical interest and infatuation with ideas may take me to things of no interest to anyone else.

I am sorry about what you tell me about Gardner, Will and Karl, but it seems that people do not get wiser as time passes. [. . .]

As for the Rubinstein and Lorr book: I think it is an important thing to do this. I think from the vantage point in which you are, you can do a lot of important things in such an article. I mean, do a real piece of education concerning organization, training, practice and research role of clinical psychology. I will be delighted to do anything you ask me to do about it, and will be glad to volunteer all kinds of ideas I have about it if—as I know you will do—you will take what anyway is up your line and drop what isn't. I would very much like to collaborate with you on something, but I do not think that this should be it. I have been too closely connected with what happened in Topeka for me to be a co-author on this. You are in a more favorable position to be objective. I would have to insist on certain things which you do not have to. I am sure you will be far more objective and feel more unfettered without my collaboration. In the meanwhile you can have anything you want to about this from me, just as much as from a collaborator. The only thing you could have from a collaborator that you won't have, is dispassionate judgment. But that you couldn't have even if I tried to collaborate. Maybe I am not old enough for that, or maybe people of my temperament die first before they get dispassionate about certain things. So: (1) give the sign what kind of stuff you would want to hear about from me; (2) give the sign to invite me just to scribble out various ideas and historical sequences as they come to me if you want to; (3) take a look at some papers I have written in the Journal of Consulting Psychology, on "Clinical Psychology in the Private Mental Hospital," [Rapaport, 1944] and "Training in Clinical Psychology" [Rapaport & Schafer, 1946?]. You may want to look over also again the psychology issues of the Menninger Bulletin: some of the articles which do not talk at all about the topic proper, do imply attitudes toward clinical psychology. I have in mind, for instance, the paper about the Rorschach test I once wrote in the Bulletin [not traceable]. Enclosed I am returning to you the two letters by Rubinstein [probably Eli Rubinstein].

Sincerely yours,

David

P.S. I just read the "Barriers and Gateways to Communication" you sent me. I am sorry—since you called it "good stuff"—to tell you that I found it profoundly irritating, superficial and wrong from the word go. In fact, it would be dangerous if it didn't sound so boy-Scoutish. If you want to look it over once more and want me to write about it, I would be glad to indeed. [This comment makes it totally evident that Rapaport could be as unsparing in his criticism as he was generous in his praise. No holding back of either kind!]

Summary—Minor Letters from
March 21 to December 31, 1952

First, Rapaport wrote about a compatriot, a Hungarian psychologist, M. H. Nagy, whom he had known in the university, to see if there might be a job in Topeka for which she would be appropriate. Apparently he had forgotten that he had raised the question before. In response, I reminded him that the position for which we had considered her was no longer open, but that I had told her about an opening in California for which she would be qualified. In the same letter, I confessed having given up "my grandiose dreams about doing some original theorizing" in my chapter for the Klopfer book on Rorschach. I enclosed part of the first draft; meanwhile (March 27) he had already written asking to see it. That letter bubbles with enthusiasm about undisclosed ideas for experimentation on communication, stimulated by conversations with George Klein and Alex Bavelas, a well-known social psychologist at MIT.

On June 2, Rapaport wrote about family matters, his travel plans, and transmitting a paper.

On July 7, I told him I was assembling his various writings about the rationale of Rorschach responding and sending lists of typos found in two of his books. He replied with apologies for not having done the first task himself and thanking me for the second. On July 23, he enclosed a letter from Nagy, indicating that she could emigrate from Canada if she had a pro forma job offer.

I wrote on July 28 that Dr. Will might agree re Nagy, adding: "Paul, Beni Rubinstein, Gerry Aronson and I have been having a series of talks on some of the basic problems of motivation theory. I have been recording some of them, and if any of the material looks interesting after it's typed, I'll send you copies if you'd be interested." Nothing seems to have come from that, however.

On July 30, I sent him a copy of a general letter sent to former staff members at Menninger's, Topeka State Hospital, and Winter VA Hospital, proposing the possibility of an "alumni organization of Topeka psychologists," perhaps with a newsletter of current doings.

Before he could respond, I wrote again on September 8 about other job-seekers and matching them with openings (including Chief Psychologist at Menninger's), asking for some feedback. I added: "This Friday, I am flying to Montana to take part [as faculty member] in a workshop in clinical psychology at Flathead Lake. It is sponsored by the U.S. Public Health Service, and [. . .] I am looking forward to it. [. . .]"

On September 12, DR explained why he could not recommend one of the seekers.

Next, there are couple of notes about getting the Schilder translation to me, followed (November 26) by my first reaction on dipping into it:

I'm frightened by the thickness of the manuscript [. . .] [but] I am enjoying it—the extraordinary scope and freshness of Schilder's mind is a revelation to me, since I haven't read more than a few pages of his before. I'm beginning to agree with all those apparently contradictory things you said about him!

Then I asked his advice about a number of job opportunities that were beginning to open. Indeed, most of the remaining letters exchanged in 1952 are preoccupied with these two rather different matters. My comments on his Schilder book are not substantive, but focus on matters of organization, format, style, etc., and though his efforts to help me find the next location in which to live and work show his warmth as well as deep knowledge of what was going on in clinical psychology, we can easily skip most of the exchanges.

Here, however, is part of my letter of December 3:

It would be very much to my liking indeed if George and I could [. . .] team up, or at least be in the same institution and have an opportunity of talking things over together. I had a talk with Gardner [Murphy] the other day, also, and he was very helpful. Incidentally, David—and this is just between you and me—I wouldn't be at all surprised if Gardner does not stay long in Topeka himself. I am trying to think of some tactful way of dropping a warning word to Dr. Will that his debonair way of making promises and blandly reneging is a dangerous pastime. Whenever I have regrets about leaving Topeka, I think of Karl and Will and the fact that they are still firmly in the saddle, and then I take heart.

I have about decided to collaborate with a couple of rather unknown [to me] psychologists in Washington, Eli Rubinstein and Maurice Lorr, in contributing a chapter to a book that they are going to write on the emergence of the profession of clinical psychology. Their general plan is to have representatives of each of a number of major institutions and types of practice give a historical summary of the development of clinical psychology in their setting. It looks now as if enough good institutions and individuals are associated with it to make it worthwhile for the Foundation to be included. I don't see how I can do it without some help from you. Would you like to make it a collaborative affair? I'd be very happy indeed if you'd be a co-author with me. In any event, I'll need to count on your help in checking over what I can put together of the history of the first ten years of psychology here at the Foundation. [. . .]

In the first of two letters dictated on December 5, after some helpful comments about my opportunities, David added:

I just received the Newsletter [of the alumni group] and it was really an eye-opener to see how many people, how widespread, and with how much vivid interest, came out of Topeka. I wondered whether one could add [. . .] an invitation that people tell not only what they are doing but what they have read (in any

field) that moved them and made them feel that they would like
to recommend it to the rest of us. I, for instance, would right now
indicate that the Tinbergen [book], The Study of Instincts, and
Hebb's Organization of Behavior, plus Lorenz's King Solomon's
Ring are excellent. [. . .]

My response (December 8) continued the conversation about possible relocations for me, more about the Schilder book, and his reading
recommendations ("completely captivated by [Lorenz] [. . .] charmed
and instructed"). I thanked him for his generous offer of help on the
Rubinstein-Lorr book.

I hope very much that we will find something more meaty to collaborate on someday. Meanwhile, I'd appreciate it if you'd do
what you suggested: "scribble out various ideas & historical sequences" [. . .] at odd moments. After I've organized a tentative
outline, I'll send it to you & we can see how I can best exploit your
willingness! [. . .] I'm surprised by your reaction to the communications stuff and hope to go into it in detail at some future date. [. . .]

Finally (December 31), appended to letter of thanks for my work on
Schilder and for a Christmas gift, came the following postscript:

You surprised me with your comment about McClelland, which
you made on the manuscript. I never thought that he would allow
himself really to theorize. Is his learning theory, which takes the
distinction between early and late learning into consideration,
worth reading? I just got Fritz Heider's manuscript [perhaps an
early draft of Heider, 1958] in a mimeographed form, and I am
champing at the bit to get to it. George sent me some material on
'Aktualgenese,' the Leipzig school experiments on the here-and-
now development that takes place before a percept is experienced in its fully developed form. Then there is a manuscript here
by Bettelheim, which contains a new interpretation of 'initiation
rites,' and then last but not least, two manuscripts from Paul. In

addition, Merton's recorded therapy hours, which I am trying to follow and discuss in letters. In the meanwhile, I am—believe it or not—actually prepared to begin some experiments, either in January or early in February. I wished I could sit down with you for a few hours and discuss them.

CHAPTER 3

Rapaport to Holt—Early December 1952

[handwritten]

Dear Bob,

I have your letter of Dec. 8, but won't answer it now. I will just begin to "scribble" as you invited me—or rather as I invited you to invite me. You don't know what you are getting into—and so stop me if it gets [to be] too much. I do not think that I can do this without personal reminiscences. Actually, I may have been waiting for just such an adoo [sic; invitation?] to write such—to gather up what happened. You will understand that it isn't meant for others to see besides yourself[53] and now you did start me on it you can spare yourself the trouble of reading it by just a brief note.

I met Karl Menninger first in 1939 [when Rapaport was 28 years old] through Larry Kubie [Lawrence S. Kubie, MD] (who after my arrival in NY gave me a few hundred letters of recommendation). Preparatory to going to him I read his "Human Mind." I was working on what became later "Emotions and Memory" and so I read those parts first. The thalamic theory of emotions was new to me and impressive—the connection to the Ucs. even newer and I did not see the evidence for the connection. The news-story style seemed to me to bespeak a master who can allow himself to illus-

---

[53] Because so many years have elapsed since Rapaport's death, and that of most (if not all) other persons mentioned, I feel that the historical value of this account outweighs my obligation to respect this expression of his wishes.

117

trate thus, using the trivial to convey profound knowledge. The man's appearance bore this out, he seemed "a man of stature." He was "ready to help" and thought he can get me to the Devereux Schools. I did not know when I sadly sat after missing my chance what I escaped. He wanted me to meet his colleagues at the Or-tho [American Orthopsychiatric Association] meeting: I met Doug Orr [Douglass W. Orr, MD] and the occupational therapist [Kreider] of the Southard School. They were cordial to each other and to me over a cup of coffee. The "camaraderie" was deeply impressive to the newcomer and the cordiality seemed to promise that I have a job just about secured. It took some rude awakenings be-fore I learned that neither was true: Orr and Kreider hardly knew each other, I never heard from them or from Karl about the job. Just let me add that my greenhorn imagination and partly their talk and partly the way people talked about Topeka to me made me imagine—the image was so vivid that I still see its details at this moment—a huge modern building, the Clinic, and a wing of it the Southard School with all the conveniences of American Technique. [. . .]

In the meanwhile something totally unrelated happened still in N.Y. which was to prove later the link that brought me to Menningers. Through Larry Kubie I met Mrs. Pollitier—a lovely grandmother who in many ways reminded me of my mother. She was the famous dermatologist Pollitier's widow and proved to be a friend of Prof. Török—a Hungarian dermatologist, distant ac-quaintance of ours whose son and his family were our close acquaintances. Mrs. Pollitier spoke a lovely soft German— heavenly music to my ears, who never [before had] heard English for [more than] a day in succession and never spoke any before his [my] arrival at these shores. She took us to the Walden School—a progressive N.Y. school—which had a weekly open house for refugees—and there she found English teaching volun-teers for us and where we found [a] German-speaking 'Kindergarten' for refugees for Hanna [his older daughter].—We met there her daughter—the wife of Louis Weiss, friend of

Rosewelt [FDR] from college and throughout the New Deal years, later the background organizer of the Hiss defense, trustee of the New School, attorney of the Psa. Assoc. [New York or American Psychoanalytic Association]. One day I mentioned that I need[ed] subjects for to get accustomed to take [i.e., administer] Rorschachs in English. She sent her daughter Elisabeth.—Later in Ossawatomie [Osawatomie, KS] I got a letter from Caroline Zachri [Caroline B. Zachry, PhD] that E. is in analysis with her and they are in an impasse—would I send her an interpretation. I did. I received a grateful note that it was very helpful—but I was yet [sic] to hear about it later. This incident was somehow very helpful to me. I never [had] thought that an analyst might need a test. Hungarian analysts didn't. They were pretty sure of themselves, at least so they seemed at that time me. Zachri's letter amazed me with its forthrightness but also made me pause "what kind of analysts are these?" Yet a [again? (erasure)] I am sure that the incident opened up new vistas of possible practical avenues.

But let me return to N.Y. I had a promise of a grant of $1,000 from the Committee for Displaced Scholars if I find a place which will give me a volunteer job to help acclimatization, and the tentative (it was made clear that it needn't be binding or even serious) promise that they [would] help me etc. if I'd prove useful. I was hunting for a job like that! among many other things: volunteer work at Mount Sinai where G. [Gardner] Murphy got me in through David Beres—review of memory literature for Macy Foundation which I got by Larry [Lawrence K.] Frank introducing me to [Frank] Fremont-Smith who wanted to see me because he was of Hungarian ancestry. He gave me this work when his effort to get me in the study of [Helen Flanders] Dunbar and husband ([Theodore P.] Wolfe—who just got all tied up with W.[ilhelm] Reich) failed because these two got into a fight at the luncheon which was to seal the deal, over what my role in the project would be, and how my material which I was to obtain was to be used by them, and I bowed out not seeing how I could adjust to this country under such inauspicious tension-conditions. (I did not know then either what luck I had—what I escaped.) K[urt] Lewin, who was then W. James visiting professor at Harvard (substituting for [H. A.] Murray in one of his many absences), was the teacher of my teacher Paul Schiller. He suggested that I see J. F. Brown—who was a student of his associated with K.U. [University of Kansas] and Menningers. The 1933 [American] Psychiatric [Association] Meetings (Chicago) gave a good occasion for it. Brown—after he first gave me an examination in methodology, philosophy and epistemology in the most German professorial manner, intro-duced me to [W. D.] Orbison who at that time worked at Osawatomie State Hospital, Kansas. He in turn took both of us to Dr. [Ralph M.] Fellows the superintendent. Fellows didn't know nothing from nothing. Except that he was trying to get his hospi-tal to be fully approved for residencies and he was about to hire Orbison[54] who was to go to Yale [PhD, 1945] in the fall, and except as a good shrewd—though none too bright—businessman, he heard the $1000 well, and saw a saving. Hands were shaken, the bargain was on. Brown [was] appointed my supervisor, research advisor and mentor.—I got back to N.Y., the promised $1000 were gone. Larry Kubie and David Levy got [another $1,000] for me then, from Mrs. D. Levy (of the Rosenwald family).

So I got to Osawatomie. It was the hottest Kansas summer I [ever] knew. In the daytime I settled for a few tests as a routine for each staff case. Rorschach—Szondi—Stanford-Binet with which I just began to be familiar: there was only Binet in Hungary and standardized only up to [age] 8. Otherwise individual tests (we would call them items here) were standardized by the few indi-vidual institutions, each for their own consumption. This had little reliability—but it put the individual ingenuity of the tester to test. Be it noted that I did not spend much time with such stuff there [in Hungary]. I was interested in epistemology and thought and considered Rorschach and all the rest interesting only for that.

---

[54] In a 1939 article, W. D. Orbison described what became known as "Orbison's illu-sion."

Though I did record that if worse comes to worse and I can't live on teaching (I did not have any idea that one can live on research) I could try to make a living on it. Frankly, I got for the same purpose a Montessori School teaching experience (Kindergarten mainly) and a diploma—and I would have had more basis to earn my living on that—though I would have probably liked it less; though arithmetic teaching in grade [school] or in High school would have suited me to a T. (I was sort of a teacher often. To Bob [Knight]'s one patient in Topeka, to most of Margaret [Brenman]'s and to one of Roy [Schafer]'s here—and there was something in my relation to my associates of the school-teacherish—it partly marred and partly informed with substance those relationships).

Orbison, who studied at KU (also his later wife, Marian Gilbert, who worked in the children's cottage of the Hospital and in the traveling O.P. clinics), brought a Stanford-Binet report sheet from there. It was like the Rossolimo[55] profiles I was familiar with (they are meant to be personality profiles) showing "scatter" of grouped S.B. intelligence items. The word scatter came from here and the determination to find a test which will [would] show meaningful scatter. I studied the S.B. scatter, felt it was both meaningful and deceptive in its measures. I went at studying its literature—and everybody had different measures and negative results. But I got a feel for it and I was sure it was worth pursuing. I think that it was clearly a method to study the "components of thought"—a continuation of my Ph.D. thesis—that excited me more than the diagnostic possibility. At nights I was trying to cover the English psychiatric and psychoanalytic journal literature from 1890 on. In the remaining daytime I planned a huge battery of tests, some of which I brought with me, others which I discovered in use here. Orbison showed me a word association list they used at K.U. in a Luria experiment [that] he himself modified (toned it down) for general use and I used it increasingly instead

---

[55] G. I. Rossolimo (1860–1928), a Russian child neurologist and experimental psychologist who worked on the development of psychological profiles.

of the Jung and Kent-Rosanoff. We still use the same—only Roy modified it somewhat. [Eugenia] Hanfmann, whom I met in Chicago, introduced me to the Vigotsky test [of concept-formation]; the object-sorting [test] I saw in N.Y. at Montefiore in [Kurt] Goldstein's use—Bolles-Rosen-Landis version. The TAT [David] Shakow had given me when I showed him the Szondi, having come to him on my way back from Lewin in Boston, to look for a job. In the meanwhile I used the opportunities [that were] present: drugs were in big use and a few young psychiatrists were bored and eager to do something. I lectured on tests and their use and involved them. So we ran series of [studies on] the prognostication [predictive value?] by and effect on tests of metrazol treatment; of histamine, of sodium amytal; story recalls under and after these drugs, [and] drawing (Bender-Gestalt, which I had from [Max] Wertheimer's papers) under similar conditions. I learned an important lesson: drugs affect tests differently according to the illness and personality of the patient.

Later in a meeting, I tried to say, when psychosomatic specificity was discussed, that drug reaction specificity may be one way to approach it. Nobody listened. Except Dunbar, who offered to publish "my studies" on this in a psychosomatic monograph. Since I had "experience" but no "solid experiments" with them, I suggested that she help finance such. That killed that on the spot; and I avoided a bad experience and mistake. I am sure that this was sheer luck. Now George K.[lein] finds individual differences in perception. These experiences were very important for me. When formulating later, at Menninger's, the first research projects, it [the specificity of drug reactions] was one of the foremost [investigative ideas] still among them. It was also discussed by Crail, Calderon and Silverman [unidentified persons] among my own research plans just prior to my joining Menninger's.—It was a way to involve psychiatrists and get close knowledge of the cases which I could not have gotten otherwise.

Another set of studies started with a case of paresis who was diagnosed schizophrenia and shocked out of his psychosis. Dr.

[Vivian B.] Kenyon discovered [that] the [patient had] paresis and became puzzled. I picked this up and induced [Milton] Lozoff and her to try it on other paretics. A cruel story. But the helplessness of watching their decay wasn't any less cruel. I knew [Paul] Schilder's paretic study superficially; the psychosomatic issue excited me; the bonafide opportunity to get "organic tests" and parallel histories from Doctors was important. And I saw some 70 paretics and got a real taste of that thought disorder and its contrast with the schizophrenic. I think I learned more about thought disorder on those Babcocks (I found the test in Orbison's hand) than in most any other place; synchronization of my own interests, or new learning opportunities, for techniques or problems, of inspiring others, of maintaining and channeling interest already existing, of trying to set goals which bring rewards, of foregoing undeserved rewards and premature publication—these I tried out first in Osawatamie. In the meanwhile, there was a Cornell-trained philosophy Ph.D.—a polio victim [Alden O. Weber], son of the local banker with whom I discussed borderlands of phil. and psych. and published some [Weber & Rapaport, 1941], getting an introduction into the literature. In the meanwhile I did my reading, so that I developed Frank Fremont-Smith's original assignment into "Emotions and Memory" [Rapaport, 1942a]. I still had help from F. F. S. (a total of some $1400) and used it to get excerpts and card files with the help of a secretary. But the feverish pace of all this activity can not be understood really without some background of the course in [of] my job. But that I will have to visit some time in the future. [Final six words mostly cut off and illegible.]

Rapaport to Holt—December 16, 1952

[handwritten]

Dear Bob,

I believe I left off where I wanted to give a picture of the background of my feverish activity.

I arrived at Osawatomie in Midsummer. There was no housing for my family and they were supposed to arrive later. I was terribly lonesome. I made the decision to rent a little flat and have them come: they did, some six weeks after me. No sooner they arrived the troubles began. The Kansas State Board of Welfare would not approve my appointment: "We want no 'furriners' here." I never found out whether Dr. Fellows had me come without clearing with the Board or whether the Board "changed its mind." I did find out soon, however, that Fellows wanted to be rid of me because he was utterly dependent on Board politics, which disregarded every interest of the hospital, of the stability of its staff etc. I also felt that he went chicken, showing how his few-worded bluster was just a thin veneer. He advised that I take the money left of my $1000 grant and go back east. I did not feel like going into the New York time-wasting, self-administering turmoil—wanted peace, quiet study imposed by conditions. I told him that I came there on invitation, a word given should oblige [i.e., since he gave his word, he should keep it]. Furthermore that I wouldn't move without consulting my sponsors. When he saw that I did not budge easy, he made two moves: he took me to Menningers and later, on my insistence, to the Board. I had already been at Menningers: Orbison and Marianne

124

Gilbert took me there on the day the bad news broke: to speak with Brown's substitute there, Dr. [Walter A.] Varvel. Varvel was shy, friendly, and the picture he gave me of the place was both uninviting and scant. Stone, the business manager, saw good business in helping; Karl was visiting too, and supported him. But none showed interest in listening to me. Later I learned that Fellows left with them the grant check. At the Board Fellows again got chickenhearted. Went in alone rather than with me. He came out blustering afterwards that they changed their mind when he told them that they will lose this good free work and Menningers will gain it.

I came out of this affair, which much depressed me, with a deep sense of lonesomeness and the feeling that I must redouble my efforts to use the year as I planned: attaining a command of the literature of the land, coming close to completing the book I was making out of the money Fremont-Smith financed, and make myself known. But there was some reservation in the latter: I was afraid to get a spurious name, and that helped. This had its roots early and was reinforced by my experiences in the inbred group of Rorschachers around [Bruno] Klopfer. A night walk with [Emil] Oberholzer after one of his seminars which I attended reinforced it; he said: what you need is a clinical psychiatric place where you can do research. The course of [i.e., given by Max] Wertheimer which I took reinforced it too: I did not want to be confined to Rorschach.

This is how it happened that my analysis of W-B [the Wechsler-Bellevue Adult Intelligence Scale], my Rorschach and perception [understanding of the test in terms of perception], and contributions to the blind-diagnostic symposia never got published and that I hardly published anything on Rorschach until Diagnostic Psychological Testing [Rapaport, Gill, &, Schafer, 1945–1946].

So when I was "retained" in Osawatomie, I began to work furiously with all sorts of tests, all sorts of cases, and with memory experiments. I also saw two schizophrenics (deteriorated) just for daily conversations and saw them blossoming out to acceptable behavior (though they remained delusional), and thus I carried away convictions concerning the nature of "deterioration" as dis-use, concerning the nature and potential of "communication"; and from my drug experience [research on the effects of drugs on psychiatric patients], that the reaction is individually variable, that the miracle drug "metrazol" does as much harm as advantage. I also carried away—besides the conviction of need for "profiles"—the observation how empty and unrevealing tests can be and how well preserved certain functions remain while the illness has wrought already disastrous havoc with the patient.

There was also another thing that I carried away. When tests be-came empty [when he realized how little could be learned from the mere quantitative scores], I began watching for finer signs; when achievement remained too good I began to watch for qualitative weakness in the passing achievement. Particularly, the relatively well preserved vocabularies of paretics on the Babcock test [of the memory of a verbal passage read to the patient] forced me to that [conclusion]. A paper by Jahercrinsky [?] which I often quoted later reinforced my thinking there. I became more and more centered not on what is said but how it is said—not on content but on formal characteristics. The Rorschach scoring provided the pattern for this, but I have given the distinction a new meaning and as I went along it became clear that what from one point of view was a formal char-acteristic could be a content from another.

But I am off on ideas again and am not telling the story. [J. F.] Brown was on his vacation, at La Jolla being analyzed by [Franz] Alexander there. He came back; I visited in brief [briefly] one even-ing with him at Varvel's house. Blustering, unctuous, professorial, he announced that he would take over my supervision. But he in-vited Orbison and me to come join them socially after the farewell dinner he was going to give for Varvel who was off to Texas A & T [probably Texas A&M—Texas Agricultural and Mechanical Univer-sity]—where he still is. This was a week later. We came, were kept waiting in another room till they—all high—finished eating. Then without any ado he brought out Rorschachs he had given and told me to interpret them. I was taken aback. It was clear that he gave these at Menningers and that he wanted to use me so he could give a good interpretation tomorrow. The records were incomplete even in the wording, location not marked, no inquiry. I couldn't help commenting that if this and that had been inquired into, depending upon whether this or that answer would have been gotten the inferences would have varied, thus and so. After my 3rd or 4th such comment, Brown—quite high—boiled over: called me a damned refugee, a Jew-bastard who owes his job to him and who, in his house at a social occasion, arrogates the right to lecture him. The two boys, Orbison—about whose schizophrenic episode from which Knight helped him out, I didn't know for years to come—and the quiet, studious Varvel; with their intellectuals' eyeglasses and reserve and talk about democracy and praise of Brown as a liberal and even pink, as a broadminded man, learned and of broad intellectual scope[56]—they sat there silent, avoiding my gaze asking for a word of help. No use! I felt. I decided to swallow the bitter pill: I interrupted B.'s unceasing railing and said that in the tradition in which I grew up this would not have been taken for [as] an offense (in truth, no occasion for it would have ever been given)—so I did not understand it and I was ready to tender my apologies. He grabbed on it: Your apologies are accepted! The bitterness I felt I can't describe; it was matched only a few times in my life. That Brown was to add later to it, I only dimly surmised at the time. But I knew that I did wish and would persist in wishing to see him humiliated, to see him, looking down from far above [him].

I knew that I will [would] have a task to get along with him somehow and yet not to serve him more than [would be] inevitable. I was determined on a quiet sabotage of the exploitation [a] first taste [of which] I [had] just got. There issued out of this experience several tendencies, as I see it in retrospect. I do not mean to say that these did not have earlier roots and did not need later

---

[56] Presumably based on Brown (1936), in which he tried to integrate Gestalt psychology, Marxism, and psychoanalysis.

supporting experiences. I mean to say, however, that a newcomer to a country—particularly this one—gains several degrees of freedom to recast his inner economy (no denying that he may lose as many degrees of freedom, too); and I mean to say that my experience as newcomer determined the form many of my attitudes later took.

First, let me say that the addressing [me] by first name became hateful to me: all these 3 people who witnessed my humiliation were calling me by my first name. I simply could not talk to Orbison for a while and when I did he took Brown's side overtly, too. Varvel (true, it was only 2 years later that I spoke to him about it) did not. Second, I was from then on determined not to let anyone around me get sloppy test records, or rely on a single test to diagnose, or fraudulently mix (as Brown tried to describe to me the patient when I asked for inquiry) clinical and test data.

[no signature]

Rapaport to Holt—January 22, 1953

Dear Bob:

Thank you for your letter of January 5. Once more, many thanks for all the help on the Schilder.

I didn't write to you so far about the Rubinstein-Lorr project. It isn't that I did not fool around with it. I wrote some 10 tightly written manuscript pages, but I interrupted it and was embarrassed to send it to you because it became so terribly personal.[57] I cannot really write systematically about themes. Too many things go into it. I cannot criticize your outline. I will tell you briefly my memory of the story.

As I remember, the first psychologist who ever was at Menninger's was a girl by the name of Leona Chidester,[58] who worked at the Southard School. If I remember correctly, the Southard School at that time took feeble-minded children. It was only around 1939 or 1940 that they discontinued that. I gather the psychologist was hired partly to make sure who is feeble-minded and who isn't, and partly to do some teaching with them. Chidester did psychometric stuff. She must have been gone already in 1938 or 1939. They had,

---

[57] This explains the fact that I never received the two long letters of mid-December 1952 and did not see them until they came from the Library of Congress along with others not in my own collection. A comparison of Rapaport's accounts of the same events and people in the earlier, withheld version, and the present one is both instructive and amusing.

[58] Between 1933 and 1936, Leona Chidester, MA, published three articles on psychiatric work with retarded children, one each with Karl and William Menninger.

however, psychological internes at the Southard School. These internes were actually glorified attendants to the children. They were not taught at all. Later on it seems that J. F. Brown invited them to his seminars at K.U. But that was not clinical teaching they got there. My first contact with such internes was when I was invited by Dr. Earl Sachs, who was the director of the school after Dr. Douglass Orr abandoned the job, apparently in 1939 or 1940—to discuss what research could be done. The discussion was inert and there was no impetus in anybody to do anything.

The next phase of the story centers around J. F. Brown. He was a pupil of Lewin for a year in Germany. He picked up a smattering of Gestalt psychology. He was involved in some social movement at K.U. and Psychology and the Social Order reflects that. He retreated from that, apparently, and went into analysis with Alexander. These were the best phases, apparently, of his activity, and he had written with Lewin a paper on reality and irreality levels and the effect of tension systems on these; he had done with Voth[59] a paper on apparent movement, and he had an epistemological flair which made him move to an integration of what he was learning in psychoanalysis, what he had learned in sociology, and what he had learned from Lewin. He had the idea that psychoanalysis ought to be made into a respectable science. The reflection of this is his having invited Lewin to the Menninger's to speak. This is reflected in an article of Lewin's in the Bulletin [of the Menninger Clinic]. His own thinking centered on the problem of frustration-tolerance and its experimental exploration. That had to do something with Maier's problem-solving experiments[60] and the attempt to give people unsolvable problems. Maybe that too is reflected in one of the Bulletins in an article. This is where

---

[59] Harold M. Voth spent most of his psychiatric career at Menninger's, becoming a psychoanalyst in 1965. He published several other research papers.

[60] Norman R. F. Meier, a psychologist who came to national fame by an experiment: he produced "neurotic" behavior and convulsions in rats by giving them impossible problems.

Karl Menninger comes into the game. Karl Menninger was at Harvard. He felt as an outsider. His professor Southard remained an idol in his eyes. He came back to Topeka, but with the idea that he will make science and outshine those who excluded him. There was a steady yearning for excellence—and for fostering excellence—in him. He grasped on Brown and Brown's idea for this reason. Brown had made himself a consultant to the Menningers. He picked up Rorschach, I don't know where, he picked up Bellevue, I don't know where, and began to test. He reported to staff conferences, usually only verbally (there were never records stating his analysis of the test, though you might want to try to see in 1939 some minutes of the staff conferences to see whether the stenographer took down what he said). He would go over to Menningers once or twice a week. If he was gone, Walter Varvel, who now teaches at Texas A. & M., would substitute for him. It is quite possible that it was Sarvis[61] on the staff of K.U. who taught Brown the testing and who taught several others—for instance, Orbison, who later was at Yale and died recently while teaching at the University of Connecticut in Storrs, and his widow, Marian Gilbert, who at the time wasn't yet married to him—the Rorschach and the Bellevue.

It was through Brown, to whom I was sent by Kurt Lewin, that I met Orbison, and his boss, Dr. Fellows, of the Osawatomie State Hospital, at the American Psychiatric Association meeting in 1939 in Chicago. I have gotten accepted at Osawatomie, and when I got there I had many difficulties, with Brown, with the State Board of Public Welfare, who wanted no "furriners," but stuck it out. I had met Karl Menninger before I got to Osawatomie, and I had met him again while employed at Osawatomie, [and] in New York. That's where he hung out in those days, being analyzed by Ruth Brunswick. My experiences with Karl were double: on the one hand, he showed that he is a man of imagination and a flair for

---

[61] Byron E. Sarvis, PhD, Assistant Professor of Psychology, University of Kansas, 1938–1939 (on military leave the rest of the time he appears on the faculty roster).

new things and liking for science; on the other hand, he was personally quite unreliable and showed it immediately. The details of this I won't put down, because this is where I got derailed in my earlier manuscript. Consequently I was very hesitant to go to Menningers. It seemed a most mercenary outfit and a most impersonal one. I was afraid to be directly under Brown's knuckles. But I did not have any other choice. I arrived, to find my worst fears all justified and yet also to find that in Karl I had a support which, irascible and unreliable as it was, sustained me through the worst times. I joined the Menninger Clinic (it was not Foundation yet) in 1940 on May 27. I prepared an outline of the testing I will be doing, and that must be somewhere still in the files. Brown added to it "Lewinian techniques" and in this form, but abbreviated, it was published in the 1941 volume of the <u>Menninger Bulletin</u>, under the title "The Role of the Psychologist in the Psychiatric Clinic" [Brown & Rapaport, 1941]. In it you will find the form of test report I used at the time. The prospectus itself originated somewhere in May, 1940. You will note that even before this, in the 1941 volume, my Szondi paper [Rapaport, 1941] was published.[62] The story of this is that Caroline Zachry, whom I already knew from before, was lecturing in Topeka and told the Menningers that I am somewhere near and how come they don't know me (Karl was still in New York) so I got invited over to the lecture and the dinner. Out of this came an invitation to lecture on the Szondi test at M.C. [Menninger Clinic], after Zachry arranged a lecture for me in New York on it, which was attended by Karl Menninger.

I would like to give you here a picture of the conception out of which this testing program grew. I came to testing partly as a matter of getting to earn my bread, and partly because of my interest in thinking. In Hungary we used "Rossolimo profiles." To me, such profiles meant that maybe we could paint patterns of

---

[62] There are so many such references, giving enough information so that they can be readily found, that most are not listed in the general reference list.

thought or achievement which will be characteristic for thought in particular, or personality in general. In Osawatomie I worked with schizophrenics and had the feeling that somehow we can't corner the schizophrenic thought disorder. So I hoped that if I worked on a broad battery of tests, I will either by profile pattern or by finding a test that was so far not systematically used, get on the trail of the schizophrenic thought disorder. Actually, I used far broader batteries at times at Osawatomie than I used later. I have been using all kinds of story recalls, all kinds of free paintings, and drawings, visual-motor Gestalt tests of a broader variety than just the Bender patterns which she brought from Wertheimer. It was the time-economics which limited me in setting the actual battery I would use. There was another factor involved too. My interest in the Wechsler-Bellevue. I should mention this also. I refound in it the advantage that lay in the Rossolimo profile idea. The Binet we used in Hungary did not lend itself to anything like this. Having arrived in Osawatomie, I found that K. U. used a kind of scatter-gram to represent the Stanford-Binet findings. I went into the literature of it, and found that any ideas about that scatter, rather any systematic ideas, have been found unworkable by those who studied it. You may have found out that there is quite a literature of the Stanford-Binet scatter. The Wechsler-Bellevue had just come out, and I found it a God-send and began to study its scatter. This made it easier for me to limit myself to a smaller battery.

At first I lay low at Menningers. I had to prove the value of testing and the battery, and myself worth my salt. In the meanwhile, I also had Emotions and Memory to finish, which I brought along from the Macy Foundation from New York as an assignment. I felt very lonesome, the only man who had real research interest there, Dr. Silverman [unidentified], left as soon as I arrived. There was one guy who tried to show some interest, but it soon turned out that he wanted to use me rather than invest anything in it, and I gave up before I started. His name was Karl Tillman [unidentified]. While Karl Menninger gave me the impression that he would support me, he was never interested in what I myself was doing.

This was the more hard to take since in Osawatamie I found, within the short year, Lozoff and Kenyon[63] and a third fellow (Ben Kowitz), as well as a philosopher, Webber, in whom I could kindle research interest and could work with. My first move was twofold. I began a seminar for the residents, to which the Southard School internes also came, and I started a seminar Tuesday evenings with the Southard School internes. The residents proved worthless. The internes were Margaret Brenman and Dubin (1940–41). I also began to give, on invitation, a Rorschach course at K. U., but it turned out that this was a move of J. F. Brown's to keep Sarvis in check by me, and to get Sarvis irritated with me, to report to Karl and the others that I am difficult, I cause trouble, I incense Sarvis, that I need his tutelage in order to be tolerable. So I gave that up rather soon. Dubin was the first to pull close to me, and Brown, he and I[64] reported the first scatter study in Midwestern Psychological meetings in Athens, Ohio. But Dubin, as fast as he adapted, proved himself also a weak sister.

The story was different with Brenman. Her interest in therapy showed itself soon and brought her trouble at Southard School. I had just begun to study [a report on] two double personalities by Milton Erickson, and he was invited then through me to the Clinic to lecture, and interest in hypnosis rose. As I remember it, Karl, Knight and I jointly sponsored Margaret's being appointed to a job at the Clinic, after her year at the Southard School was over. She was supposed to test part time, and do hypnotic experiments part time. She showed her mettle even before that, undertaking some research with interrupted tasks at the Southard School. We had some money for this from the Bevin Foundation. This study never got completed.

---

[63] See Kenyon, V. B., Rapaport, D., & Lozoff, M. (1941). Note on metrazol in general paresis. *Psychiatry, 4*, pp. 165–176.

[64] Brown, J. F., Rapaport, D., Dubin, S., & Tillman, C. G. (1941). *Analysis of scatter in a battery of tests.* Paper presented at the meeting of Midwestern Psychological Association, Athens, Ohio.

At this time I had an office in the Clinic building which I shared with Brown when he came twice a week for half a day. Now we were moved to the White Cottage. Upstairs there were patients, downstairs were we. Margaret and I had an office each, she had a hypnotic laboratory, there was a bathroom not yet converted, and there was a small lecture room where we met for the resident-interne lectures. Southard School had three internes by that time: one was the son of Rich, the Milwaukee psychiatrist, one was the girl Schneider who wrote the first concept formation paper with us, and is now Rich's wife, and the third was a southern girl Courtney Roetgen. These were the first internes who with my help did study some and really did a piece of research at Southard School. Margaret soon petered out as a tester. She was bored to tears with it, and for me she wasn't precise enough. Helen Henderson, who later became Bob Knight's secretary, was my secretary at the time. It was this dingy little place in which our whole development got dreamed out, down in the downstairs of the White Cottage. (The southeast building facing the Monument House.)

Margaret was doing a study on fairy-tale recall in hypnosis, the Bevin study on interrupted tasks with children, sick children, and began to go to K. U. for her doctor's [degree]. Brown lorded it over her pretty hard, yet she managed to bring together a thesis which dealt with interrupted tasks in hypnosis. This is reprinted in the "Hypnotherapy" volume in the appendix [Brenman & Gill, 1947]. Margaret also took on some of her experimental subjects, who were secretaries, for therapy, and began to have controls over them [i.e., began to get supervision].

This was really the pattern that we followed later. We brought in somebody who had some kind of promise, sponsored their making their professional way, and slowly shifted them into a position to learn the clinical stuff as they wanted it. Somewhere around this time came Suzanne Reichard, whom I hired on Macy money which they gave me to explore the battery of tests we were working on. She was put into the remodeled bathroom. The war preparations were picking up, and I got additional money to hire a further assistant. So if I remember correctly, Margaret came in Sept. 1940 just when I came to Menningers; she became a staff member on a research appointment with junior quality [status], going to K. U. in September of 1941, that's the time we moved to the White Cottage; Reichard came somewhere in mid-1942, and Roy I met for the first time Christmas 1942 and he arrived early in 1943. In the 1942 <u>Bulletin</u> in March you will find already some report of Margaret's research in progress .

Merton arrived, as I remember it, in July 1941, around the same time when Margaret was taken to the Clinic. We warmed up relatively soon, because I remember that in September I showed him the first draft of the manuscript of <u>Emotions and Memory</u> and he discussed it with me and corrected certain things. In the same year Margaret and her husband Bill [William Gibson] undertook to give English shape to my manuscript. Merton also showed considerable interest in hypnosis, but they two were considerably at odds with each other. Margaret felt that Merton is trying to horn in on her possession, and Merton felt that Margaret is trying to be a therapist without having had training for that. It was an extremely slow process by which they managed slowly to come to some kind of terms with each other. But I know for sure that Merton would already [have] come to the White Cottage to the back room there where Margaret had her hypnotic laboratory. It was there that they two produced results in the first joint case of anxiety hysteria [. . .] [Gill & Brenman, 1943]. Also Margaret began to be called in on other cases where the therapists were stumped and hypnosis seemed advised. Out of one of these cases resulted the report of the treatment of a 71-year-old woman [. . .] [Brenman & Knight, 1943]. Indeed, this whole issue was devoted to hypnotic stuff. The other important case was that of an adolescent anorexic [. . .] [Brenman & Knight, 1945]. Larry Kubie came to lecture on his method to elicit hypnagogic states, and around this time it was that Margaret presented at a private meeting at Larry Kubie's house in New York, the treatment of the first case of hypnoanalysis done by Merton and herself. This was her "coming out" party and I was sitting there awful happy.

It is around this time that the first research committee was organized. A note I have in my possession indicates that it was in the executive committee meeting of the Menninger Foundation on February 18, 1943, that the research committee was appointed, with me as chairman, RPK [Knight] and Merton as members. It was Margaret's research that awakened RPK's interest, and the date of Merton's appointment already indicates that Merton and Margaret had been coming to an understanding about their research by this time. It is also around this time that Hacker[65] arrived at the Foundation, and he began to show some interest, partly in amnesia studies and partly in hypnosis. We attempted to involve him, but it never was quite successful. [See, however, p. 10, below.]

The hunt now for research funds for the hypnosis study began and in the course of the year 1943 we obtained New York Fund and Macy Foundation and Hoffheimer Foundation support which continued then for '44, '45, '46, I believe, and the support was then taken over by the USPHS, which support continued until last year, that is, five years.

In the mid-summer of 1943, Bille Escalona arrived. She was to be hired at the Southard School as a psychologist and therapist. She was hired also one third time to the research department, originally, to do some kind of Lewinian work. But by this time Suzanne Reichard left, and on the request of the family agency she had started some infant testing. Later Bille took this over, and instead of doing Lewinian work, slowly it shaped up that she did in a major part of her time increasingly less work at Southard School and more and more with us in infant testing and [adult] testing, and began to develop, involving Mary Leitch slowly, what later became the infant study. It seems to me that sometime in 1944 she came to that point, more or less around the same time when we moved from the White Cottage to the Foundation Building, which was hatched out actually for the hypnosis, infancy research,

---

[65] Frederick J. Hacker, MD, later became a well-known Hollywood psychoanalyst.

and psychology department, though social workers and others were also put in there. It was our idea really, the whole building, and a considerable part of its financing also. Around the same time in 1944, it was that Sarah [Paleyeff, later, Schafer] and [Martin] Mayman came as internes. By this time the diagnostic testing study was going great guns and they did some of the footwork on the statistical tables and graphs for us. Elaine Grimm and Murray [not identified] came the next year. Around the time Sarah arrived, Grace Collett of the Harding Sanitarium, was with us for a summer.

This would tide us over '45–'46, that is, to the beginnings of the Winter Veterans Administration Hospital and the School of Clinical Psychology. That period you may know from your own experience, and there may be several other people who may know about it. It was around the time the school was established that the research department grew to some size, and Margaret and Bille took over the psychology department, Merton and I establishing the research department. Particularly in '46–'47 Merton and I tried to get many people—this is how [Rudolf] Ekstein & Dr. Rubin were gotten. We were not very successful, and that's how we hatched the Foreign Fellows plan for '47–'48. You may remember how [Lucas] Kamp, [Benjamin B.] Rubinstein, [Nik] Waal, and [C. V.] Ramana did or did not pan out.[66] You may also remember that this was the period in which the selection research got started.

The dates are again reasonably reflected in the Menninger Bulletin. In the May, 1943 issue, you find a special psychological issue

---

[66] The first three of these were MDs, Kemp from the Netherlands, Rubinstein from Finland, and Waal (a Wilhelm Reichian) from Norway; plus Ramana, a psychologist-psychoanalyst without a doctorate from India. He once explained to me that few candidates in India had doctoral degrees, and therefore they were given unusually long training analyses (!). I was made Rubinstein's research mentor, the beginning of a long, close friendship (see Holt [ed.] 1997, editor's introduction). Though he became one of the finest psychoanalytic theorists of his time, Beni never got an empirical research project off the ground.

reflecting the testing program. You can see there how Roy got into the scatter frame of mind very fast, and what Suzanne Reichard
did. The same volume shows that Suzanne Reichard tried to collaborate with Margaret also, on [a] hypnotizability study
[Brenman & Reichard, 1943]. In [the] 1944 volume of the Bulletin
you already see, in an article written by Bille and me, the outlines
of the children's psychological service, and some of the research
problems. You also see Mary Leitch drawing near us. The May
1945 issue was again devoted to psychological matters, and you
see there how our general attitude to the Rorschach crystallized,
and how we went at rationale and scatter issues in other tests, for
instance, in the new army individual test; there is a note also that
we were getting interested in vocational things, but this never
materialized quite. At this time, the manual copies of Diagnostic
Testing[67] were out, and we had the greatest influence we ever
had on other psychologists. This is also reflected in the other articles that were included by outsiders in this Bulletin. This was also
shortly before the appearance, at the end of 1945, of the first volume of Diagnostic [Psychological] Testing [Rapaport, Gill, &
Schafer, 1945], followed soon after in 1946 by the second volume.
Around the middle of 1945, Roy got taken away from us for about
a year by the army. Already in the previous two and a half years I
had been fighting a more and more losing battle against his being taken away. Finally it was no more possible to hold it. The
1946 volume of the Bulletin shows Margaret and Merton, and
Merton with Karl Menninger, writing on hypnosis. The project was
going hot at this time. This same volume shows the beginning of
Winter Veterans Hospital. In the 1947 volume you will find in the
March issue the inaugural address of Karl Menninger for the
School of Clinical Psychology, dating the inauguration as of October 21, 1946. In the same volume, on page 60, there is a paper
reflecting already the ego psychological turn of mind in the hyp-

---

[67] Shortly before the big, two-volume work appeared, a military version was published
in two slim paperback books (Rapaport, Schafer, & Gill, 1944–1946).

nosis research, and it is also the only paper to which Hacker contributed [Brenman, Gill, & Hacker, 1947].

This ego-psychological turn was forecast variously before. A lecture of mine (1942, I believe—Tillman was still there) on "The Awakening of Insight" [Rapaport, 1942c]; a psychoanalytic lecture series (1944–1945) on Special Problems in Ego-Psychology, and Diagnostic Testing marked the steps in it. But note, <u>Emotions and Memory</u> was untouched by it though I was already then preoccupied with it. Looking over this volume [10 of the *Bulletin of the Menninger Clinic*], I note, on page 43, Paul Bergman's review of <u>Diagnostic Psychological Testing</u>. Paul must have come somewhere early in 1943. He had a dingy office in the Southard School. He was extremely dissatisfied and began to think in terms of studying something. We had at first bitter clashes about psychoanalysis, then he tried to study other kinds of things, and I lent him a hand. As his difficulties with the Southard School and with psychotherapy in general increased, he increasingly tried to study other matters; the incidence of hernia in cases of mental disorder, management of anxiety in children, etc. It is my memory that soon after we came over to our new building from the White Cottage, Paul Bergman got an office with us. It is also my impression that around this time he began to get interested in non-directive [psychotherapy], and therapeutic experimentation in general. Once again, you can see how somebody, either present in the place or joining for a certain purpose, slowly shifts under attentive eyes with the help of those who have some say-so about arrangements: Bob Knight helped.

In the 1948 volume of the <u>Menninger Bulletin</u>, you find the second hypnosis issue, with two articles, one by Merton and the other by Margaret and Bob. You also find a reflection of Bille's work in therapy with Southard School children, even after she already was with us in our building. She was supervised by Hawkins.[68] I notice that I overlooked an issue, namely, the July issue of the 1947 vol-

---

[68] Mary O'Neil Hawkins, MD, a training analyst of the Topeka Psychoanalytic Institute, and at one time vice president of the American Psychoanalytic Association.

ume, which was also a psychological issue, and described for the first time the whole program of the School of Clinical Psychology. I should note here that in '46–'47 and in '47–'48, after the return of Dr. Will, the Foundation was organized in four sections: clinical services, administrative services, educational services, and research services, Bob [Knight], John Stone, Karl, and I being the general directors of them, Will being the coordinating general secretary. I think that hereby I have given you a picture of some of the chronology and the coming in of the key people. Maybe I simply omitted that Mary Leitch came to us somewhere late in 1943 or early in 1944. About the arrival of the people who came with the Winter General, you know enough; I mean now you, [Milton] Wexler, [Robert] Challman, Roy's coming over there, Mayman's coming over there, etc. You probably know about [Walter] Kass's and [Gerald] Ehrenreich's arrival around the same time, and George's arrival about that time, too.

All of these people had Roy's training in clinical work [i.e., were trained by him in testing], and had very little to do with me.[69] I may have introduced them to it only. But Roy did the real work with them. All the others, excepting these few and the Winter people, all of whom had only conference work with me, had been through the mill with me, which included their sitting in on my tests, my sitting in on their testing; discussion of how and why I did things and how and why they did things; checking of scoring together; interpreting each test separately, including all the objective features as well as the "tune of the record"; attempting to achieve an integration of what was learned from all the tests; insistence of blind diagnosing of every case and every feature as much as possible. In fact, attempts to diagnose from a single test without recourse to the others. Those people who have been through the wringer with me had many scores of reports, if not

---

[69] My own vivid memory was that Rapaport played a critical and predominant role in teaching diagnostic testing to the 1946 recruits to the VA Hospital staff. That was, however, during Roy Schafer's absence.

several hundred of them (some did that much), corrected by me, word by word, phrase by phrase. My two main ideas here were to achieve a real discipline in immersion in the test material; and to achieve a real self-critique which should be a balance and a check against self-deceiving interpretations. The latter point was always the sorest one to my mind. Excepting those who wanted to interpret mechanically on the basis of a book, of the people whom I knew closely (Winter people excluded here) only Roy was little tempted to use external information and self-deception.

My original conception of the [psychology] department was to build a place where testing and its contribution would be appreciated, and to teach a few people to do the testing in accord with the two principles mentioned above. The accompanying idea (just as strong as the main one) was to create an opportunity for real psychological exploration of psychiatric phenomena. I knew that in a clinical setting this would not be possible if clinical usefulness was not simultaneously demonstrated, and clinical competence was not acquired. I felt that clinical competence cannot be acquired by psychologists without using the avenue of testing. As time passed, a third point emerged, namely, that one has to give sufficient freedom to people to find the area in which their ingenuity can work, and that we have to find psychiatrists who will be also interested in research and will be our companions in it. Thus we had to raise our own psychiatrists. A fourth point came up, namely, that we were sorely burdened and had to introduce new people, bring new people to ourselves, in order to relieve us of the big burden of the everyday grind, in order to have research possibility. More and more it proved that we have to have systematically freed time, and I reached out for external grants, but I had to have the right people also. We got a number of good people, but the general run of the applicants was not good. We felt that this is because we do not offer credits. When the Veterans Administration came along, we set quite strenuous requirements to them and these were at first granted to us. We set these strenuous requirements because we felt that we would be all swallowed up by the duties of working with a lot of people. By this time we were the center of attraction for many people and we wondered whether in a few years we won't get enough post-graduate people anyway, and why bother with graduate education. It was, however, our feeling that one has to instill what we have to offer earlier than on a post-graduate level. All the promises of the Veterans Administration progressively petered out as we went along. The financial position and views of the clinic were such that nothing the Veterans Administration could possibly have offered would have made up for it. The fact is that no educational institution can charge fees and pay teaching salaries on the scale private or institutional practice of psychiatry and psychology charge nowadays.

In some ways this was a disappointing experience. It was disappointing also because one began to realize how much we would want to teach our people, about developmental psychology, Gestalt psychology, Lewinian psychology, psychoanalysis, etc., in order that they have the equipment that it would take to become really good research workers in the field, and really good clinical workers. Yet this development added a fifth point. The predecessor of this point was the need to give enough freedom to people to shift around to areas where their ingenuity can really blossom. This [policy] shifted Margaret from internship with children to testing and experiment to hypnotherapy and psychotherapy, Merton from psychosomatics to hypnosis to psychotherapy, Bille from therapeutic work with children and Lewinian experiments to infant testing and infant investigations, etc. It was in line with this [policy] that, with the influx of more and more people, the need to give experience in therapy for psychologists increased progressively. Margaret really broke the ice in this respect, and Bergman's coming added to this. But really only the teaching program could break up the remaining ice floes that crushed the attempts we made in this direction. The underlying economic reason was, however, a different one. The feeling was that psychologists, when becoming analysts, might remain more "faithful" to and more steady in the place than otherwise medical men do. The need for research workers to have psycho-analytic training, and that must include therapy experience, also contributed. Fundamentally, however, the entrenched position of psychologists—having worked themselves up from the bottom, and having proven useful and trustworthy—was the most important factor in our succeeding in this.

The picture would be quite incomplete if I did omit that these developments were greatly aided and abetted by broader scale historical events. I have in mind the war and its sequelae. On the one hand it was the beginning war preparation that moved the Macy Foundation, after an initial rejection, to give us the first grant, out of which <u>Diagnostic Psychological Testing</u> developed. Let me put down for the record that <u>Emotions and Memory</u> was written on a total of a $1,500 grant. <u>Diagnostic Psychological Testing</u> was written on a $4,500 grant. Though it is true that the Macy Foundation contributed to the publication of <u>Emotions and Memory</u> by buying 200 copies to the tune of $600, and contributed to <u>Diagnostic Psychological Testing</u> another $700 in travel allowances, etc. It seems to me that we worked best, and at least I worked best, on the least amount of money, that is, when I had only a shoestring. Another point which I felt quite strongly about always was to start people on a sufficiently low level so that their status-consciousness does not rob their flexibility. People coming to me on a higher status—Kass belongs to these—find it more difficult to let their hair down, admit what they don't know, and don't prevent by pretenses their own assimilating new points of view, new procedures, and new knowledge. This is part of the reason why I always opposed that psychologists must get a Ph.D. before they become practicing psychologists. This was one of the reasons why we wanted to have younger people, and not just post-graduates to work with us. This was one of the reasons I felt that people should, if possible, not be hired for a project, but introduced slowly and helped along to find their area, rather than to profess it in advance and be stuck with it, and have to quit when their ingenuity peters out in the area they have predetermined.

Another way in which the war helped us a great deal was that the psychiatric manpower was greatly depleted and the less rigid seniors, Karl and Bob Knight, stayed while Will was gone, and many of the younger stuffed shirts weren't there either, and we shared—in fact, took the lion's share of the responsibility of—running the place. I remember times when we had people on the [psychiatric] staff like Dimont, Friedman, David Abrahamson, and other excellences, when decisions about patients had to be taken more on the basis of what Roy or I or the internes reported than on the basis of the psychiatric workup. Both this practical fact and the sharing of responsibility contributed considerably to our maturation and to the consolidation of our position.

A third way the war contributed was that it pushed the completion of the research project on diagnostic psychological testing to conclusion. This had regrettable consequences also. In a way, we were always working against a deadline that Roy might be called away any time. We could not avail ourselves of all kinds of external help or getting additional material to make the insights which we had really stick: by reliable material and good statistics. On the other hand, however, we did provide, by this pressured output, to the psychologists in the armed forces the only real guide they had for a long time. Our manual attained a 10,000 copy circulation and a popularity which then swept me into the secretary's chair of the newly formed division of clinical and abnormal psychology. I imagine you will be surprised to learn that at that time Marquis[70] tried to create a liaison with me and used the psychological issues of the Bulletin of the Menninger Clinic as one of the important arguments for creating and obtaining more places on various boards for [clinical] psychologists than they had before. In fact, that was a time when Marquis was introduced by

---

[70] Donald G. Marquis, an outstanding experimental psychologist. He became President of the American Psychological Association in 1948.

me to several places in the Federal Security Agency and in the USPHS. Those places did not know about the American Psychological Association in those days. The first Research Study Group [of NIMH, to evaluate research grant proposals] was full of dynamic people. Only [G. R.] Wendt[71] was there from the other side. Now the opposite is the case. How the Veterans Administration and its education efforts played into any development I have already mentioned and you know yourself also.

Looking over your outline, I notice that you want to talk about administrative structure. It was based always on a direct personal contact of mine with anybody and everybody, though certain divisions of labor were slowly introduced and then people had a double contact with the person who was in direct charge, as well as with me. This was the situation with Bille Escalona as far as children were concerned, and Roy as far as adults were concerned. Later on, Bille and Margaret took over the whole psychology department and were my liaison to the School of Clinical Psychology, while Merton took over with me the research department and was my liaison to some of the projects and individuals. But throughout I kept contact with everybody and their work, and was a scout both for talents and deficiencies.

Then I notice that you want to mention semi-blind testing. This was not introduced until sometime in 1947. It was not introduced for training purposes at all in the whole time I was there. The trainees had to work entirely blind.

I notice that you want to talk about the Division of Clinical and Abnormal Psychology. Originally there were two divisions, and I was the secretary of one, the clinical division. One had the clinicians, the other had the teachers. I think that I was elected to this one division secretaryship in 1945 for the term of '45–'46. I did all the leg work for unification, and the new division was born, and I was elected for a three-year term '46–'49 to be the secretary of the division. I believe it is correct to say that I established the financial

---

[71] Another prominent experimentalist.

structure, the newsletter, the committee structure (Dave Shakow had the lion's share in that), the regional meeting proposition, and the preparation for summer courses. I made myself quite unpopular with fighting against the Ph.D. level requirement, which is now accepted through [across] the board. I was always afraid that it would result in a stuffiness, in private practice, and in inflexibility of people who are raised in academic environments where they do not get the clinical training necessary. I waged a battle for better representation of the clinical division in the APA councils. I did not get to the first base even with that. In a meeting called by the Macy Foundation in New York, in a private conversation Marquis and [Neal] Miller made a curious offer to make personal agreements about personal representations of the right people to be nominated and elected for the various boards and committees. Since I was not interested in that, I laughed in their faces and asked whether that's what they call democratic organization. That was that.

I notice that you want to write about psychoanalytic training. Margaret and I have broken the ice there. Margaret by her therapeutic successes, and I in the various seminars. From the very first on, I was invited to participate in these seminars, both in the clinical ones and the theoretical ones. In the beginning, particularly in the reading seminars, I came to play an important role because I knew the literature and often better than the person presiding in the seminar. Sooner or later I began to give these seminars also, at least some of them. Margaret's therapeutic successes opened the way for her to get a regular analysis, and to be accepted as a member of the association. I never tried or aspired to that in those years. Later on, the power position we had established made it possible for us to establish the principle that psychologists will be given training in proportion to their numbers, as related to the numbers of the residents in the school of psychiatry. If I remember correctly, Schlesinger and Ehrenreich were the first two accepted. By the way, this was the door through which Ekstein made his arrival to the inner councils of the Topeka Psychoanalytic Institute. Merton and I brought him especially with analyzing of psychologists in mind.

You may want to know something about the interpersonal workings of all this. Some of this I have indicated through the story of how people came. In final analysis, however, the way the things shaped up was this: (1) It was usually I who picked up the ideas of others and took the initiative and action, or helped to implement them. (2) It was usually Merton who criticized and brought into the open weaknesses of things, while I would be prone to see the good side and try to throw in help to develop it. (3) While I took personal interest in everybody, my approach remained usually quite impersonal and administrative. I wanted to have administrative order and saw first of all the interests of the whole place in front of me. (4) Margaret and Bille brought an entirely new note into this. Margaret brought a personal warmth of human relation, and Bille a principle of respect for individual liberty. I came to rely in any decision on all three of them, because things got so complicated that my good personal intents clashed with administrative interests, Merton trimmed them critically, Bille stood on principle, and Margaret informed it with a kind of human touch and sensitivity for what goes on with people, that of the rest of us only Merton had, though he let his critical and sarcastic proclivities get the better of it at times. I think it is fair to say that each one provided inspiration and ideas from their own vantage points, but somehow I remained the motor of execution.

I believe that you may want to be reminded that there was a period in which we did occupational testing and psychological advisory testing for the Kansas Rehabilitation Service. I think that this died out after Margaret and Bille took over the department. But I am not sure. Our relationship to the Kansas Family and Service League was a very important factor in the development of our infancy project. Bille can tell you the whole story of that.

Well, for the moment this should suffice, and if you have any specific questions, please do not hesitate to tell me. I am sending a copy of this to Margaret, and if she feels moved, she might make some comments on it, so that you can see her way of recollecting it. Maybe you even want to send to Merton a copy. He likes the reminiscences and I am sure he will like to give you his slant on it all. Roy may have a lot of recollections which may set some of what I say right. Though it may be that in his transition from one job to another he may have a somewhat colored attitude to the past.

If all this is too much, and not what you wanted, just throw it away.

> Yours,
> David

Holt to Rapaport—May 21, 1953

Dear David:

I see that it's almost a month since your last letter to me, and I have not properly responded to it, if at all. You know what a busy time it has been for me, and perhaps you know something about the problems I have been struggling with. I would like very much to get your advice about some of them.

The Menninger Monograph series has just been turned over to Basic Books, and we have decided that we want to go along with them. That is, our book on the Selection Project will be one of the Monographs and will be published by Basic Books—a good outcome for us, I think. I like very much what you said about them, and I would be interested in having some closer tie to them as an advisor; perhaps I should wait until I get to New York before I consider that very seriously as a possibility to work on. As a matter of fact, I was thinking of writing to Mr. [Arthur] Rosenthal. He asked my advice about books they might want to distribute, and I thought I'd suggest King Solomon's Ring and perhaps The Study of Instinct. I was also thinking of telling him about Louisa's manuscript, though I am a little uncertain about the propriety of that. She is pretty well committed to Knopf, I think, but I believe that the book will be just the kind of thing they are looking for—something combining psychoanalysis, psychology, and social science, though it may be somewhat too theoretical to be a big seller. [. . .]

I was in California a couple of weeks ago; I got up to San Francisco and Berkeley for Sunday and Monday, May 3rd and 4th. [. . .]

In San Francisco I stayed with Bob Harris, getting to know him and his wife and increasing the already great admiration I have for him as a person and as a psychologist. He wanted me to take over his job next year while he will be away on a sabbatical, and I was very sorry not to be able to do so. I had another very stimulating morning at IPAR [UC Berkeley's Institute for Personality Assessment and Research], just seeing Don MacKinnon long enough to say hello, but having a long talk with Dick Crutchfield, with Bob Harris himself, and a rather brief one with Frank Barron. It's a very interesting set-up. I didn't learn nearly enough about it as an institution, and hope to go back there before long to find out more about how it runs as an organization. (You see, I am getting interested in this kind of thing; I believe that the more I learn about what makes good research settings good to work in, the better job I can do at NYU.) The impression that I have, which may not be justified, is that it is a very harmonious group of individualists. They discuss things with each other, they share common subjects [research participants] and trade findings or at least make use of each other's data to some extent, and yet the whole thing seems to remain a collection of one-man projects, rather than anything truly collaborative. It's rather remarkable, I think, that quite a few publications have emerged from this group, but all of them are by single authors! (There is, of course, a joint monograph in press, but it's been in press so long that I'm starting to disbelieve in it.) Maybe this is indeed the way they work, and maybe it is a very good way to work. I want to find out. [. . .]

Really the main thing to say about Los Angeles is to tell you what a beautiful time I had with the Klopfers. I stayed in their house the entire time I was there, and had numerous opportunities to talk with Erna as well as with Bruno. I found her to be a most delightful, warm, utterly unaffected and unpretentious person. I thought of calling her simple, and yet I don't think that would do her justice; I think she's pretty bright, and is a person of rather broad and serious interests. We made contact first in talking about music, for she was quite a singer in her time. This is what I read between the lines, for she is a very modest person, quite without vanity.

Bruno seems to me a little more complicated. On the one hand, he treated me in an equally generous and open fashion, really acting like a kind of warmly loving father toward me. At the same time, he is a good deal more narcissistic than his wife, though I think a good deal less so than I would rate myself, and at times I had a little the feeling that the generosity was beginning to be overwhelming. I would have been more comfortable if Bruno had not put himself out on my account quite so much. Possibly there was a trace of reaction-formation in it or something of the kind, but I don't feel like pursuing this idea in the least. Throughout our contact on this book [i.e., Holt (1954)], he has been as completely honest, generous, and considerate as anyone could be, and I got some even stronger impression of all these virtues from our direct tête-a-tête relationship. We discussed a number of issues pertaining to the Rorschach, and I went at his discussion of M with no holds barred. It was very gratifying to find that he was able to discuss these issues entirely on their merits, apparently feeling in no way threatened by me and yet really listening to me and being willing to modify his thinking to incorporate some of my ideas.

Perhaps Dave Shapiro has told you about the meeting at which he gave his thoughtful and well written paper. You know that the paper contains many ideas whose most important ancestor is yourself. In discussing this paper, Bruno indicated a real willingness to learn from your and Roy's ideas, and the meeting as a whole was in my opinion a stunning success. Not only did Dave deliver one of the best papers I heard on my trip, but the level of discussion in general was good, and I felt that there was a real meeting of the Klopfer and Rapaport sets of ideas about the Rorschach there.

Then, on Thursday morning, I went along with Bruno to the VA Mental Hygiene Clinic where he serves as a consultant and met the small group of excellent trainees with him. We discussed first some theoretical ideas (about M, referred to above), and then a concrete case. Again, Bruno and I were far from seeing eye to eye on everything, but I didn't feel in him the least competitiveness nor personal need that his ideas prevail simply because they were his.

I am telling you this in such detail, because I have had the impression in the past, gained I believe mostly from you, that Bruno and his bunch were rather a power-conscious and competitive group, with whom you didn't feel you could communicate very well. Perhaps your own feelings have changed; perhaps Bruno has mellowed a good deal in the past 15 years; perhaps my relative youth and my strong desire to be liked by him played some role in our forming such different impressions.

I am afraid that I am getting almost the reputation of a Pollyanna with you, by stories like this. Maybe you should think about the unconscious motives that may lie behind my telling you things like this, such as a need (which I would be loath to recognize) to compete with you and show you how much better I am at getting along with people. Anyway, the fact is that I did like most of the psychologists I met out there. Certainly my admiration for Ruth Tolman goes beyond what is usually expected that a man will feel toward a woman nearly 30 years his senior! I must say, though, that I still don't like Jean MacFarlane, in spite of the fact that she's been quite decent toward me and seems to be a close friend of Ruth's, and that I didn't care much for Bert Forer and his wife.

I don't know that there is a great deal about the [American Psychiatric Association] meetings themselves that bears re-telling; you've probably heard most of it anyway. I met some very smart and interesting research psychiatrists, who asked me why I didn't get around more and see them in their own settings. This made me start to think that when I am in a position to ask for a budget, I will want to include a good deal of money for travel. I get a good deal out of such visits as I have been able to make, and would like to do more of that kind of thing.

I still have not written to Rubinstein and Lorr about that article on the history of psychology here. As I believe I told you, I tentatively offered it to Walter Kass and then withdrew it, yet I don't really want to do it myself. I'm sorry that the whole thing came up; I hate to disappoint you about it. I do think I could make something out of it, but it would take much more work than is at all feasible. I simply have to put all of the time I can find on the [Selection] project, and as soon as a draft of our book is written that I will feel like letting other people see, I will want to leave. I hope very much indeed that that will be before September. But I suppose the really crucial consideration is that I don't really want very much to do it. What you say about how I might be able to find myself in it is somehow flattering and enticing, but it's hard for me to see how that would happen. You say you want to see me write a history; well, I am about to plunge into writing a history of the School of Psychiatry and the whole impact of that and related activities on the local scene. I'm much more interested in that, even though I don't yet see how I can do anything terribly meaningful with it. We had a conference with Karl today, incidentally, in which he was in one of his best and most helpful moods. He was really quite inspiring in the way he went at our poorly organized outline, showed us how we could make it a good deal tighter, with suspense and some impact. He laid a great deal of stress on the importance of getting the reader into the thing by showing him the broad picture of the social scene and the concrete setting, to give an idea of the importance of the project.

Perhaps you have had a chance to talk to George since his trip here. As you know, I worked on him pretty hard, and had some talks with Stuart Cook which were encouraging. Stuart is now working on the NYU administration to see if he can't wangle an offer out of them for George that would be attractive to him. I think there is a good chance that George and I might be able to do more together than the sum of our separate efforts in different places, and I honestly believe that if NYU comes through the way I believe they will that George does not have as good prospects at Pittsburgh or at Bethesda. I hope that you will get a chance to give him your views on the Bethesda set-up, because now that Dave Shakow has definitely decided to go (this at any rate was the scuttlebutt at the convention) it begins to look very good on paper. Of course, the next few weeks should tell an important story as far as their appropriation is concerned. I had a nice talk with [Henry W.] Brosin, who told me that he was going to testify before the Senate about the appropriation and was not worried about the outcome, but talking to people since, I find that others are much less optimistic and feel that the Public Health Service is up against a different situation this year than they have faced in a long time. Even if they do get by all right, there would always be that Damocle[si]an sword, and certainly the medical staff they are getting together are coming to it with a very brief time perspective.

Perhaps the really crucial issue about NYU is money. If I had the kind of budget at my disposal that George is promised if he goes to Pittsburgh, I believe that the decision would be much easier for him. As it is, I have decided to try to begin raising funds on the strength of a very general program rather than for specific projects. This is a matter about which I very earnestly hope for advice from you. I wish very much that it were possible for me to come out there and talk it over with you. There are many reasons, some of them personal, why I can't contemplate a trip east until the manuscript is really well under control. Anyway, let me try to tell you something about my thinking on this.

I wrote Bille at some length in a more personal way as well as writing her a formal letter submitting a request for funds, an approximate copy of which I enclose. I was uncomfortable about this letter, because I wanted very much not to presume on my friendship with Bille, and I wanted to let her know about this feeling without making it too much of an issue. In a way, I feel close enough to Bille to feel fairly free to ask her advice as well as to make a request to her in her capacity as Executive Chairman of this fund [Foundations Fund for Research in Psychiatry, Yale University, 1951–1955], and I certainly have enough respect for Bille's integrity and her ability to do her job without being affected by personal considerations.—Well, anyway, I submitted this request and I hope that they may invite us to be more specific about what kind of money we want. It seems to me almost presumptuous to make this kind of request, and I believe that it may be unconventional, yet I believe very strongly in this type of support for research: that is, providing several years' support for people who are likely to produce and who present a generally promising statement of direction. I just talked to Al Baldwin, who is a kind of consultant to the Ford Foundation, and he told me that he didn't believe that the Ford Foundation was yet ready for people to approach them with proposals of this kind. Does that coincide with your impression? And do you have any other suggestions about possible sources of funds, sources that might be approached in this sort of way? I certainly don't want to plunge in with a half-baked proposition and jeopardize the chances of future and more tangible proposals. Nevertheless, this [enclosed] statement makes sense to me and I hope it may to other people as well.

Thanks for your offer to read our manuscript; I'm sure that we will have a good deal of it at least if not the whole first draft by August first. We already have a couple hundred pages of preliminary drafts, but most of them will have to be extensively rewritten. I do hope that you get your trip to Israel. You mentioned in your letter your hope that I would see Norm Reider and Hanna Fenichel; I met the former only once at the time he came back stage after the Freudian Follies [the latest in a series of musical satires, in which I performed as Oedipus!], and don't know Mrs. Fenichel at all. So I didn't see anything of either of them on this trip.

I hope that your health is better, David, and that you are taking care of yourself. I'd better stop this long letter before it too becomes an assault on your endurance!

Affectionately,

Bob

Rapaport to Holt—May 26, 1953

Dear Bob:

Thank you for your long letter of May 21. I well understand the delay and did not feel impatient about it.

I am glad that you like the Basic Book idea, and that they got the Menninger Monograph series. I think your own will also be probably in good hands with them. I would like to use this issue as an example to clear up this question of personal relations, Pollyanna-ism, etc. You see, I wrote to you forming and conveying a good impression about this setup. I do not mean to take it back now. But I would like to tell you that I myself have many reservations about [Arthur] Rosenthal and [Nicholas] Freydberg and the setup itself. Nevertheless, I have spent considerable time and energy, and put considerable thought into it, to give criticisms, suggestions, and contacts to them, as well as to support them in some contacts. Why did I do it? I did it because I think that the book publishers and the book market are not in harmony with the interests of the reading and writing professional in our field. I did it because this is the only outfit where I see some hope that they might come close to the interests of the reader and writer in the field. I cannot help that by nature I see at least as much of the negative sides of people and situations as I see of the positive side. It is in the nature of people, institutions, and the general social setup that they do have the devil in them. I can't help seeing it, perhaps because I know quite a bit about the devil in myself. The only thing that can be said in my favor is that my seeing the black side does not prevent me from seeing some of the good side, and if it be of any sizeable amount, to throw in considerable energy to bank on it. This is what I am doing about the Basic Books, and this is what I have been doing with people with whom I was associated. Particularly since I tend to engage strongly, I will choose very critically. I do not consider what you say about people to be Pollyanna-ism. It is possible to consider my attitude a misanthropic one and it is my fate to struggle against its becoming that. Your attitudes are such that if you will have to struggle against anything, it will be against Pollyanna-ism. You will be up against it when you will begin to organize your own staff. You are enviable in that you can enjoy a lot of people and see the best in them, and apparently pull it out of them. You can enjoy Klopfer, who to me shows his most vain, patronizing, and intrusive aspects. You can enjoy his paternal trends, while I cannot take a father and need one not. But don't forget that there is a difference between enjoying the best sides of people and making the type of investment which a head of an institute has to make, in the people he gathers around himself. Surely it is relevant in this connection what you write about the McKinnon setup [IPAR, headed by Donald W. MacKinnon]. It makes a great deal of difference whether you want to have an institution in which you influence people deeply and assume a responsibility of leadership more than administrative. You know that by temperament I needed to do that. What you will need to do by temperament I do not know. From your comment on the McKinnon setup, it seems that you are attracted to the type of setup where there is a group of equals whom you do not need to influence. Not even here at Stockbridge, where I am certainly amongst my peers, can I try to keep away from, what I would call, theoretical and in a way spiritual influence, though by no means am I alone assuming it and several of us pool it. But the difference is not as great between these two types of setup as one might imagine. The selection of the people with whom one will work, whether one will take spiritual leadership or only [an] administrative one, creating a fraternity of individualists, in either case there is a question of selection. In either case the work of the others and the publications of the others, and the public relations of the others, have an important influence and reflection on the one who stands in the center. This is a matter quite different from being able to enjoy and bring out the best from others in social contacts. The scientifically best is not brought out of people except by very great investments. Even then only out of people chosen very critically. If one does not want to make that investment, but wants to be a peer among peers in this respect also, then one has to choose probably even more critically or more intuitively. I think you are right that you want to travel around as much as is just possible. I think you will want to come here also to see what the inner dynamics of the situation is here. It is a complex one, Bob Knight, Erik, Margaret, and myself each playing very different roles, and the whole series of others playing roles far more than just that of the supporting cast. It is in this very sense that I thought that writing a history might make you face a number of issues of this sort. But please do not feel that you let me down. You gave me an opportunity to write out something I had never gotten myself really to pull together, but just permitted it to live in me. You do not have any obligations in this respect toward me. I am sure that if you steep yourself in the history of the school of psychiatry you will also find similar problems at the roots.

I saw George a few days ago at Perry Point. He told me about the offer you and Cook made to him, and told me also that he has to go and see [I. Arthur] Mirsky [Department of Clinical Science, University of Pittsburgh School of Medicine] first to clarify the situation and his obligations. So I don't know what he is going to do. The money problem is a serious one. I think that in general that fund Bille is connected with is prone to relate favorably to the type of request you made (particularly if the money involved is not going to be too big). If I were you, I would try to contact the Carnegie Fund and Charles Dollard. You know they have a psychologist in charge there also. Maybe Brewster Smith can help you to figure out how to go about it. I would, in your place, go up to Morrison of Rockefeller's [Robert S. Morison, Director of Medical and Natural Sciences, Rockefeller Foundation] together with Cook and talk to him about it. I do not think that the Ford Foundation is unapproachable for this type of thing. The record shows that they have given to this type of thing. But again, there is a question of the approach, and I do not know it. I wonder whether Cook and you could talk directly to [E. H. "Jack"] Hilgard about it. Hilgard is relatively close to the sources there.

I am delighted that Dave Shapiro gave a good presentation, and that there was some understanding between you and him on the one hand and Klopfer on the other. I was always bothered by Klopfer having taught a lot of people who had no business and no prerequisites to learn the Rorschach. I felt that he was selling it cheap and keeping it skin deep. I did not like their keeping away from rationale, and I did not like their avoiding reference to us. But all this seems so very far away now. I am interested in entirely different things. Did you get my reprints regularly, and my papers? I am working now on a new paper on activity and passivity, and have been trying to experiment some. When you come around to these parts we will have further opportunity to talk about them.

> Yours,
> David

Summary—Letters from First Half of 1953

Since the period covered by this summary coincided with my last months in Topeka, I was largely preoccupied with the transition and with frantic efforts to finish off the first draft, together with Lester Luborsky, of our book on the Selection Project (Holt & Luborsky, 1958). Most of the correspondence with Rapaport therefore concerns those matters and may be briefly summarized.

A letter from me of January 2 thanks David for a gift and turns to his Schilder manuscript:

> I am sorry to have to tell you that as time went on I lost some of the interest in the book that had been excited in me earlier. [. . .] At the top of his form, Schilder is wonderful, but at other times it just doesn't seem worth the effort of reading him. [. . .] [But] certainly there are many books published which have a good deal less in them. An example [. . .] is Dave McClelland's [1951] book. You know how harsh my general judgment of the book was, yet there are some ideas in it of real merit and worthy of your attention. [. . .] [E.g.,] his chapter 12, entitled <u>Motivation: experimental approach</u>. Even here, there is a good deal that is thoughtless.

Then I wrote about an attractive offer from NYU, and talked of other possibilities (Pittsburgh, Yale, Harvard). It was good news that David would soon start doing experiments, a wish to discuss them with him, perhaps on a forthcoming eastern trip.

Three days later, more editorial suggestions about the Schilder book. I enclosed a hastily written outline of the chapter for Rubin-stein-Lorr. Noting that "I have read through part of the voluminous files that exist [at Menninger's] on the doings of psychologists since Pentateuchal times," I added my suspicion that "much of the real meat is missing."

In his reply of January 9 (thanks and comments about my job pro-spects), David hoped I might come to Stockbridge, perhaps to give a "seminar" and "It would be awfully nice to have a good long talk and to have your reactions to my ideas and plans. I need some cold water thrown on my enthusiasms. I think you could do that without me feel-ing deflated by it."

In the enclosed copy of his letter to Shakow, after urging that he con-sider offering me a job, Rapaport added (on January 22):

I know few people, beside you, who are as conservative and fair-minded, and yet immersed in the spirit of dynamic psychology, as he is. When I say [that] [. . .] I mean: so little blinded by partisan-ship. I am sure you know that while I am keenly aware that my partisanship blinds me, and at times even know where it blinds me, and at times I am even ready to fight against this blindness, nevertheless by temperament and perhaps [al]so by choice, I would rather remain a partisan with all that entails. I am glad only that that does not force me to deny the attraction fair-mindedness has for me, nor to abandon my respect and affection for those who can afford to be partisan and fair-minded both.

My next letter (January 29) thanks him for the "fascinating reminis-cences" in his letter of January 22, which would be "an enormous help to me." I asked for his permission to show it to several interested friends. The rest is concerned with pros and cons of job possibilities. I also asked him about a rumor that he was planning to move to Israel.

His response, on February 2, gave permission for me to show his last letter on the beginnings of psychology at Menninger's to anyone inter-ested, but on this condition:

> If you would tell them [. . .] that this was dictated into the Dicta-
> phone, was not corrected for content, not meant for anybody else
> but you to see, originally; thus, it is not a fair assessment of the
> role [of clinical psychologist], of the capacity of people [men-
> tioned], of my interest in them, or even of my feeling toward
> them. It was meant simply as an orientation in the history, to you.

He then gave me some good advice about how to choose among the job options, concluding with a postscript asking where I heard about his "moving to Israel," which, he said, "In this form for now it is not true at all."

The next item is a generic letter from me (on March 24) sent to my friends summarizing the job search and announcing the decision: directing the Research Center for Mental Health, NYU. In addition to an apology, I added a note to David, sorry to hear from Paul Bergman that he had been unwell and "may visit Israel to consider a job there."

The reply, of April 14, sends congratulations and word that "George is about to go to Topeka" for a visit. He is still undecided about several possibilities; Rapaport hopes that there will be "a feasible combination at NYU for him also." The rest concerns:

> A new book by [C. H.] Patterson [1953], about the Bellevue-
> Wechsler. The utter stupidity of all that is being pattered about—
> and Patterson is apparently the summary of all patter-scatter, is
> really irritating. I am wondering whether or not you would have
> the yen to write something theoretical on this matter, either by
> yourself or jointly with me. [. . .] The whole problem of rationale is
> what should be discussed.

It now seems odd that my response of April 17 does not even mention that possible collaboration, but it describes such a busy life in my last Topeka months that it is clear that I could not have accepted. I wrote at some length about the difficulties Lester and I were having finishing a first draft of the Selection Project book. I reported that Bille was leaving for a foundation job, and that, "partly as a preparation for my new job, or as a kind of beginning of it," I was reviewing "the Hilgard-Kubie-Pumpian-Mindlin [1952] volume." It seemed inappropriate for me to write about psychology at Menninger under these circumstances, so I had tried to get Walter Kass to take it on. There was little time for me to finish reading the manuscript of Roy's [1954] book; "I think that it's going to be one of the very few best books on the Rorschach." And I asked Rapaport if he could find time to read the manuscript of our Selection book, which Basic Books might publish.

On April 22, David responded:

I am glad you are dealing with the Basic Books. It is a young outfit and may, if supported , become a type of publishing house which we do not have at present on the American scene. [. . .] They need an advisor and you would be the ideal person. They offered it to me, but I did not feel that I should accept money from them. I can help them much more if I [don't]. [. . .] I am interested in [. . .] [helping] them grow into a real publishing-house which pioneers, sets the pace in the field instead of crawling after it, which will publish soft-cover books cheaply, etc. I will be delighted to read your manuscript [. . .] [starting] on August 1. If I can get the money, I will be going around the end of September to Israel [and will read it there]. [. . .] I will probably spend some 10 weeks around there. It may not surprise you that I am just as critical of Hilgard's as of Kubie's contribution. When you consider it from the point of view of the basic psychological theory of psychoanalysis, you will find that Kubie has little if any grasp of that.

He then tried to persuade me to do the chapter on the history of clinical psychology at Menningers. I was just the person for it, it would be good for me, etc. He didn't care much who I got to do it if I wouldn't, but would "make one reservation": "No direct quotes from what I wrote, nor attribution to me in a direct fashion. [. . .] This reservation would not hold for you because I would rely without reservation on your taste."

It is amusing to contrast this passage with his later negative reaction to my draft of a short history of the Menninger Foundation in a chapter of the book manuscript (see letter of August 27, 1953). The present letter ends with some more talk about the unsettled plans of George Klein and David Shakow.

In another short letter of June 29, I tell Rapaport that there is hope of getting George Klein to NYU, and praise Roy's [1954] book, which I just finished and thought "far and away the best book on the Rorschach." I had been working hard on the Selection book, and complain that "In a way, it is almost <u>more</u> work, having Les [Luborsky] for a collaborator than it would be to write it all myself. I know that is a terribly arrogant statement, and I wouldn't say it to anyone else besides yourself."

For the record, let me note that, probably because the Selection Project was not of greater intrinsic interest to him than it was to me, Lester showed in our joint work little of the remarkable talent for research on psychotherapy, which brought him so much deserved acclaim from his peers in later years.

Rapaport to Holt—July 28, 1953

Dear Bob:

Thank you for your letter of July 22. I am looking forward to seeing your first chapter. [. . .]

I have no files whatsoever concerning the research projects in Topeka. All that has been in the Research Department files and should be there now. As I remember it, we first obtained a two years grant from the Veterans Administration for this study. I am under the impression that it was in 1946 and 1947. If I remember correctly, we started the whole thing in order to finance on the one hand the intake procedure, that is, the selection procedure, by using it as research data collection procedure also. I think it was in consultation with Jim Miller that the idea to turn this selection procedure into a research came up. At the time they were very interested in getting us going on a school of clinical psychology and when I told them about financial difficulties, they made all kinds of such financial suggestions which I would now call finagling, to make it possible for us to get started. You may not know it, but I was not interested in starting a school of clinical psychology and it was the joint pressure of the Menningers on the one hand and Miller on the other, that drove us into it. We did not really make an application; it was really from Washington that we were given this. I think somehow the support was then relegated to be a part of the money that was given to Michigan [for the similar project of Kelly and Fiske]. But I cannot be sure of this. Later on, when the Veterans Administration research moneys had

166

been subordinated to a National Research Council's top committee jurisdiction, then [John C.] Whitehorn and [James G.] Miller
came down to study what we were doing and to form an opinion
on it, whether they should further support it. At the time it was a
touch-and-go affair. But this is all I remember; my effort then was
to transform it into a real research project, getting it out from the
intake interview financing sphere. That is how you and Luborsky
got into it then. [. . .]

      Yours,

        David

Rapaport to Holt—August 27, 1953

Dear Bob:

The new batch of manuscripts arrived. I read Chapter II and I am hastening to write you about it. Since you want to hear the unembellished truth from me, I will give it to you: this chapter simply dismayed me. It is unbalanced, injudicious, righteous and judgmental. It barges in everywhere where even angels would fear to tread on tip-toe. I do not mean that many of us do not hold opinions, prejudices, feelings and attitudes like those expressed here. But here they are expressed as proven facts. Now you know very well that I do not mind myself treading on as many toes as is necessary for something I believe in. But to write something that treads on every God-damned toe when one wants to get a sympathetic audience to listen to what factual findings and serious considerations you have to offer—that's not just a mistake. Besides offending many people whose interests will be tactlessly intruded upon, this presentation cannot but antagonize all people who are judicious. Instead of assuming a tone of understatement which sketches difficulties—the tone here is contemptuous and condemning; or else on the other side, when Karl Menninger and Will Menninger are mentioned, it is ass-licking. Uncertainty about evidence is marked by adjectives and extreme assertions, as well as irrelevancies. To me it seems that the whole chapter is wrong from the word "go." It has to be started over again, to my mind, with an eye to the objective difficulties of psychiatric ignorance, slow development of psychiatry, the mass burden on state hospitals, the unattractiveness of salaries. Al Deutsch[72] and Goren, as much as we are fond of them as persons, must not be treated as gospel but rather as indicators that what you judiciously pronounce, has been and could be stated in far more extreme terms. What Will Menninger and Karl Menninger did must be described without insinuating that it would not have happened by the sheer weight of historical circumstances, but could [have] come about only because of these two geniuses. (I do not mean here to go to the opposite extreme but seek rather for a balance.) One reading this chapter might gain the impression that everything is known and that the writers subscribe to shock and lobotomy without reserve. The paragraph on page 16 is a good example in point. Instead of discussing first the factual finding which is reported perfunctorily on page 17, in a most journalistic fashion an inquiry was reported which was no [real] inquiry and dignified by the word "discovered." I have marked quite a lot of sentences with question marks. Also I did it for terms. These are not to be construed as the only points which are questionable. I marked the most jarring ones for examples. There is hardly a line in this whole chapter which does not offend my taste. This is not the question of the issues discussed but rather of how they are discussed.

Well, you can imagine that I would have been pleased if I would not have had to deliver such a tirade. But you also can see—I imagine—that I would not do this would I not have been really outraged. There is somehow a wrong outlook on society in this, a wrong outlook on psychiatry, no perspective [on] what this book is to serve (I do not know what it is to serve but nothing is served by this chapter). This is journalism of the poor sort—I mean a fighting but insecure sort. Oh, well, hell, why should I pile

---

[72] Albert Deutsch (1905–1961) published exposés of America's public psychiatric hospitals in the newspaper *PM* in the 1940s and in his 1948 book. He also wrote a less sensational history and edited an encyclopedia on of mental illness in the United States. I assume that Goren played a similar role, but have been unable to trace him.

it up! It is much better to write a dull report than to jazz it up in this phony way.

I hear from Margaret that you will be here early in September and I am looking forward to seeing you.

Yours,

David

Holt to Rapaport—September 11, 1953

Dear David,

My immediate reaction to your blockbuster of the 27th last was to tell you to go to hell and at the same time to give you a lot of excuses and reasons why I did that chapter the way I did. I do not think that either of these two reactions is very constructive, and I believe I will be able to assimilate your criticisms without them. I think that you were unnecessarily harsh, but I know that that is your style, and I do not hold it too much against you. I am grateful to you for your frankness, and I believe that I shall end up agreeing with almost all of your criticisms. I hope you realize what a tough job it is to write something like this. I worked very hard to try to liven the thing up, and it is rather bitter to find that this earns only your contempt. Yet I believe you are right in saying that it is better to be dull than to be phony.

It won't be early in September that I will make it up there but it will be as soon as I can. I want first to find an apartment and to get myself more settled generally. When will you be leaving? I am afraid that it is soon, but at least you may be able to stop by and see me here before you sail, if you embark before I come up.

Yours,

Bob

Summary—Letters from Second Half of 1953

The first letters in the second half of 1953 are taken up with talk about problems of getting on with the Selection Project book, and chat about friends. David was happy (July 3) that I like Roy's book: "I hope you tell him. My praise was clouded with lots of critique. [. . .] He is really pioneering." On July 22, I sent him a draft of the first chapter of our book, asked for information about how the Selection Project got started, and responded to the paper he had just sent (an early draft on activity and passivity [Rapaport, 1953d])—I was able to read only the first eight pages, but had many notes already.

He responded to my request about the origins of the Selection Project in the letter of July 28. On August 5, he thanked me for the chapter and commented:

> 1) The invention which you use to get away from a dry description of a trainee's course is a good one. 2) The text is lively and readable. 3) [. . .] There is an overtone of "sweetness and light" and an implied overpraising of the setup at the Menninger School of Psychiatry. I find it hard to put my finger on it. [. . .] Somehow a "best of all worlds" air about it all. [. . .] The danger is not merely that it will sound [. . .] [like] propaganda, but somehow the bitterness of realities may slip by sugar-coated. [. . .] Here one of your virtues may be turning into a vice. [. . .]

In response a week later, I agree that the point is well taken: We will try to change it but it is tricky, we have to please or at least not offend many people. The rest is gossip about mutual friends.

Three days after the painful exchange of August 27 and September 11 came David's response to chapter III, which he felt deserved a milder form of the criticism of chapter II. The chapter lacks integration but "can stand very well on its own." My response of September 15 emphasizes the difficulties we face. "KAM thinks that we put the school in an unfair light to devote such space and emphasis to the disaffections of the residents." He thinks them minor and that he irons everything out in his talks with them.

> It's really pitiful how little he sees of what is going on right under his nose. The Fellows tell me that these talks of his made the situation seem even more hopeless to them, so that they simply gave up in disgust trying to do anything about their grievances. But can we say that? [. . .] At the same time, we are attacked on the other flank by Rudi [Ekstein] for whitewashing the school. [. . .]
>
> [Les and I may decide not to try to describe the MSP in such detail] if we can't do a completely fair and rounded appraisal. [. . .] It is very hard to avoid implicit or explicit approval and disapproval. [. . .] We can't conclude, I think, that since no one is pleased we must have stumbled on the truth.

The rest of the letter concerns planning to go see him and some personal news.

The letter of September 23 shows that the visit to Stockbridge did happen and "was both stimulating and relaxing." Most of it concerns our first contact at NYU with the graduate students of clinical psychology, "an interesting group. Someone here remarked [. . .] that the best ones are very good indeed, but that the lower limit goes down somewhat further than it does in a number of other places; it is easy to believe both statements. [. . .] only about one applicant to the clinical program out of ten was accepted." Finally, "Bon voyage, David, and don't work yourself too hard."

There follows a gap for the rest of the year. Obviously, George and I were preoccupied with learning new ropes and getting our Research Center off the ground.

CHAPTER 4

Summary—Letters from 1954

Rapaport's letter of January 12, written "on the first day of my return to the office" from Israel, dealt first with a bureaucratic matter, then "a word of greeting [. . .] and to tell you how glad I was that you and Elvira met several times [. . .]." The rest dealt with an invitation to speak at the NYU departmental seminar.

My reply on February 3, dealing with both issues, came after another weekend's visit, at which we had discussed applying for grant support of the Research Center. I reassured him that despite a misunderstanding, George "is as fond of you as ever and will very sincerely welcome the opportunity to get your thinking on some of the problems we will be working with."

His next (February 5) continued the effort to find a good time for him to come to New York to give a seminar and also attend a lecture by Anna Freud. I offered him a consultation fee to help make the trip. His comment on a recent visit by me suggests that these letters contain little of substance because we were now able to have discussions face to face.

On March 1, I reported having visited both Topeka and California. George had just returned from a longer but somewhat less comfortable visit to Menninger's than mine was. I expressed ambivalence about our grant application to the US Public Health Service for support of our research program—not yet well enough thought through, but it has to go in. Final word on Rubinstein-Lorr chapter: Marty Mayman did it; not good, not bad.

David's next (March 17) came after a visit to Topeka also. He found there "a very nice group, but one which has no real leadership." Meanwhile, "I made a negative decision for the time being, on the invitation of the Hebrew University."

My response of March 18 answered some questions about how to crowd in, on the same day, the NYU seminar, a consultation with George and me, and the Anna Freud lecture. I expressed concern about having learned from Margaret and Bill Gibson that Erik Erikson was in a Boston hospital for an operation. In California I had attended the American Orthopsychiatric meetings, where I spent an enjoyable evening with Bille at her party. "Quite a number of people were discussing Bill's book [the novel *The Cobweb*] which we had just read. I find that it stays with me remarkably—I keep thinking about those characters, which I suppose speaks for their vitality and for the psychological truth of their predicament. In way I was more impressed by the human wisdom and the psychological insight in the book than I was by the writing."

On March 22, Rapaport wrote that he had heard from David van Lennep, who was coming to Denver and wanted help in arranging a seminar in Topeka. Could I contact someone?

I replied on April 1 that I had done so, and that we needed a title for his own May 5 talk, plus other minor planning details.

At last, April 14, I sent him a copy of our grant application to the Ford Foundation, "a slight revision of the one . . . to USPHS." We hoped to discuss it with him on May 5. I sent Erik "my warm regards and wishes for a speedy recovery."

After all the preparations, I had to send regrets on May 7 from all of us "that your health didn't allow you to speak here this week." I reported on visits with Dave Shapiro and his wife, the Wheelises, Mert and Charlotte Gill, and on Anna Freud's lecture.

In a letter dated May 14, David reported on his recent but brief illness, and talks at Riggs by Bille (not good) and Roy (excellent). About our application to the Ford Foundation: "I found it thoughtful and interesting. I hope that they will be sensible about it."

After four months, a letter from me expressed excitement at "the word from George that you might be interested in an adjunctive professorship here." I introduced to him "an old friend of mine, Dr. Rosemary

Pritchard, of London, England," who was going to Riggs to learn about the best modern clinical methods. And I wrote that we had had a very good meeting with the subcommittee from the Study Section of the USPSH. They had invited us to submit a supplement with a revised budget, which seems more likely to succeed.

A brief note from Rapaport on September 21 said rather cryptically that "These are difficult weeks for me." He was going to be in New York on October 7 and hoped to see us.

On September 24, I reported on the business of an Adjunct Professorship. We love the idea, but Stuart Cook (our departmental chair) says that NYU won't pay anything unless he gives a course here, can't even reimburse Riggs for time spent supervising a student's dissertation. It looks as if we can take care of the last point from research funds.

His response of September 29 said: "As long as I have one or two students (good ones!) only and I do not have to come to New York, I do not care about money." He had to cancel the October 7 visit but hoped to be up to it later.

He was; a note from me on October 19 looked forward to seeing him a few days later. His letter of October 27 indicates that he did come, but frustratingly there was still no substance. Apparently we talked about my memory experiments and Rorschach manual; he wanted to learn more about them. He sent the Riggs collection of papers.

I sent some material he had requested with a cover note, on about November 13, also asking for "a statement from you on the topics or areas in which you'd be willing to supervise [doctoral] theses, such that it could be directly quoted to the students." A handwritten note of November 24 thanks me for it, adds that he has sent the staff seminar notes to Merton, who is "very interested in several aspects of these issues. [. . .] Things are not easy right now for me."

Holt to Rapaport—October 28, 1954

Dear David:

I enjoyed our talks, but I felt afterwards that I could have made much better use of your presence if I had prepared for it. Actually there are quite a number of problems of psychoanalytic theory that have been bothering me, since I have recently been going over the Interpretation of Dreams[73] rather carefully and noting down most of the difficulties I had with it. I do hope we will be able to find time to discuss some of these matters at a future meeting either in Stockbridge or here in New York.

Let me tell you just briefly what I did on memory. It was when I was reading [a translation of] Poetzl [1917] and [Charles] Fisher [1954] and thinking about those problems that it occurred to me to try to find out whether passages that were read to a subject for immediate reproduction might not be partially scotomatized and parts not consciously recalled might be recovered in dreams. Consequently, I plunged right into an attempt to test this hypothesis, using six or eight people who were around the office—colleagues, research assistants, and secretaries. I made up three passages after the model of the learning efficiency story from the Babcock test, trying to keep the same general structure and number of elements, but varying the themes. One of them concentrated heavily on symbolic anal material, another on

---

[73] The *Standard Edition* was just coming out at that time, starting with volumes 4 and 5, and we at the Research Center were all reading it with close attention.

themes supposedly associated with urethral fixation and a third on voyeuristic-exhibitionistic material. I did not use oral because I knew that Roy had done so and wanted to make use of his experience if I worked [i.e., did further research] in that particular area.

The procedure was rather simple: I got an immediate recall, and then asked my subjects to tell me any dreams they had that night on the following morning. Very briefly, the results seemed to be quite negative as far as the main hypothesis was concerned, though the experiment was faulty in many respects and not a good test of it.

Nevertheless, in the course of doing this I discovered quite a number of things that I did not know about immediate memory for meaningful material. Largely it was based upon discussion with my subjects in which I tried to draw them out on how they recalled the material, what difficulties they had, and the like. I am sure that you will have encountered all of these facets of the problem, but I would like to list the points that struck me particularly.

One thing that I had never thought of was the different way in which subjects might use imagery in remembering a passage. Some subjects who had vivid visual imagery reported that it made it easy to recall some stories, which could easily be translated into a series of images, while the [different] structure of other stories in this respect made their visualizing proclivities a handicap. It became evident that the task of memorizing a story, or at least of recalling it on one hearing, was a very different one for a subject who had vivid visual imagery and a subject who had practically none, at least for certain forms of these stories. Since I am quite a visual person myself, doubtless this influenced the way that I composed the passages.

Another thing that was particularly striking was the effect of the grammatical structure of sentences. In one of the passages, I included an inversion of the normal order of words. The reasons for it are irrelevant, but I am glad that I did it because it created such a unanimous effect: every subject made more mistakes in recalling this sentence than in the rest of the passage! I don't happen to have the originals of these stories at hand, but as I recall it myself, the sentence went: "Where a great stream pours from an opening in the mountain, a waterfall he discovered has been named after him." Actually, the sentence doesn't make quite perfect sense, though I think only an English teacher would really cavil at it, but the implicit expectation that the sentence would be like the others in starting with the subject and proceeding uneventfully to the predicate seems to have thrown all the subjects off. This of course is something that would be easy to test by rewriting passages, keeping the same content (one could probably even use exactly the same words) but introducing inversions or other variations of sentence structure and testing their relative memorability.

There were certain phrases used in some of the stories which came through again and again where the other elements in the stories would drop out. Perhaps to some extent this is a matter of imagery, but I think that there is some sort of saliency that goes beyond just that. For example, the paired words <u>slimy mud</u> were recalled by most subjects, though the imagery here if any is probably kinesthetic, and people are not supposed to have very much kinesthetic imagery generally. Of course, that is a kind of cliché or familiar pairing of words which may give it a relative advantage. These considerations prompted me to think that even in trivial pieces of prose made up for the purpose, there may be features of literary quality, or the kinds of considerations that literary critics have in mind in judging prose, which affect memorability. In general, I had the impression that there would probably be a good relationship between readability (and also Flesch's human interest measure[74]) and the ease with which something could be remembered.

---

[74] In *The Art of Readable Writing* (1949), Rudolf Flesch published his Human Interest formula along with his Reading Ease formula. The former is a sum of the percentage frequency, in a text, of "personal words" (e.g., names, personal pronouns) and of "personal sentences" (e.g., those that address the reader, sentences containing dialogue).

I believe it would be possible to show that the Aristotelian unities have empirical validity in this respect. Certainly the concreteness of incident and the extent to which a passage contains a readily grasped story-line seems to have a marked influence on its memorability.

In a couple of instances I got delayed recalls from subjects in a not very systematic way, but just enough to bring out a couple of instances of "reminiscence." This is an intriguing phenomenon, one that we have had to deal with in our own attempts to repeat the Poetzl experiments. For example, in connection with the mescaline experiment on George, I showed him at 1/100 of a second, a slide of a courtyard in which was standing an equestrian statue. The statue blends perceptually into the façade of the buildings behind it, and is not easy to grasp; George did not see it, or rather did not report it in his attempt to describe what he had seen immediately afterwards. When we returned an hour or so later to the same test, he gave essentially the same description of the picture and made essentially the same drawing that he had done the first time, and then suddenly had the idea that there might have been a horse in it. It turned out that this horse was the one thing that seemed to have been recovered in the dream he had that night, of which he could report only that it had been about an Indian and a horse. Of course, I got the idea of having him do this delayed recall because Poetzl had done it and had also found similar reminiscence effects. Sometime I want to look up the literature on this phenomenon, which is a most intriguing one.

Coming back to the playing around I did with memory, there were also considerable differences in the extent to which subjects strove for internal consistency and meaning, which in turn depended I think, partly on their attitude toward the whole experiment. Secretaries who participated under pressure and without interest made no effort to reproduce anything meaningful. The pressure was not explicit, but when I asked them if they would like to participate, they seemed to be unable to say no, even though it seemed quite clear that they didn't really want to do it. Perhaps, then, this failure to get involved showed up in their failure to make sense out of the passage, though there was probably also quite a difference in the general level of intelligence or verbal factors between them and the graduate students. There may have been some effect of the status hierarchy here, too. At any rate, I found it difficult to empathize with this attitude of reporting unrelated snatches, or fragments which were confabulated in a meaningless way. It also happens that I did not instruct the subjects to try to get the gist of the passage, and they may have had the idea that it was more important to pick up words than to get the sense. Working with different sets of that kind also seems like an obviously necessary variation of this sort of work.

Finally, some of the subjects reported that there were subtle shifts in content, even in these relatively unitary passages, which introduced some kind of surprise which caused them to lose what they had grasped at first. This along with some of the other observations points very strongly to the importance of the particular anticipations that the subject has in this special task of immediate auditory memory. I believe that many simultaneous sets or anticipations are probably operating in a subject, many more than he could consciously verbalize unless you violated some of them. Some exist before you say anything; others are undoubtedly evoked by the initial impact of the first few words. Indeed, if it were not for the flexibility and pervasiveness of sets operating in this way, it would be very difficult for us to understand each other.

The more I think about these problems, the more complex and intriguing they seem to me. Yet I don't foresee any immediate chance of working on them myself. I hope you can get a good student to work with you on some of these things.

With my warm regards to Elvira and yourself—

Bob

Minutes of Staff Seminar—October 28, 1954[75]

GSK, HL [Harriet Linton, a staff member] and RRH met briefly, beginning the discussion of some of the points in the section on primary and secondary process in the seventh chapter of the Interpretation of Dreams. (Page references are to Vol. V of the Standard Edition [SE] of Freud.)

RRH led off with a question about two paragraphs on page 597, where Freud says that "two fundamentally different kinds of psychical process are concerned in the formation of dreams. [Apparently he refers here to primary and secondary process, though he never says so explicitly.] One of these produces perfectly rational dream-thoughts, of no less validity than normal thinking; while the other treats these thoughts in a manner which is in the highest degree bewildering and irrational." In the following paragraph he says: "In hysteria, too, we come across a series of perfectly rational thoughts, equal in validity to our conscious thoughts . . . [there is] complete identity between the characteristic features of the dream work and those of the psychical activity which issues in psychoneurotic symptoms. . . ." In this passage, Freud seems to be saying that the primary process is involved only in a defensive way in the production of dreams and neurotic symptoms, while the thought-process producing the latent

---

[75] This and the following document are routine minutes I took of two staff discussions, which were sent to Rapaport because they addressed theoretical issues about which he then commented in two subsequent letters.

thoughts underlying the hysterical symptom or the dream is "perfectly rational and valid," just like "normal thinking," which sounds as if he means secondary process. Actually, we decided, in his effort to convince the skeptical that underneath the apparently nonsensical and random vagaries of dreams and symptoms there is something intelligible and determined, Freud overstated his case. Consideration of any particular dream and the dream-thoughts involved in it shows that these can be stated in orderly, perfectly intelligible sentences, but are prime examples of drive-directed, autistic thinking.

It seems therefore reasonable to say that there is indeed a difference between the thought processes that result in dream-thoughts (or the "thoughts" underlying a hysterical symptom) and the processes which produce the manifest dream or symptom, even though both of these sets of processes must be conceived as primary in type. The important distinction seems to be that the dream-work or symptom-work is a <u>defensive</u> use of the primary process, while in the underlying thoughts the primary process is not used in a defensive way. This way of looking at it clears up a number of difficulties.

There has been something of a controversy in the psychoanalytic literature, with Jones, for example, taking a definite position that the primary process is always a defensively organized stratagem of thinking, while Silberer [Rapaport, 1951, Chap. 8 & 9], for example, upholds the view that at least the primary process mechanism of symbol formation is not defensive but is a function of certain states of consciousness. Freud may be quoted on both sides of this controversy, like so many others in the psychoanalytic literature. According to the present view, [the] thinking of the infant and young child (which Freud has clearly said was primary in character) does not have to be conceived of as defensive. The fluid and arbitrary transitions, the illogical structure, and the rest of it can be viewed as the necessary result of the fact that counter-cathectic controlling mechanisms are only beginning to be formed, so that drives have pretty much free play and cathexes are freely mobile. Later on, then, the fact that the mind has this type of functioning always potentially present can be used by the developing ego defensively, in a strategic regressive retreat. Perhaps we can say that the primary process is being used defensively only when there is regression, though this would not be a sufficient definition.

This distinction led us into a consideration of the concept of drive-organization. Drive-directed thinking is apparently always primary, but not all primary thinking is in any clear or obvious way drive-directed. Rather, it seems possible that structural considerations alone may suffice to account for the primary nature of some thought processes. Thus, in schizophrenia, it seems very doubtful that the statement "Brazil is in Argentina" is autistic in the sense of being wish-fulfilling; rather, it seems to be the outcome of a structural derangement; a loosening of conceptual boundaries in memory organization. We discussed contamination in the Rorschach in this light: the classic example: "grass-bear" may indeed in some obscure way be drive-determined, (unfortunately we simply don't know enough about the patient to know the answer to this), but it seems a fairly safe supposition that this is simply due to a fluid state of affairs in which separate ideas are not kept separate. The association to the shape and to the color came to mind more or less simultaneously and the cathexes of these ideas being freely mobile, they were combined in a single contamination or condensation. Thus, the concept of "freely mobile cathexis" seems enough to account for the primary nature of some kinds of thinking.

The question was raised whether this conclusion necessarily committed us to the energy model. This was a question that perhaps may be pursued fruitfully in greater detail later on, but our immediate thought was that it did not. The same phenomenon might be describable in terms of Hebb's concept of perceptual identity: the establishment of a kind of constancy, so that a [mental representation of a] particular thing is that thing rather than just a shifting pattern of momentary stimulation. According to

Hebb [1949], such identities must be built up by learning before the simplest recognition can take place. This looks as if it may be another way of referring to the phenomenon of freely mobile cathexis and the lack of what Freud calls "thought-identity."

Pursuing this thought further, we decided that it would be logically impossible for such identities ever to arise in an organism that had no ego rudiments, no primordial capacity for reality contact or for restraining the free mobility of cathexis even a little bit. Repetition could not lead to any kind of learning if there were no stability whatever of the resulting traces, and thus the organism could never develop object constancy (which is probably a closely related concept to "thought identity"). Thus, this train of thought leads to the same conclusion reached by Hartmann et al. about the presence of ego rudiments in the original "undifferentiated" phase.

GSK raised the question whether the mechanisms of condensation, displacement, etc. might not also have a developmental history. On the one hand, this idea seemed plausible enough, if these mechanisms were thought of either as [parts of] Id or an unconscious ego (an issue which remains to be fully discussed), if both are thought of as differentiating from the primordial undifferentiated phase. On the other hand, Rapaport describes condensation and displacement as the inevitable results of the free mobility of cathexis existing in infancy. Perhaps the real point here is that the <u>defensive use</u> of these mechanisms is something that has a developmental history, while the occurrence of the phenomena themselves may date from the very beginning. (When we use the term "mechanism" we imply that there is some kind of purposive use of a phenomenon like displacement or condensation, which doesn't have to be thought of as a mechanism at all in the infant, or perhaps in non-defensive primary process thinking generally.)

There was some further discussion of the energy model, mostly by way of touching briefly on some of its difficulties. For example, the concept of <u>discharge</u> seems to have a number of problems, perhaps even fallacies. On page 598 [SE, V], for example, Freud speaks of "the power of movement" as "<u>the</u> path to discharge." (Emphasis mine.) Thus, it is questionable whether a dream can be thought of as providing any opportunity for discharge, though we had the impression that somewhere Freud said or implied that at least small amounts of discharge could take place through it. This raised the question of the <u>function</u> biologically of the primary process; we decided that this was a very difficult matter, and that even though it might seem in itself not to have much survival value, it might be a necessary by-product of some other important feature of the organism which did have important survival value. Thus, if the apparently useless and even dangerous capacity for hallucinating the need-satisfying object were not present in the infant, it might not be possible for a thought to develop at all as a substitute for action. It may well be that the only alternative to having our peculiar and unhandy kinds of instincts would be to have the rigid instincts of animals, with their built-in adaptiveness to reality and their limiting effect on any but that particular built-in adaptation—or perhaps not to have any innate drives at all, which would seem to leave an organism in too inert a state to develop into anything.

In discussing the fact that the concept of discharge was based on the model of the reflex arc, which Freud followed in creating his own construct of a psychic apparatus, GSK raised the question what difference it might have made in Freud's model building if he had known what is known today about the incessant activity of the nervous system. For Freud, the nervous system was a passive, reactive structure reducing stimulation to a minimum. This seems to require a tension-reduction theory, which runs into many difficulties; even a theory implying an optimum level of tension has its problems, too (another topic for future discussion); whether or not it is possible to retain the general model of the psychic apparatus that Freud described while adopting the idea of maintaining an optimum [level] of tension instead of a minimum remains to be worked out.

[In] the next meeting, we decided that it might be profitable to discuss in more detail the operations of condensation, displacement, and symbol-formation. GSK also suggested the problem of whether or not social-cultural influences are solely secondary in nature, or whether they affect the primary process in any way other than the contents with which it works. RRH suggested that a comparative study of psychoses in different cultures might be one way of approaching this question, and HL said she would look up some material on this question from Ralph Linton [her father].

Minutes of Staff Seminar—November 11, 1954

All five members of the group were present and took part in a discussion that began with a report by RRH on his talk with Lois Murphy and her group [in Topeka] on the problems of applying the concepts of primary and secondary process to the productions of children of nursery school age. Two major types of problems were described: first, problems caused by the multiplicity of phenomena encompassed under the general concept of primary process, which makes it very difficult to combine observations or measurements on, say, the degree of drive-directedness, of fidelity to reality, of logical structure, and of the presence of the dream-work mechanisms. The second class of problems is caused by the difficulty of scaling quantitatively any one of these dimensions.

In discussing some particular examples that Dr. Murphy had presented, GSK made the point that one has to be very careful to adopt the child's own frame of reference or understanding what it is that he is doing. Thus, even though it looks more unrealistic and therefore more "primary" to put a toy horse on a toy table than it does to put a toy dog in a toy bassinette, the child may be using these objects in a way or with meanings that do not correspond to those present in the adult's mind. This was pointed out as being similar to another problem that was discussed: how much weight to give the unrealism of an initial assumption in play, which, like the original absurd premise of a paranoid train of thought, is then followed by consistent and logical development of ideas.

(Other problems raised in the Topeka groups and not discussed at the staff meeting were how to handle the problem of time-relation—the extent to which temporal realism was maintained or flouted, and the underlined, global use of objects and toys. Under the last heading may be considered phenomena reported by [Lucas N.] Kamp [Menninger child psychiatrist] in his work with the World Test. Certain young children play with all of the toys of the World Test without regard to their content or meaning, simply lining them up in rows higgledy-piggledy. Here it doesn't make any particular sense to look at this in terms of realism, for example, since the behavior is entirely different from that of the child cited earlier who knew very well that the toy horse was a toy horse and was putting it on the toy table for that very reason. In the Topeka group, we discussed these two different types of primary processes with reference to H. S. Sullivan's distinction between prototaxic and parataxic thinking. Prototaxic thinking is primitive, undifferentiated, pre-verbal, and pre-logical; it is reminiscent of the phenomena described by Werner and Piaget. Sullivan uses the term parataxic to refer to defensive uses of the primary process by adults primarily. Whether the difference is great enough to warrant this kind of distinction or not, some kind of systematic account has to be taken of errors and anomalies of thinking due to developmental immaturity.)

The discussion of the mechanisms of condensation, displacement, and symbolization began with an argument that displacement is the most irreducible of the mechanisms. Thus, a symbol can be looked on as a special case of displacement, in which the cathexis belonging to the thing symbolized is displaced to its substitute, the symbol-image. Similarly, in many kinds of condensation where a single image or idea is said to carry the cathectic charge of many different chains of thought or ideas, one can conceive this as a displacement of the cathexis from the latter to the former. Thus, the notion of displacement seems to express in purest form the underlying conceptual idea of free mobility of cathexis. Yet there is a residual meaning of condensation: it often results in a change in the structural characteristics of the image or word itself.

From here we went on to an extended discussion of the concept of condensation. Proceeding from the example of the image of Irma in Freud's dream, which he said was "a collective image with, it must be admitted, a number of contradictory characteristics [representing] other figures which have been sacrificed to the work of condensation, since I passed over to <u>her</u>, point by point, everything that reminded me of her," (page 293) the point was made that it is very difficult to distinguish between over-determination and condensation. Freud was aware of this and made what we considered only a weak defense against it. That is, disposing of the argument that anyone else associating to a particular element in a dream might bring extensive chains of association just as the dreamer does, Freud points out that the dreamer's associations do lead him back to the dream itself. This, however, could be attributed merely to the fact that it is his own material; it certainly leaves us with no criterion to distinguish a condensation from any instance of over-determined thinking—as all thinking must be considered to be, anyway. In another context, Freud does suggest such a criterion: sensory intensification. On page 595 he speaks as if every instance of condensation in dreams can be identified by this hallmark, yet he does not use the concept consistently in this way, referring often to condensations where there is no particular intensification of a sensory kind. BR [Benjamin Rubinstein] pointed out the difficulty of using this criterion as a sign of condensation, since in another context Freud uses it as a sign that a displacement has taken place: when a particular part of a dream has a peculiar sensory intensity, this may be due to displacement of emphasis as a defensive stratagem. BR went on to point out how difficult it is to distinguish sensory intensity from affective intensity in dreams. DS [Donald Spence] cited instances in non-dreaming behavior where peculiar sensory intensity seems to have quite different causes, such as "sensory starvation." In sum, the criterion of sensory intensity, then, is neither unique to condensation nor always found in association with it, for which reason it can have but little utility. It did seem possible, however, that we might be able to use it to some extent in the tachistoscopic situation,[76] where an A and B figure are manipulated so as to produce a compromise formation and where apparently such sensory intensifications do occur.

Another criterion for the recognition of condensation was discussed at some length: the presence in the image itself of diverse elements, or the fusion of more than one image into a new one. We discussed certain examples made familiar in mythology and folklore, such as the centaur and faun, and others which may be created in a playful or humorous context (such as a drawing of a hand made to represent a woman's face and called a "handmaiden"). HL [Harriet Linton] made the point that such images or concepts may be quite acceptable because of this context, but that does not make them any the less primary in nature. Condensation may be bound[77] ("sublimated") by a playful or aesthetic frame of reference, and may be achieved through a controlled regression in the service of the ego, but these aspects of the process should be considered separately from the issue of whether or not it is to be conceived of as primary process. RRH reported that he was making such a distinction in attempts to apply these concepts to the Rorschach, and finding that they helped make clear distinctions between GSK's "flexibly controlled" and "constricted-control" cases from the Harvard thirst study. Condensations or responses apparently involving some degree of condensation did appear in the protocols of the flexibly controlled subjects, but always with an intellectual, mythological, or other artistic or playful justification (including "Disneyism," describing animals as having human characteristics but in the tradition of animated cartoons and the like.)

---

[76] In experiments we were then conducting, we used a tachistoscope—an instrument into which a "subject" looked, receiving flashes of controlled brevity and brightness, of image A followed by a longer exposure of another image, B, which usually blocked awareness of A, though it often had some influence on the subject's report about B.

[77] This was written well before my study of the manifold meanings of this term in Freud's writings (Holt, 1962a). I would now say "controlled."

There was a fairly extended discussion of the different form varieties of condensations or near-condensations found in Rorschach responses. It seemed to RRH that the important considerations in arranging such things in a series was the extent to which the subject kept the two ideas separate and the extent to which he created a new concept to go along with the fused percepts. Such a series might be, for example, (Card VII, usual popular movement): subject sees the figures as two women, and then says, "They also could be two dogs." Here there is a complete separation of the two ideas, though one follows the other in quick succession and they are stimulated by the same area. At the other extreme would be: "Dog-ladies," with human and canine characteristics being seen simultaneously in a fused image accompanied by the fused concept. It is not so easy to line up all of the intermediate cases in an unambiguous way. There was some discussion of what to do with the case, for example, of an obsessive wavering back and forth between "looks like a woman—no, it looks more like a dog—but then it. . . ." It seems very difficult also, to draw a line at any particular point on such an empirical series and say: "Beyond this point condensation is involved." RRH suggested conceiving of condensation as a continuous variable, something that might be present to a greater or less extent in any thought product, which could thus be scored quantitatively. (Cf. in this connection Rapaport's [1961, Chap. 1] suggestion with reference to "apperceptive fusion" ([Narziss K.] Ach) that "closer study of such phenomena may demonstrate them to belong to one continuum with the Freudian mechanism of 'condensations'.")

It seemed that we were tending towards a definition of condensation in terms of a fusion of disparate elements into a new image. An unresolved question was the extent to which such an image had to be unrealistic to deserve the name of condensation. Is a child who looks like both her parents to be considered a biological condensation, and is the recognition of the similarity in any way a condensation? The answer, at least to the second part of the question, is obviously no. But suppose someone knew both of the parents and had not seen the child, yet drew a phantasy image of what the child of these two parents must look like, producing an image realistically combining the features of both parents; would that not be a condensation? The point seems to be that it probably would not be <u>recognized</u> as such without further knowledge of its context, while the drawing of the "ape-man" on p. 369 of Boring, Langfeld and Weld's <u>Introduction to Psychology</u> could be clearly recognized as a condensation without knowledge of its context. Similarly, a Rorschach response may involve the condensation of several images but as long as the product is realistically acceptable, it would be extremely difficult to spot it as such, and even if one had the associations that would bring out its multiple origins, it would be difficult to distinguish condensation and over-determination. Thus, it may lead to a conservative definition, but it seems useful for working purposes to restrict condensation to cases where there is distortion or arbitrariness in the resulting image. In this connection, we discussed the response of one of GSK's patients to a picture which he showed us. In this rather peculiar painting, part of the fur garment being worn by one of two fighting men protrudes between his legs in the position of a penis but with exaggerated size and darkness. He had shown this picture with a very brief exposure; the patient said it was two men wrestling; "one of them has a sword." From his knowledge of the patient and her attitude towards men, GSK felt that this percept, "sword," was a condensation involving the unconscious image of a penis. It was pointed out, however, that her interpretation was a much more reasonable one than anything else that might have occurred under the circumstances, and would probably be a modal response from a normal population. Due to the peculiar nature of the picture, therefore, it was something like the incongruous pictures used by Bruner in an experiment where he showed that people tended to wash out the incongruities on tachistoscopic presentation. Thus, the criterion of what is <u>distorted</u> and what is <u>realistic</u> has to be considered rather carefully, and sometimes in terms of consensus rather than the examiner's own point of view when he has a chance to study a stimulus in a way that the subject does not.

RRH said that in his thinking about condensations he had frequently run up against the idea that a mobility of cathexis was centrally important in any question of whether an active thought was primary or not, and that he had found it very difficult to think of any operations [observations] that would correspond to this concept. Perhaps the concept was really a second order one, on a level of generalization where no direct operations should be expected. Thus, it seems to be an abstractive generalization from the mechanisms of displacement, condensation and symbolization, which extract what they have in common and expresses it in another language—that of the energy theory. DS suggested that this concept, free mobility of cathexis, might have the status of an intervening variable. BR took up this suggestion and said that he would like for us to go into that question at greater length in the future, to try to get clear on just what the conceptual status of this notion was, and thus into the whole question of the necessity for the cathectic theory in general. GSK thought that there might be some instances in which the cathectic theory resolved or illuminated some problems dealing with primary process, but had to fall back on the idea that its main usefulness might be in providing a unity of language to discuss many diverse phenomena. This is a topic that we shall take up at greater length in a future meeting.

For the next time, it was decided to continue with the discussion of the mechanisms of condensation and displacement, attempting with the aid of these minutes to decide on some specific definitions or formulations. It may be possible thereafter to tackle the problem of the conceptual status of <u>cathexis</u>: what it contributes, whether it is redundant or enables us to solve any conceptual problems.

RRH

Note

These discussions give a good glimpse into the help many people gave me in the development of the scoring manual, originally just for applying the concept of primary process to understanding Rorschach responding, later as a means of reliably and quantitatively measuring manifestations of the primary process in thought products of various kinds. (See Holt et al., 2009, Vol. 2.)

Rapaport to Holt—November 16, 1954

Dear Bob:

Thank you for your note and for the material you sent me. I will react here to it (excepting for the manual,[78] reaction to which I have to postpone at the moment), addressing myself to you, though I mean most of this for George also. The reason I postpone reacting to the manual is that my health has been playing tricks and I am overburdened with problems as well as work. I will be looking forward to your writing to me or sending me the material on your memory experiments.

To the minutes of your seminar. Let me start where you quote me, at the bottom of page 2. If I phrased the point the way you quote me, then I regret it, though I do not intend to retract it. Let me explain. You may remember that I make a distinction between "drive organization of memory" and "conceptual organization of memory." Let us assume that we agree on it that conceptual organization of memory has "schemata." If you agreed on this I would add that "drive organization of memory" has also schemata. Let me add to that that schemata in my terminology would be "apparatuses," "structures." That you realize this is clear where you refer to Silberer. That I realize it will be clear to you when you note that Silberer himself did not say what you say about him in the last paragraph of your first page. I generalized Silberer's findings

---

[78] I had sent a copy of an early draft of what became the manual for scoring manifestations of primary process thinking (Holt et al., 2009).

in an attempt to demonstrate that this is what he implies: states of consciousness. In his terminology there is something purely quantitative which stands for this. I do not know what happens in the infant. If I take Piaget as a witness for that, then I with you together will assume that from the beginning on there are structures and structure building, and that the primary process is as much a matter of structures as is the secondary process, but that not only the ego and the id but drive and structure are not so clearly differentiated in the so-called "undifferentiated phase." Freud tried to describe the primary process purely in terms of drive. With the aid of Hebb, you can describe it purely in terms of structure. If you ask me, I will answer, this is more a question of choosing frame of reference than of anything else. After all, we are seeking concepts to describe phenomena and interrelationships. I fully agree with the first half of your first paragraph on page 2. Neither "grass-bear" nor "Brazil is in Argentina" needs to be drive motivated. If you look up [i.e., in] either "Diagnostic Testing" or "Organization and Pathology of Thought" you will note that I am most of the time careful (and who of us is not careless?) to indicate that all that can come about in a drive-motivated fashion can come about also as a structured phenomenon, as a manifestation of a structured state. Indeed, already in "Emotions and Memory" [Rapaport, 1942] I have pointed out such differences between loss of personal identity and fugue states on the one hand, and retrograde and anterograde amnesias on the other. Let us add to this that I agree fully (and in my seminars I discuss it thus) that "Freud overstated his case" (your second paragraph on the first page). The latent dream thought which is perfectly rational is nothing else but what would happen if the latent dream thought would become fully systematized without censorship intervening in secondary-process terms. The primary process manifestations in the dream are there because the secondary process is not working. This not working is due to the censorship. The primary process mechanisms themselves are not due to censorship. I do believe that Freud implied this in a few places but implied the opposites in more places. I am not at all sure that Merton is not right when he speaks about regression in terms of "the higher mental processes are countercathected." That is to say, a barrier is set up against the thought processes taking their usual course and being translated into secondary process terms.

In this sense the primary process is not a "defensively organized stratagem of thinking" but rather the manifestations of the primary process in dreams and psychoses are a result of certain defensive processes.

Just one more word on this matter: Page 3 talks about the tension reduction theory and the difficulties about the optimum level of tension and minimum level of tension. Once it is clear that there are structures present from the beginning on (and as you know, I have always made quite a point of thresholds as structures being present always, because without such structures no energy and no tension can exist—nor do I believe that such structures can exist without tensions), it will be clear also that we cannot ever speak about a minimal tension but only an optimal one relative to the thresholds and relative to the defensive countercathectic organizations which are mostly in essence organized around these thresholds to heighten these, or at times to lower them too.

While some of this may have sounded like an "urge to quote myself," please give me the benefit of the doubt and try to see it as an effort to link what you are concerned with, with a number of issues that I have been concerned with and tried to work out. Assume for the moment that I was trying to be helpful by indicating in what terms I have tried to struggle with the same problems. If I would have more leisure it would have come out less peculiarly.

To indicate in brief the topics in which I would be willing to supervise theses: I would be willing to supervise these in any area of thought organization and pathology of thought, provided that the student is ready to study that area of literature which I consider relevant to all such problems and which is indicated by

"Organization and Pathology of Thought" in general terms. This could include associations, memory, problem-solving, creative thinking, daydreams, dreams, any god-damned stuff as long as it is understood in what frame of reference it will be treated.

  With warm regards,

    Yours,

      David

CHAPTER 5

Rapaport to Holt—January 17, 1955

Dear Bob:

Thank you for your letter of January 12 and for the "minutes" [of November 24, 1954] which arrived soon after it. These minutes are really rich with many problems and considerations. I wished I would be energetic enough to organize my reactions concisely and write them out for you. I am afraid I am not. I am about to go to the hospital for some minor repairs. At several points in reading these minutes I wished we could sit down and read the VIIth Chapter together. I have just re-read it for my Institute course. I enclose here the outline which I made for that course [not found]. Maybe we can go over this outline of the VIIth Chapter together one day.

Here nothing much, our experiments are moving ahead very slowly. The Piaget Epistemology[79] Vol. I is 2/3 done. Our [Riggs staff's] group-research is trying for the first preliminary reports [...].

If and when I get out of these doldrums—I have a paper on Identification and one on the Defense Concept[80] prepared for to write. Activity-Passivity still incomplete; Hoax business waiting for further work.[81] Merton and I started a paper on Metapsychology

---

[79] A reference to an incomplete project of some kind. Rapaport never published a translation or commentary on this work, which may be the one mentioned below also.

[80] Two other abandoned projects, or perhaps work that led to one of several papers on ego psychology.

[81] Neither of these was finished and published in Rapaport's remaining years, though the former appeared as Rapaport (1953d). He was fascinated by hoaxes, collected materials on

[Rapaport & Gill, 1959] and I have an analysis of Piaget in the works somewhere.

Please keep sending me the minutes. Even if I do not react to them now, when we meet we could well discuss them.

Yours,

David

---

many of them, and told me that in them lay buried something of metapsychological significance he hoped eventually to figure out.

Rapaport to Holt—February 28, 1955

[handwritten]

Dear Bob,

Only today did I find your outline of the theory of primary and secondary processes [dated Oct. 1954].[82] It must have separated from the memo on [staff] conferences with which you sent it. I was impressed by it. It has elements of what I think the project Koch suggests will require. It would be interesting if you and/or George would feel like joining me on it. They give a full year for completing it. I don't see that I can undertake it alone. They want a framework which is alien to me and to master which I do not have the yen. I think you two have that framework and understand me and the topic. I do have a fair mastery of the latter, though I am not sure whether anyone including me has a history of the sort this project requires.

Greetings,
David

PS. I have read also the manual on "Neutralization" [primary process] scoring, but somehow I did not get into the spirit of it and do not have suggestions or ideas about it.

---

[82] That particular document has not survived.

Holt to Rapaport—March 15, 1955

Dear David:

I have several unanswered letters from you, and would like to comment on all of them. Thanks for your kind remarks about our minutes and about the schematic outline of primary and secondary process. I have the feeling that we are slowly getting somewhere. It's just as well that you didn't devote any particular effort to the manual on the Rorschach, since I and Joan Havel[83] have just completed a new version which considerably outdates the one I sent you. If you would like to see it, I'll send it along as soon as it is dittoed.

Thanks also for your kind words about my review [a longer version of Holt, 1955]; I had not thought of trying to publish it, but maybe I will—if you will clear up one matter you referred to in your letter of February 25th. You made some rather allusive remark about a weakness you felt in the review, and I don't really quite get the point. You say: "You ride the statistical point hard and though you make several allowances, the one that I would consider fundamental you do not touch. Now we have the nursery open, now we have methodological sophistication—and yet we

---

[83] Joan Havel, PhD, a social psychologist who had participated actively in the research and publications of the Research Center for Social Relations at NYU, then worked with me for several years at our sister Research Center for Mental Health, helping to develop the scoring manual for the measurement of primary process thinking. After leaving, she continued to publish under her married name Grant. See Holt & Havel (1960).

do not have a clear and systematic view of the clinical method, nor any surety that we can get along without it. (In some senses this is the problem of idiographic lawfulness vs. the nomothetic one.)" Are you saying that I don't take full account of the fact that the real status of the clinical method is still unclear, so that we can't fully describe what it gives us in terms of Mill's canons and other methodological paraphernalia? After writing this statement, I am not certain that I wholly agree with it. Perhaps I am taking an over-simple view of just what the clinical method is, but I don't think that I want to retreat from the position that the inferential processes are ultimately statistical in nature. Maybe that ought to be broken down a little bit: we might say that there is first of all the process of getting an insight, putting together observations into a coherent whole. This certainly is not a fixed statistical matter, but one of an esthetic nature, and which we are guided by the elegance and economy with which elements may be fitted together to form a convincing totality or pattern. Perhaps part of what you mean by saying that we still do not have a clear and systematic view of the clinical method refers to the way in which our own unconscious enters into the construction of these insightful unities, or perhaps you mean it more generally than that. In any case, I feel that this is just the first step, the illuminations which must be followed by verification, and it is verification that is always a necessarily statistical matter. Mill talked about verification; so far as I know, he had nothing to say about the ways in which we first discern the possibility that A may indeed be associated with B in some necessary way.

Thus, I would say that Freud was a most masterful insight-getter and propounder of valuable hypotheses, but that he had an insufficient grasp of procedures for verification of these hypotheses. I suppose that the clinical method is as good a method of getting verifying data as any other, but I don't see how it can escape from the statistical requirement, and I don't think that you disagree with me on that, most likely. Anyway, would this kind of modification improve the review, as you see it? Incidentally, I am going to be talking to Hacker's group in Los Angeles about these matters next month, and shall have to think them all through a little better and state them in a somewhat more expanded form for that lecture.[84]

I was glad to know that you and Elvira did try to reach me while you were here in New York, sorry that you didn't succeed. I have been awfully busy evenings in the last couple of months. I hope very much that by now you are all over your convalescence and feeling fully up to your usual killing work schedule.

As you can see, I have been saving the hardest part for the end: the matter of Project A. To give you my general conclusion first, I think that the job as a whole is probably worth doing, and I hope that you undertake it. Moreover, I'd like to help if I can do so, and I think George wants to also.

From here on it isn't so easy. The whole thing strikes me as probably the most difficult of these theoretical jobs that Koch is handing out, and I think that you ought not take him too seriously when he talks about a one year deadline. I spoke to John Eberhart[85] about it briefly the other day, and he mentioned spontaneously that Koch had said to him that he hopes to be able to get the things back in two and a half years. Nevertheless, there is no getting around the fact that a great deal of work would have to be done, and I think the main question with George and myself is whether we couldn't arrange it so that we would work on the parts that we would be concerned with and hoping to do something about theoretically anyway. We ought to get together, the three of us, and talk it over in detail. Also, I think you should take

---

[84] It was not published as such, but was one step toward my 1962b paper.

[85] John C. Eberhart (1907–1990), PhD in social psychology, Northwestern University, became one of the elder statesmen of psychology. From 1961 to 1981, he managed the research complex at the National Institute of Mental Health. There, Eberhart promoted an environment of scientific freedom of inquiry in clinical psychiatry, psychology, and other disciplines. He was an organizer of the Boulder Conference (1949), resulting in the scientist-practitioner model of clinical psychology. For years a member of its Policy and Planning Board, he represented the APA on the National Research Council.

Koch up on his offer to discuss the thing, and try to clear up a number of points. One of the most troublesome ones is the matter of boundaries: should you confine it to Freud? That might be somewhat too narrow. At the other extreme, to try to encompass all of psychoanalytic theorizing would be a lifetime job for an army. Perhaps Koch will agree to let you set your own boundaries. I gathered from the tone of the accompanying matter that he will be quite agreeable to your propounding a somewhat different approach than the one proposed in the outline. The latter is obviously written primarily with one kind of person in mind: the man who constructed the theory himself, like Tolman working on his own theory. I think you ought to feel quite free to approach the general problem from your own standpoint, trying to take the spirit of the specifications rather than their letter.

I have made a number of notes on specific points about the outline, which I think I will just dictate for whatever value they may have to you. They are first impressions when reading the thing over, mainly trying to consider how big a job it would be.

(1) (a) Background factors: This could be approached in terms of Freud himself, using the [Siegfried] Bernfeld and [Ernest] Jones material and the evidence of the Fliess letters, on influences and genetic circumstances; or, the emphasis could be on general influences on psychoanalysis as a movement, the internal conditions and peculiarities of it as a scientific and educational system, and the effects on the theory (for example, of intellectual isolation, non-institutionalization, lack of training in research, methodology and theory formation, etc.). (b) This should not be too difficult.

(2) (a) This would be very difficult, though you have made a start. I am doubtful that the dependent-independent variable approach is really applicable, but I doubt that it is really necessary. As I see it, in psychoanalysis many variables are independent for one purpose, dependent for another in a different context.

(3) This gets really rough! It is usually not explicit; will involve a good deal of change in the proposed outline, or else many assumptions about which lots of analysts might not be happy.

(4) Largely irrelevant, as psychoanalytic theory stands. This perhaps could best be disposed of quickly: it's largely qualitative and verbal as I see it, though perhaps subtler formulations can and should be made.

(5) This, especially (c) is a controversial point in psychoanalysis. Yet the outline suggests a good many things that can be said about the present lack of quantification and kinds that could be introduced.

(6) (a) Can be fairly quickly answered; (b) would get speculative but could be done; (c) brings up again the question of scope and Koch's intent. If he wants your own version of psychoanalysis and your views on axiomatization, etc., that would be legitimate, but if he wants you to try to piece together what Freud's views might or must have been on these issues, then that would be very hard to do. Perhaps he would be content just to have some ideas on these points clearly identified as not being necessarily representative of psychoanalysis as a whole.

The material covered under topics (7), (10) and (11) look as if they could be done without too much labor. (8), however, would be a lot of work and of possibly dubious value: repeating [Robert] Sears'[s] study [pioneering survey of psychoanalytic research]. (9) is very important and very tough—only (d) could be done without a lot of work. On topic (12), I think it would be difficult to speak for all of psychoanalysis here.

Let me close by mentioning a piece of good personal news: I just got a very nice apartment overlooking Washington Square North. I shall move in June 1st, and am looking forward to it very eagerly. I hope to see you and Elvira there before long. With my affectionate greetings—

Bob

Rapaport to Holt—May 31, 1955

[handwritten]

Dear Bob,

Just a brief note, to keep in touch. I hear from George that you had a very good trip and that you wrote a circular letter about it. Could I see it? In the meanwhile, many thanks for your Seminar Notes and for the Poetzl.[86] Do you intend to publish the latter? I have some ideas—maybe we should discuss them. Where will you be in the summer? Maybe you come up for a week-end?

In the meanwhile, before I get to reacting to your Seminar Notes, I am sending you a paper I wrote. This is still pre-final and any suggestions, comments, appraisals and criticisms will be much appreciated.

I began work on the Koch draft. Do you want to see it piece-meal, or should I wait until it is all done? As you know I did not commit myself to it and this is just that exploratory draft which we agreed on.

In the meanwhile I am invited to write for a Freud centenary volume: "Freud's central role in psychology in general." I have no decision yet. What would you think about it? What topics, points, should be taken up? I'd really be grateful for your comments—and ready to reciprocate!

Here not much news: Hanna after much indecision, decided to finish off college this summer in Colorado and to spend the year

---

[86] I believe that this was an unpublished translation of Poetzl (1917), done by Harry Fiss, a staff member at the Research Center, referred to in a previous letter.

she gained by summer courses in San Frisco [sic] in secretarial school, learning something breadwinning and biding her time before further decision. Elvira finished her thesis problem and is awaiting her professor's reaction. I am still convalescing, but beginning to work—it was dreadful not to be able to. It was "a has been" feeling.

　　　　With my best to you
　　　　David

I have been approached by a young publisher, whose other—literary—ventures I am familiar with. I enclose the correspondence. [Not preserved.] You will see that I tried to dissuade him from psychological book publishing, but suggested a monograph series which is an old hobby horse of mine. Basic Books wouldn't do it. The man wants to meet me on June 8 for lunch. What do you think of the whole thing? I hope you don't mind that I mentioned you? Are you interested? If you are, how about answering me pronto so that I can write to you more about my ideas? Or call me up? Maybe you'd like to be in on the luncheon?

　　　　D.

Holt to Rapaport—June 14, 1955

Dear David:

I can at last get around to a fuller answer to your good letter of May 31st. We don't have any definite plans about publishing the Poetzl; my feeling is that it would still need a good deal of work to be put into really publishable form, which would include having someone like yourself (and there is no one else like yourself!) check it over carefully to see that the sense is not distorted. It would be necessary to reproduce the pictures, and I don't think that that would be particularly easy since they are not too clear in the original. Nevertheless, if you have ideas about getting it done I would be happy to hear them. (Incidentally, only after the thing was dittoed did I notice that I hadn't edited the translation of the title; I believe that it would read much better as: "Experimentally elicited dream-images in their relation to peripheral vision.") I did put this remark of yours together with the correspondence with the man you are trying to talk into doing a monograph series and suspect that the latter might be what you have in mind. It would of course take just this kind of publication, and the problem with any existing outlet is that one would have to pay to have it done, which just doesn't seem worthwhile to me.

You ask about my summer plans. They are primarily to get the first draft of the selection project book done. If I can find a more attractive place to work on it than New York without incurring a lot of expense, I may try to get out of the city for some time, but I am thinking about my California trip as my real vacation. I shall have a week with Dorothy and Cathy in Berkeley before the APA meetings and then of course, the week of the meetings themselves. Lester is going to be in a house on the New Jersey seashore, and has given me a general invitation to spend some time there with them; I may take them up on that to some extent. But I would like very much to come up to Stockbridge for a weekend sometime. One reason that I can't be more ambitious in my plans is that I am investing everything I can in getting established in my new apartment, for which I am having to buy quite a lot of furniture. It looks as if the result is going to be well worth it, however.

I am glad to hear that you are at work on the draft for Koch. I am counting on seeing [it], but I'd be glad to leave it to you either to send it to me in pieces as you complete them or as a whole, whichever way you would prefer to handle it. I can well understand your desire for suggestions on the task of writing about Freud's central role in psychology in general; the task is one of a large enough scope to buffalo me. The title, incidentally, is a rather odd one. Freud can be considered to have played a central role in psychology only if one arranges psychology around him at the center; if we look at the psychology of the past fifty or sixty years in its own terms, Freud, I believe, would have to be seen as operating on the periphery—sending out powerful waves of influence, to be sure, but none the less peripheral. My ideas about what these waves of influence have been are conventional enough: the impact of his insistence on a thorough-going determinism in mental life, the conception of unconscious mental processes, the enormous role of motivation in all of psychological life, and perhaps most recently the impact of the structural point of view. For my taste, a paper of this kind is most attractive and stimulating if the author succeeds in backing away from his subject enough to get a really broad perspective on it, to see types of general and subtle influence that are not so obvious as the ones I just alluded to. Thus, perhaps it is ultimately to Freud that we have to attribute the convergence of two approaches to the human being: the one from psychology and one from medicine or psychiatry. Surely it is hard to conceive of the growth of clinical psychology as a science and as a profession at this time if Freud had never lived. Could we not also speculate that the trend towards private practice in professional psychology owes something to the accident of Freud's having developed his ideas and his techniques outside of an institution, setting up a model of professional practice that has been followed by psychoanalysts and now by psychotherapists more generally? I suppose it is fair to say that within psychology as a science concern for problems of personality—for central life problems rather than strictly scientific questions about the operation of isolated structures or functions—is an important trend of the past decade. It is easy to say that Freud must have had a lot of influence on such a development, but of course hard to demonstrate it to the satisfaction of anyone who is not already convinced.

One of the things that has struck and interested me is what I perceive to be the fact that in the realm of motivation and its central importance in understanding human behavior, the major type of influence seems to have come not from what Freud said literally about the instincts and the way they operate but rather from what is much more implicit in a great deal of his discussion of psychological matters. For his instinct theory, as I understand it, is an astonishingly anachronistic, mechanistic, un-dynamic apparatus of peripheral stimulations pursuing a reflex arc type of path. His much cloudier formulations about the Id, his murkier statements about instincts and their subtle transformations and penetrations (many of which do not seem to be very easy to reconcile with the theory of instincts set forth in the three contributions) have been much more influential. I am reluctant to admit that it is their very lack of good definition, their very ambiguity and inconsistency that has allowed these notions to retain the core of thinly grasped truths that they always had, saving them from the sterility that might have been imposed by Freud's physiologizing.

I am afraid that's all I can do on that broad topic for the moment. Let me turn now to your paper, "Cognition, cognitive organization and consciousness."[87] I read it with great pleasure and feel enthusi-astic about it. It is one of the most interesting of your papers, and I think its implications have far-reaching significance. As far as the great bulk of it is concerned, I follow the argument easily and ad-miringly, and have only a thin scattering of typographical and similar points, which I will put at the end of this letter. The only sec-tion I found problematical was the one numbered I, at the beginning. I started to have trouble on page 2 where you say: "But memory organizations are by no means the only such (I would take out the word <u>such</u> here) cognitive organizations. For instance, the grammar and syntax of language reflect a great many such organi-zations. Take, for instance, the modes." In this context, I thought you meant what is sometimes called <u>mood</u>, "a set of categories of verb inflection" such as indicative, imperative, subjunctive, condi-tional. Yet on rereading, I get the impression from pages 2 and 3 that you used linguistic modes to illustrate general behavioral modes a la Erikson. I am not sure that the correspondence is com-plete, though the words coincide. Intrusiveness (one of Erik's modes) seems more closely related to a style than to a linguistic form like the subjunctive mode. Thus, I think that your footnote where you first refer to Erikson will be confusing, with its unex-plained reference to "body-modes" and its implicit assumption that grammatical modes are in some way coterminous with behavioral modes.

My next problem is with the concept of style. On page 3, in the second part of the first paragraph you try to distinguish style from the other kinds of organization by saying that styles do <u>not</u> "strike us first of all with their ubiquitous presence in some form, or to some extent, in all members of the species." I think that the point should be made differently: Any aspect of behavior is organized in general ways (e.g., drive-organization, conceptual organization) and in idiosyncratic ways; the latter we call styles. This difference shouldn't be confounded with differences between faculties or

---

[87] Published as "Cognitive Structures" (Rapaport, 1957a).

types of cognitive function. There are styles of remembering and of speaking just as much as styles of perceiving, conversing or dreaming. And the latter three, as types of cognitive organization, are just as ubiquitous as the former two. Thus, just as memory may be organized conceptually or motivationally, so too with perception. Memory as such is not a type of organization of cognition any more than perception, or creative thought, or dreaming. At least, it is a type of organization only in a special and different sense from the way you have been using it.

On page 4, it's not clear where the concept of style leaves off and "choice of symptoms" or defense begins. If a person makes habitual and excessive use of repression, is that in itself a style? I think to say so extends the meaning of the word unduly, though I am not sure about this. Certainly an excessive repressor behaves differently from a person who uses repression little and isolation much; such differences would meet any usual criteria of style. By this way of thinking, a style is not necessarily a defense because it is a broader category including not only the latter but types of "coping" or adaptive behavior which are not defensive in the narrow sense, and also expressive behavior without any discernible adaptive significance. If used thus, however, style is not such a good concept to refer to a way that cognition is organized. Rather it cuts across in a different dimension from the others you use; it refers to what is in-dividualizing rather than to general ways of organizing cognition, like memory-organization, linguistic organization, etc. Your usage of the words "unique" and "typical" in the last sentence is not clear. You mean unique to the person or unique to the moment? Typical is a somewhat vague term, and it isn't clear to me how it is related to rate of change.

I would like to study the paper over further and think some more about the concept of cognitive organization. I have a vague feeling of discomfort about it which has not yet crystallized into any definite critique. Meanwhile, however, I can offer a few more brief comments on the paper. On page 8, I was a little surprised to hear that clinical study had showed that the basic drive motivating the <u>crucial cognitive phenomena</u> of all three phases was murderous hostility directed towards the wife; not towards the self also? Particularly in the third phase, I find it hard to relate the "crucial cognitive phenomena" to hostility to the wife except through a number of intervening layers.

On page 9, aren't schemata the building units of memory organization rather than a term for the latter itself? Thus, in the third sentence on the page, I should think it might better read ". . . to designate the essential units of enduring memory organization . . .". In the note on that page, the second sentence ends in an ambiguous word, <u>these</u>. Does it refer to the <u>drive</u> (as it seems to), or rather to the appetites, etc.? While we are on that note, the parenthetical expression "(discharge bound)" seems very ambiguous to me, since it carries echoes of "tonic binding" which is a connotation quite the opposite of what I believe you mean; something like "discharge-oriented" might be closer to the sense, though it is awkward.

Jumping over to page 22, at the end of the second paragraph, I wonder if this is a legitimate use of the concept of projection. Certainly displacement is involved in the creation of this internal image, but as long as it is internal, can we really speak about projection? And what is <u>substitution</u>, as separate from displacement and symbolism? On page 29, your reference in the third footnote to "Regression in the service of the ego" is obscure. On page 38, in the third paragraph, where you speak about ranking the cognitive organizations, you talk first about the frames of reference without specifying what kind you are referring to; wasn't something omitted here?

On page 39, when you were discussing the state of mind of your schizophrenic patient, I thought it might be related also to other-directed credulousness (Riesman)—lack of strongly cathected beliefs, and intense need for some kind of bond with others or a tendency to introject them, together could result in a feeling, when one hears something from another person, that "This is my opinion. This is true."

Instead of trying to write out what the various typographical and stylistic changes I am suggesting are, I will simply return to you the copy of the paper that you sent me. I'd like to have another copy, or course, but if you are planning to publish it soon I can wait for a reprint.

It's awfully good news to hear that Elvira has completed her thesis already; I am eager to hear how it is received by the faculty. Please let me know as soon as there is good news. I am sorry to learn that you are still convalescing; I had hoped that that would be behind you by now. At least you won't have as long a time of it as Bille did.

As you know, I just moved into a new apartment, and about the time I finish getting settled down there we are going to be moving our offices, so I am afraid that these sheer mechanical details of life are going to take up a good deal of my time over quite a period when I would rather be doing more productive things. I have not learned the secret of keeping enough of my time free for study and research and writing, though I am not down-hearted about it.

With my affectionate regards to yourself and to Elvira,

Bob

Rapaport to Holt—August 5, 1955

[handwritten]

Dear Bob:

Thank you for your letter of Aug. 1. Frankly, the reason of my not commenting on your paper was that I did not read it till this day—today I did. The reason for that—in turn—was that I was supposed to write this "experimental" system paper and by your title I judged that I might limit myself to reading it in your framework or to my response framework without attempting really to roam freely and take a good look at what is in my mind's landscape. I hope you will find this a forgivable weakness if you consider that this is a nouvelle task for me and one which instills awe in me. I doubt even now whether I dared to roam as freely and take as new looks as I wished or even perhaps as I could. At times I wished I would be somewhere far away, alone for this. This is not my usual way—I like to read while working—this time I didn't; I like to discuss—this time I didn't. But now I was stymied on the mensuration point and when your letter came I picked up your paper.

I am not surprised that your paper[88] was criticized, though I am surprised that it was as sharply criticized as you indicate it. What I mean is that I agree with the essential point: exploration and theory making vs. validation and theory consolidating being

---

[88] "Freud and the Scientific Method of Psychoanalysis," read to Hacker's group on April 22 and later in Topeka. It was never published, for good reasons laid out here.

two phases of the job of science and that the work of Freud was on the first side in the main and that the second is still ahead of us. But I feel that the thesis was put forth in a fashion which had several unfortunate features. First, it was burdened by an "analysis" why Freud did it that way. To analyze the analyst's analyst is a tough job at best and will not yield to an attempt which has another aim in mind (here—your thesis). I do not think that even your usual judiciousness could have pulled this job off when your hand was tilted by the intent: to set out and support your thesis. I will come back to this point. Now it should suffice to say that a structural flaw of the paper's conception demanded more than you—or for that matter, in my opinion, anyone—could have given it. From the point of view of tackling the man Freud, you <u>had</u> an ax to grind. I am sorry that—probably unwittingly—you got into that position.

    <u>Second</u>, you also got yourself into a position of having to explain that you do not blame. That says that you did not succeed— to your own feeling—not to blame. Indeed, you didn't. If you would have, then the dire fact that <u>nobody</u> succeeded yet to present a systematic plan for the validation of psychoanalytic propositions (by the way, it is incorrect to say that one case of no seduction in a neurotic, or one case of seduction in a non-neurotic would have settled the issue—vicarious functioning and multiple outlets, as well as the indeterminacy of the criteria of <u>resolved</u> repression would intervene here) would have emerged clearly from the paper. It did not. It is to my mind a fact that while we know (or know about, or know of) "the" criteria of scientific method, we still do not know how to apply them to psychological life in those of its areas that matter most. We do not know, for instance, how to apply them to the validation (verification or falsification) of the Freudian propositions. Maybe we are too impatient and slowly the random applications of the method and the incidental partial successes will jell. . . . At times I think this is so. At other times I feel diffident whether it can ever be done. At other times I want to transport psychodynamics research into the therapy room, with-

out making it therapy research. At times I feel that research on automatization may be the key to the validation problem; once the former succeeded, the latter will offer no difficulties. . . . But be this as it may, I think your paper here gives a slanted picture by omission of this stress.

Third, I really think you do injustice to Freud with an unbalanced presentation of personal characteristics. So did Jones to my mind in an opposite direction. Puner did it in a devastating way in the same direction as you do. Please do not misunderstand. To my mind Freud is a legitimate subject matter of critical study. All criticism—no holds barred—has justification. But such attempts need more space, more broad base of presentation, so that no apologies be necessary, but the statements speak for themselves.

Fourth, on p. 19, your expressions "pity," "misfortune" are rather unfortunate and must be symptomatic of something that you intend. They do seem to imply that we (or you?) know how insights should be gained and imply that all he did could have been done by one not "twice burned."—Somehow here historical perspective is lost and the measure is the ideal of the scientific method. Anything that does not lead to it must be pitied, is a misfortune. I know I am exaggerating this, but I do believe there is a true kernel to this. Note, you e.g. criticize Freud's statement on reflex arc on grounds which he actually avoided in introducing the Ucs in the reflex arc. This is no crime, but shows how the task was somehow disproportioned.

I hope you won't resent my frankness, at least you know I read it with care and real interest. I think it might really help me in writing the mensuration section.

Hoping to hear from you—other points later, leaving for Mexico in 36 hours.

> Yours,
> David

Copy sent to Dr. Gill

Holt to Rapaport—September 27, 1955

Introductory Comment

In this and the two following letters, I went over an early draft of Rapaport's response to an invitation from Sigmund Koch to contribute to his massive "Project A" an evaluation of psychoanalytic theory (see note following letter of February 8, 1955, Holt to Rapaport). The copies of these letters retrieved from the large collection of the Rapaport papers, donated to the Library of Congress archives by his widow shortly after his death, contain large check marks in the left margins by many paragraphs. Evidently, that was his way of keeping track of his work on the manuscript as he went over my critique, point by point.

I began editing the three letters conveying my critique of the manuscript by reading through the letters and the final text of "The Structure of Psychoanalytic Theory," side by side. It was gratifying to see how seriously he took my points, but the task also impressed on me how clear it is that my contributions were those of an editor rather than a collaborator! Without the original text, it is of course impossible to know just how much it changed by the time of publication, or indeed the extent to which alterations stemmed from Rapaport's own reflections and how much from the critique of others, notably Gill, Schafer, and Klein. I have not had access to their criticisms and suggestions, some of which may have been spoken and not written. Nevertheless, it is evident that in a number of instances Rapaport took my advice, while we agreed to disagree on some of the most fundamental issues. Those very disagreements fueled a large part of my subsequent work on theoretical problems of psychoanalysis.

On re-reading my notes about the comparisons, I feel that they would be of little interest to readers of these letters, so have omitted them. For the dogged scholar, I have put copies of them, filed with these three letters, in the archives at the library of the Austen Riggs Center and at the Library of Congress.

Dear David:

It was a great pleasure to be able to be host in a very small way to Elvira, and please tell her that she is most welcome at any time.[89] I only hope that I'll be able to see her on some of her visits.

I have your new chunk of manuscript, bringing the total up to 136 pages. (And just now, the end of it.) Getting out the first installment, I see that although I had made numerous notes, they are probably getting cold, and so I had better start sending you some reflections and reactions now, even if I am not able to cover very much of the manuscript.

I think I have already told you that I like this work and already find it useful, so that I hope you will go through with it. I also like the brevity and condensation and hope that you will not be persuaded to expand it very greatly. I find the succinctness of this telegraphic, almost outline-like mode of presentation attractive and refreshing. By the way, do you want me to spend any time on stylistic and grammatical matters at this point? I have written in a few suggestions of this kind, but it does slow me up somewhat.

On pages 4 and 5, when you took up the Zeitgeist, you neglected to mention the theory of evolution and the whole ferment that that caused in the intellectual world of Freud's day.

On page 12, I'm not sure just what you have in mind as "the basic independent variable psychoanalytic theory postulates," but I suspect that the first statement ought to read: "And thus not available to manipulation and measurement by any techniques

---

[89] Elvira was then working at an office in the NYU mathematics department. Our arrangement was that I gave her a key, and she was able to take afternoon naps in my nearby apartment. Since I was at work then, I never actually saw her.

known to Freud," or the equivalent. There are methods for approximately measuring intangible and internal variables now; most assessment researches have succeeded more or less in doing so, following the lead of Murray [1938]. In the Explorations, he and his co-workers did quantify psychoanalytic variables like "degree of super-ego integration," "amount of conflict between ego and id," the extent to which a person used the various classical defense mechanisms, and the like. You might consider it "a circumstance that led to this state of affairs" (the failure of quantification to make headway within psychoanalysis itself), that the analytic movement started and has continued apart from the academic psychology departments in universities, where such measurement techniques have been worked on. On reflection, however, I think you may be referring to libido, and I'd agree that it is not so far measurable.

With reference to page 13, isn't there a clear statement in "The Project" that psychoanalysis is a general psychology, embracing the study of normal as well as pathological behavior? Of course, it wasn't called psychoanalysis, and this is only a curiosity in one sense, except that it shows the early development of a broad conception of this task on the part of Freud.

On page 16, I have the uneasy feeling that you are attributing to Freud something that he wasn't at all clear about, if indeed he didn't actively espouse an incompatible viewpoint. I don't see that there is any necessary relation at all between the demand that the explanation of dreams fit into a general theory of psychological life, and the proposition that "no behavior stands in isolation, but rather all behavior is that of the integral and individual personality." The difference is that between the properties of the theory and the assumed properties of the organism, about which the theory talks. Watson, who was as particularistic and atomistic as anyone in his assumptions about behavior, would still have accepted Freud's criterion for a dream theory.

I wish I could be shown more concrete evidence that Freud had an organismic viewpoint; I am more impressed by his espousal of a number of implicitly anti-organismic propositions. For example, the instinct theory contained in the Three Contributions. But I believe that Freud did not say anything directly on this issue as such; certainly he did not in anything that I have read. I believe that his starting premises were drawn from an atomistic and mechanistic physiology, on the one hand, and from a humanistic interest in literature and human nature broadly on the other. My impression is that he only slowly and painfully moved towards an organismic viewpoint, and that usually in quite implicit ways, with many reversals. Yet the organismic viewpoint did seem to be implicit in a number of aspects of psychoanalytic theory, as you point out, and Freud did seem to be able to allow the most anti-organismic aspects of the theory mostly to die quietly by neglect.

In the middle of page 19 you say "that certain behaviors do . . . cease to be shaped further by their recurrence" as if this were entirely equivalent to the statement following: "They become automatized, relatively autonomous from their genetic roots." I'm not sure that these two statements mean the same thing. The more situationally determined behavior is, the more it is shaped by the particular circumstances under which it occurs. Automatization is only one type of autonomy; it leads to rigidity, whereas behavior which is autonomous in the sense that it is mostly determined by the demands of the situation rather than by instinct differs from automatized behavior in being flexible and by definition highly attuned to the immediate situation.

Near the bottom of page 23, do you mean to say that "the drive is conceived . . . as the causal agent which becomes active only when specific environmental conditions (presence of the drive object) are fulfilled"? This denies the observation (a) above, the apparent spontaneity of behavior. It would appear to deny the inner periodicity of drive, the way it waxes simply from disuse. Do you mean to say that the drive is gratified only under these specific conditions?—It strikes me that the last two sentences of the first paragraph on page 24 are unnecessary for the audience of this book, which has quite enough theoretical sophistication not to need these elementary propositions spelled out for them.

On page 27, second paragraph, isn't it more accurate to say that the primary regulative tendency of the primary process, the pleasure principle, is towards attaining an optimal level of tension? I thought that it was the Nirvana principle that tended towards an absolute lowering of the tension level.

At the bottom of page 28 you say that "the conceptual relationships of these energies to Lewin's valences and forces is obvious;" do you really think that there is a close conceptual relationship? It seems to me no closer than to any other theory that uses the words "force," "energy," or the like. Certainly the similarity between the concepts of cathexis and of valence are slight and the differences great. At the top of page 29 you say that it is not ruled out that some actual biochemical energy exchanges may be discovered in the future corresponding to the ones inferred by Lewin; I thought that he did explicitly rule out such a possibility. Also, isn't it fairer to say that "no useful methods of quantifying any of these economic considerations have been advanced," since there have been some crackpot methods suggested or reported.

I feel moved to express one of my private foibles when I come to the section beginning on page 36 where you discuss reality. It always offends my over-nice grammatical sense, the way psychoanalysts use reality as an adjective, when there is a perfectly good adjectival form of the word: real. A more substantial suggestion is that you introduce somewhere early in this discussion a definition of the term reality as it is used in psychoanalysis, as referring to external sources of stimuli. There is a possible source of confusion in the fact that reality is often pitted against fantasy, on the one hand, and on the other hand used to refer to that part of the world that lies beyond the boundaries of the individual's skin. In the latter usage, there is no intention to imply that intra-organismic events are not real—I suppose, as a matter of fact, that it is not counter to psychoanalytic usage to speak of the fact that a person actually has a lesion somewhere in his body as part of "the reality situation" (ugh!).

I think your choice of metaphor on page 37 and in the section that follows it was a little unfortunate, where you speak of a "two-faced conception of reality." The term "two-faced" has implications of dissimulation which, although irrelevant, might be confusing, and you get into some trouble with maintaining the consistency of this metaphor later on.

On pages 40 and 41, there are a couple of references to the ego that make me a little uneasy. You say that the ego is "in general" a regulator of behavior; I find this not a very meaningful statement, if drives are also "regulators" of behavior. You don't make it clear just what this notion of regulation refers to. It doesn't sound as if you mean merely "determinants"; but if you distinguish drives from the ego, then I would have thought you would say that drives instigate behavior, while we conceptualize its regulations in terms of the concept of ego. Then, when you repeat the familiar phrases, at the top of page 41, that the relation to reality is crucial to the ego and that the ego crystallizes around the Perceptual-Conscious System, I wonder again just what this means. This crystallization metaphor particularly troubles me.

At the top of page 42, it's unclear what you mean when you say: "The ego is the organ of adaptation, which operates by the reality principle, a special case of that broader reality principle, termed 'fitting-in'." What is it that is a special case—the ego? The reality principle? What is it that is termed "fitting-in"? As I read the sentence, you were saying that there are two reality principles, though on my first reading I thought that you were saying simply that fitting-in was fitting-in. This, however, is mainly a matter of stylistic clarification. Further down the page, you cite several concepts of Hartmann and say that they provide the framework for the understanding of the development and the function of the secondary process "(unlike Freud's conception of the secondary process)." Do you mean to say here that Freud described the secondary process without giving us a sufficient framework to understand its development and function? The point is apparently a little too much boiled down here.

In the second paragraph on page 44, you use the word "anaclytic" in an unusual spelling and a rather obscure sense. It would help most readers if you were to replace this by something less recherché.

Whom did you have in mind when you said on page 45 that some dissidents "came to conceive of adaptation as adjustment"? I thought that Adler, Sullivan, Horney, and Kardiner alike would reject any such statement. Maybe you don't mean it to refer to them, but in the context it sounds as if you do. Anything <u>can</u> be overestimated; it seems to me that you are trying a little too hard at the top of page 46 to be decent to the dissidents, and thus do them too much honor, so I have suggested a slight rewording. (Mostly I am letting the enclosed and marked up manuscript speak for itself in that way.)

In the last paragraph on page 46, I don't know whether you meant to be exhaustive in describing Erikson's conception of society; I don't believe that you are. I'm not particularly happy with the phrase "economics, institutions, and ideology": economics refers to a number of institutions, and probably has no more reason to be singled out from all of the institutional bases of society (such as the power structure, or the non-ideological aspects of religion) than any other. I was impressed by the way that Erikson took into consideration the concrete geographic setting of each society, also, which helps emphasize the point that he is not talking about an abstract instinct.

So that is about all that I have at the moment on the first chunk of manuscript. I am a little reluctant to part with it, because there are many things I would like to read and think over at leisure, particularly what you have to say about primary and secondary process. So I am counting on you to let me have a copy of the next revision.

One more word for Elvira. Dina Rubinstein[90] will be delighted

---

[90] Dinah Rubinstein was the lovely and gifted wife of Benjamin B. Rubinstein, like him a Finnish Jew. Rapaport brought them to Topeka as part of his effort to build up his Research

to hear what she said about the apartment, because she was very instrumental in getting it to look like something. She found the chair and the fabric in which it is upholstered for me—the one that Elvira admired so. I am sure she would be delighted to hear from Elvira about it.

There's too much to discuss to try to get started on anything outside the limits of this immediate topic, so let's save it. Hoping to see you before too long—

Yours,

Bob

[P.S.] I see from your letter of September 27 that I have concentrated entirely too much attention on the trees—even underbrush—and have neglected the forest. I'll take a wider look at the rest of it.

Department with foreign fellows. Multitalented, she tried out several occupations in Topeka, where we became good friends, and later in New York, including that of interior decorator. She had a good soprano voice; she and I learned several Lieder written by Beni, performed them at parties, and even recorded a few. Later, she found her true vocation as a photographer; the Museum of Modern Art has some of her prints.

Holt to Rapaport—November 9, 1955

Dear David:

   This letter has been much more delayed than I had hoped; I have finally just had to put other work aside and decide to get this out. As it is, I don't feel that I have been able to give enough consecutive time to it to have a clear over-all picture of just how the whole thing fits together. Consequently, my impressions about the architectural questions you have raised are not as well based as I would like.

   Anyway—I believe that the organization the manuscript now has is an arguable and usable one; it would surely be less work to make do with this than to reorganize the whole thing. Perhaps you could find out whether or not the others are going to be cast in this mold. If a number of them are, that would be a justification for your doing so also. I don't think you should simply follow other people's lead, but I don't see enough being gained by your putting in a great amount of time to restructure the whole thing, to make it worthwhile.

   If you wanted to make some minimal reorganization, here are a few suggestions. The sketch of the theory (pp. 13 ff.) might come even nearer the beginning than it presently does. You might also want to precede it by an introduction in which you explain something about your unique predicament in this undertaking, having to write about a theory which in most part is not your own, and moreover one the limits of which are exceedingly vague and definable according to various positions. Then you might include some statement to the effect that your sketch of the structure of the theory is a synthetic and inferential piece of work which it might be hard to find chapter and verse in Freud to support in some parts. If I were you, I would explicitly recognize the fact that many analysts might not agree with some parts of the Gestalt and organismic statements (b and c).

The section on "The Nature and Limits of Psychological Prediction" seems to me might well be re-oriented a little. I believe that what Koch wanted is what kinds of prediction are contemplated in the theory and provided for. You rightly point out that psychoanalysis has been mainly concerned with explaining already occurred events rather than predicting events to come; my impression is that the main predictions analysts make have to do with behavior in particular sequences of analytic hours. In the theory as Freud set it up, there seems to be no concern with certain types of "microscopic" prediction of fine detail. Thus, in analyzing behavior, we have the paradoxical state of affairs that much attention is paid to relatively "trivial" matters, like slips of the tongue and dreams, while very little is said about the prediction of ordinary adaptive behavior. Under this state of affairs, I think that one can superficially get the impression that psychoanalysis is concerned with the explanation of behavior in its most minute details, but this would not be true. The interpretation of dreams does give principles for explaining many aspects of dreams, but the aim was always to get to the kernel, the underlying dream thoughts, the dynamic essence of the matter, rather than exhaustively to account for all aspects of the dream. Erikson [1954], in his Dream Specimen article, has made a big advance towards such a comprehensive undertaking, however, as far as dreams are concerned. Nevertheless, the general trend in psychoanalysis has been to explain and predict only in terms of dynamics and the larger sweep of life events. Thus, as I see it, psychoanalytic explanations (and thus, potentially at least, predictions) have been concerned with the very aspects of behavior that were ignored or disregarded by academic psychologies; the two have been complementary.

I get the feeling, also, that psychoanalysis mostly simply has not faced this issue—has not asked of itself the question, to what extent is psychological prediction possible?—so that you have to extract the very good points that you make from between the lines, as it were.

The section on independent and intervening variables needs re-thinking and re-writing. In this connection, I would recommend that you look at Else Frenkel-Brunswik's [1954] recent long article on psychoanalytic theory; I don't seem to be able to put my hand on my reprint at the moment, but I remember being impressed by her discussion of the hypothetical construct vs. intervening variable issue as it relates to psychoanalysis. That isn't entirely the same thing, but those considerations are relevant.

I believe that what you write beginning halfway down p. 49 slightly misconstrues the issue about independent variables. The term independent here does not mean that the variables are empirically or even theoretically separable cleanly, one from another. As a matter of fact, I haven't been able to find exactly where this terminology (independent and dependent variables) comes from. It doesn't seem to be in Cohen and Nagel [1934], though it is prominently used in Marx [1951] (Psychological Theory). I suggest that you read the article by [Edward C.] Tolman on pp. 87–102. Here (particularly on p. 89) he gives a very clear and straightforward discussion of what he believes the important independent variables to be. He lists "(1) environmental stimuli, (2) physiological drives, (3) heredity, (4) previous training, and (5) maturity," with behavior as the dependent variable. Now, obviously, physiological drives and heredity cannot be disentangled, to take only one such pair, yet these all stand on the causal side of the cause to effect equation (or, as [R. L.] Ackoff [1950, with Churchman] more elegantly describes it, the producer-product relation). And that is, I think, what is essentially meant by this particular distinction.

Therefore, much of your discussion becomes irrelevant. I'm sure that Tolman would agree in his system that "the systematic exploration of mutual dependences and independences of the determiners" is a major problem, in spite of the fact that he speaks of the determiners as independent variables. Personally, I don't see that it makes particularly good sense to ask of a theory what are the independent and dependent variables; this is the sort of thing that you want to know about an experiment, rather.

I don't think that you are right in your assertion that "independent variables are often . . . discussed with the implied assertion that they must be amenable to controlled manipulation." They are the factors in a complex set of interdependencies that are manipulable either directly or in experiments of nature. Thus, we may want to study the possible relationship of skin color to some particular performance (as in the "racial difference" studies); to do so, we select subjects who happen to be differentiated in that respect and thus, in a sense, manipulate or achieve a spread on this variable, even though it is not accessible to direct manipulation. Therefore, I think you are charging through an open door in this paragraph. I have said this clumsily and at too great length; the main point is that everyone would agree with everything you say after your third sentence and the implication that you see in the term isn't there, to my knowledge.

On p. 53, you say: "When the perceptual apparatus functions autonomously, then the drives as intervening variables will not be involved." I think this statement is a little misleading, seeming to suggest that there can be psychic functioning without any motivation. What you mean, I believe, is that only <u>neutralized</u> drive energies are involved in autonomous functioning, but that is not the same thing as saying that the drives as intervening variables don't come into play. (Cf. George's [1954] theoretical treatment of motivation in perception.)

In the next section, I find myself a little unclear on just what is meant by <u>assumptions</u>. Certainly the concept of psychic determinism, or the concept of psychic forces, must fall under this heading. But when we start to get into matters like censorship, defense, the instinctual origin of forces and so forth, I begin to wonder where assumptions leave off and other kinds of concepts take over. My unsystematic conception of it was that the term "as-sumptions" was restricted to a relatively small number of very basic unprovable notions, which could not be defined operation-ally. But here the weakness of my background in logic shows up; I don't know how to distinguish an axiom and an assumption, and I find that Cohen and Nagel don't help me. It does seem to me, however, that not all of the concepts of a system are assumptions and that you need to be quite clear on the question of just which of the early concepts Freud used should be called "initial assump-tions."

In line with the above point of view, it seems to me that on p. 58 the second assumption cited is perhaps better stated as: "The assumption that unconscious processes are in some cases psychic or mental." Since clear operational definitions can be given for the existence of some kind of unconscious processes, they don't seem to require an assumption; but the really disputed point arises from the much more moot proposition that they are psychic in nature (rather than, for example, purely physiological). The evi-dential grounds are accordingly much more indirect, though I believe that they are essentially stated in your paragraph.

At the bottom of p. 59, you have quite a conglomeration of stuff listed as the fourth assumption. In it, the only thing that seems to me really an assumption is the proposition of instinctual drives as forces. The rest of what is listed seems to me much more a matter of secondary theory construction.

My note on p. 61, in case my handwriting is not legible, argues that "evidential basis" can only mean the kind of fact that seemed best conceptualized by a particular assumption. The observations you cite in themselves did not directly force the adoption of an energy concept—it came from physics and physiology and seemed helpful, though I am personally, as yet, open-minded about the possibility of its continued usefulness in the system. One of the things I hope to get around to someday is an examina-tion of the effects on the psychoanalytic system of replacing the energy concept by some other kind.

On p. 68, as well as earlier, you speak about S-S linkages; don't you really mean R-R, which you don't mention? I don't really grasp what could be meant by S-S. This requirement seems to me particularly inappropriate to psychoanalytic theory, if it means anything more than simply to give some examples of the way that variables are linked up in the theory. I agree that it doesn't make sense to select "<u>chief</u> empirical independent and dependent variables," but I don't really see why you bring in this S-R terminology.

On p. 70, my note to the fourth point in the second paragraph is to the effect that the explanation given seems to me insufficient to account for the embarrassment. The latter seems to require also the assumption that the subject had conscious values denying hostility, opposing any overt manifestation of it in the situation, and also opposing loss of self-control. On the whole, I like this example and your handling of it very much. At the end, however, on p. 71, I am not so happy with your handling of it.

As I point out in the margin, I think that you have set up an artificial question. The problem is not which is <u>the</u> independent variable, but which variables are independent and which intervening. It is certainly clear enough what the dependent variable is: the behavior in question, the slip of the tongue. And surely the "external stimulation," as you put it, must be an independent variable; and therefore, the problem reduces to the status of the motivational and controlling-defensive variables. At this point, it occurs to me that Koch is requiring a distinction to be made between independent variable and intervening variable that I am not really familiar with. Thus, in the context of experimentation, what we set up as the independent variable may be something that is an intervening variable in the context of a MacCorquodale and Meehl [1948] discussion of methodology. Maybe you had better appeal to him directly for a source that will clarify the meaning he expects you to adopt for these terms. Otherwise, it seems to me very likely that various participants in this total enterprise are going to be using the terms of his framework in different senses, and will perhaps create unnecessary confusion. I mean by this last remark to propose that you suggest to Koch that he inform all of the others, as well as yourself, just what definitions he wants you to use for the crucial terms in his outline.

On p. 76, you say, "If what the person experiences as his life-space is our basic information about E, then E is an implicit function of life-space and P." (Note, incidentally, that Lewin uses the capital letters throughout.) I think what you mean to say is that E, that part of a life-space not comprised by P, is an implicit function of "the hull of physical facts," and P: in other words, E is a construct by the person from the raw material given by objective stimulation. It's necessary in this discussion to be perfectly clear that E does not refer to what the S-R theorists call S.

Again to transcribe my scrawl, at the bottom of p. 77, I disagree with you on the issue of autonomy in relation to the need for intervening variables, and say that instead, the need for intervening variables is a function of observational methods used. Skinner [1953] doesn't need intervening variables because he forces behavior into a narrow compass where S and R can be directly related mathematically. The more freedom we give to the organism (that is, the more we concern ourselves with non-experimental behavior) and the more we look at all aspects of behavior—not just measurable aspects of short time segments, but qualitative patterns that may be seen only from a perspective of whole days or weeks—the more we need to postulate intervening variables to account for the complex relationships between such independent variables as stimuli, constitution, past history, and behavior. I also raised the question whether we must consider an independent variable an intervening one when it is response-inferred (i.e., definable only by inference from response).

Now we move into the very difficult issue of measurement and quantification. To begin with, on p. 79, I was surprised to read your statement near the top of the page about bound and mobile energy. It sounds as if you are treating mobile as almost equivalent to kinetic. I see no necessary relation at all between the status of energy as bound or mobile and involvement of the motor apparatus. Is not the energy involved in the dream-work mobile? Yet surely nothing mobile [i.e., no movement] is "tripped" in the formation of the dream. Moreover, I was of the firm impression that the great preponderance of action undertaken by ordinary human beings involved the expenditure of bound rather than mobile energy—beyond babyhood, anyway. Moreover, is it really correct to speak of bound and mobile as two separate forms of energy? I thought of them as polar extremes, ideal types like secondary and primary process and, in fact, corresponding closely to the latter pair of terms, being the energy-language for the same events. Thus, we would speak always of a degree of binding, or a relative state of mobility. But in doing this I am explicitly equating the notion of binding and that of neutralization or sublimation, following the assumption that the imposition of controlling structures tends to transform the raw, mobile energy of the drives into more desexualized and de-aggressivized bound forms or derivatives, corresponding to increasingly autonomous motives. Have I been confusing matters that actually have separate meanings?[91] If so, I have to revise a great deal of my understanding of metapsychology, which fell into place for me when I read your recent writings on the subject.

At the bottom of p. 80, I don't know what you mean when you say that superego, ego, id, and environmental factors cannot be considered actually independent. They are theoretically and logically independent, even though, of course, they are linked in an empirical relationship, but the same is true of acceleration, space, and time. The fact that the concepts refer to various aspects of the same behavior need in no way mean that they are not independent. Here I think you are falling into a kind of methodological empiricism—assuming that concepts cannot be independent because they refer to various aspects of a Gestalt. This is similar to [Gordon W.] Allport's [1937] error in denying that it is possible to

---

[91] It became apparent that I was; see Holt (1962a).

use generalized variables at all in the study of human beings, because each human being is unique. The empirical difficulties of
measurement that you cite at the end of the first paragraph on p.
81 seem to me more to suggest that the concepts themselves are
poorly defined. This seems to me to be the basic problem with
regard to quantification in psychoanalysis. Until the concepts
have been thoroughly clarified, their present state of partial or
complete overlap and their general lack of clear empirical referents (see my discussion above of binding, neutralization, and so
forth) is replaced by a coherent structure of variables with clear
conceptual and operational definitions, measurement will be exceedingly difficult.

I like very much the way you confront the issue of the so-called
experimental studies of psychoanalysis, starting with p. 83.

On p. 84, the discussion of the interrupted task problem suddenly reminds me that you have spoken very little, if at all, about
the concept of tension and the very disputed business of tension-
reduction. As a matter of fact, in your sketch of the theory I believe you succeeded in avoiding this problem (and the closely
related questions of the dual instinct theory, the pleasure- and
Nirvana-principles) completely. This is just an aside; I hope that
you can succeed in not taking up these very vexed questions. The
last few lines of this page, incidentally, don't make sense, apparently because of typing errors.

On p. 86, I'm not at all clear what you mean by the sentence in
the middle of the page, which I have lined and question-marked.
But then, you never explained what you mean by dimensions or
dimensional quantification, yet this clearly is a very meaningful
term for you and one that is central to your argument. You owe it
to your readers to be perfectly explicit about the distinction you
see between a dimension and a variable that is quantified ad hoc.
With regard to this particular experiment by [Jules D.] Holzberg,[92]
I should say that the experimenters quantified whatever came

---

[92] Not easily identifiable, but eliminated from the published version.

readily to hand, without apparently worrying very much about methodological issues. The measurement of aggressive tension seems to me particularly weak and questionable—using the efficiency of learning tests involving aggressive material. That seems awfully indirect and inferential. (Incidentally, your statement, "The controls will not apply in the learning task," is ambiguous—I just figured out what you meant.)

I don't think your discussion of factor analysis is very satisfactory; mostly it betrays your prejudice rather than contributing to clarification. Certainly factor analysis seeks dimensions blindly, but it places its faith on the very fact that many different kinds of quantification—the measurement of variously constructed tasks, ratings, and what-not—are used. If order emerges from such chaos, and if the same kind of order seems to emerge from various investigations, using partly the same tasks or measures and partly different ones, than this is some guarantee that the factor emerging from all of these studies has some claim to be considered a dimension. I think this sounds like a better argument than it is, because it overlooks the big subjective element in the choice of factor analytic method and in the process of rotation, not to mention the process of naming the factor. Certainly, many factors seem to be artifacts and to have little sensible claim to the status of dimension. The argument grows more impressive when there is a convergence of a variety of studies, such as [Raymond B.] Cattell [1946] has tried to demonstrate, but I don't think that it is fair to attack factor analysis for starting out with arbitrary quantifications rather than the measurement of definite dimensions, when its aim is to discover dimensions by the manipulation of deliberately arbitrary quantifications. On the whole, however, I think your discussion would be stronger without mentioning factor analysis.

On p. 89, you merely state your belief or faith that studying the problem of learning will make a dimensional metric possible. Your speculation about Hull, Dollard, and Mowrer is clearly an aside to yourself and not something that belongs in the finished manuscript. But you do have some kind of obligation to explain why and how studying a particular problem will lead to dimensional quantification; it isn't at all obvious.

Incidentally, I think a fourth possibility might be included in the first paragraph on p. 89: that certain aspects of psychology or psychoanalysis are amenable to dimensional quantification, whereas other aspects are not. This seems to me the most likely choice.

In re-reading the discussion on pp. 89 and 90, I begin to see that you have said something about what you understand a dimension to be, but I wonder if the choice is only between such elegant and far-reachingly useful variables as those in physics, on the one hand, and mere ad hoc quantifications of whatever comes handy on the other. The kind of structural-functional theory found in physiology, for example, is quite successful and in many respects rigorous, yet none of its variables can meet your criterion of expressing both structure and function in the same terms, so would have be to be relegated to the wastebasket of the ad hoc. I am certainly naïve about theoretical biology, but I can't see any way that it would ever be possible to express organs and their functions in a single set of dimensions.

Nevertheless, I begin to see on p. 90 how you are doing what I just asked you to do with respect to learning.

In this discussion, you seem to assume that the only process by which structure arises is learning, something that I am sure you don't mean to do. Certainly genetic and maturational processes play an important part in the formation of structure, but one that can hardly be distinguished from that of learning.

If I understand correctly your point about the hierarchical location of structures and functions that are involved in experiments, it seems to me that it should be possible to do this if one has a clear grasp of the theory, even if the quantification involved is strictly ad hoc.

On p. 92, your general statement about the kind of quantification is unclear. Moreover, I don't see how this is a different type, possibly because I haven't really grasped your point. It seems to me just as much ad hoc as anything you have discussed up to this point and that you are confusing what is being quantified with the type of quantification being done.

Your description of George's first experiment [Klein, 1954] is, I think, a little misleading. You say that he "measured cognitive (ego) style polarity" and that "the cognitive style was an ego-function (or structure), the presence of which was assumed to have been reliably measured." This seems to imply that he had firmly in mind some psychoanalytically-based concept of an ego-function, and then found a measure of it. As you know, actually, it was the other way around: he began with the task—the Color-Word Interference test—and got a hunch that it might be separating subjects on a significant dimension (oops!—I'd better say "variable"). The name ultimately given to the polarity depended on the empirical relationships found between the Color-Word test and quite a number of other different tasks. From the beginning, however, it was strictly an ad hoc measure.

Later in this long paragraph on pp. 92 and 93, you speak a couple of times about "the relationship asserted by psychoanalysis," between drives and defenses, as if some single statement of such a relationship existed somewhere. I would like to know what this relationship is, if indeed you meant to say it this way; otherwise, this is just a roundabout way of calling attention to a minor verbal unclarity.

Because I don't follow you on your basic requirement of an acceptable dimension, I can't go along with the top of p. 94. It seems to me that one should condemn only the refusal to recognize our ignorance of what we are measuring and whether what we measure will or will not turn out to be useful for the advance of theory.

At this point, I'd like to express some general reflections about the problem of dimensions or other quantitative variables in psychology and psychoanalysis. We always measure what we can. Sometimes we choose to find measures or variables which turn out to be useless for many purposes. Thus, if we defined phlogiston operationally enough to measure it, we would find as Lavoisier did that it had paradoxical properties and would begin to suspect that there was something wrong with the theory. It was the effort to measure it precisely that led him to this discovery, as a matter of fact. Variables always proceed from some theory, even if only an intuitive one; in the latter case, it's often hard to see through the implicit assumptions of common sense to what the theoretical model really is. But we can work on only the clarification of theory on the one hand and its application to empirical problems as rigorously as possible on the other. Doing so will ultimately prove some variables both internally consistent and externally reliable in yielding predictable results. Others will fall by the wayside, and we will recognize that they were only possibly measurable, but too complexly constituted to be useful building blocks in the theory. Thus, mass supersedes weight, and in general, common-sense intuitively graspable properties of physical objects gradually are replaced by more abstract and widely useful properties. These we call dimensions, if we wish, but it seems better to me not to speak about them in such a way as to imply (as your discussion seems to) that there is some sharp qualitative difference between dimensions and other measurable variables. Are all of the measurements in physics confined to dimensions? I don't think so, and I think that physics couldn't get along without this non-dimensional quantification.

Thus, my view is that we must always start out with "ad hoc variables," but that we must specify operations of measurement for our theoretical variables wherever it is appropriate to do so; as long as we have a lack of such agreed operations, any particular one will seem arbitrary and ad hoc. Because of the anarchical situation in psychology, this seems likely to continue for quite some time, with the same unfortunate consequences that would exist in physics if some people measured distance in yards, others in centimeters, and others in a third kind of unit [e.g., cubits], without there being any generally agreed-on operations establishing the equivalence of the various units. Anyway, the ultimate usefulness of the centimeter-gram-second dimensions comes from the theory; there could have been no way of recognizing that they were measuring dimensions (in your sense) rather than ad hoc quantification before the theory was developed to the point where all of the phenomena in question were interrelated. It may very well be, therefore, that some of the ad hoc variables we are using today will ultimately turn out to be dimensions, but this need not happen for them to be useful to a scientific psychoanalytic psychology.

At the bottom of p. 94, I have suggested some changes in your analysis of independent, intervening, and dependent variables in [Seymour] Feshback's [probably 1954 or 1955] experiment: the insult was the main independent variable, it seems to me that the intervening variable was the aroused aggressive drive and related cognitive mechanisms, while the fantasy activity—the stories expressing aggression—correspond to the dependent variables.

On p. 95, you speak of repression and isolation as "drive-reducing ways." I'm not clear what you mean by this expression; it doesn't seem the same as what Feshback is talking about, where reduction seems to mean discharge. I agree very much that it may well have been a fortuitous choice of subjects who had the right drive level and the right cognitive structure to produce these particular findings.

P. 96 is most admirable, but I think you should not talk as if drives could be directly manifested except [i.e., only] through some kind of behavior. You don't mean to imply, do you, that a physiological manifestation of drive or its manifestation in overt behavior (e.g., slapping the experimenter's face) would be a more direct drive manifestation than the verbal behavior? It would be a question of relating manifestations of drives on verbal and nonverbal levels.

I have a feeling that there are still some issues in the whole problem of quantification that haven't been covered; I believe I adverted to some of them in my earlier comments on the first part of the manuscript. But we can talk about these matters when we get together, if you'd like.

On p. 98, a minor point: From my memory of <u>New Ways in Psychoanalysis</u>, Horney [1939] did not stick to clinical issues to the exclusion of systematic ones; I would put her along with Sullivan and Rado.

I like your polemical discussion of axiomatization very much and hope you keep it in very much the present form. I found it quite enlightening. I only found the last sentence of it puzzling and unclear. And I wonder, as an afterthought, whether you have squarely faced the basic issue of clarifying the theoretical structure of psychoanalysis. Reducing it to axioms, etc., may not be a meaningful undertaking (though I think many of your own attempts have helped and are a kind of partial statement of psychoanalytic axioms), but there are other kinds of theoretical systematization and clarification that psychoanalysis certainly does need.

On p. 115, third line, where you speak of motivation, you mean I presume the motivation of development, rather than all motivation.

Skipping now over a great deal of material, because I agree so thoroughly with most of it, a minor point on p. 126: in your second paragraph, first point, you say that the experimental evidence of the system "would seem conclusive in terms of the usual canon of psychological experiments." I wonder what you mean by conclusiveness here; my impression is that experiments have covered only a few scattered parts of the theory, and very few of them have been very conclusive in terms of anybody's standards.

I think that you handle the problem of the dissident movements in psychoanalysis and of Carl Rogers[93] with exceptional fairness and judiciousness: you show how there is something good in all of these people without being patronizing to them and without offending the orthodox ones either.

---

[93] Carl R. Rogers (1902–1987) was best known for devising and teaching a method of individual psychotherapy called "client-centered," based in part on the work of Otto Rank.

On p. 131, I thought it would be helpful if you could insert a backward reference to the place where you cite the data that make the economic and genetic theories necessary.

On p. 132, perhaps you should take into account David McClelland's contribution on this point of the non-extinction of neurotically-learned behavior. Taking off from the point of inconsistent discipline, he put his rats through probabilistic reward-punishment schedules and obtained stable learning which was proof against extinction. I don't know that this is embarrassing data for psychoanalysis, however.

It seems to me that plenty of data are inconsistent with a number of Freud's early formulations. Part of this problem of what is embarrassing to psychoanalytic theory and what isn't depends on your definition of what is psychoanalytic theory. Since you are using a relatively broad and inclusive one, and since you are perfectly straightforward about the fact that all of this sprawling theory has not been well systematized, it is hardly surprising that many people feel that a great many psychoanalytic propositions have been refuted by data. See, for example, Ben Rubinstein's [1952] paper on the insufficiency of the psychoanalytic instinct theory. As long as there isn't a statement of psychoanalytic theory that clearly replaces the outmoded and disproved with the new, this confused situation will remain. There really is a need for such an encyclopedic summa, marshalling psychoanalytic theories in order on each topic, indicating how and why they were changed, what systematic and theoretical evidence there is on each point. But where is our St. Thomas to write it?

The embarrassing situation you mention on p. 136 seems to be reducible to what I have been so frequently describing as the lack of definitive definitions (both conceptual and operational) and the lack of a clarified restatement of the theory, cleared of underbrush.

One issue that I think has been overlooked in all of this is the place of verification-research in theoretical development. In other words, I am riding my current hobby-horse, expressed in that paper that I read to Hacker's group;[94] I certainly don't think that it is the answer to the problems of clinical research, but I believe that this distinction between hypotheses-forming and hypothesis-testing research has some place in a discussion like yours.

This still feels very incomplete to me, in spite of the fact that all three of us (you, me, and my secretary) are undoubtedly exhausted at this point. But it's the best I can do at the moment. I hope there is something here of use to you, or at least that we can have some good discussions over a few of these issues.

Cordially,

Bob

P.S. Now I see why it seemed so incomplete—I had put the last installment under a pile of other papers and found it only after dictating this. I'll try to polish it off tomorrow. [. . .]

---

[94] Cited in Rapaport's monograph as Holt, 1955. *Freud and the Scientific Method of Psychoanalysis.* Unpublished manuscript.

Rapaport to Holt—November 17, 1955

Dear Bob:

Thanks for both of your letters. I was both impressed by and grateful for your long letter and the generous detail of your critical comments. I felt enlightened by most of them and felt that I will have to give it considerable time to digest them. I think you could help the paper a lot both on the "variables" and the "quantification" section and I do hope you will—and will join me on it altogether through these. I know you have little time—but let us try for it.

You are right: I did decide to go through with this, but with much ill ease, feeling that in many ways I will be out of my depth and I will have to work hard to find (or regain) the ground under my feet. I do count—but with understanding of your situation— on your help on this.

I will accept your invitation for March 7. I hope to link it up with other business so that I should need no expenses paid. Thanks for your invitation to stay with you—I accept and look forward to see your quarters. Topic: wouldn't [it] be the best if I do not prepare anything but your boys prepare to ask me questions and I will try to answer them? Or else I'd need some information what of the things I can talk about would be of most use to them? How would it be if [I. H.] Paul and I present our present research? I, a theoretical introduction—he a report on methods and findings? But, please, take this only if it "fits." There is only one reservation I must make: you know I am still not well and you must count with it that if the week would

246

prove physically very bad I'd have to renege. As you know to do so is against my religion and temperament—but you must share responsibility with me for this contingency—I can't take it alone by no[t] mentioning it here.

From George not a line in several months. What is the matter? I hope you can reassure me that it is merely a great load of work. [. . .]

With many thanks,
David

Holt to Rapaport—November 21, 1955

Dear David,

I have finally been able to finish your manuscript. The final pages are magnificent! You rise to eloquent heights in discussing the barriers to theoretical advance; this section [pp. 142–144 of the published monograph] will make a stunning close for the monograph (for such it is) with very little alteration.

Section (c), starting on p. 137, seems to me less satisfactory than most of it. I feel myself the need for more clarification about the definition of <u>assumptions, principles,</u> and the like before I can be quite sure just what is needed for this section. Surely also you need to make more explicit what you mean by "existential propositions" and their place in the system. I don't see how overdetermination can be considered an existential proposition, nor an assumption that permits more testing than has already been done. The whole section was too brief—it left me feeling that you had left much unsaid, and that you could have added the needed words on why just these few propositions were the "principal assumptions" for testing.[95]

Section (10) seemed to me very good on the whole. I have no comments beyond those on the margin of the enclosed sheets.

---

[95] I find it difficult to locate the portions of the published work that correspond to the manuscript I had in hand. It seems most likely that Rapaport revised chapters 10 and 11 of the monograph rather extensively. It is possible that comments in the above paragraph had some effect, but it is impossible to be certain, especially because at least three other persons were providing critique.

On p. 160, I suggest two more aspects of the system to discuss: [1] The problem of an adequate brain model—a physiological and anatomical substitute [I think I was groping for a synonym for "model"] to link purely psychodynamic (and psychic-structural) problems to somatic ones. [2] The expansion of psychoanalysis into a general psychology, absorbing and integrating other branches. Both of these were on Freud's agenda at the time of the Project, and though he renounced them pretty clearly on some occasions, he never really gave them up.[96]

Section (12) (a) also seems over-brief and not sufficiently thought through. Much of what's in it refers to theoretical problems of such a nature that they don't seem to point to any one kind of data. But I think that this part will probably fill itself out naturally enough as the rest is revised and extended.

The next subsection, (b) [cf. pp. 137–140 of the monograph], suggests the possible discussion of a number of rather delicate matters—chiefly having to do with the situation of psychoanalytic theory and science as the (alleged) private property of the psychoanalysts—and among them, of the American Psychoanalytic Association. The fact that this system, along amongst all others being discussed, developed outside the universities as the part-time hobby of over-worked medical practitioners, and all of the special "psychology" of the psychoanalytic movement, are surely relevant to this section.[97] Talking about these matters dispassionately and disinterestedly would be highly necessary and very difficult, but if you think it should be tried, I have the beginnings of a brief manuscript on it which I'd be glad to turn over to you. Under this heading might be a place to mention the need for a thorough stock-taking summary of the system, which as it stands is hard to master and work with by virtue of the size of the literature that contains it, the amount of dead wood, anachronism, contradiction, and irrelevant materials therein. (I don't think

[96] Evidently, Rapaport did not feel ready to take on these two difficult challenges.
[97] They are discussed at length in section C., pp. 140–142, which he added.

you can make your final indictment of the experimenters without admitting these very great obstacles that lie in the way of "coming to grips with the theoretical system of psychoanalysis.") Other obstacles are the lack of adequate definitions of concepts, the lack of a clarification of the nature and limits of the clinical method, and again the political, economic, and emotional peculiarities of the psychoanalytic movement that hinder such clarification, systematization, and advance.[98]

That concludes these scattered reflections; as usual, the manuscript contains marginal notes, random stylistic suggestions jotted down when the spirit moved me, and indication of minor unclarities.

I am eager to hear your decision and to learn what the other readers have advised. I remain convinced that you can and should do it. Meanwhile, let me wish you and Elvira and Julie a happy Thanksgiving.

> With warmest regards,
> Bob

---

[98] I am not sure what unpublished manuscript of mine I was referring to here. But the paragraph lays out a program of the work I undertook in the following three decades or so, especially after Rapaport's death (Holt, 1989).

Rapaport to Holt—December 9, 1955

[handwritten]

Dear Bob,

I just read your rebuttal to Mayzner.[99] Let me first tell you how I enjoyed your hospitality and our conversation and that I considered your rebuttal judicious and fair. I think it does a real service. The only point I am not sure of is whether this book is not a book of science. I am not so sure that the early books on medicine which did not prove anything (to take your example) or the books of naturalists (e.g. medieval Bestiaries) were not books of science appropriate to a given phase of science. This is not so different from your point on medicine, but it does go beyond the necessity for such with a view on future development. I'd insist with Pico della Mirandola[100] that all [every] human product is [at base] a human thought, worthwhile on its own right in the development of human thought. And I would insist that what we are (in this case, Roy is) doing is science of a certain sort. That the canon these boys try to foist on us prematurely is a distinct danger: it might throttle the science (I think it has been already often successful in

---

[99] Holt (1956a). Mark Mayzner received his PhD in Industrial Psychology at NYU in the 1960s, but was interested in clinical issues, and sent some letters to Rapaport, which are in the Stockbridge archive. Rapaport's reference to "this book" means Schafer (1954), which Mayzner had criticized in his review.

[100] Count Giovanni Pico della Mirandola (1463–1494), an Italian Renaissance philosopher whose Oration on the Dignity of Man is sometimes called called the "Manifesto of the Renaissance."

doing so). But this is a detail and unimportant in the larger scale of your rebuttal.

        With best greetings,

          David

Summary—Brief Letters from 1955

The year starts with a handwritten note of thanks from Rapaport for a Christmas gift. "I am still under the weather and hope to get out by an operation sometime this month." He then asks if there might be a place on our staff for Irving Paul, who has been working with him. My reply on January 12 thanked him for his gift, and regretted that there was no place for Dr. Paul with us because "our budget is already overstrained. [. . .] I had a very good visit with Merton during my recent visit to Berkeley. I found him and Charlotte in excellent spirits. [. . .] They are very happy with little Ben," their new baby.

My February 7 response to David's letter of January 17 dealt with his illness and hopes that the operation might not be necessary, enclosing a review (Holt, 1955) and brief comments on RCMH work. David's reply of the 18th indicates that he was recuperating from the operation. He explained briefly why he declined to sponsor an NYU student's proposed dissertation ("not in my immediate field of interest [. . .] [and] the foggy character of the concepts").

On February 23, he briefly commented on a longer version of my review of the Fliess letters and encouraged me to submit it to another journal [I did not]. "I cannot write more. Just started to go to the office half time and I am tired."

We exchanged substantive letters on February 28 and March 15. Then, in an exchange of notes (March 23 and 24), David proposed, and George and I accepted, that we meet at the Biltmore Hotel, where he would be staying for the psychoanalytic meetings, to talk about the American Psychological Association's recent statement about psychoanalysis. (There is no record of what was said.)

On June 6, I responded to Rapaport's letter of May 31: You are "full of ideas as usual." A full response has to wait (and it did, until June 14), but "my feeling about editorship [of a monograph series] is too much like your own for me to be interested in this venture."

On July 25, David wondered if his first draft for the Koch volume had reached me, what I thought about it and the feasibility of working with Koch's outline. More specifically, "could the four of us [presumably he, Gill, Klein, and I] do it jointly?" He also wrote:

> Going over the cognition paper [Rapaport, 1957a] to give it final form, I have been dwelling on your letter about it and wanted to thank you for it. It was very helpful in half of its suggestions. About the other half: they seem to be disagreements between you and me and I wished there were a chance to discuss them in detail.

I reported on August 1 that our group and the whole psychology department had just moved (from the old "Bible house," across a small square from a department store—both demolished long ago—to a small, former hat-band factory building at the heart of NYU on Washington Place), to quarters I described as "better looking than the old, but cramped and in many ways not wholly satisfactory." I had not had time to finish his draft of the "Koch piece" which was to become Rapaport (1960). So far, I wrote:

> I can report that it impresses me strongly favorably, that the job seems to be feasible, and I have not yet found evidence that you have any marked need for the rest of us to do much more than criticize and polish.

Then I spoke about negative reactions in Topeka to my paper ("Freud and the Scientific Method of Psychoanalysis"), about which I had been hoping for David's evaluation. I had spent a week working with Lester on our book manuscript, and hoped to see him soon at the American Psychological Association meetings in Los Angeles.

An exchange of three letters followed on August 5, September 27, and November 9. On November 10, David had not yet received my long critique written the day before, and asked for "your final reaction to the System MS; and an indication whether or not (and on which parts) could I count on your <u>collaboration</u> if I undertake it. [. . .] I have to make a decision around the 15th of this month."

In responding on November 15, I explained that a visit from a relative had made it impossible for me to finish his manuscript, but hoped to in a few days. I had not accepted his "generous offer to share in it collaboratively" because of my obligation to finish work on the Selection book. If publication is held up, "I might be able to [. . .] work on the section on quantification, perhaps the part on the role of independent, intervening, and dependent variables, and perhaps the section on experimental design for tests of assumption." Of course, I wanted to follow the work closely and "make whatever critical contribution I can. [. . .] It is hardly conceivable for me that you should abandon something so magnificently begun." Finally, I invited him to come talk to a group of graduate students and faculty on one of four spring Wednesdays.

My next letter, written November 21, seems to have been written before I had received his of November 17. I wrote the next day, after getting that letter:

> [I am looking forward] to doing as much as I can on the monograph. [. . .] This has been a big day for me, as chairman of our Seminars Committee: [. . .] [I just got] a letter from Heinz Werner, also accepting, and our next speaker is Köhler. [. . .] So you see, you are in good company. I shall be delighted to have you stay with me. [George was pleased by David's decision to accept Koch's invitation.] As you surmised, he has been heavily snowed under by a tremendous load of work. I marvel at the number of things he is involved in and the amount he manages to get done on them all; under the circumstances, correspondence—even with closest friends—is bound to suffer.

In addition, omitted here are several letters to and from Elvira about visits and arrangements for her to use my apartment on occasion.

CHAPTER 6

Rapaport to Holt—January 23, 1956

Dear Bob:

I have so far read Chapters VII, VIII, IX and X. I have found it easy reading so far. That is, easy in general, though I felt that in various places the recommendation made in the footnote of Chapter VII, on the first page, namely that the reader should grit his teeth and read on, is not the most fortunate one and that a few footnotes explaining the general idea of the statistics would have been really called for. [It was deleted.] The easy reading puzzled me. I was not sure whether it was so well done, or whether it was mainly helping one over the humps without plumbing them. I have made some remarks to this effect. I have also made, on some of the points, simply stylistic and content remarks. I would like to pick up some of the points one by one.

Chapter VII, Page 2: I made a note. What I meant by it was discussed later at one point by you, but I wish you could see your way clear to deal with it throughout in a consistent way: it is quite possible that any assessment of psychiatrists which might exclude them from training or from practice, may not be justified excepting on the very extremes of the distribution, because only training, and with some people prolonged practice, will bring about the flourishing of the potentialities which make them good practitioners, or otherwise. This is the general question which may be put: in what respect are assessment procedures interferences with the freedom of the individual? I do not mean to be a boy-scout. I know that with the increasing complexity of society, the individual's freedom must lose and as a matter of fact, with these losses there is a gain certainly to other individuals, and some to the person himself. But the problem is one well worth facing in a general discussion of assessment, and you have faced it in these four chapters only at one point, which I will—as I get to it—signify later, and I think it should be in a way one of the red threads going throughout it.[101]

Otherwise I have no comments on Chapter VII, excepting on page 36 I thought that the point which you attribute to me has been spelled out by me in greater detail in "The Principles of Projective Techniques," and in "The Principles of Non-Projective Techniques," and to some extent in the Congress paper, "Theoretical Implications of Diagnostic Testing Procedures."[102]

Chapter VIII, Page 7, the first paragraph: I felt should be spelled out in considerable detail. I do not believe that your average psychiatric reader will see the point clearly, and I believe actually that thinking it through and writing it through will bring many things into focus. For instance, it could be expanded in clear relation to the point I have tried to make in connection with the previous chapter.[103]

Chapter VIII, Page 10: I have made a comment which may seem to you to contradict fully what I have pointed up in both of my above comments. I have noted there that it may be possible to find a pattern which indicates the potentiality for that type of pursuit into which, in final analysis, reality factors will lead the person. I mean to say that if we would be real knowledgeable, we might discover that out of the various experiences to which one is exposed, we [could] choose for skill and occupational development the one which corresponds to a certain combination of our

---

[101] This point came as a surprise to me, though it is quite a valid one if neglected in most of the literature on occupational assessment. It is a reminder of the young Rapaport, who had been a social reformer and fighter for human rights.

[102] All of these references (Rapaport, 1942b, 1946, and 1950b) were added.

[103] I believe that the material on p. 113 of Holt & Luborsky (1958) was added in response.

potentialities. Now while this may look as contradictory to the previous points, what I mean to point out is simply that there are here two poles between which the whole problem of assessment is stretched out, and that these two poles should and could be worked out more in depth to the advantage of your general considerations.

Page 44: is an example where it would be well worth it to spell out the meaning of the statistical concepts, but I think that this is just one which I singled out and the whole manuscript could well be gone over for such points.

This chapter, Page 49: you will find a note indicating that the preceding sections of this chapter are prone to slow down the reading. If I were you, I would rewrite them in great brevity and directness, so as to make reading [meaning?] obvious to a psychiatric reader, and put the details into footnotes.

On Page 51: I made a note about something that has worried me repeatedly in reading these chapters. The increasing correlation of the supervisor's and the peer's evaluations are interpreted by you as follows: "Clearly there is a common core of something measured quite independently by both." If I would be absolutely certain of this I would be happy. It is, however, quite possible that in the course of time a tradition was established in the school as to what constitutes desirable residency and peer's and supervisor's ratings became increasingly correlated as the crystallization progressed. I do not know precisely what the alternative that I am suggesting here means for the general picture, but I feel it should be thought through.

On Page 53, at the bottom: I commented raising the question whether the superior and the adequate people (who showed competence in training) might be [more] preoccupied with further training and further study in their post-graduate years, than those people who did not show competence in training because they were in the whole thing for money.

As to Chapter IX, my first remark is on Page 7: at this moment I cannot find which is Class 4. I am wondering whether or not this class was the first class to which people applied in masses who were not veterans. If this is so, the high rejection rate may be due to the fact that we have been accustomed to a more mature man among the veterans. It would be interesting in this respect to know whether the ratings given by the tests were the higher ones in this class, or whether the ratings given by the interviewers were. Also [what is] the correlation between the rejections and the ratings, both by the interviewers and the testers. The data supplied in the following do not directly answer this question. Somehow the anomalous position of this class among all the others requires, to my mind, some elaboration and exploration. Is it possible that this is the first class which was not tested by me, but by others? The fact which you mention, that this was the first group chosen for cross-validations, emphasizes the necessity that this point be explored in detail.[104]

On Page 16: I reiterated a comment which I have made before. The question accompanied me apparently throughout the reading. Concerning the table which follows Page 16, I have raised the question whether or not the ratings by interview[er]s and by testers and their recommendations, which are in the parentheses, differ statistically significantly from the ratings of the other people who were accepted. I am raising this question because it seems to me that this table might well serve as an example for those points where I feel that my ease of reading this whole material is partly due to the fact that I am being helped over the humps, and the writing does not really explore the manifold problems that are implicit. For instance, here if it is really true that this group of severe personality disturbances in general has been rated more highly in every which way, and statistically more highly than the other accepted people, then you have in that some kind of extreme characterization of the factors which are considered by the

---

[104] The data do not support Rapaport's impressions about ways Class 4 differed from others. He also did not consider the fact that the situation in Winter VA Hospital settled down a good deal after the first few years of getting under way.

rating groups, testers, and otherwise, to be the best psychiatric material, and it might show also that this best psychiatric material is highly fragile to personality disorders. The whole problem of internal differentiation, its necessity for psychiatric practice, and the fragility which goes with it in many cases, would be somewhat explored here by going into, at least in a footnote, the details of the test findings of these people. Or into the interview findings of these people. I think this would throw an analytic, microscopic spotlight on the difficulty of the job of selection and rating. I know I am a bit cryptic about this, but I would like you to come back at me if you want me to elaborate on it.[105]

On Page 17 in this chapter: I marked statement #4 as unclear. It is specifically unclear to my mind in its wording, but it is also a good example for the type of stuff I have been protesting against earlier. I think that it is really necessary to spell things out so that everybody can understand it who reads it.

Now for Chapter X: I have very little comment to make on this chapter, excepting one to the initial paragraph of it. Please believe me, that I will not be offended if it stays the way it is now. But I am wondering whether the impression this paragraph and several others before give, is really the one you want to give. To my mind there is no question about it, that the final design is your brain-child. Nor does there seem to me to be doubt about it that the vague way I originally conceived this business was very different, and in most respects falling far short of what you did. Yet somehow the way the situation is presented, it does not seem to quite do justice to the actual story.[106]

On Page 19: I am questioning whether the [. . .] "Minnesota multiphasic personality inventory" was not used because "you were not experts in its use." You do not mean to say that it

---

[105] The issue is complicated by the fact that Rapaport's impression that this group contained many with severe personality problems was not well founded.

[106] The text was so much altered after the comments in this and similar letters that it is difficult to find passages to which Rapaport objected.

couldn't have been learned for this purpose, just as fast or faster than any of the other things you tried out? You do not mean to say that we did not have a distinctly negative attitude towards it, derived from the study of its literature? Also it does give the impression as though these would have been considered, when I don't know whether or not they were considered, but while I remember the others being considered I do not remember that these were ever considered, either the Minnesota multiphasic or the drawing.

Nor can I sympathize with the formulation of the last paragraph on Page 19. As I remember it, we started a discussion of concepts and it became very lengthy and some people begrudged the time for it. It was really a matter of lesser evil (as against the time-consuming procedure) that the thing was allowed to lapse and commonsense definitions were adopted. The last two sentences seemed to me—in this context—particularly unfortunate. While in the context of a general discussion of psychoanalytic theory it would be quite appropriate to point up conceptual unclarities, and while in a detailed discussion of the concepts we have been dealing with it would be very interesting to point up that there are several ways they can be fitted in meaningfully in the psychoanalytic framework, the way this appears here is out of context and really does not give the right impression.

On Page 22: #17 seems to indicate that there were only men in this assessment population. If so, that should be indicated because otherwise this sounds odd. But it is my memory that there were at least three women, if not more.[107]

Concerning Page 25 and my comment on it: I would like to note that it would not be a simple "waste of time" for somebody to gather the energy to shed some light on the implications and not to slough it off as a "workable and helpful" set of concepts. It

---

[107] Though for the final Predictive Study, it was judged desirable to limit the sample to male, white, natives of the United States, 17 women actually received training in the MFSCP between 1945 and 1954 (Holt & Luborsky, 1958, Vol. 2, p. 397).

would be good to spell out some of the rationale that lies behind them, at least in the fashion of the footnote.

The phrase I marked on this page is one which rubs me wrong, particularly. While it is quite possible that this was a Northern invasion and that countering it stopped a general line of Russian policy, it is not so certain that it was not something provoked by the South, and it is quite certain that we acted before we talked about it with the United Nations, and that the United Nations simply rubber-stamped what we did. But above and beyond whether this statement is factually correct, the question is: How does it belong here? Why shouldn't a simple sentence that the Korean war came [i.e., began in 1949] take its place here. [It did.] As you can see from my comment, I find it simply offensive.

As you can see, Bob, while I am trying to do my best, I am not touching on the meat of the manuscript. Somehow it is either so excellent that there is nothing to be said about it, or I do not have the know-how to look at it critically, or (and this is the possibility that I mentioned repeatedly) you do not really explore some of the depths that lie in this. It may be, however, and it probably is, a combination of all three things. I doubt that I am so ignorant that I would not notice gross things which deserve criticism. The few points which I picked show that somehow there is an inclination to avoid the depths of problems where you hit them. And I do think that it is a very serious, honest job and [the] carefulness and undefensiveness about it impresses me very much. I certainly would have a very good conscience about it in general, if I would be one of the responsibles [those responsible for it].

I hope that I will soon be able to deliver my comments on the rest to you. Unless you are going to drop me a note to tell me that it is of no use to you, what I am sending to you comment-wise. You may want to look over the manuscript which I am returning herewith, because there are some minor question-marks put there, on which I didn't feel like commenting.

Yours,

David Rapaport

Rapaport to Holt—February 23, 1956

Dear Bob:

After some interruption, I again settled down to continue reading your manuscript. I would like to go over it quickly.

Chapter XII

Page 1. In the beginning of this chapter I am missing, in the discussion of what was said about psychotherapy, a discussion of the observation common to many of us, that there is a characteristic obsessive streak to the people who come into this occupation.

Still concerning this first page, I have the feeling that somewhere in the last two paragraphs on this page it should again be made clear to the reader what it is that you will compare. Otherwise, he might not quite follow what you begin to say in the very last paragraph.

Page 4. In the top ten lines you speak about the reason why the inadequate candidates were less frequently commented on. There is another possibility, namely that there are simply less verbal formulations amenable to those who speak about these people, to say anything about them. This is a matter of what gets conceptualized in a certain atmosphere and what doesn't. This issue may have had quite a role here. Do you have any way to check this?

Still about this page: the big footnote lists the things which I commented on most frequently. I do not know whether it is of any use to you to point out that these were the outstanding, obvious test characteristics.

Page 6. Again the footnote (I am a bit abashed that I am commenting too much on the parts which refer to me): I have the feeling that this phrase "informs me" is stuffy and could be put in a less distant way perhaps.

Page 9. In the paragraph before the last you end with mentioning that "liking" turns out as a good predictor of competence. It would seem to me that this would deserve a pause and a bit of thinking. There are many possibilities here. First of all, the people who are liked may blossom and flourish more freely and bring to bear more of their own person, since they are accepted as persons, than the others. Thus, being disliked may be productive simply of the negative result. On the other hand it is possible that the personal liking of a person or of a group is directed towards a person who "fits in" or is "similar to" the liker. If this were so, then the best selection would be to have an outstanding man, who has strong likes, select the people with whom he feels like working. Now history shows that in some cases this actually worked in the past. History, however, also shows that some people under these conditions have chosen weak "yes-men" to surround themselves with. In addition, this would bring up the question how the situation is modified if there is a group whose liking is to be attained. If their liking would have to be [were] a criterion, then the likers would have to be a rather homogeneous group. Is there any evidence that with the increasing homogeneity and crystallization of the school, the liking becomes a better criterion for success, than previously? I am not suggesting that what I am saying here should be in the text, or in what form it should be. I am suggesting, however, that this is the type of stuff which I am somehow missing in this otherwise very clear presentation.

Page 12. In the first paragraph you discuss the lack of differentiation by Rorschach scores. May I point out that since the population is highly polarized, namely it is quite an obsessional group (at least to my mind), the score differentials are thereby highly obscured.

Still concerning this page, namely to the second paragraph of the page. You conclude that skill as a psychiatrist does not go along with age. I would certainly object to this. I find it hard to state the reasons for my objection. My experience is that the skill in psychiatry increases with age in general. If I were to be asked, I would say that there are three types of people among psychiatrists: 1) Some who show their skills early, increase these skills with age, and this improvement keeps up. 2) A second type, whose interests may show early or late, and their skills similarly, but after a gradual improvement to a peak, it slowly or fast dwindles out and they become very stereotyped and do not keep on improving. Indeed they fall off. 3) There is a third type who show little or no improvement in skills, having started with an early show of skill, relative skill, or having started with an early conspicuous lack of skill. While you get the result which you seem to be getting, I can explain only that you have a narrow range of ages and indeed no material of the sort from which you could draw a warranted conclusion like this.

Still on the same page, to the very end of this second paragraph. If possible I feel even more strongly about this last sentence. At best what you could say would be that your material seems to suggest this, and that it is a material consisting of the external aspects of health and conventional adjustment. Again, I feel that your material is too limited. Chiefly it is already subject to a high social selection. Actually if you look at the contemporary scene of psychiatry and psychoanalysis, you see that a bigger bunch of screwballs has never been gathered into one occupation. Moreover, some of the most influential ones have been rather peculiar people. Consider, for instance, [N. Lionel] Blitzsten,[108] [Harry Stack] Sullivan, and many others.

<u>Page 13</u>. First of all to the footnote. The issue that you discuss in the second part of the footnote would really deserve a full-scale

---

[108] Blitzsten (1893–1952) was analyzed in Vienna by Otto Rank before immigrating to the United States. As a Chicago psychiatrist-psychoanalyst, he promoted Rank's ideas.

discussion of the issue. The examples you give here are most enlightening. One in a way yearns to have had more of this spread throughout the material, though in some places, particularly concerning score manuals, you have given such.

Page 17. The last paragraph: this general-atmosphere effect of the ability as a psychotherapist issued from the values held in the Topeka group. This value problem in itself deserves some discussion.

Chapter XIII

I really have but one remark or a question in mind: I wonder whether or not Morrow's section is not repetitious of something that appeared earlier in an earlier section. This was my memory. I am not against repetitiousness but this seemed too repetitious. In general, I believe that this chapter shows up even more clearly than the previous ones the great care and factual ingenuity that went into the study.

Chapter XIV

Actually it turns out that this may be the most difficult chapter for me to comment on. I marked a few places here in this chapter where you did just that kind of, stopping and considering as I somehow felt lacking in some other places. In the meanwhile, the major discussions of Design II are very wearing, and one somehow wished that just at these points it would be interrupted with some kind of an attempt to explain or facilitate a digesting of all the negative results. I also felt considerably bothered by the brief concluding summary on Page 38. Your ending conclusion is not clear to me: what is it precisely you recommend? In general I have the feeling that when one is faced with such a series of negative results, somehow it should be spelled out in detail what these do mean and what these do not mean for the tools used, for the solubility of the problem tackled. I really do not know precisely what I want, but this chapter seems so far the most difficult one for me to imagine that readers will get the impression [from it] that you intend to give. I am not even quite sure that I know what impression you did intend to give.

Chapter XV

In contrast to Chapter XIV, Chapter XV I found not only palatable but highly interesting. It again gives a sense of how much work you have done, how thoughtful and conscientious and inventive you have been in checking things. Your discussion of the halo-effect was particularly interesting to me, since it comes back to some comments I made earlier about liking the material. The Wechsler findings I found very enlightening. Less satisfactory did I feel was the Rorschach discussion: I would have wished that there would have been some way to explain the failure. Some way to show what was different about those DR's [responses to rarely noticed details] or their context in one class against the other. The least satisfactory thing about the chapter seems to me the last page and a half. And this for the paradoxical reason that a most important issue is joined and yet not as sharply explored as one would wish it would be. You know, if it wasn't this late in the game I am not sure but that I would suggest that each chapter be reread and the major problem that it tackles, its general significance and the results it arrives at concerning it, be stated leisurely and in the general way of a writer talking to an intelligent audience in the beginning of the chapter. But it is late in the game and I mention it only because it might give you some idea what it is that leaves me somewhat unsatisfied, even in a chapter which otherwise has quite fascinated me.

      Yours,

        David Rapaport

Rapaport to Holt—February 28, 1956

Dear Bob:

Finally, I am coming to the last lap.

Chapter XVI

Page 2, In the second paragraph you speak about the two men who [i.e., the validity of whose predictive ratings] reached respectively the 5% and the 1% level of confidence. I am wondering whether these two men were men who were highly influential in the intake and in determining the atmosphere of the place. It seems to me that one of the points one could make possibly (but you have to check me on this) about the results is that, given a strong influential person, his selection of the men whom he likes will result in a population which he likes, and therefore will result in a population whom he will readily teach and who will readily learn from him, and change in the direction in which he wants them to change. I wonder whether I am making my-self clear here, but I cannot do anything but leave it at this.

Page 3. It would seem that if you agree a person's bias is what leads him to observe correctly facts that pertain to the bias, and if we assume that the men who were making judgments here were good observers, then the only place the trouble could come in would be in turning the observation into prediction. It would seem then that the major area of future research should lie in the observation-prediction relationship. But this is the point precisely where the greatest dependence upon external events seems to lie. In a sense one could assert that only a man who can then proceed to do the educational work on the person who was selected should make a prediction, because he is the one who would take the responsibility of turning the assets or qualities he saw into those qualities, emergence of which he predicted. I know this is a screwy conclusion but it would be well worth thinking through.

On this same page I am worried about what you call the "comforting fact." You see, I know from experience that when I take a stand upon my own vision of a situation, I usually take an extreme stand, and if somebody else takes another extreme or a mediating stand, it helps me to see the possibility of the stands of others and to modify my own. This is indeed a process by which a modest amount of truth emerges, but not from pooling of errors, only from the pooling of extreme weights given to correct observations. Is it this process which is represented by the statistical averaging you are discussing? Is it not possible that what happens is simply a statistical artifact by which the averages are better "fits" than anything else, without any reference to any essential process?

Page 4. I again have the same concern as I had on Page 2: you talk about the interviewer's competence as a psychiatrist, and I am wondering about his weight in the whole setup.

Page 6. I am wondering whether Interviewer B did not make his overestimations because actually all these estimations were relative estimates, the baseline of which was some kind of self-rating, and the mechanism by which the rating was achieved was to relate the person observed or judged to the interviewer's self-estimate. Now, if the self-estimate of a person is very low, then he will tend to overrate. Does this mean anything in this context?

Page 7. I would like to make the same point to the three beginning lines of this page: What if Observer D had such a front and overestimated this front as an asset because it served him well in his life?

Page 10. The third paragraph calls for examples and I certainly felt that that would be good.

Page 12. Top paragraph: the overestimations, while not excessive, are still impressive. I am wondering whether what happened here simply was not that the assets, on the basis [of which] estimations were made, were such that [they] did not get nourishment in the training period, and therefore did not bring the results which were expected of them, and thus the [predictions were] overestimates. Here [. . .] a training problem [is] possibly involved.

Page 18. I object to #3 on the same grounds as [. . .] before. The last paragraph of #3 puzzles me. Is it so that, simply statistically, by the nature of this population the reject vote would tend to make the person a better judge, because of the population's low standards [of suitability]?

Chapter XVII

Page 6. On this page there is a heading, "Personological Assumptions." I was not very clear how the issue raised here differed from the genotype issue already discussed. But with this minor exception I found this chapter very interesting, very straightforward, and instructive. The same holds, to my mind for Chapter XVIII, which I also found excellent.

Dear Bob, I wonder why we haven't heard from you in a long while?[109] I am also wondering whether or not the date of March 7—that is, a week from tomorrow—is a fixed date, or whether we could simply skip it? I would like next to come to New York when you and I can already do some of the work on the "Systems" paper. I realize that I have contributed very little with these comments (except maybe some unnecessary trouble) on these chapters, but this is the best I know how to do it at this time.

I was in New York last weekend but between Merton and Shakow, who both were there, and a lot of work to be accomplished, I did not manage to get in touch with you. So let me hear from you.

Yours,

David Rapaport

---

[109] My brief letter of February 27, concerning the March lecture, had not reached him when he wrote these pages.

Rapaport to Holt—April 18, 1956

[handwritten]

Dear Bob,

Sorry over the news.—The more reason for you to come up and for us to have some good talks.—I must be still short: not too well physically or otherwise.

Glad about both your decisions: book and FFRP.—You two Bobs[110] are judicious and can do good jobs on such committees: I am impulsive and make things difficult for myself and others.—If there will be things you'll want to have my ideas on, you'll be welcome to them.

Colby [1955]: I read it and didn't understand it. Sure I am only that—while he may be well worth listening to and I will try again when I review him for "Science," next Fall—he <u>did</u> <u>not</u> listen to psychoanalytic metapsychology. Well, it is not easy to listen to that one, but then nobody is obliged to write on metapsychology. If you want to see what Merton and I did on systematizing that [Rapaport & Gill, 1959], you are welcome. But since I have only one copy it must be carefully handled.

The best to you,

Yours,

David

---

[110] The other was Robert P. Knight.

Holt to Rapaport—July 26, 1956

Dear David:

Here's the manuscript, more or less marked up.[111] The suggested changes are almost all stylistic and grammatical; I don't think there is a single matter of substance on which I felt any strong difference. On page 156, point 12, I didn't quite agree with your first statement about the clinical theory, implying that you thought the state of data collecting was in rather satisfactory shape, but then you took care of most of what I had in mind by the last paragraph of the section, some pages later. I certainly agree that in terms of a direct contribution to theoretical advance, there is negligible importance in establishing clinical psychoanalytic conclusions on sound research bases. I wonder, however, if in a slightly different meaning of "strategic" it may not be of long run value to the theory if a start could be made in just this aspect of psychoanalysis. I have in mind the sort of thing that I discussed in my [unpublished] paper on "Freud and the Scientific Method of Psychoanalysis": systematic instead of haphazard collection of case data, attention paid to considerations of sampling and elementary precautions to reach conclusions that are not the result

---

[111] From the text that follows, the paper seems to have dealt with problems of the relations between clinical psychoanalytic theory and research of various types. Among Rapaport's publications of 1956 and later, no such paper appears in Gill (1967). I have not had an opportunity to search for it through the Library of Congress collection of his unpublished manuscripts.

of wishful thinking or tracing the outlines of preconceived ideas on scanty data and the like.

But this would be of value principally on the assumption that one of the factors blocking theoretical advance in psychoanalysis is the low state of research training and methodological sophistication among most psychoanalytic investigators. I agree with your vigorous and telling indictment of those sections of psychology that worship the scientific method too much and try to replace thinking and observation by following the rules in the book. But it's not my impression that this is much of a problem of the clinical psychoanalytic researcher. It seems to me that most psychoanalysts would heartily applaud what you have to say in that particular section and would use your arguments to buttress what is another kind of anti-intellectual position: a resistance against any kind of precision and control in thinking or in gathering data.

What is needed is as usual some kind of middle ground. I believe that people have to be trained enough in the disciplines of scientific method so that they are no longer anxious lest someone catch them being sloppy until the essential features of the scientific method become so ingrained that the investigator can proceed flexibly and can improvise as he goes along. I see it as the same thing that obtains in any art: one has to learn the discipline of representational techniques before he can flexibly and comfortably abandon them for good reason. One has to know the classical rules of harmony before he can write music that violates them, not out of ignorance but deliberately. Just so, if the psychologist tries to be free, creative and flexible in his investigative approach without ever having learned the rigid text-book models, he is likely to equivocate his findings, foul up his data with unnecessary biases, and introduce avoidable error. If he is so terrified of unavoidable error that he sticks to the text-book model and investigates trivia only, then he is falling into the trap that you so clearly point out. But I think that the other danger exists too, and that it needs to be brought to the attention of the psychoanalyst just as the worship of the scientific method needs to be pointed out to the psychologist as a danger. So I would hope to see a plug for the hard middle way—the combination of discipline with freedom, of rigor with flexibility, of sophisticated knowledge of the technical procedures with an understanding that the safety gained by adhering rigidly to them is sterile.

On pages 160 and 161, I didn't really follow your argument about participant versus direct observation. (This incidentally does not seem to me a good antithesis; the two terms are drawn from quite different frames of reference, and are likely to lead to some confusion. The opposite of direct observation is reconstruction; direct observation may or may not be participant, and the same goes for reconstruction. I don't know a good term to oppose to participant observation; I suppose it might be something like "outside observation.") But it isn't clear to me just how you thought of complementarity as a relevant issue, or how transformation rules could be set up to help us get from one type of observation to the other. Your example suggests to me that you are really thinking about the difficulties of getting from data gathered in one theoretical frame of reference to data gathered from another, and the difference in methods becomes quite secondary to the basic difference, which is in concepts. The Piaget example gives me this impression because, as you point out in your footnote, the methods are really not so very different, and the problems of putting Piaget's observations together with those of psychoanalysis seems to be mainly that they have been conceived in different theoretical systems.

In short, I can conceive that the dilemma that you describe ("whether the yield of the method of participant observation and the yield of other methods can be related to each other by conjunctive rules of inference or must be related by disjunctive rule of complementarity") but I don't see that you have demonstrated that this is in fact an issue or a problem for psychoanalysis.

Towards this end, I tried to combine on page 166 some of the material you had omitted from the previous version with this one, because I thought it read a little more smoothly before or was clearer. And then, as I noted in the last margin, the last paragraph somehow has a slightly anticlimactic tone to it; it fails to maintain the invigorating spirit of what just precedes it. I imagine that if you will simply come back to it after a few days, you will be able to rewrite it in such a way as to give it the proper touch.

So much about the paper, except to say again that I think in all parts of it there has been steady improvement from one draft to the next, and that I feel it is a highly valuable document even though perhaps not the best you could have done with another year or so to ripen it.

[. . .]

Crusa and I are going to Tanglewood this weekend, so we shall probably stop by and see you sometime on Saturday or Sunday.

Best,

Bob

Rapaport to Holt—November 15, 1956

[handwritten]

Dear Bob,

Good to hear from you even if only on direct provocation. No, you have no reason to be peeved at all: you can't expect me to want to comment without invitation. I understand the pressure you are feeling—and all I wanted was to make sure that you know that I am around and interested. Your silence seemed more than just too much work.

Berman:[112] I wonder whether the group experience and its effect would not be best tested (against the effects of teaching) by testing increased ability to solve problems which are pertinent or increased ability to profit from experience. In this respect I regard the situation somewhat similar as [George] Katona [1940] regarded it in the experiments reported in "Organizing and Memorizing."—I would prefer this approach to any of the proposed testing and observation that L. B. mentioned here.

I would be inclined to take a bunch of people who had one

---

[112] Leo Berman (1912–1958), a Boston psychoanalyst. In the American Journal of Orthopsychiatry, 1963, vol. 33, pp. 132-135, there was a report of a memorial meeting of the Boston Psychoanalytic Society in which Joseph J. Michaels reported on Berman's major achievement, the application of psychoanalytic group psychology to the disciplines of education, psychiatry, social work, mental health and preventive medicine. Because of his interest in developing some scientifically controlled research, I served as a consultant to him for a few years. Rapaport and I had received a specific proposal from him which is briefly outlined in what follows.

year of teaching and would test their ability to profit from experience; would divide them into two groups—one to have group experience, one to be "control," and would then test them afterwards again for ability to profit from experience. Obviously, the nub of the matter is a well designed test of the ability to profit from experience. I would do this by exposing them to an experience in a field of psychiatry which they were not so far exposed to, but the experience (either actual or one written to be read) would be such that it is related to the course of one group and [to the] group experience of the other. I then would ask them questions to explore whether the experience was integrated to the course material (or to the group experience) and whether the latter (either of them) developed further under the impact of the experience.—If this is not clear—ask. The reason I prefer this is the same as that for L. B.'s inclination to regard his group experiences as <u>educational</u> experiences.

[. . .] I am asking my secretary to see whether you got my two discussions of Lifton's brainwashing papers which are related to sensory deprivation.

Stuart Miller is concerned with the theory of sensory deprivation. It may pay you to talk to him. I think Wolff, Miller and Elkind, each would be well worth to be heard by your group.

> Yours
> David

Holt to Rapaport—December 13, 1956

Dear David:

I'm returning your review of Colby,[113] somewhat marked up, though not very much so I see on looking it over again. Since we had discussed the book [Colby, 1955], the review didn't contain many surprises, and I hardly need tell you that like everything you send me it is thoughtful and full of meat.

I do have two criticisms. First, I seem to remember that this is for Science [. . .]. If so, I'd think that it is not very well addressed to this particular audience. [. . .] I think the balance between related matter and critique, on the one hand and a straight exposition of what is in the book and what it's all about on the other hand is too heavily dipped in the former direction. Moreover, you discuss matters that are simply not of very much concern to the general scientific reader, part of the time. In short, it sounds fine as a communication to me or to Mert or to George, because we know these issues and why you are concerned about them; I was going on to say that someone from another discipline might be puzzled, yet I find that this general impression, which was left with me after reading the review, doesn't hold up on looking it over again. [. . .] I guess you are under no compulsion to tell anything about

---

[113] Kenneth M. Colby (1920-2001), an American psychiatrist-psychoanalyst, was best known for his application of computer science and artificial intelligence to psychiatry. In particular, his computer program PARRY simulated a paranoid schizophrenic who could carry on limited "conversations" with others.

the details of Colby's model, but the criticism that [you don't] give a good idea what the contents of the book are still stands. I have made some changes on Page 3 which may redress the balance a little.

My second major criticism is that I think you're a little too hard on Colby. Your little paradox in the sentence that spans pages 3 and 4 is slightly misleading. True, Freud's <u>theory</u> is dynamic in its core, but we are discussing here models, and the tripartite model makes up only a very small part of the theory, and not the dynamic part. Colby tries to keep the dynamic part of the theory but to change the model. I don't have any other specific suggestions for ways to make it less critical; it just sounds a little odd as it stands that you say so much that is negative, so little that is positive, and yet urge that the book be read.

Best,

Bob

Summary—Brief Letters from 1956

On February 27, I wrote at some length about a talk Rapaport was to give at the NYU Graduate Seminar. A couple of days later I wrote apologizing for not having yet thanked him for his comments on the Selection Project book. I also commented on a just-received rough outline of the NYU lecture, ending: "But I recognize that these criticisms are petty and probably inappropriate because of the fact that this is a rough outline rather than a paper."

He gave the lecture on March 7 and stayed overnight in my apartment. He wrote on the 19th, explaining that he was delayed in thanking me for my hospitality because, "Just as soon as I got back here came the news that my Mother died . . . The rest you can imagine." He added:

> Thanks for the "Hypotheses etc." of 1-18-56. [That letter not preserved.] They are indeed closely related to what Merton and I have been thinking, though the issue of double relative autonomy as Merton puts it sheds additional light on it all and I do think that it makes your experimental plans very worthwhile over and above McGill. [A reference to Bexton, Heron, & Scott, 1954.] Are you going at it? Do you want to discuss it with me?

A letter from me, written the next day, mainly concerned my revisions of the Selection book. I was trying to use both his comments and the issues raised by Meehl (1954). "I think things would be a lot easier for me if I didn't have such diverse loyalties: I want to be true to a clinical point of view and, at the same time, maintain as much methodological rigor as possible." In a postscript I noted that his letter with the sad news had just arrived, gave condolences, and asked to defer a discussion of our experiments "until the MS is well in hand."

The spring of 1956 was a very eventful one in my personal as well as professional lives. Crusa and I were both struggling with the inner problems that had prevented us from taking the step to marriage. Some time in early April, there was a brief break in our relationship, about which, it seems, I expressed some pain in a handwritten note (not preserved); Rapaport responded empathically on April 18. I answered on May 14, saying that the break with Crusa was brief and "we are on a sounder and more solid basis than ever before." To try to clear up my neurotic blocks to marriage, I had found a therapist, Hyman Spotnitz, who however was unable to schedule me for more than a few hours before the fall. I reported that I was going to give a paper in early June in Stockbridge and hoped that he and I could have a good talk. Soon I would send a copy of a long version of my review of Colby, and hoped to read the draft on metapsychology by him and Merton. Finally I reported the good news that both of our applications for support of our program at the new Research Center were likely to be awarded.

Rapaport responded at May's end, apologizing for the delay, because of "trouble in my Montreal family, Washington lectures, and chiefly feverish writing on David Shakow's and my 'Freud's Influence on Psychology'" (Shakow & Rapaport, 1956). Irving Paul was looking for a job; perhaps we should take a look at him.

My reply of June 12 implied that we had been in contact by phone and that I had asked him for independent evaluation of Spotnitz, about whom I had doubts after only an hour or so. In the imminent trip to Stockbridge, I would talk with Dr. Paul. No surviving letters concern that visit. A note from Rapaport dated July 2 thanked me for comments on a paper, probably the draft (with Gill) on metapsychology. On July 10, I merely sent the title of the first report of research from the new RCMH (Klein, Spence, Holt, & Gourevitch, 1958), a copy to follow. And a note from Rapaport of July 12 implied a recent visit and enclosed a section of his monograph for comments.

A gap of over three months followed my critique of July 26. On November 12, Rapaport asked, "Why this silence?" After reporting about his recent contacts with mutual friends for whom I was also acting as a consultant (Leo Berman and Grete Bibring), he remarked: "For Gods sake, send me the plans [for our sensory deprivation project]! Don't you want to hear my ideas about it?" ending, "How are you? What are you doing? How is the charming young lady? When do I see you?"

I responded quickly and apologetically, saying that we were starting "an intensive period of data-gathering for a couple of months" though I was planning a Christmas visit to my girls in California and had started analysis with Mrs. Charlotte Feibel,[114] whom I liked. (No word about my swiftly quitting Spotnitz after he had blandly suggested that I use grant money to pay his high fees, which struck me as unethical.) I promised to send the experimental plans as soon as we could spare our one copy,[115] and gave hasty responses to his other questions, pleading time pressure.

---

[114] Charlotte Feibel (1901–1973), a lay analyst, lived and practiced in New York City.
[115] Recall that digital copiers and fax machines did not exist in those days.

CHAPTER 7

Rapaport to Holt—February 6, 1957

Dear Bob:

I read your project outline with a great deal of interest. I am in a dreadful hurry, but I want to jot down a few points which you may have thought through long ago but which impressed me as I have been reading. Since you are building a special equipment for this purpose I wonder whether you have any possibility to put in a television camera not for photographing but simply so that you can see what the man is doing even though you don't have a one way vision screen. I don't think that the one way vision screen is the ideal thing in this arrangement.

Moreover, I have been thinking about this: if you want to test your subject for Rorschach, then it would be best for that test and for other tests to have a screen onto which various things get projected automatically, so that for instance he looks at the Rorschach without moving and takes various attention tests. Among these, I would include not only digit span tests but also a variety of others which I will be glad to write to you about if you write to me specifically asking for them.[116]

I am very interested in what you will be getting. Another thing that I have been thinking about in wake of our last conversation was whether or not your subjects know how long it will take for them to be in this condition. I think it may make all the difference, actually. It seems that for instance in concentration camps, those

---

[116] Unfortunately, we were unable to adopt these useful suggestions.

people survived who had somebody outside in a relatively safe position, that is, not subject to the same kind of torture and disappearance.[117] Also in prisons those people managed best who did not have associates who could have either actually testified against them or who could be said by the investigators to have already "confessed." I think these are relevant considerations.

Stuart Miller here is trying to put together the general survey of all the literature in this area and has been reading a great deal. I wished one day you would get together with him. Likewise Peter Wolff is quite involved in this whole "nutriment issue." How this is a nutriment issue, if you wouldn't remember it by chance, then from my memo on Lifton's paper you might be able to see it. I am also about to complete the first readable version (this will be the third) of the autonomy paper which I gave in Topeka, which covers the area theoretically to some extent. [. . .] In other ways it is quite ambitious. I will send you a copy when I get around to finishing it. All my best to you and that notorious greeting which you don't like to convey.[118]

> Yours,
>
> David

---

[117] Here Rapaport forgot that ethical and practical considerations made it impossible not to tell participants how long they would be in confinement.

[118] I cannot quite recall what this final jocular jibe refers to.

Holt to Rapaport—May 3, 1957

Dear David:

Let me start by an attempt to clear my own thoughts through a restatement of some of your points. If there were no autonomy of the ego from the environment, but a complete dependence on it, robbing man of contact with the environment would put him wholly at the mercy of the drives. This was the basis of my first hypothesis about the effects of isolation. It assumes that, since we are relatively dependent on the environment, if contact with reality is cut the autonomy from the drives cannot be maintained and secondary process will give way to primary. In other words, that the autonomy of cognitive, secondary processes from the id was secured and maintained by a dependence on the environment. It underestimated the strength of the ego, the organism's capacity for self-sustenance and thus the far-reachingness of its autonomy. This has been brought home to me by Leo Goldberger's work.[119] His isolation experiment has yielded results that are inconsistent with the hypothesis in three ways, while generally supporting it: a. subjects don't immediately, on severing the contact with the environment, regress—it takes time; b. with any given amount of deprivation of reality contact, there are individual differences in the amount of regression; c. as between individuals and over the course of time, different (secondarily autonomous ego-, or secondary process-) functions are affected to different degrees and

---

[119] His dissertation research, later published as Goldberger (1961).

at different rates. (This last seems to me an important source of evidence that primary and secondary processes are not unitary, but heterogeneous concepts.)

Page 8: for some time, I've been [made] vaguely uneasy by the "apparatus" terminology. The more we study perception, the less sense it seems to make to speak of a "perceptual apparatus." That implies some kind of structure devoted to this particular function. To a degree, of course, there is specialization of bodily structure (particularly of brain structure) for such functions as perception and movement. Muscles, tendons and bones are important parts of "the motor apparatus," I suppose, along with the muscular innovations and "motor areas" of the cortex, and an indefinite amount of other brain tissue in addition. In the brain particularly, however, there is a lot of non-specialized "mass action." It seems to me especially arbitrary to single out and classify together "threshold apparatuses." I'm not sure I understand what is meant by drive-discharge or its threshold, ditto affect-discharge. The usual meaning of threshold is the absolute or differential limens of perceptual psychology— which would presumably be part of "the perceptual apparatus." The consummation of drives (and so possibly, drive-discharge thresholds?) requires the functioning of all the other apparatuses mentioned. All told, it seems that much confusion is caused by the apparatus terminology. Wouldn't we do better to stick to calling perception, memory and motor action <u>functions</u>? The bodily structures associated with each one are the province of anatomists and kindred scientists; and we should move very cautiously in denoting any generalized function a psychic structure, for there we are treading close to the bog of hypostasis [I should have said misplaced concreteness]. True, any function goes on in a structure, is limited, facilitated, guided, etc. by structure, which <u>may</u> be defined as that which performs these services. But there are similar dangers in such definitions, which look away from what they supposedly denote and give only secondary properties of it. (Thus, if one defined Boulder Dam only by Lake Mead, he wouldn't know its primary properties: its dimensions, how it was built, its materials, etc. For the most part, this is how we define psychic structures, however.)—Is the secondary process an apparatus? Is the ego an apparatus of apparatuses? Where do we stop in automatically assuming a special structure (apparatus) for every function we may choose to single out? We must have independent means of defining psychic structures in terms of their primary properties, or we're faced with the logical prospect of an infinity of them in any person. (Like the old static, taxonomic "instinct" cul-de-sac.)

Page 9: Erikson's modes need to be examined to clarify their relation to cognitive styles. To varying degrees they may be independent of what George [Klein] calls "content" (in the case of a mode, independent of zones, I suppose), so that what he is saying about cognitive attitudes and cognitive styles in the paper he is giving today might well apply to modes.

Page 11: Autonomy from the environment is defined by the extent to which behavior is a function of the organism, not the stimulus conditions or situation, as I see it. From this formulation, it would follow that any enduring organismic determinant of behavior is a "source and guarantee" of autonomy from the environment. To a usually inconspicuous and often trivial degree, these may be aspects of bodily structure: the crippled person's hobble is built in, not by drives but by his deformity; the myope's manner of peering—and perhaps many other aspects of his behavior—are partly caused by the structure of his eyes (interacting with the drives, of course). Then, if behavior is shaped by such individual psychic structures of primary autonomy as thresholds, these also guarantee autonomy from the environment; see George's paper on cognitive attitudes in this respect, since what he says may stand for all other autonomous psychic structures. As you yourself later point out, memory structures play a particularly important part, for it is memory that enables us to create an imaginal world if we're cut off (or if we cut ourselves off) from the real one. I would differ from you on the role of memory only in stressing its structural aspect rather than its role as self-stimulating nutriment.

To the extent that all of these structures have primary autonomy, the drives may be said not to be the ultimate source of
autonomy from the environment. I suppose in a sense, however,
it's legitimate to say that the above mentioned structural sources
of autonomy from the environment are not <u>ultimate</u> guarantees,
because they represent only the machinery, not what makes it go,
though here George's new formulations would part company
with you. I agree about the ultimate role of drives, because it
seems to me that if we imagine a person deprived of stimuli from
without and deprived of instinctual drives, then no matter how
elaborate his internal structures, he would be just a stationary car
with no gas in its tank. George is arguing, with Hebb [1949], that
there is only one kind of "gas" for the human machine: the energy
released by oxidation of food. This energy is then channeled (and
perhaps recruited) by motivational structures, of which the drives
are only a few; cognitive attitudes are others. The difficulty with
this position, as I see it, is that it makes it hard to explain transformation of instincts like displacements; how come a repressed
drive acts like a capped flowing well that finds other outlets?[120]
And how can this formulation account for the periodicity of
drives? I am really addressing those questions to George, not to
you.

The structures I have mentioned may have primary autonomy
from the drives, but they have much less primary autonomy from
the environment. Certainly Brozek's studies show that the soma-
totype is not autonomous with respect to the literal nutriment a
person gets.[121] And of course the recent experiments and observations showing the dependence of more figurative kinds of
structures on infantile stimulation are relevant here. I don't think

---

[120] I had not yet realized that this assumption lacked a good foundation in data.

[121] Josef Brozek, a Czech who came to the US in 1939, is best known as the psychologist on the team of researchers (Keyes, Brozek, and Henschel) who carried out the ground-breaking Minnesota Starvation Study, published as *The Biology of Human Starvation*, by the University of Minnesota Press, 1950, in two volumes.

we can ever speak of absolute autonomy from the environment, therefore, only relative autonomy.

Brainwashing and especially thought reform is a procedure calculated to minimize autonomy from the environment. Starvation may have similar effects (see below).

Page 15: Goldberger's data suggest that certain stylistic "structures" are more resistive to change—less dependent on stimulation or reality contact—than are secondary processes. I wish that Hebb's data could be examined from this standpoint, or that we could get another group of subjects for intensive study with a much longer period of isolation, asking which structures are least affected, and in what kind of order are they undermined by isolation? With only eight hours of isolation, in many of our subjects some of the most fragile-seeming functions (attention, concentration) make a very fast comeback, and may even be better at the end of isolation when retested (compare the learning results of Vernon and Parry).[122]

In general, I <u>feel</u> (I can't yet formulate it very well) that the <u>nutriment</u> conceptualization doesn't fit the facts very well. Part of the time it seems to mean something like what we refer to by the metaphor of "grist for the mill."—Machinery rusts if left unused, needs something to work on to keep it in good condition, just as a muscle needs use not to atrophy. But that suggests that we should look for the oxygen that does the rusting of psychic function (and perhaps the water that catalyzes this rusting) in our situation; just what is the atrophic process? I'm reminded of the forgetting issue: active interference rather than trace decay seems to be the answer. The use of a term like nutriment instead of one like grist seems to me to imply that there is some constant <u>building</u> of structure, not just the use of it.

If repression is weakened in isolation (and it does seem to be because we get "deeper" stuff, though maybe that's a function of a change in inhibition rather than repression), does this imply that repressive defense is nourished somehow by the presence of ordinary

---

[122] What I meant was Hoffman & Vernon (1956); see my letter of May 16, 1957.

reality-contact of a non-specific sort? The grist for repression is pre-sumably repressible impulses, and there's every reason to suppose that they are even more present in isolation than outside of it, though on second thought I suppose that isolation represents a sit-uation of being removed from temptation for at least some subjects. I find that kind of non-specific nourishing function harder to under-stand for repression than, for example, to accept the idea that attention or concentration need the nutriment of objects to be re-garded. What I don't understand is how one can tell in a situation like this whether the emergence of something that was formerly re-pressed is due to the weakening of repression, or to the strengthening of the impulse, or to the removal of another, not usu-ally noticed control, reality-contact? Unfortunately I can't take the time right now to try to pull together my thoughts on the notion that contact with an external reality may serve many of the same functions as internal controlling structures. Perhaps this is a familiar enough idea; if so, I'd appreciate being steered to some references on it.

Pages 15–16, re hypnosis and the reduction of autonomy from the id: this doesn't sound so convincing, because hypnosis is not notorious for being a drive-dominated state—in fact, quite the opposite. The hypnotist takes over the task of external control and does so very effectively: the subject isn't likely to start raping and murdering; there's even quite a controversy over the hypno-tist's ability to induce him to steal or act out other impulses against which he is usually defended. No, I don't see terribly much id-dominance; the hypnotist can get the subject to use his primary process, to hallucinate, dream, etc., but in a sense the subject thus has even more control than usual, in the sense that regression in the service of the ego is cited by you as an instance of ego auton-omy; he can turn on or off either primary or secondary process. According to your formulation, it would be hard to understand how feats of concentration and intellectual labor could be carried out under hypnosis. (Of course, I don't know the literature well— are there actually well documented instances of hypnotic hyperfunction of a strictly secondary process kind? I wouldn't regard hypermnesia as such.)

Page 16: how good are our studies of stimulus intake in depression and mourning? May it not also be the other way, too: that some withdrawal from external objects (stimulation) is useful to conserve energy for the work of mourning? Mourners resolutely turn away from new, stimulating activities; they seek solitude and quiet to meditate, and perhaps if they are forced to keep up a busy, highly stimulated life, they don't do the work of mourning very well. I don't know the clinical facts on that.

Last sentence of paragraph one, page sixteen, is unclear to me: which structures? Why is the nutriment concept necessary to make therapy conceivable?

We must carefully distinguish between nutriment of internal controls (structure building) and the availability of external controls. What seems to be super-ego control of moral behavior may be to a large extent dependence on external controls. (Compare here Riesman and Witkin,[123] and the externalization-internalization issue as formulated by the authoritarian personality group.) I'd answer your examples with [those of] Anne Frank's father and other inner-directed characters with well internalized superegos and strong senses of identity. You yourself refer to them later on in the paper (page 32 ff.). In your examples, I don't think you refer specifically to people who show surprising ability to resist circumstances that cause apparent atrophy of the superego in others, but I'm sure that you would admit their existence. Under such circumstances, isn't there similar stimulus-nutriment for everyone, both the craven and the hero? From where does the superego get its nutriment in such instances—surely not from itself? I read the implications of Erikson's

---

[123] David Riesman, Harvard sociologist, very well known at the time as author (with Nathan Glaser and Reuel Denney) of *The Lonely Crowd* (1950). Herman A. Witkin was author of the concept of field-dependence vs. field-independence and methods for measuring it. See, for example, Witkin & Goodenough (1977). George Klein, a good friend of Witkin's, considered it a cognitive style which he often used in his own research.

work quite differently. If one has a firm sense of identity, then he is no longer so dependent on the pressure and opinions of others. In fact, I think there's good experimental evidence for this viewpoint in the work of Asch, Barron and Crutchfield[124] (which I tried to summarize in my brainwashing paper [Holt, 1964]).

Page 18: I'm inclined to a different view of echolalia and echopraxia, which I agree are crucially important examples, though I feel a little abashed about stating my hypotheses since they are based on an almost total ignorance of the subject. I read somewhere—I think it was in Sorokin's autobiographical account of experiences with starving Siberians—about similar behavior in non-catatonic people, which inclines me to think of it as symbolic oral incorporation. A starving man is no more a victim of "massive blocking" of libidinal and aggressive drives than a man prostrated with physical illness, yet despite their similarly weakened states, echolalia and echopraxia are not seen in the latter condition. I suspect that in schizophrenia these symptoms may be: a. a kind of expression of extreme regression to the oral sucking stage, b. a restitutive effort to rebuild by identification a shattered ego, but an effort that fails because there is too little to build on or too little cathexis for what is introjected; c. an extreme of "schizophrenic empathy" in which the patient cannot resist the impact of another person, who captures his defenseless psychic apparatus which is not manned by any workable sense of identity.

Page 18: often the aim of brainwashing is to extort "confession"; promises, threats and beatings do not work as well. See the testimony before the McClellan Committee on this point.

Page 19: it's not clear to me what you mean by "nourishment for memory." Actually, I understand this [Chinese thought reform] as an attempt to undermine memory via an attack on identity and belief, the inculcation of a new value system, and the steady input of competing "facts." What Orwell omitted, I think, is the systematic attack on identity, and also some of the features of brainwashing

---

[124] Asch (1952), Barron (1952), Crutchfield (1955).

technique that produce the "acute" phase, as against the "chronic" phase which is more emphasized by Lifton [1961].

Page 20: Is a concentration camp "barren of stimulus nutriment"? We have to be careful in using these terms. It's monotonous in a number of respects, but not like the cell of a Russian prisoner, nor the situations of Lilly[125] or our subjects.[126] Also, I think you underplay the role of physical and physiological influences in these coercive situations. I believe that they are very important in weakening the capacity of the person (or ego, if you will) to be autonomous with respect to anything. You can weaken a person so much that he no longer responds to or in terms of the usual drives, but I doubt that this state could be called one of autonomy. Under such circumstances, extreme passivity and compliance have been reported; the person is under the domination of the environment almost completely. I suppose in a sense you might call this a special case of "blocking the instinctual drives," since the drives are unable to function in an exhausted and enervated organism, so he doesn't have them to fall back on, to mobilize him. [. . .]

On page 21, you say that maximized deprivation, danger and fear "enlist the drives . . . as the prompters of surrender"; I don't see how either sexuality or aggression are enlisted. Did you have something else in mind? I should subsume this condition under that of exhaustion, which I've just been describing. I'm surprised that you mention a relatively subordinate matter like the deprivation of privacy, and say nothing about attacks on identity as such. Finally, I don't care for the formulation of your fifth point. You have never described what you mean by nutritive; now you introduce the concept of "non-nutritive instructions and information"—something that is very much in need of clarification. Since I don't find the "nutriment" concept very congenial

---

[125] John C. Lilly, MD, at NIMH in 1954 devised an isolation tank of warm salt water for some of the earliest studies on sensory deprivation.
[126] Leo Goldberger and I had done a series of studies (Goldberger & Holt, 1958, 1961a, b; Holt & Goldberger, 1959, 1960, 1961) at the Research Center for Mental Health, starting with his dissertation. In each, volunteer participants rested on a bed in a soundproof room with halved ping pong balls over their eyes for up to eight hours.

anyhow, maybe I should hold my peace, though it seems to me that forcible indoctrination provides what I think you mean by nutriment for the formation of unwanted structures to replace the others that are systematically torn down. In this instance, I think that it is seriously confusing the issues to talk about "stimulus-nutriment" in a context where you have been discussing isolation experiments, for there the term stimulus is meant quite literally, and here I think it is metaphorical. Someone who is being "struggled" [subjected to "thought reform"] in a Chinese prison is certainly bombarded with highly figured stimuli of all sorts in all his senses, and one certainly cannot say that the abstract structures of the ego are robbed of contact with the type of stimulus that has built them.

There's a good deal of repetition on pages 23 and 24, and I think you push the concept of autonomy a little too far—as you yourself recognize in the first paragraph on page 24, yet you go right on in the second paragraph speaking of autonomy in the way you just criticized.

Reading pages 27 and 28, it strikes me that many learning theorists would say that what you call "stimulus-nutriment" is only reinforcement, or in some instances practice. If the concept is retained, it will be necessary to distinguish it carefully from these learning concepts.

On page 29, I see that you are making distinctions between the different kinds of nutriment, such as I just called for. But I wonder how far you can go in calling anything that fosters or promotes something psychological as "nutriment." The more broadly it is used, the more it seems not to be a technical innovation but merely a loose metaphor.

I was very interested by your statement on pages 33 and 34 that structures may be nourished from drives and from the superego. Unfortunately, you merely state this without working it out in any detail. I don't really see how reference to drives or the superego helps very much; I wish you could expand on that.

Page 38, next to the last sentence. This seems like a paradox: counter-cathectic barriers to the discharge of tension are, by definition (as I understand it), a part of the ego, but you say that "a non-autonomous ego . . . does not regulate the tension." What I think you mean to stress is that insofar as this defense is redoubled automatically as drive tension rises, it is not operating as an <u>autonomous</u> ego function. I guess it is essentially just a matter of verbal expression; although the regulation of tension must remain an ego matter, it may at the same time be in turn regulated by the id, although the second usage of the word "regulated" is slightly different from the first.

Because I haven't yet finished the paper on activity and passivity, I am not convinced that your attempt to treat the metapsychology of the autonomies via activity and passivity is the best strategy for accomplishing that task. From what I've read of both papers, I have the feeling that the old issue of the <u>will</u> is still plaguing us. Its revenant refused to remain interred when the dread curse, "pseudo-problem!" was pronounced over its grave. And I don't think that the discussions of activity, passivity and the autonomies will wholly placate this restless spirit.

I suppose what I'm saying is that your paper opens up many problems, only sketching out possible solutions to many of them. It's already a long paper and shouldn't be expected to solve all of the problems it identifies; merely to call attention to them is a large contribution. I think I would like the paper a little better, though, if it explicitly recognized that on a number of issues, nothing more has been done than to point in the general direction where solutions may be found.

Altogether these reflections have been fragmentary and not brought together very well, a fault that I am tempted to attribute entirely to the haste with which I have prepared them. Perhaps there will be more matured ideas after the staff discussion; if so, I'll write them to you, even if the deadline is passed.

Yours,

Bob

Comment

Trying to follow what feels like a tortured argument more than half a century later, I see here some of the many ways in which it was slowly becoming evident to me that Rapaport's basic project was impossible: to bring together and make internally coherent and orderly the elements of Freud's basic theory, metapsychology, while maintaining fidelity to scientific methodology and relevance to observations, mostly clinical but also those of disciplined research. Of course my relative youth, plus talents and scholarship so vastly inferior to those of a revered mentor whom I also cherished as a friend, put me in an eventually untenable position. I could and did point out inconsistencies and implausibilities in his drafts but not raise fundamental questions about the inherent feasibility of the whole project. Uneasy though I was about concepts like instinctual drive, psychic structure, and the generally unquestioned ego-id-superego triad, I was far from ready to challenge, much less to abandon them. I doubt that I ever understood my own unease in just these terms at the time.

Rapaport to Holt—May 10, 1957

Dear Bob:

Thank you for your letter of May 3. You will see that it was of considerable help to me, when you read the revised version of the [ego autonomy] paper. But I am not fully through yet with the revision and want to write to you [now] only since you indicate that soon there may be a discussion of the paper.

As to the first big paragraph on your first page, I must say that it hammers on an open door. If you will look over the paper you will note that I did not even speak about the sturdiness of autonomous functioning, but only about its breakdown, from the varieties of which I tried to make inferences concerning the mutual relations between the autonomies. I am still considering to put in something about the sturdiness of the autonomy which you stress, and about the role of cognitive processes in the maintenance of the autonomy from the environment, both of which I sorely neglected. But as you say later in your letter, I couldn't possibly discuss all the issues. Otherwise you will note that I have referred now in two places to your communication and your and Goldberger's work.

As to your big comment concerning page 8: I find your point very interesting. But let me make two comments about it. First of all, as you yourself know it was not my job to make here a change in terminology. In this respect then, for my paper the question is beside the point. Secondly, I think that your argument is well taken, the only thing that you are not demonstrating is that one can follow your argument to the bitter end and arrive at a conceptual framework consistent with the conceptual framework necessary for the rest of psychoanalytic thinking. Several of the problems you bring up must sooner or later find a solution, but they must find a solution responsible to the rest of the theory. That, I think, was not taken into consideration in your comments, but then they were comments apropos a paper.

More or less the same thing applies to your comments on my page 9.

Concerning your comment as to page 11, I would feel that you are driving the point of autonomy from the environment too far. I did not define it as "the extent to which the behavior is a function of the organism and not the stimulus conditions." I defined it as the degree of independence from the stimulus conditions, that is to what degree the stimulus determination can be postponed, avoided and modified. Now you could very well say that I did not make this a sharp definition. That is true, but again I was more interested in sketching the broad outlines of the conception in symmetry to the autonomy from the id than anything else. I have not yet seen George's new formulations. I trust that they are as thoughtful as usual. If he is forced to part ways with some of the formulations that we more or less held in common, that will certainly give reason to rethink quite a bit. This rethinking is sure to be fruitful, though it is not certain that it will not result in revisions not only of what I have been writing but also of George's point (your questions to George makes this rather clear).

Your stress on the relativity of the autonomy is well taken and I have sharpened that point up.

Now as to page 15: This is again that matter of the sturdiness of autonomy. I nowhere asserted that any deprivation results in immediate destruction of structures or even in full destruction of their autonomy, I was not even convinced that the effectiveness of all structures is reduced by deprivation. The whole point is that I did not go into these things at all. But I would be interested to know what is the Vernon and Parry reference.

As for your comment which goes from the third to the fourth page of your letter, I think that you will be in full position to judge the nutriment issue only when you restudy Piaget very carefully. I do not give a fair picture of it. It is very important in this connection to keep in mind the Riesen experimental material also.[127] I think you are right that what I mean by nutriment is very different from grist for the mill. The last sentence of your paragraph implies this already. The learning-theoretical assertion that forgetting is "active interference rather than trace decay" seems to me to be an unproven contrast. I am not sure that it does not raise a fictitious question. But this would go too far to dwell on.

Now to the second paragraph on your page four. The whole repression issue should be discussed. I would not say that the contact with external reality may serve the same functions as internal controlling structures excepting when the internal controlling structures are too weak and one has to find external props, which is frequent enough in pathology. When this is not the case the external reality supports these structures and nourishes them. I wouldn't even say that this is an altogether "familiar" idea (you raise this question in your last sentence). I would however say that the kind of interpretation I give of repression here is quite consistent with the one that one would reconstruct from Freud's "Papers on Metapsychology" and "Repression" in particular, once they are put into a contemporary context.

Concerning your comments on pages 15 and 16, I would suggest that you ask Merton to send you manuscripts he has and you will see that indeed as you suspect the appraisal of hypnosis that you give is not necessarily correct. I don't say that it is not an arguable interpretation but it is not the one we have come to assume, considering both theoretical and empirical connections.

---

[127] The reference is to A. H. Riesman's early experiments (later published in Riesen & Clark [1973]) on the cognitive delay observed in chimpanzees raised in darkness. Much like congenitally blind persons who, when vision is restored later in childhood, for some time cannot really see, Riesman's subjects learned only very slowly to accomplish simple visual tasks.

Your comments on page 16 go into the whole problem of depression. [It] is a most complex problem, I would love to talk to you about it.

As to page 5, your second paragraph on this page has its answer in a later section of the paper.

As to your big paragraph concerning page 16, on page 5 of your letter: I would certainly question whether the identity concept should be used here causally. I tried to argue this point in the new version of the paper. Indeed the problem is: how identity itself is maintained, and I believe that it requires a high level stimulus input. I think that I am in total harmony here with Erikson and I believe that the Asch, Barron and Crutchfield material does not contradict my point.

As to your comments on page 18, I think that while one might question the psychiatric view and psychoanalytic view of the catatonic conditions I discussed, your suggestion about them is far more questionable and not consistent with the clinical impression. May I also point out that your three points are purely in terms of "content" and thus not relevant to the points I am trying to make. Actually the whole autonomy issue could be expressed throughout in such content terms. Indeed these content terms, as well as many others, could be simply the form which my interpretation would take in any concrete case.

These are obviously only the points to which I take exception and you will see how much was really helpful to me.

Let me say one thing about your paper on "Brainwashing."[128] As a survey it is very helpful. You have referred to a number of things which I was not familiar with. Stuart Miller [1962] is working on a broad review of the whole literature in these matters. The thing that I am bothered about in this paper is the use of "identity" as the ultimate explanation. I believe, and letters of Erik make me think he would agree, that what I have been trying to do with the autonomy issue and with activity and passivity are further

---

[128] An early draft of Holt (1964).

specifications of the identity issue without which there is no real metapsychological status to be attributed to the concept of identity. For this reason I find the paper—though interesting and useful—theoretically quite weak. Now it is possible that this is simply because I wished you would have digested my paper with a more positive attitude and would have taken a theoretical stand on the brainwashing matter. It is possible however in turn that I am too impatient with this and the phenomenology should be worked on for much longer before any such theoretical attempts can be accepted as the one I made. Hard to say which is the truth. It would be very good to get together and thrash this matter out thoroughly.

In a way I wish that you people [i.e., the RCMH staff] would not discuss the present version of the paper and wait until a new version is available.

My best to you.

Yours,

David

Comment

That lack of "real metapsychological status" in the concept of identity was, for Rapaport, a critical weakness in the concept, indicating how thoroughly committed he was to the central importance of metapsychology in Freud's work. In retrospect, it strikes me as paradoxical to require of a concept, before it is acceptable as a causal variable, that it attain status in the very part of psychoanalysis that is hardest to test empirically, making its causal efficacy most difficult to establish.

Holt to Rapaport—May 16, 1957

Dear David:

Thanks for your good letter in response to my slightly confused and confusing one. I call it that because I was not very clearly focused on discussing your paper as a particular paper in my effort to be helpful in its revision, but let myself ramble over some of the issues that were touched on in it, and particularly in the first paragraph (the one you characterized as hammering on an open door). I was just talking out loud trying to pull together my own thoughts about some of these matters and re-stating some of your arguments for myself. Thus, I had no intention of accusing you of thinking that sensory deprivation would result in immediate destruction of structures; I only verbalized this for myself to bring it to mind that I had not made any provision for some continuing inner control. There is no "Vernon and Parry reference"; I was quoting from memory and trying to refer to the study by Hoffman and Vernon [1956]. I'm enclosing a little bibliography put together by Leo Goldberger, which contains this reference and others that you may not have run across.

I wasn't seriously suggesting that you try to abandon the "apparatus" terminology for this paper, but I did want to raise for our consideration the question of what this terminology implies. You're perfectly correct in saying that we have to consider also what would be implied by giving it up; this is something I certainly intend to do, but it is not easy nor the work of a few moments thought.

I realize that you did not define autonomy from the environment in the way I did at the bottom of my second page; this was a definition I was proposing (as the final phrase of that sentence showed). I recognize your right to define it as you yourself wish, but I would like for you to consider whether there might not be advantages to doing it my way. The main such advantage is that it focuses our attention on structural determinants of which it is otherwise easy to lose sight.

I was a little disappointed that you did not go into the issue of nutriment. It was afraid that you would recommend the study of Piaget—a task for which I have little time and little appetite, since I find Piaget such hard going. I suppose there is no escape from it, however. Even before I do that, however, I wonder if you could not comment on the issue I raised about nutriment versus external control. The critical question that I see here is: how can one distinguish between regressive and other effects due to a lack of nutriment and such effects when due to a failure of external control? I don't see how they can be distinguished, myself.

Thanks, I'm going to write to Merton and make another attempt to get some manuscripts from him.

I agree that it is quite a tricky matter to decide when a concept should be used causally and when discussion of that kind should be reserved for more elementary structures or processes to which something like identity might be reduced. I don't agree, however, that "the problem is: how identity itself is maintained." That is a problem, but my acquaintance with the brainwashing literature and related stuff convinces me that your statement, "it requires a high level stimulus input" will not hold up if you are using the word "stimulus input" in the way it seems that you are. The whole question of the proper definition of stimulus is a very tricky one in these deprivation studies, however. I still remain impressed by anecdotal accounts suggesting that when identity is firmly grounded and well built, it not only has extraordinary resistance to the most determined and ingenious efforts to tear it down, but that it does seem to serve as a protection against other kinds of functional losses. And structural losses too, perhaps I should add.

I certainly share your gently expressed judgment that my brainwashing paper is theoretically weak. I am pleased that you managed to get anything at all out of it, and was not surprised to learn of your disappointment. I think I could do a better job on the theoretical aspect of it now, and could have done better then; but you must remember that I was able to read your paper only the day before I gave my own, after it was all written, and that I was talking to a lay audience and so felt that it would be inappropriate to try to go more than quite superficially into the theory of the phenomena.

We had our [staff] discussion [of his draft on autonomy]—a rather confused and rambling one, out of which I don't think anything much came that will be helpful to you. I'm enclosing a copy of the minutes of this meeting [not preserved] that were taken by one of our research assistants. The main thing I got out of this discussion was a realization (if I may use that term) that the concept of autonomy is not in itself an explanatory one with much "real metapsychological status." I feel even more strongly about autonomy than I do about identity that it is a descriptive term summarizing a set of more specific considerations, which are the ones metapsychology needs to deal with.

I'm sorry that I was not able to digest your paper with a more positive attitude, but you must remember that I wrote you about the few points of disagreement or the points on which I was unclear, rather than about the great body of the paper, which I found helpful and useful.

We will not have a further discussion of the paper until the new version arrives, though we only began to get into it last time. Do you suppose that you could again send a least a dozen copies so that we could all read it? More important, would you consider coming down to meet with our group and discuss it after we have had a chance to read it? We would of course pay your travel expenses and a consultation fee. You may know that Peter Wolff is coming in a few weeks to talk with us about Piaget; I'm looking forward to that quite eagerly. Our group is thirsting eagerly for theoretical knowledge and stimulation, but they raise difficult basic questions that go beyond George's or my capacity to deal with effectively and which make me long to have you on hand to clear things up.

I spent two nights the early part of this week completely absorbed in Alger Hiss' book, In the Court of Public Opinion.[129] I found it fascinating in a blood curdling kind of way, and I am convinced that he is the victim of a monstrous miscarriage of justice. I strongly recommend the book and hope that it will get the widest possible reading.

Yesterday I had a letter from Morton Levitt, inviting me to contribute to the book he is editing, Readings in Psychoanalytic Psychology [Levitt, 1959]. He mentions your name among a list of excellent looking contributors; what are you going to give him? He asks me to submit a paper "which would deal with the relationship between psychiatric theory and projective techniques." I imagine that "psychiatric" is a slip and he means psychoanalytic; but I am not terribly eager to write on just that topic, even though I would like to be in the book. I have been wanting to try to review the theory of primary and secondary process and try to develop some ideas about it that are kicking around in the back of my head; do you think that would be an appropriate topic for me to suggest?

With warm regards from Crusa and myself—

Bob

---

[129] New York: Knopf, 1957. Hiss was a neighbor whom I knew slightly, living in the same New York apartment building. That disposed me to give him the benefit of doubt.

Holt to Rapaport—October 21, 1957

Dear David,

I spent some pleasant and fruitful hours over the weekend reading and ruminating about your paper, Psychoanalysis and Developmental Psychology [1960].[130] I may say, first of all, that it made an immensely better impression on me reading it than it did when I heard it. Indeed, I'm a little puzzled by this discrepancy, and am at a loss to understand why it was so hard to absorb by ear, except for the fact that it was so long. But it reads well and makes a solid contribution.

I am sending back the copy, because I made quite a number of minor editorial suggestions, which are most easily conveyed in that way. I want to take up some other, more extensive, points now, in no particular order.

To begin with, your concept of "intrinsic developmental factor" is one that is central to a good deal of the argument, yet it is undefined and its meaning is not obvious to me. It's true I have a rather vague idea, derived from a couple of readings of the paper itself, of what it is you're getting at, but I think you owe your reader something more than that. Thus, it is not immediately clear how drive is such a factor.

At the top of page 4, you speak about Freud's idea of the relationship between instinct and intelligence; this is very interesting,

---

[130] The paper was published in Kaplan & Werner (1960), after a number of further revisions. See also Gill, Chap. 64.

and an important idea, but I wouldn't know where to go in Freud to find what he has to say along these lines. Could you add references? (preferably rather specific ones).

Much of the argument raises the question in my mind of just what audience you intend the paper for. Brewster Smith tells me that you have submitted it to him and has asked me for a copy of these comments, which I told him I was writing to you. I don't feel at all certain in my judgment of these matters, but I have the feeling that a large proportion of readers of the Journal of Abnormal and Social Psychology would find much of what you say unconvincing. In large part, it seems to be written for psychoanalysts. Now I know that you should not be expected to take on the task of educating all of your readers in psychoanalysis if they haven't read Freud, but you should think about the question of what the paper's impact is likely to be if in fact most of the people who encounter it have a skepticism about psychoanalysis that is in large part compounded of ignorance. When you speak of drive as an a priori organizer of experience, for example, many of these readers are very likely to think that this means that Freud espoused a theory of innate ideas and behavior patterns—instinct in a certain naive sense.

This brings up considerations of a somewhat political kind, really. If Brewster wants to make a point with the publication of a theoretical article by you, and if you want to say something to an audience of psychologists, then I think it would be better done by a paper that presupposed less intimate familiarity with psychoanalytic theory. If it were a choice between this paper and nothing, then I would say let's do whatever is possible to make this paper suitable. I'm not sure that I can think of another one that would be more meet, but how about your paper on Hartmann and Erikson [Gill, Chap. 58]? Or even the new autonomy paper [Gill, Chap. 57]. You see, this present paper could go into an analytic journal with very little work done on it, but it would hardly be fair to the journal, its readers, or yourself to print it substantially as it stands in the Journal of Abnormal and Social Psychology.

On page 5, I feel that you make the genetic method look a good deal easier and more trouble-free than it is. You don't mention the fact that it depends on the process of interpretation, which has never been proved to be reliable as between different interpreters.

I wonder if the section on the ego as an intrinsic developmental drive-restraining factor wouldn't be stronger if you bring in the idea of intelligence as an innate, maturing set of capacities. I think it might be worth describing in some detail how the development of intelligence serves to restrain drives, since this proposition will be novel to some readers. Incidentally, it strikes me as rather remarkable that stimulus-response theories, to my knowledge, take no systematic account of intelligence, as they take no account either of the dual nature of mental functioning; and learning theories of the Hullian kind have no systematic place for intelligence.

On page 8, and in general throughout, I had a slightly uneasy feeling that you seemed to be overplaying the degree of corroboration of psychoanalytic theory. You have certainly collected some interesting and instructive parallels, which do much to support the idea of convergence, but I feel unsure that it is safe to say that they corroborate psychoanalytic theory.

Would it be possible to add, in a paragraph or two, a brief statement of what the "developmental matrix" is for the theories of Piaget, Werner, and Hebb? I don't know any of those theories well enough to be able to say what it is, and it would increase the value of the paper to me to have that information included.[131]

On the back of page 12, I scrawled the following note: it seems weak to say that the conception of development as consisting of a series of phases has been corroborated. That is hardly more than a matter of definition: anything that changes can be described as going through phases. The reader is likely to say, so what?[132]

I liked very much your resolution of the troubling peripheralism

---

[131] The concept of developmental matrix does not appear in the published paper.
[132] This is an issue I considered in more detail some years later (Holt, 1998).

of the drive theory in the Three Contributions [Freud, 1905], at the bottom of page 14.

I liked very much the summary of ethology in the next section, and the convergences cited are impressive indeed. But in view of the fact that ethologists work with infrahuman animals, and particularly because of Hartmann's persuasive arguments about the differences between human and animal instinct, it seems too much to say that ethology corroborates psychoanalysis. Rather, I would say that its findings parallel those of psychoanalysis. To some degree the parallel may make the analytic theory more plausible, but strictly speaking all of the relevant propositions would have to be established independently on human beings.

Parenthetically, let me explain that I converted your word "commonalities" on page 25 to "common elements" because of the fact that you mean the latter and the English word commonality does not have this meaning; its closest meaning is "generality." I know that psychologists increasingly talk this way, but what they are doing is adopting factor analytic jargon and by analogy extending the use of the word commonality in a way that the dictionaries haven't caught up with yet. It's the kind of unnecessary polysyllabic jargon that makes psychology so difficult for the outsider.

When we come to the third part, I am less happy with the paper. To begin with, it does not seem to me much of a victory that other evidence confirms the general idea that secondary process develops out of primary process. Surely this was not an empirical study [i.e., finding] of Freud's, it was merely his conceptualization of something "discovered" long before and generally known from common sense, that children are less sensible than adults, that undeveloped peoples (of former eras or of uncivilized parts of the world) are more superstitious and less rational than educated men [persons!] in high civilizations. What Freud did was to produce a conceptualization of grand sweep and simplicity, which ordered all these observations together with those he had made of neurosis, dream, and fantasy— and to relate these conceptualized phenomena to his metapsychology, particularly the cathectic dynamics and economics. What is "corroborated" by the studies you cite is that primitive, childish, and magical ways of thinking give way to rational and realistic ones not in a saltatory but in a gradual, evolving way. Freud's dichotomous concepts if anything tend to obscure this continuity. Your statement on page 35 almost reduces to the absurdity: "Freud discovered that adult thinking emerges from childish thinking, and the independent observations of other thinkers corroborate him."

I doubt that "the study of myths, philosophies, and the origins of sciences is a promising method for the investigation of the development of the secondary process."[133] It teaches us how these thought products develop, but does that enable us to reason directly to the changes in the producing processes? An affirmative answer seems dangerous to me, because (a) the transitions to the thought products of one era to those of another are interindividual (whereas those in ontogeny are intra-individual) and (b) such products—even primitive myths—are the work of adult intelligences, which have perforce learned to deal with reality by the very virtue of their survival. In the individual, however, his first primary processes are the work of an intellect that has had only a few skirmishes with reality. The myth-makers and their successors all had fully-developed synthetic, organizing powers and were relatively free of difficulty in maintaining the constancy of ideas; so the evolutions that took place were from one reasonably stable system of ideas to another, and such changes could proceed by processes like the examination of internal consistency, which may be beyond the individual child. Thus, such studies would probably have never led Piaget to some of the discoveries he made from direct work with children, though it was possible for him, after the fact, to trace resemblances.

Another reason I found the final section disappointing was that it does not live up to its advance billing (page 1, where you

---

[133] The passage does not appear in the final form of the paper. This is one of several ways in which Rapaport accepted my suggestions.

say that you are going to "try to clarify the developmental relation of awe to thought"—it merely reiterates that one precedes the other). It remains unclear to me why you chose to emphasize the notion of awe, which appears dragged in by the heels and distracting. Perhaps you could have made the points that one is a feeling of fear and wonder, containing (at least implicitly) a desire to understand as well as an attitude of humility—and this gnostic component is the germ of the secondary process and its propulsive force. Awe in the face of the universe implies first an extensive knowledge (compared to that of the infant) about natural phenomena, an hypothesis that there is order of some type underlying or contained in them, and an implied wish to find and state the principles of that order. By such an argument, the system-building, rationalizing (and thus concept-forming) aspect of the secondary process grows out of an emotional root.—But as I read you, you only hint at all this, and I am not sure even that it is what you mean. Maybe it [an explanation] was in the first, long draft, and you overlooked the fact that you deleted it.

Page 35, last paragraph: I don't see that you have shown how Freud's methods of investigation and theory building are in agreement with those of developmental psychology. You have shown convergences and similarities between other bodies of knowledge and psychoanalysis, in the theories themselves but not in the methods either of observation or of theory-building. Thus, the similarities between theoretical propositions of psychoanalysis and ethology are striking, but the methods of the two sciences are at least superficially different. At least, you have not stressed the similarities of method (which could be done), nor is it necessary to your argument.

On page 36, your summing up (first paragraph) doesn't quite accord with the emphasized points in the body of the paper, and includes as a "basic concept" a method—the genetic approach, which is surely not a basic concept.

I still fail to see what the great contribution of Totem and Taboo was to developmental psychology. The concept of the two processes and the development of one from the other was given in the Interpretation of Dreams; the notion of societal and cultural evolution, the growth of civilized conceptions from primitive ones was at least sketched out by the first social Darwinists (e.g., [Herbert] Spencer). On rereading, I wonder if your point is not that Freud espoused the idea that the primary process may produce a system of thought, a world view, and that this system-building aspect is what develops the secondary process (compare the sociological concept of "the strain toward consistency"—[Max] Weber?) but this seems to me a matter of definition again. I'd prefer to point to the existence of such a tendency as evidence that one aspect of the secondary process develops early and autonomously, being akin to the notion of inborn ego-rudiments. It remains essentially unexplained where this rationalizing tendency comes from and how it grows; it is clearly a prime constituent of intelligence, one of the unique features of human as opposed to animal intelligence, and surely related to the capacity for abstraction, true symbolic thinking, and concept formation. Simply to say that it is part of the primary process, and thus that the secondary develops from the primary process, seems to me a rather arbitrary and empty feat, one that is perhaps based on failure to remember that secondary process is an abstract, idealized concept, as is primary process. Thus, all of what exists in the thinking of children, savages, and madmen is not primary process, any more than it is true to maintain that scientists use the secondary process exclusively. And therefore, the germ of the secondary process in the system-building aspect of childish and primitive thought is not ipso facto primary process. Freud saw this clearly in the realm of dreams; thus, secondary elaboration (or secondary revision) was not considered an aspect of the primary process, but a rudiment of secondary process invading the dream work. But this is the very same aspect of thought that transforms simple fantasies into a connected sequence of myths forming an implicit cosmology.

The procedure of putting this synthetic function into the definition of the primary process merely postpones and conceals the real problem of how the primary process develops into the secondary process. Maybe the answer is that the germs of the secondary process exist independently from the beginning, as apparatuses of primary autonomy, and although they are concealed by the prevalence of primary process and seem to be its handmaidens at first, merely spinning it into impressive products of the imagination, they ultimately have to renounce this original alliance—their inner logic forces the development of a system of logical rational thought. The latter should no more be identified with secondary process than dreams, fantasies or other productions of the primary process should be identified with it; that would be methodological empiricism, or hypostasis.[134] Instead, we should recognize clearly that these products are the operational base on which the abstract conceptual structure of the theory of primary and secondary process is built, and the latter are intervening variables, not observables.

Please bear with me if I charge through open doors in some of this last; I got going and wanted to get down some of these thoughts. I hope, anyway, that this makes it clear why I can't follow the argument of the third section as well as the first two. [. . .]

Cordially,

Bob

---

[134] I should have said "the fallacy of misplaced concreteness."

Rapaport to Holt—October 23, 1957

Dear Bob,

We have just hung up and I have written to Smith.

Let me say this: if you'd have submitted a paper somewhere and I would have been asked to advise on it and I would have felt the way you did ('that is not the place for the paper')—I'd have certainly first called you up and given you a chance to explain <u>why</u> you submitted it and to convince me that I am wrong, or else to give you a chance to withdraw it before I transmitted my criticisms which I was asked for.

I realize that this is a matter of temperament, I realize also that mutual relationships of such long standing as ours have complexities, particularly when one is in the process of reviewing one's relationships. <u>But</u>: were it not that I have known you long, feel respect and fondness for you, and trust you, I would not have been able to find this amusing like a <u>slip</u>, but would have taken it as an <u>action</u> and not one of a friendly sort.

I write this so that when we meet we do not have to go over it. Naturally, if you will feel like going over it, I shall not object.

       With best regards

       David

Holt to Brewster Smith—October 24, 1957

TO: Dr. M. Brewster Smith
FROM: Robert R. Holt
SUBJECT: Rapaport's paper on developmental psychology

Dear Brewster:

   I'm sorry about having to recall the copy of the letter; after I sent it to you, I realized that the tone of the whole letter was too personal and much of its contents too private for it to be appropriate for me simply to send you a carbon.

   Let me tell you more directly my thoughts about the suitability of this paper for the Journal of Abnormal and Social. When I first thought about it, somehow I completely overlooked your statement to me that Dr. Rapaport had said that he would want to spend eight or nine months revising it, and I thought about it in terms of the suitability as it stands. That was a rather stupid lapse on my part, and the fact that the paper as it stands doesn't strike me as suitable in level of sophistication in psychoanalytic theory presupposed for the reader, is irrelevant. I am sure that, if he wanted to, Dr. Rapaport could rework this paper in a way that would communicate adequately with our readers. As I told him, however, in a telephone conversation, my feeling is that it would take more work than would probably be worthwhile.

   I hope that you won't be discouraged by two false starts, and that you will still give a friendly hearing to a theoretical paper from Dr. Rapaport. I hope to get a chance to discuss with him a little bit in the near future what sort of papers might be most appropriate for this purpose.

Cordially,

Robert R. Holt

cc: Dr. David Rapaport

Rapaport to Holt—October 29, 1957

Dear Bob:

I was very sorry that you and Crusa couldn't make it here Saturday. It was a very nice evening. I missed you and you would have enjoyed it.

I received a copy of the letter you wrote to Smith. I want to make two points clear: 1) I had nothing to do with your decision to ask your letter back from him. When you brought up this idea in our telephone conversation I refused to entertain it. My reason was that it would have used our personal relationship to induce you to doing something which cuts into one's pride. I rather chose to withdraw the paper, than to do that. 2) I want you to remember that over and above this whole issue I appreciated your letter. I thought that all of its <u>specific</u> points were correct and helpful. The disagreement was over the major points and chiefly over the conclusions you drew from them. Frankly, I feel rather proud that my friends do not mince words with me and feel free to dish it out and to pull no punches. Let me assure you that in my revision of the paper most of your points will find their reflection. Please give my best to Crusa and I hope by now you are well.

       Yours,

         David

Summary—Brief Letters from 1957

On February 26, I asked Rapaport's opinion about publishing a brief account of the main findings of the Selection Project in a psychological journal (cf. Luborsky & Holt, 1957). Nothing seems to have come of it. The next day, he sent some information about a possible job for Crusa.

A note from Sue Annin on April 23 asked for any final input to the Koch monograph (I did not have any). A week later I sent a postcard about George's search for a reference, and on May 14 another brief letter about personal matters. In that I said I was sending a long version of my own review of Colby's 1955 book (Holt, 1956b), adding:

> It's not altogether clear to me what you mean by "he did not lis-
> ten to psa. metapsychology"—just that he does not have an
> expert familiarity with it? If he commits any real blunders in this
> respect, I failed to find them, but since my grasp of metapsychol-
> ogy is very far from expert I wouldn't expect to.

In a May 21 letter, Rapaport continued the discussion of autonomy and nutriment briefly. He expressed disappointment about Morton Levitt's (1959) proposed book, and said he was withdrawing his own paper. I had been considering reviewing the theory of primary and secondary process for that book; he suggested that I write it first and then think about where to publish it. This letter contains the first reference to George's plans for the *Psychological Issues* monograph series. Then, after an expression of regret about Robert W. White's "excursions into Adlerism," came these words:

Bob, I hope that we do not build walls between ourselves by bluntly talking out about weakness in each others' papers. I want you to be blunt with mine and I will be blunt with yours or [there] will be nothing. For all that, I am not sure but that you are right about autonomy and about identity that they really are in a sense descriptive terms. Yet the term descriptive does not quite apply because there lies in these terms a true amount of generalization which ties many phenomena together and allows the field to be mapped out. This is somehow different than your description. I wished I knew precisely how it is different.

He ended with thanks for calling the Alger Hiss book to his attention; he will read it despite some reluctance.

My letter of July 2 reported "a brief visit from Peter Wolff, who gave an excellent talk to our staff on Piaget. . . . I think I understand a number of issues better now." Then hopes for a staff discussion with Rapaport on the new autonomy paper, and summer plans. I reported gossip from Topeka about imminent departures:

The Menningers' talent for finding good men is surpassed only by their capacity to drive them away. . . . They are so threatened whenever someone begins to emerge as a potential successor that they manage to get rid of him, though it is perfectly obvious that the long-range health of the institution demands they train someone to follow in their footsteps.

Paul Bergman was leaving, too, for Bethesda: "What a buoyant soul he is, and how attractive it is to see such mature wisdom combined with the ability to bounce gaily back after a series of harsh blows!" Else Frenkel Brunswik told me she might go there too. A brief report about the commemoration of the Harvard Psychological Clinic's founding and a forthcoming tribute to Murray, to which I hoped Rapaport would contribute. Finally some words about a reading course in metapsychology with "Sheldon Bach, one of our best assistants. . . . It's quite a splendid experience to see a first-rate young mind coming to grips for the first time with a set of important ideas and getting really excited by them."

A quick response from Rapaport on July 8, after acknowledging a week's illness, commented positively on all the above topics. "If the two years Wolff and I put in on [Piaget] will serve to loosen up the . . . lack of understanding, then we will have done something which should have a remaining impact. You might think that I could have spent my time better, but in my own self appraisal this is good enough a 'midwife' job."

He then asked my help in starting his paper "about genetic psychology and Freud," to be given at Clark University:

> What kind of books and papers am I supposed to know about ge-
> netic psychology besides Werner. . . What are the principles of . . .
> developmental study? How does it differ from simply historical
> study? How does it differ from study in terms of learning. . .? [. . .] I
> would very much like to hear your opinion on it and hear what I
> should cover if I want to give a picture on present day develop-
> mental psychology or genetic psychology and Freud, and both
> Freud's influence on it and a comparison of Freud's genetic psy-
> chology with present day genetic psychology.

Finally, he recounted having finished a seminar for the Western New England Psychoanalytic Institute on "Advanced Metapsychology," as well as an elementary one, both of which would be transcribed. (I was later to profit greatly from studying these and all of his other transcribed seminars on psychoanalytic theory.)

The letter ended with thanks for my first comments about his Activity-Passivity manuscript, and upbeat comments about the work of several mutual friends: "quite a few things ripening."

My response a couple of weeks later sent my regrets about not to be able to help with the Clark paper, genetic psychology being "an area in which my own ignorance is vast," but hopes to see him in September.

A note from Rapaport on August 1 sent along some textual corrections for Leo Goldberger's thesis outline. My reply at the end of the month reported three wonderful weeks with my daughters in Hawaii, then addressed his review of Bruner et al. (1956), with a few stylistic suggestions, and this comment: "Why do you suppose Piaget went overboard so enthusiastically for this book? Is it perhaps because he is out of touch with the issues of method in terms of which this work seems to be so fallible? I hope you will send a copy of your review to him."

A brief exchange of notes in September regretted missing one another and anticipated Crusa's and my visit to Worcester to hear the developmental paper.

Finally, a Christmas card reported the good news from Crusa and me: "We're getting married on Dec. 27! Another proof that analysis does some good."

CHAPTER 8

Rapaport to Holt—January 15, 1958

[handwritten]

Dear Bob and Crusa,

First of all let me, for all four of us, wish you the best, much happiness and contentment, to your marriage. For myself, it is a special pleasure to have the news of your decision; I have thought that you are two people who can go and grow coming closer together and likely more than the average to avoid both boredom and estrangement which dog so many of the marriages we see. To many, avoiding these pits is a task to be faced when time and again it is skirted and it is a noble one: but you may not even find it to be a task, since you enter it as mature people.

This note is so late because we found it here on our return from the Caribbean where we spent 3 weeks on Grand Caiman. It was sun, bathing, beach, storm: refreshing.

[...]

Before vacation I worked with Merton 9 days and we hammered out a workable draft of our "Reassessment of Metapsychology." [First draft of Rapaport & Gill, 1959] After some polishing I'll send it along. We are rather pleased with it. Now we have to get a short version (this is 45 pages) for presentation at NY. Psa. Soc. in March. At the same time, I have the job of the last smoothings of the Shakow-Rapaport [1964], which is growing to a monograph's dimension.

Finally, let me thank you for both of us, for the lovely gift book you sent: it is a pleasure to see and handle.

Best wishes to the New Year
David.

PS. Enclosed the paper just published [Rapaport, 1958, in first issue of *Bulletin of the Menninger Clinic, 22,* 13–25.]

Rapaport to Holt—January 22, 1958

Dear Bob:

First of all, many thanks for your comments on the Miller controversy.[135] I am awaiting Mert's and George's reactions and I have already here Roy's which is quite a bit more critical of me than yours. He actually makes several of the points you have made in your original letter of [on] my review. It is so good to have friends, and in a moment of quandary when one's inner mirror is rippled, the mirrors they hold up to you are invaluable. But don't misunderstand me, all this is only the external indication of how much they have become for you part of your inner mirror, otherwise you couldn't possibly look into the mirrors that they hold up to you at such moments and see in a meaningful way what you yourself are doing.

From the formal point of view my main comment goes in a way without saying, since this is a first draft of your review:[136] it is diffuse and thus is not focused. Likewise, your phrase in your letter "purple passages" obviates the necessity to criticize these. Yet I have marked a few of them which jarred me particularly: "human interest," "hair-raising," "profoundly sustaining," "commendable," "rejoicing." Some of these are simply purple as you realize, others

---

[135] See discussion of letters of January 15, 16, and 17 in Summary.

[136] Rapaport here abruptly turns to comments on my review of Jones's biography of Freud, Vol. III (Holt, 1958), a draft of which I had just sent him. Most of his subsequent discussion deals with the entire three volumes, however.

are "hackneyed" and you need to penetrate them all again to dis-cover the real thought and feeling that you meant to convey.

The very first paragraph raises the question what is so impres-sive about this book. I think that your last sentence says it: it is indeed hard to imagine a psychologist, psychoanalyst or any oth-er really sensitive human being who would not profit by it. But why? Here I think I find you only partially correct and somewhat diffuse. As I see it, you are right on two points: the massive chron-icle of facts, many of them insufficiently and some of them altogether not known; and secondly what you called "human in-terest," and which if penetrated will, I guess, boil down to the struggles of life of a unique human being. As for the exhaustive summary and appraisal of the entire scientific output, while it is indeed a staggering job, in a sense I feel that it is neither fish nor fowl. Too technical and yet in a way deceptively simple for the lay reader, and of too little penetration to be—what it gives the im-pression of being—"definitive." And yet you may be right, we ought to be grateful for it because there is nothing like it extant. This is a moot point. I myself think that Jones has tried too much. I wish I could compare it in a leisurely way to other "life and works" to see how it would stack up against them. It seems to me that without such an empirical approach we are really left without a measuring rod.

Now let me come back to the two points on which I agreed because there I see also the main deficiencies of the book. Just like I wonder whether the summaries of the work he gave with their pretensions of "definitiveness" are the real thing, I am also wondering whether the chronological impression of "exhaustive-ness" is real or illusory. I wonder first of all whether "life" is to be such a chronology. You touch on this matter in both of its facets. On page 4, the third paragraph unequivocally accepts Jones' claim. As I indicated, I consider this to be a moot point. But in the second par-agraph, particularly towards the end of it, on page 7 you take more of a view like mine concerning the "life"; you say that you ex-pected from Jones, the psychoanalyst, an interpretation. I think that while this implies the same criticism as mine, I would not have put it this way. I would say that I would not have minded interpretations if they fulfill certain criteria.

What criteria? To my mind a "life" of a man requires a certain kind of writing which should not and must not be replaced either by "chronology" however exhaustive, nor by "psychoanalytic interpretations" however cogent. I would not have minded a section here or there akin to sections of Erik's review of the Fliess letters or of his Erma dream paper, or of his "The First Psychoanalyst" which deals with Freud's personality. But these would have had to fit in a framework of events of Freud's life so told as to let the personality emerge through the telling. Interpretation as well as chronology can easily interfere with this. Let me say that the very fact that at the end of the second volume Jones found himself constrained to insert a chapter "Character and Personality" is the best testimony to his failure in this respect and reflects best what I feel is missing. If you read carefully this chapter (Vol. 2 chapter 16) then you will see that in it he selects "traits" and gives examples for them, but cannot reach any integration. Perhaps only the discussion of "credulity," or should we call it "gullibility," has something about it which does not stay on one level but somehow vertically plumbs the relationships between interpersonal relations, personal characteristics, creativity, etc. How any of the characteristics of Freud really hang together and how he makes sense as a human being you do not get from Jones. And this is where the criticism of the second point on which I agreed with you ("human interest") comes in: it seems to me that it is the lure of the unique personality, Freud, which you labeled with that term and which penetrates in spite of Jones rather than because of him. It seems to me that towards the end of the first paragraph on page 8 you come to this criticism. Likewise in the second paragraph on page 8 you try, only too briefly, to make up for what Jones failed in. I really don't think that the review can do so. In a way you continue doing the same thing in the third paragraph on page 9.

Before I go on to other matters I would say that the last sentence of the review really sets the spirit and tone of your review. I don't think it is worked out in the review but I do sense that this is the intrinsic message throughout it and I think it is a fine one, one of the crucial ones and I am glad with your choice. I will have soon to say a number of things about it to show how Jones failed us in this respect. I think in the paragraph which goes from page 8 to 9, but particularly in its beginning you come closest to hitting a tone homogeneous with that very last sentence.

Now back once more to the criticism which I just abandoned. Let me add that your quandary in the first big paragraph on page 6 seems to me to corroborate and find its resolution in the very point I tried to state. The trouble is not simply that Jones was hero-worshiping, or that he did not include negative facts concerning Freud (you stated correctly that this is not the case). The trouble to my mind is that these things are not brought to a relationship to each other. I tried to point out how different it looks where such a relating is attempted, as for instance when he talks about Freud's credulity and [quotes]"Strachey" on it. But even on that point he remains limited and does not explore it in full scope.

I couldn't agree more than I do with the big paragraph going from page 6 to 7. Both his obtruding himself on us continually, particularly in the second volume, and his attitude towards the members of the committee, which you characterize cogently and very briefly, are points which struck me forcibly. But it seems to me that they really show how Jones failed to write a "life."

Did he try anywhere really to envisage how people must have felt in relation to a man who started out on something which opened up their imagination, provided them with a goal in life (ideology) which they could devote themselves to, who plumbed depths with a zest so that he must have been experienced by them to be always many steps ahead of them, in relation to whose system—which was never systematically stated—they found themselves necessitated to state the fruits of their own imagination and observation, in relation to a man who "needed them" but who was sufficiently independent of needing them only "sub specie" of the common scientific ideal, etc., etc. Do we see Adler, Stekel and Jung arising this way? Do we see Abraham, Jones, Rank and Sachs arising this way? Do we see Ferenczi arising this way?

Is all this ever clearly related to and elucidated in the light of the fact that he quotes repeatedly, namely that Freud felt strongly that he himself can evaluate ideas with a reasonable speed only if they are his own, and that in relation to others, since his system provided little checking opportunity, he had to be slow and uncertain? Why aren't we told directly that he tried to trust and accept all new ideas within this limitation, and he tried to separate personal relationships from theoretical or ideological diversions and succeeded in doing so again and again at least for a while, but not in the final analysis; and do we find the question raised, who could have, under these conditions, managed longer? Do we find it elucidated what Binswanger[137] has so strikingly shown and what in the first letter in the appendix of the third volume is illustrated, namely that all young people could count on his good will and encouragement, even—as Binswanger points out—a bit beyond absolute factual proof that Freud had as to their worthwhileness or the worthwhileness of their ideas: do we find it elucidated that therein lies an identification with this young man and the feeling that the trust given to him when he was young by people like Breuer and others indeed in a sense engendered his creative potential? Do we see all this related to his greater wish to have friends than to be the sole source of new discoveries? Do we see the man's struggle between trying to distinguish between what is a new contribution of his friends and what he would want to see, as marvelous, and what is no factual contribution? Do we see the

---

[137] Ludwig Binswanger (1881–1966), a prominent Swiss psychiatrist and lifelong friend of Freud's, contributed to a Festschrift in honor of Freud's 80th birthday (Binswanger, 1936), which I have not been able to read, but seems the likely source of this description of Freud.

gullibility involved in all this and its relation to a man's feeling this way in a new field that he discovered but has not mapped completely?

I don't know whether I am making it plausible to you, what I have in mind here. But I think that you can see that these are human terms with which you and I and you and George and Roy and I and the rest of us are familiar out of our personal experience and which makes immediate human sense though it is not burdened down by chronology nor achieved by "interpretation." This is the stratum between data and interpretation which I think a "life" has to strike. It has been [i.e., would be] written in general human terms which are familiar to man, quite aside from any interpretation, and which can be documented by chronology but cannot be replaced by chronology, though it can be destroyed by overemphasis on such chronology.

The trouble here is something on which you touched when you spoke about the literary style of Jones. He just simply is not a writer. He did not use the prerogative and did not accept the duties of a writer: to create a living organism out of the dead data. I think one of the fallacies in the whole thing was that these data are not all dead, and [the?] man's grandeur and suffering and human failings were still all too alive in the documents for Jones and he thought that he will "let them speak." Well, they do speak fragmentarily, but they do not speak on the whole.

Another one of my pet peeves about this whole biography is that it is so complete in its appearance and weighty that one is never sure how Jones has selected. Again you have touched on this several times under the heading of Jones' credibility. But beyond the credibility there is the question of the selection principle, which does not emerge. You asked for the statement of "limitations" and I think that behind that the question is the same: how was this selection made? Why does he have to assert simply that Mrs. Freud was such a marvelous woman and the relationship was marvelous? Why do not some events and data speak about that? Why do we not learn anything about what the relationship to Minna

Bernays was? I don't have in mind here the silly gossip, nor Bettelheim's [1957] pointed (bull in the china shop) question. I am willing to believe that this unusual man had a purely Platonic relationship with this woman. But what was the relationship like? Why did he find it so interesting to be so much with her, his sister-in-law? I can well understand that Anna Freud still living would make it difficult to state that [i.e., discuss] the relationship to her, but why can't he have a few real elucidating anecdotes which would have shed light on this? Why is there no word about the character of the relationship to Hartmann, when we are told that he was one of the favorites? Why not anything about Kris? And if he has none of that, why not—as you put it—state directly the reason?

Another one of my pet peeves is that it is quite impossible to get a picture of this man if—as Jones gives none—one has no picture of the social, political, economic, cultural atmosphere of the Austro-Hungarian monarchy and of Victorian Vienna in particular. How can a life be without that? How can it be human without that?

I think that for the moment, I will let this be all. I wish that you would take all this as nothing else but an attempt to underscore some of your points in a fashion which might serve to indicate relationships between these points, in the hope that you will mold your review so that it be focused on a few points or on a few points and their corollaries and let it not remain diffused. I would not want you to understand my letter as urging you to adopt my views on it, though any that you would adopt would be no more than a strengthening of one or the other points you have anyway made somewhere. Nor would I want you to understand that I would like you to make a scathing criticism of Jones. I think I will do that anyway probably, after he is dead, in a very long discussion of these books. I think that the man was struggling to get finished before the bell tolled for him and I think I would myself want to respect that limitation imposed by life (and death), though I would have liked it much better if the man would have said so directly. I mean to say, if the man would have seen his limitations as he does not seem to. If I have any wish, I would wish that you characterize the book as what it is and what it does for us and distinguish if from what it does not do. I think this is what you tried to do and I am trying to sharpen the point and this is the process—insofar as I can—of your molding this into a focused, clear, easily surveyable review.

My best to you,

David

Rapaport to Martin Mayman—
January 28, 1958

Note

This letter to Martin Mayman was contained both in my and the Library of Congress's collection. It is an example of Rapaport's custom of occasionally sending copies of letters from, and his replies to, third parties to a small group of his friends who would be interested in the issues discussed in them.

Dear Marty:

Finally, after working in San Francisco with Merton, after a vacation of three weeks in the Caribbean, and after catching up with things and polishing up the first draft of the paper on metapsychology which I finally completed with Merton after five years of batting it about, I got around to reading your material.

Let me say, first of all, that I was very gratified with the quality of writing, on which I would like to compliment you strongly and warmly. One can't write this way if one did not reach a maturity and security in some segment of one's understandings. Let me also say that the problem you had set for yourself interested me very much, and so did the test concerning early memories and the image association test. You might be surprised with my ignorance, but I heard these only mentioned and never saw them discussed or used. Indeed, I would be hard put telling who initiated these. Won't you let me know? The use you make of them seems to me also impressive.

Now on the critical side, since this is probably what you want to hear from me. My main complaint would be that you did not so far digest Erikson's concept of ego identity, nor the self concept as it is being cooked up by Hartmann [1950] and Jacobson [1954]. Now do not take these tragically, because I must admit that I did not quite digest them either. I am just one jump ahead of you, just enough to be able to tell you that you did not digest them. Let me say, however, that I realize that you started the research project clearly indicating that you want to chew through the literature yourself and one of the aims of the project is to give you an opportunity for doing that simultaneously with gathering empirical material. May I suggest that the ego psychology seminar transcript and the just finished advanced metapsychology seminar transcript, both of them edited by Stuart C. Miller, have attempted to come to grips with this problem. I must admit freely that they did so not quite successfully. The limitation was partly that of seminar time and partly limitation of insight. These abstractions are too new to master and to make abstractions from them which bring [approach?] them on the same level, or to the same common denominator. I would strongly advise you to try to get some help (no solution or answer, only help) from reading these. I am reasonably sure that if you write to Miller he will supply you with them, though regrettably only at self [i.e., our] cost. These are so expensive that we cannot possibly begin to give them away, even to the closest circle.[138]

Let me say a few words about them here only: if you would have come to grips with Erikson's ego identity concept, then your material would reflect that this concept is a psychosocial concept and is not discussible without the social and ideological problems. It is a kind of integration of impulses, defenses, identification, role identifications, occupational role identifications (in this respect, Kai Erikson's [1957] paper in one of the recent issues of Psychiatry may be enlightening) in such a way as to fit into a social niche. For

---

[138] Happily, I was able to buy and study all of Rapaport's transcribed lectures.

example, when you discuss your case of the nurse, the nurse's role would not appear alone in terms of a defense position, but it would also appear as a fitting of a social niche compatible with the [i.e., her] impulse-defense balance, schooling and experience, self-estimate, intellectual capacities, special skills, activity-passivity balance in the sense that the give and take balance is tilted to the "giving" end. Moreover, it must be pointed out that in this activity-passivity balance, in the self-estimate I referred to, and in several other of these facets, this social niche satisfies superego requirements also. Finally, I have to point out that it is insufficient to say that the basic impulse-defense balance finds expression in this occupational choice. It must be pointed out that the higher level derivative or autonomous motivations, for instance those for tenderness, as well as for other higher order correspondents of sexual motivations, aggressive and dominance motivations, all must be simultaneously fitted by the social niche which in this case is that of the nurse.

Let me apply this [approach] to what you say about the "transference paradigm." The reason this patient behaves towards the doctor like a nurse, reporting about another person, is only in the broadest sense a transference phenomenon. Only in the sense of paratactic[139] relation to other people, and not in the classical sense. Now please don't take this as a criticism, but rather as a clarification. I hold no belief for what should or should not be called transference. I hold a belief for clarity in this respect. There

---

[139] Rapaport did not intend the usage in linguistics but that of Harry Stack Sullivan, a psychoanalyst whom he rarely quoted and of whom he had, at best, an ambivalent opinion. That founder of interpersonal psychoanalysis substituted for Freud's binary classification of modes of thinking into primary and secondary processes, the three concepts of prototaxis, parataxis, and syntaxis. I believe that Rapaport recognized the value of distinguishing preverbal, incommunicable vagueness, plus inability to follow the rules of ordinary thought and language (the prototaxic level), from parataxic distortions of the kind Freud emphasized in discussing the disordered cognitive functioning in dreaming and schizophrenia. Syntaxic experiences can be accurately conveyed to others in language, a concept that largely overlaps with the secondary process. Both spellings, *paratactic* and *parataxic*, are found in the literature.

is much to be said about reconsidering the whole transference conception. Let me point out to you that there may or may not be [a set of personal-historical reactions to] a specific infantile object or a condensation of a group of such, which is thus transferred to the doctor and in relation to which the patient displayed the behavior you described. I am reasonably sure that Erikson would see in this rather an identity defense (and you hint to such a thing yourself) than a "transference paradigm." I imagine in the classic sense you would get transference only once, as you express it, "you broke into this pattern." If you reread Erikson's [1956] big identity paper you will see that, to his mind, identity has its own unconscious parts and related defenses which need not consist simply of an integrate of the specific defenses against specific impulses. It may or may not coincide with such specific defenses and their integration, it may be a relatively independent defense operation. Naturally, even then it will emulate and use already existing defensive positions and methods and means. I can't push this here any further; I would hope, however, that I will have, by what I wrote, opened the door a little bit for a further integration, in your own thinking, of the classic and the Erikson concept.

Let me make some similar comments on the Hartmann-Jacobson conception. There you must realize that they introduce that conception for the explanation of narcism.[140] As you yourself mention, they speak about self-representations in contrast to object representations instead of [bringing in the concept,] ego. Clinically, they are on an altogether safe ground because we know how to make a distinction between id narcism, ego narcism, and super ego narcism. Theoretically, they are rather out on the limb because it is a very hard thing to conceive of a self which has all these three aspects and yet has representations, which we have come to think [about] in terms of something as a part of the

---

[140] Again, Rapaport uses a neologistic simplification—introduced by H. A. Murray (1938)—instead of the conventional spelling of *narcissism*. Perhaps he was merely echoing Mayman's (unavailable) text.

"inner world" and thus a part of the ego. It is possible that this will necessitate to make our picture on these matters quite a bit more complicated than we managed to boil them down to so far. Be that as it may, you have to realize that just like this [i.e., in your discussion of] identity, you will have to deal here also with unconscious and id stuff related to the self rather than a self that is a super organization, the underpinnings of which can be simply treated in the classic terms of ego-id balances. The practical significance of this is that the relationship between what one reconstructs directly as the "self-image" of the person and "image[s] of others" of the person is in a much more complex relation to the basic id and defense balances and to the self as a psychoanalytic concept than your discussion of it would let on.

This is all I can say for the moment. I am grateful for the opportunity to think about these things. I am glad that what you sent me was as clear as it was and particularly as well written. Do not hesitate to write to me again if any of this is murkier than it needs to be by the very situation in the theory.

I would like to know what gives around you, what my old acquaintances are doing and in general what the world is like, looked upon from your place.

With best wishes for the New Year.

       Yours,

          David

Rapaport to Holt—January 29, 1958

Dear Bob:

I have read the Goldberger-Holt [1958] paper and would like now to comment on it. Before I do so I would like to suggest that you send a copy of it to Dr. Stuart C. Miller at Riggs. I will return this copy to you so that you can see the markings on it.

My two main impressions on the critical side (on the positive side I found it interesting in its data) are: 1) the preliminary character of the writing, which shows up in much poor expression, prolixity and lack of clarity. You will find both of these marked though by no means all of them and I will comment on some of them. 2) The paper hovers in its character between phenomenological description and the attempt to decide on a few things.[141] The decision tendency rests on the skimpy introductory part and on the discussion part. The body of the paper is not shaped to it but remains on the phenomenological description level except that talk about the primary and the secondary process and related things indicates that there is more than just phenomenology that you want to tackle. I think that if you really want to indicate

---

[141] This odd antithesis, which persists throughout the letter, basically means to contrast factual descriptive writing and drawing conclusions about theoretical issues. Though he was familiar with the work of E. G. A. Husserl, whose life span coincided almost completely with Freud's, and the school of transcendental introspective philosophy he founded, Rapaport used Husserl's neologism loosely, even misleadingly, and mainly as an alternative to the theory-based discourse he preferred.

what the issues are that should be decided then the middle part should be organized accordingly and the first and the last part should be reinforced.

In the first part (first two pages), the rationale of form responses is not discussed sufficiently to make it for anybody (including me) clear from what he reads how this matter comes in here.[142] Don't misunderstand me, I see how it comes in, but I wanted to read that rather than imagine it. But major shortcomings of this first part to my mind are that there is no reference to the fact that the very situation on the psychoanalytic couch is in a way the prototype of all these things about deprivation and even if this would be only a systematic and not a historical statement, even then nobody who like you had that experience and grew up in the frame of reference of it can omit saying that his thinking about sensory deprivation experiments has been conditioned by the explicit or implicit knowledge of what the demobilization and "relative" sensory deprivation on the analytic couch makes. In other words, your thinking about this whole matter did not start with the Rorschach form responses or with Goldberger's sensory deprivation experience.[143]

Likewise, there is a basic assumption involved upon which all your phenomenological observations and all your attempts at mak-

---

[142] There is no such mention of "the rationale of form responses" in the final text. Since the early draft to which Rapaport was responding has not been preserved, only the finally published version, many of his comments are bound to seem off the mark though they helped shape the available text.

[143] Leo Goldberger and I felt that discussion of such matters was out of place in what was planned as a rather conventional and not very extended report of his dissertation research. Uncharacteristically, Rapaport throughout this letter disregards the fact that Goldberger was the senior author and primarily responsible for the text. From prior discussions, he knew that Goldberger, a Canadian who began his graduate studies at McGill University, had been a subject in an early research on sensory deprivation, which played a major role in his choice of a dissertation topic. It is possible that Rapaport mistook a reference to *formal aspects* of Rorschach responses (which played a large part in my primary process scoring system, used by Goldberger in his research) for a concern with "form responses."

ing decisions is based. All those primary process-like and related phenomena that have made the observations of sensory deprivation experiments so striking are called by you primary process-like phenomena because you approach them with the assumption of their id origin, drive origin, etc.[144] The implication obviously is that we usually attribute these to increased intensity of drives or decreased solidity of controls and defenses and here we are encountering them in a manipulable fashion. By manipulable fashion, I mean we encounter them under conditions [in] which we can elicit them at least in part at will. Without stating what the primary process is, without stating the question how it is that what we usually expect to find under such and such condition now appears under these conditions, and without stating that the significance of these experiments really is that we might experimentally directly approach, now, these phenomena which we used to have to go after in nature and take them where we find them, you cannot really approach any decision making process.[145] Partly the great hopes one could have attached to these must be scaled down after what you observed; partly, however, something of these expectations is fulfilled by what you found. I think even if you would want to preserve your paper in the realm of discourse of pure phenomenology

[144] A curious, rather arbitrary assumption. I don't think that either Goldberger or I, in our usage of the concept of primary process, assumed that its manifestations necessarily originated in id or drive processes. Rapaport seems not to have been aware of the critical role in the dissertation project played by the manual for scoring primary process manifestations [finally published as Holt et al., 2009], by then well elaborated, which Rapaport had not studied in any detail. Goldberger used it to analyze his subjects' Rorschachs, and it guided his successful attempts to devise reliably scorable aspects of thinking in the free verbal texts of subjects' verbalizations. The manual operationally defines primary process both as "drive-dominated thinking" and as formally deviant thinking under the influence of condensation, displacement, etc., each scoring category grounded in specific quotations from Freud.

[145] It remains unclear to me just what he meant by these repeated references to decision-making processes. It seems likely, however, that he means deciding theoretical issues. If I replied to this letter and took up any of these uncertainties, my response has not been preserved. Since the published text shows none of the deficiencies detailed here, his critique must have guided our revisions.

[sic!], even then you would—I feel—be obliged to state some of the preconceptions for which these observations are of such significance. But, if you want to proceed to some tentative decision making or, as you try, to indicate what type of decisions should be made sooner or later, then you certainly are obliged to do this. (I don't think that this should be difficult to do even if you totally disregard what I tried to write about this in "Ego Autonomy: A Generalization." [Rapaport, 1958] Actually the whole thing could be done on a much simpler level than [the one] on which I tried it.)

I want to say something on the side about the self-selection factor that was introduced in the gathering of your population: this factor might give a very highly slanted picture of what happens in general. I would say that while your individual differences study combats this somewhat, it certainly cannot combat it completely. I think one ought to try it once, at least on such a limited scale as you did it, with a "captive population." Secondly, I think that once you have a population which is self-selected, as you had this time, it ought to be tried what will happen if you do not give the subjects the out that they can leave whenever they want to. Thirdly, it seems to me that the experiment should be repeated with people who have once gone through it. The reason for this is that after they have reported what passed, you can by instructions get them the second time to report all experiences pertinent to all of those types of experiences which they have already reported. So what you got incidentally in the first time you will get systematically in the second time, without your having called their attention specifically to any specific type of experience, simply by having reinforced their attention to all those things [to] which they have spontaneously attended to begin with. I think that would be the only way to really get some kind of statistically processable assessment of what the experience was really like.

I even would toy with the idea that, after such subjects had a preliminary run, I would hand them records of other subjects (but only after they have reported their own experiences already in detail both concurrently and in a retrospective fashion) so that they know what all others experienced. I think I do not need to dwell at length on the significance of this. I am sure that you know the pitfalls of this kind of thing also, but it's worth thinking about.[146]

On page 10, you will see my note in which I am inquiring how much these subjects keep up a continuous patter; or how much do they use patter to allay their apprehension and to keep up some kind of pseudo-communication to keep themselves from phantasy or imagery, etc. Do you have data on that?[147]

On page 13, you will note that I felt quite critical of the big paragraph. Its logical analysis of the situation is lacking sharpness, the phrase "suggests" is one that leaves one up in the air whether or not, simply by count and inspection this is not a fact rather than just a suggestion, and the conclusion appears lame because it does not say what you should do with these [data] once you have them.

My comment on the top of page 15, is one I have already made in somewhat more detail above. The end of the paragraph on page 20 is very important, it seems connected with what you report on the end of the third paragraph on page 21. Are these the same subjects? These points are also linking up with the whole problem of interpersonal communication that you discuss elsewhere. They should somehow be put together and their implications explored.

The comment on the end of the first paragraph on the top of page 21 certainly misses the point and is rather confusing to boot.

---

[146] In his suggestions about future research, Rapaport shows his lack of any experience in experimental studies, the degree to which their design is circumscribed by ethical and various practical considerations. Nevertheless, they are interesting as indicants of his ideas about modifications that would explore various issues, which are thought-provoking despite their impracticality. And he shows a rare concern for the generalizability of findings from small groups of people not arguably a representative sample of any definable population.

[147] This issue is discussed extensively in the published version.

I am coming now to the discussion section. As you will notice I referred again to the lying flat on one's back in psychoanalytic treatment. On page 24, I found the second big paragraph quite unclear. The first sentence suggests that in the McGill investigation [Bexton, Heron, & Scott, 1954] there were tests in the course of the experiment also. I did not realize that you did that too. Did I overlook something?[148] The third sentence suggests that the tests were not reliable and not calibrated to each other. Now I don't see how the fourth sentence then follows. You should have some kind of independent calibration of the tests and make the discount then on the results you obtain.

The paragraph going from page 24 to 25, I find quite unsatisfactory. I am not speaking about the last two sentences, which I do not understand even though they seem to refer to something I wrote. First of all it is not defined whether you mean ego activity in relation to the external environment or whether in relation to drives. It would be necessary to spell this situation out a little bit to make it clear if you at all want to refer to it. But you really don't need to if you keep the level of discourse to the phenomenological. I suspect that you will get into my stuff if you go away from that and want to do something more ambitious. The thing that I find unsatisfactory about this paragraph is the analysis of the difference between the digit span and the arithmetic tests on the one side, and the type of learning and those tasks which show impairment. It should be possible to make some kind of conjecture by analyzing the type of task that was well performed and those which were poorly performed. It is possible that the difference lies in the fact that what is needed for logical deductions and such (internal apparatus work and nutriment) is exhausted while such things as are needed in digit spans etc. are not. Then

---

[148] Comments like this, of which there are several, raise the possibility that the copy to which Rapaport was reacting was defective. It is not credible that he would have overlooked a critical part of the procedure, nor that any draft would have omitted it. It is unclear what he meant by an "independent calibration of the tests to each other."

you could analyze this in terms of what little we know about apparatuses vs. attention cathexis.[149]

I come now to the section which ends on page 29, particularly in the top paragraph of 29. I see that you are trying to reach something important here. But to save my life I do not really understand your argument. I wish you would reread that part and state to me clearly what you are arguing. I am fully ready to believe that there is here a difference between visual and auditory intensity and figuredness [e.g., structure] on the one hand and sense of reality on the other. But I do not see the proof of it. Nor do I see the proof, other than a logical conjecture, for the assertion in the third sentence. What strikes me the most, however, is that the last sentence of the paragraph disclaims the validity of the hallucination problem here, while the second sentence of the second paragraph brings this whole issue back as a valid one in connection with the predominance relations of the primary and secondary processes.

Now for the last sentence of the second paragraph: obviously you are dealing here with the matter of external and internal nutriment. You have been touching on it previously when you discussed the availability of input in the form of memory supplanting the sensory one. I doubt that this is simply memory. You see, the funny thing is that some people told you that they were

---

[149] The published text does contain discussion of this issue as well as several others raised by Rapaport. It is evident that one of his major dissatisfactions is that we did not attempt to address the kinds of theoretical questions with which he was preoccupied. In part, we responded in the paper's second paragraph, as follows: "There is value, we judge, in adopting Freud's concepts of primary and secondary process, as rough first approximations, to refer to regressive and mature types of mental functioning. We shall, however, reserve a full discussion of the theory and the relevance of our data to it in another place" (Goldberger & Holt, 1958, p. 99). In none of our several subsequent publications, however, did we invoke the kinds of metapsychological concepts (e.g., nutriment, attention cathexis, psychic structures) he missed. I do not believe that Rapaport ever fully recognized the fact that metapsychology deals with a level of abstraction and remoteness from everyday reality that makes it impossible to relate its propositions to empirical data. I had not yet fully realized it, either.

searching for something to think about, or rather one could put it that they thought about something to think about. Now isn't it a funny thing that they all have memories, we all have them: why don't we get them up when we want them? From the study of boredom we have some evidence about this: take a look at Fenichel's [1941] boredom paper in his "Collected Papers." But I do not mean to say that the same conditions hold for this situation also. Some of them may hold. And actually Fenichel's answer to the problem of boredom is an ex parte [i.e., biased] answer. We should be able to give a better one. I do not doubt that it is a question partly of being fed memories instead of sensations. But I think this is only partly true, and even then the answer that they fed themselves with memories is an answer which conceals rather than reveals the issue at hand, because apparently there must be some kind of structures available which permits such feeding by memories. One of the important uses of this type of experimentation is that it might just shed light, once the questions are sharply enough asked, on some of these structural conditions.

Again I would like to say that I might have been harsh on something which is after all a first draft. But I know that you won't mind and will hear in the sharpness rather the interest than anything else. You know this is the kind of thing I have been trying to think about very hard in connection with the Miller letter [see Summary of Brief Letters of 1958]. It is just hard to explain this kind of thing: but a certain kind of sharpness is an expression of intellectual interest. There is nothing that can replace it.

You know, I just read in the new Contemporary Psychologist the review [Alfred L.] Baldwin wrote of [Robert R.] Sears' book.[150] This is the sort of thing which I detest. It isn't that there are no devastating criticisms in it, it isn't that there aren't definite praises in it, it isn't that he does not call attention to things that are in the book and are worth while to know. What it [i.e., the problem] is, is

---

[150] Sears, R. R., Maccoby, E. E., and Levin, H. (1957). *Patterns of child rearing.* Evanston IL & White Plains NY: Row, Peterson & Co.

that it does not give a unitary point of view of a man concerning the creation of the other man. Now you might argue that to make a "unitary point of view" might paint the book black or white. But this is not really true. A unitary point of view is like giving a water level from which good and bad, valleys and hills, drop and rise in a meaningful systematic relation to each other. This is what Baldwin's review did not do for me in connection with that Sears book.

Well, it is very late in the evening by now and I better quit on this. I hope what I had to say will be of some use to Goldberger and you.

Yours,

David

Holt to Rapaport—February 21, 1958

Introduction

There follow, in addition to the letter, below, three others (those of March 4, March 13, and March 24), all concerned with metapsychology and specifically with several versions of the paper Rapaport and Merton M. Gill wrote during this year. They include one exchange between me and the latter (copies of which went to the senior author).

In a note of early January, 1958, Rapaport wrote to me, revealing that the version he sent to me was a briefer version of the first draft (which I never saw):

> Before vacation I worked with Merton 9 days and we hammered out a workable draft of our "Reassessment of Metapsychology." After some polishing I'll send it along. We are rather pleased with it. Now we have to get a short version (this is 45 pages) for presentation at NY. Psa. Soc. in March.

Though the term appeared often in psychoanalytic papers of the middle of the last century, it does not pop up often in the contemporary literature. Readers may well be unsure about just how it is being used here, especially because the Rapaport-Gill paper used it in an unusually restricted sense, while I and many others understood it as coterminous with the basic statements of psychoanalytic theory.

Freud's many comments on metapsychological issues, plus the extended works that deal primarily with metapsychology, comprise an ill-defined but considerable part of his contributions to theory. On page 796 of the published version of their joint paper (in Gill, 1967, chapter 72), however, the authors limit their purview to "Chapter VII of *The interpretation of dreams*, the 'Papers on Metapsychology' . . . and the 'Addenda' to *The problem of anxiety*." Freud was inclined to consider it the most important part of his theoretical work, but never attempted the task of assembling, reviewing, and systematizing its various pieces. Most psychoanalysts viewed it as the most difficult (and thus, probably most profound) part of Freud's work, and relatively few even attempted to make further contributions to it.

In his final years, Rapaport worked collaboratively with Merton M. Gill (1914–1994) in a way he never did with anyone else. I don't recall feeling envious, because I too had a high estimation of Merton's intellect; his wonderful, mordant sense of humor, coupled with extraordinary charm and charisma; his persuasive way of speaking in a deep, resonant bass voice; and his immersion in psychoanalysis: its practice, teaching it both clinically and didactically as a training analyst, and through a much broader familiarity with its practitioners and literature than I ever had. Most of these facts, including the wide respect by the psychoanalytic establishment that Gill enjoyed, made him an ideal partner for David. During the years after Merton left Stockbridge, they spent many an extended weekend getting together for intensive discussion and writing (and exchanging jokes). This paper is one of the major products of that collaboration. I know from conversations with both of them that each especially cherished it. Another product of the collaborative work begun in the present paper was to have been a joint monograph, which Gill completed on his own (Gill, 1963). As he notes in its introduction, "I took a progressively greater share of the work until finally, a few months before his [Rapaport's] death, he persuaded me that it would be appropriate for me to be the sole author."

In the end, that monograph focused almost entirely on the topographic point of view and the topographic model of the "psychic apparatus," as compared to the structural point of view and the model presented in *The ego and the id* (Freud, 1923). Rapaport and Gill took an unusually narrow view of what the term "metapsychology" means, restricting it to a consideration of the basic assumptions of the "general theory." Writing alone, Gill broadened its scope. True, Freud did at times give it the narrow interpretation, but when one looks at all of the passages in which he used the term (as I did in my 1983 paper, the final version of which appears as Chapter 2 in Holt, 1989) it is clear that most of the time he identified it with the substantive propositions of the general theory, expressed in the concepts that make up the three points of view.

Looking at Gill's 1963 monograph today, I am struck by two somewhat antithetical qualities. On the positive side, he showed an admirable openness to relevant data (e.g., results of experiments at the Research Center for Mental Health on the effects of unnoticed perceptual inputs on reported experiences) and to subtleties and complexities that are incompatible with the usual sweeping statements about relations among consciousness, preconscious ideas/contents of various kinds, and the degree to which communicated thoughts/perceptions have the identifying characteristics of the primary process. On the negative side, Gill appeared little troubled by the fact that few if any of the propositions considered are testable in any specified way. Only about a dozen years later he began to publish a series of papers rejecting metapsychology and then turning to what I believe an illusory substitute, hermeneutics, also unconcerned with empirical verification.

Taking this historical perspective, a contemporary reader may wonder why these two remarkable men felt that the task was worth doing. By what standard was it necessary or even desirable to identify the assumptions underlying psychoanalysis as a theory? Just three years previously, Rapaport had been much concerned with similar matters, in response to the invitation from Sigmund Koch to take part in the American Psychological Association's Project A (see letters from 1955). Happily, I recently found, in a scanned copy of *Psychology: A Study of a Science* (Koch, 1959), available online, an outline of topics prepared by Koch for participating authors. Among the Suggested Discussion Topics are:

    a.   degree and mode of quantitative and mensurational specificity towards which it is desirable and/or feasible to aim

b.   type of formal organization (on some such continuum as "explicit, hypothetico-deductive axiomatization, informal exposition") considered best suited to requirements for systematization, at the present phase, in the area selected by the systematist. (Koch, 1959, p. 667).

It is evident from his 1955 letters that Rapaport did not feel completely satisfied with what he had been able to produce, which three years later was not yet in print (Rapaport, 1960a). It seems likely, therefore, that the present work was in some part an effort to let the other shoe drop.

Let me add, however, my present belief that it is important to clarify the fundamental philosophical, or *metaphysical* assumptions on which a science is built (Holt, 1989, Chapter 14). Freud did not, I believe, ever study metaphysical literature, and the surveys and comparative expositions of various extant systems that have been very helpful to me did not exist in his day.

I began to feel uncomfortable with and to challenge some aspects of metapsychology quite early, as the reader will have noticed already, probably before many other followers because of the unique nature of our relationship. It should be evident by now how he encouraged me to think through knotty passages for myself, not to be hesitant to challenge any of his ideas, Freud's, or those of psychoanalysts generally, and how I thrived on that freedom. Still, I did not publish direct attacks on metapsychology as such until the 1970s, well after Rapaport's death and after the publication of the *Festschrift* in his honor (Holt, ed., 1967). Meanwhile, a large proportion of his other principal collaborators and students (e.g., Hartvig Dahl, Morris Eagle, George Klein, Benjamin Rubinstein, Roy Schafer, and Donald Spence) became dissatisfied with metapsychology and proposed a variety of replacements for it. A growing number of psychoanalysts outside our circle had also been criticizing one or another aspect of metapsychology for a good many years.[151] At last, a good many of us joined in a direct attack (Gill, M. M.,

---

[151] After George Klein's sudden and untimely death, Gill and Holzman (1976) edited a collection of essays in his honor, with the somewhat misleading title, "Psychology versus

& Holzman, P. S., 1976). Before long, one began to see frequent state-ments to the effect that metapsychology is dead, which is the contemporary consensus. Nevertheless, concepts that are not usually recognized as grounded in and a part of the general theory as Rapaport described it, such as the ego and the unconscious, remain in general use.

In the present letter, discussing an early draft of the joint paper, it will be easy to see that I was far from ready to challenge any of the basic premises of metapsychology, instead pecking away at less fundamental inconsistencies and unclarities.

Incidentally, I have not taken specific note of the fact that many for-mulations and other aspects of the text to which I objected here do not appear in the published version. In light of the authors' acknowledgment in its first footnote of the many colleagues who gave comments and sug-gestions, I can hardly claim that changes were made because of this particular letter.

Dear David:

As usual, I'm going to leave the positive mostly unsaid, unfair though that may be, because I'm pressed for time and want to get my criticisms down for you. But be assured in general that I think the paper is first-rate and a very important contribution.

I won't go over my textual corrections and suggestions; I might just remark that the first two sections are very clear and fi-ne for oral presentation, so far as I can see. The rest of it is quite condensed; this does not necessarily mean it can't be presented that way, although I think it does mean that much of the detail will be lost. When you talk about how the assumptions are implic-it in various propositions, none of that is self-evident and it all requires considerable reflection, so it is likely to be mostly missed; again, I don't think that is necessarily a reason to drop it.

On page 5, I begin to have some troubles. Your second as-

---

metapsychology." Though it begins with Klein's (1969) explicit abandonment of meta-psychology for an expanded clinical theory of sexuality and contains a few other critiques, most of the essays don't fit the title but deal with various of his other interests.

sumption about forces would read better, I believe: "The attributes of psychological forces are their direction (goal) and magnitude." I don't believe that it's a proper use of the word <u>definition</u> as the proposition stands. In general, I am a little bit confused about the difference between the dynamic and the economic points of view, as you present them here. As I read Freud, he says that as soon as we talk about the quantities involved in forces, we are getting into the economic point of view. You quietly introduce quantitative considerations with regard to forces into the first point of view in your second assumption, and then make the economic point of view one that has to do with work rather than quantity.[152] It seems to me that this is a more far-reaching change than you admit. Perhaps you will want to discuss that in the longer paper.

I have noted in the margin of page 5 that you might want to expand the central paragraph somewhat to make clear the nature of the goal, as some kind of transaction with or relationship to an object, not the object per se. Thus, the goal of a hunter is not food, but eating; food is the goal-object.

If I were you, I would handle the problem of the third and fourth assumptions by stating the third one as I have suggested, and then saying that it is an open question whether or not this assumption is sufficient in itself; it may be necessary to add a fourth assumption of the kind that you have listed. I would be reluctant to see this happen, because I suspect on a purely intuitive basis that it would create difficulties for the system at large. It seems to me that this assumption discards the possibility of ever dealing with forces quantitatively. I suggest that it may be possible to understand all of the psychoanalytic propositions you cite on page 6

---

[152] In the published version, the critical defining characteristic of the economic point of view is *energy* rather than work, while the concept of work appears most prominently in propositions concerning forces. The authors never confronted the basic problem, that if physics is to be the model for a psychological/metapsychological theory, it would be necessary to find analogues for *distance* (presupposed by *velocity*) and *mass*, as well as time and direction, which are less problematic, in order to measure magnitudes of forces.

in terms of the controlling structures rather than the forces themselves. Thus, what is referred to in the concepts of fusion and defusion may be interpreted via counter-cathectic structures organizing the ways that the drive energies are channeled and expended, rather than requiring an assumption about the forces' interactions themselves.[153]

If you merely want to give the impression that your economic point of view is the same as Freud's, I suppose you can leave page 7 the way it stands; but if you want to show clearly that it makes explicit what is implicit in Freud's formulation, then you need to do considerably more explaining. I wonder whether it doesn't necessarily follow that if you postulate psychological energies, you must also postulate psychological work, which in turn would get you into some kind of further necessity to define some sort of psychological distance through which forces operate. I am uncertain just how far one has to go in making the analogy to physical concepts complete, but I don't think that you can introduce the concept of work without defining it. As long as it goes undefined, it seems to imply the physical definition, which clearly is not meant; it's the muscles that do physical work, not the psychic apparatus and its energies.

I'm not a good enough physicist to be quite clear on just when we need the concept of force and when we need that of energy. My feeling about it, however, is that when Freud talked about psychological forces he [usually] meant energies. I think I'm going to have to reread my physics, however, before I comment on this issue any further. Incidentally, is an instinct a psychological force or an energy? As I understand it, it is a force, operating (doing some kind of psychic work) by means of cathectic energy.

It strikes me that the first paragraph at the top of page 9 is a

---

[153] Matters were further confused by their use, in the final version, of the concept of *work* in propositions (c) and (d) about the interaction of forces. Indeed, the correct statement on the next page (801) that energies "(by definition) are directionless quantities" makes it impossible to treat work as subject to vectorial addition.

very important one, and again its statements are by no means self-evident. It seems quite a remarkable conclusion that this assumption "makes it superfluous to postulate alongside the pleasure principle, a constancy principle, a nirvana principle [or] a repetition compulsion." I look forward to a full exposition of these claims in the long paper.[154]

I'm puzzled by the fourth assumption on page 9; you speak as if neutralization is something other than desexualization or deaggressivization, and I don't follow at all the second sentence of the paragraph. Again, I hope it will be possible to replace the messy concept of the transformation of psychological energy by a structural one.[155] This is something I would like to work out at some length with you some time.

It seems to me it is implied in what you say at the bottom of page 10 about the mechanism of the primary process. One of the great values that I see for this systematization is just this kind of simplification of concepts that it may lead to. I think you will have done psychoanalysis a great service if you do in fact sweep away the unnecessary cobwebs of the nirvana principle, the constancy principle, etc.

In general, I wonder a little bit about the methodological status of <u>assumptions</u>. Should they properly include definition? I feel that the second assumption on page 11 is something new in this paper; for the first time we have a straight formal definition. I wonder if it wouldn't be desirable to have two separate bodies of propositions: assumptions and definitions.

I have recently become somewhat dissatisfied with your proposition that structures are configurations with a slow rate of

---

[154] Instead, it was left unclear how "psychological energies are subject to a law of entropy."

[155] The point about neutralization was adopted. Electromagnetic energies may be transformed into qualitatively distinct forms, e.g., light into microwaves, but always with an entropic loss. My suggestion of replacing the assumption that psychic energy undergoes qualitative transformations by structural ones was not adopted; in retrospect, it seems a half-way effort obviated by the more sweeping critique of metapsychology that proved necessary.

change. That seems to me somehow to miss the main point. Let us take an example from physics or the physical realm. A chair is a structure; it is true that the substances in a chair are not fixed and unvarying, and that there are processes characterized by slow rates of change that gradually bring about the dissolution of the chair. But I think we say then that this process of a slow rate of change was one that destroyed the structure; it was not the structure itself. Structure, I believe, is a concept that implies the disposition of parts in a manifold; I am quoting inexactly from Angyal [1941]. I think his statements about structure deserve a careful rereading. Your definition, for example, would imply that the slow oxidation of iron is a structure, because it is characterized by a slow rate of change, whereas the flame of a candle would not be a structure since it is a configuration with a rapid rate of change—indeed, a steady configuration of rapid rates of change. It may be, however, that the term you mean to emphasize in your second assumption is "configuration," and "of a slow rate of change" is merely meant to be an incidental modifier, not essential to the definition. Thus, in a plasma tube where a fusion is being attempted, the pinch effect is certainly a structure, although it takes place at an incredibly quick rate of change. It's a structure because it's a configuration; that is, a disposition of discriminable parts (themselves processes) in a manifold—in this case, the familiar space-time manifold. The nature of the manifold presupposed by psychoanalysis needs ultimately to be explored or stated in assumptions; that will be a difficult nut to crack. But I think it is strictly implied by the concept of psychological structure and we cannot escape from the necessity to define it.

On page 12, I wonder if the fourth assumption is stated in the best way. I would think about it in this way: wherever we can distinguish a relationship of subordination or subsumption (hierarchy), these are operations that define structure, because they are operations that state a configuration in an implied manifold.

Incidentally, I hope that you somewhere in the longer version explain the way that all the psychoanalytic propositions cited here relate to the assumptions. These statements are mostly quite obscure to me.

On page 13, I am puzzled by the word "defining" in the definition of the genetic point of view. I suppose you mean "relevant" or something like that; whatever term is used conceals problems that will have to be dealt with. Just what antecedent events constitute the essential genetics in psychoanalysis? How does one isolate the genetically relevant from the "saprophytic"? The statement from Freud that I have bracketed seems to me relevant to the subordinate, not the major clause of the preceding sentence, which is what makes it confusing. I guess on second thought it can stand as it is; I was dubious about it because the genetic point of view seems to me so very implicit.

The problem of the term "defining history" crops up again in the first genetic assumption and again on page 14. I think you need to say something more explicit and intelligible in place of this phrase.

At the bottom of page 14, I have suggested that you remind the reader what the term "epigenesis" means; I had to just go look it up myself. It strikes me that there is probably a controversy at least implicit in psychoanalytic theory between the epigenetic and the preformative points of view.[156] I'm sure that Freud can be quoted to support the latter; his espousal of the Lamarckian point of view seems to be consonant with preformation rather than epigenesis.

As I notice at the top of page 15, the third assumption seems to me a proposition that is very close to testability and thus perhaps not of the same methodological status as the other assumptions.

As I have noted in the margin at the bottom of page 15, to say "<u>potentially</u> active" seems to imply that everything [in a person's]

---

[156] In attempts by early biologists to account for the development of organisms, the epigenetic assumption is that an embryo develops progressively through various stages from an undifferentiated egg cell. The preformative assumption was that development was primarily the enlargement of a miniature but complete version of the organism.

past that might have an effect on anything does affect everything. I think what you are driving at in this assumption is
essentially the same point that has been made in no. 3: that the
earlier forms are potentially active, which <u>means</u>, I think, that they
may "co-determine any subsequent psychological phenomenon."
What seems to be added by the fourth assumption appears false to
me: the "sum total" conception (which connotes a denial of a
configurational, parallelogram-of-forces point of view), and [also
false] the idea that everything potentially active is kinetically active.

On page 16, I wonder if the adaptive point of view is not in a
way also implied by Freud's statement, in the seventh chapter,
that the reflex arc is the basic model of the psychic apparatus, for
this implies input from environmental stimulation as an essential
aspect.

I was a little confused by the way you state the assumptions of
the adaptive point of view; I feel now that the way you started the
first two was a sort of rhetorical device, which seems to me a little
out of place in a set of formal statements. The first assumption, taken
literally, contains an assumption and a definition, and is thus "dou-
ble-barreled." I must admit that I did not notice in reading that you
talked about "adaptedness" in the first assumption and "adaptation"
in the second assumption; I think this distinction is likely also to be
missed by your auditors. I incidentally also felt a little unhappy about
the definition of adaptedness; it seems to refer primarily to the verid-
icality of perception. How about defining it as "the relationship
between organism (including its psychic apparatus and the phenomenal reality that constructs) and environment..."?[157] Unless, of
course, you want to have the narrower definition; I can understand
how you might, since you don't particularly want to refer to the fact

---

[157] In retrospect, I notice that what is explicit here—my suggestion that adaptation by its
very nature implies that the entity that adapts is the organism or person—is little more
than implicit in the rest of my critique. The authors accepted, with little dissent, Freud's
own focus on internal (mental) processes in his writings on metapsychology. As many
critics have asked, Where is the person in much of Freud's theorizing? (which took into
account the habitat or ecosystem only incidentally and as an afterthought).

that the Arctic fox has white fur as an example of adaptedness. Why not call it psychological adaptedness or something of the sort, then? I don't quite see what is gained by the statement that either adaptedness or adaptation "exists at every point of life"; as I note at the bottom of page 17 this seems a rather pallid assumption, which ought to drag along with it the assumptions that "psychological forces exist at every point of life" and "psychological structures exist at every point of life" etc. Thus, I would say that numbers 1 and 2 both essentially consist of definitions.

In general, I feel that the assumptions for the adaptive point of view are the least satisfactory; they are all less single-pointed than the others, and don't seem to be quite on the same level of generality. Number 3 seems to be a very general biological statement, just as numbers 1 and 2 might be; number 4 is two different statements, neither of which sounds to me exactly like an assumption.

As I've noted at the bottom of page 20, I agree with your feeling that a set of assumptions ought to be supplemented by a set of definitions, and I would emphasize the fact that you have included definitions in your assumptions.

Although I have been quite critical, I don't mean to imply that all of the points I raised have to be taken into account in some way before the paper is suitable for oral presentation. I don't think it is even necessary that your readers understand everything in the paper, as long as they get the general idea. I think they will even if you make no revisions, and will be appropriately impressed with this as a basic contribution to psychoanalysis.

Cordially,

Bob

cc: Merton M. Gill

Rapaport to John J. Sullivan—March 9, 1958

Introduction

Dr. John J. Sullivan was a colleague at NYU in the department of Educational Psychology, ambitious but prone to biting off more than he could chew. His (never published) paper has not survived and I have only a dim recollection of it. This letter is included because it shows so much about Rapaport in one page: his willingness to help others, even if undeserving; his utterly straightforward but not hurtful criticism, covering many aspects of a draft; his kind of advice: often concrete and detailed. It would take an examination of the thousands of his letters stored at the Library of Congress to know how many such responses he wrote to requests from persons unknown to him, but I feel certain that there were hundreds. This one, too, I would not have seen if he had not sent me a copy, because of our acquaintance.

Dear Dr. Sullivan:

I read your paper finally. I take it, that you know—though I do not know you—that I shoot straight. You asked for comments: here they are.

1. The merit of the paper is exclusively that it shows interest in a point, which is important and little studied.

2. The main deficiency of the paper is that you know very little about Freud and little even [about] Breuer.

3. The "methodological" intent is excellent. Its execution is amateurish: indeed, you yourself indicate that you designed some of it ad hoc.

4. The second weakness of the paper is that it does not do what it promises and fills instead half the space used, by methodological considerations.

5. There are factual errors in abundance. These cannot become clear to you without reading the <u>From the Origins of Psychoanalysis</u> [Freud, 1950] and Jones [1953–1957] and the 7th chapter of The Interpretation of Dreams [Freud, 1900, pp. 509–621]. If you want me to list them [the errors of fact], let me know, but it would be better to talk about them <u>after</u> you read the mentioned material.

6. For such an endeavor to be successful and for it to stick, you would have to write in detail and document by quotes. This way, it is <u>opinion</u> expressed and no more.

7. It so happens that I have worked some in this field. If you really want to work in it and not just to dash off a few papers, what I have done in it can be made available to you.

To the question, what could strengthen <u>this</u> paper: (a) factual quotes to bolster <u>every</u> assertion; (b) junking it and studying the material.

If you do want to penetrate the jungle of problems you touched on, I'll be delighted to help you in any way feasible.

Sincerely,

David Rapaport

Holt to Merton Gill—March 13, 1958

Dear Mert:

I suspect that David may have sent you copies of the letters I wrote him about your metapsychological paper, both the long and the short versions. I should have done so myself; in any event, I want to let you know a little about my reaction to it and also that of other people. For I was at the New York Psychoanalytic Tuesday night when David made an excellent presentation of the main points.

To start with this last matter: the place was packed and the audience seemed very appreciative. Certainly all of the discussants praised the paper highly—all, that is, except Sperling,[158] who spoke up from the floor with an ignorant objection that only showed his own confusion. Hartmann, Kubie, Schur and Chuck Fisher[159] all praised it and recognized it for the extraordinary contribution that it is. From what I heard of the audience reaction, they were respectful and impressed, in some cases a little dazed or not fully comprehending. I think the paper has to be read for its full impact.

Well, I read both versions and heard a slightly different one last night that clarified a few further points for me, and I want to tell you that it is one of the most stimulating papers that I have

---

[158] Otto E. Sperling, MD, New York psychoanalyst.
[159] Heinz Hartmann, Lawrence S. Kubie, Max Schur, and Charles Fisher: all prominent contributors to psychoanalytic literature.

ever read. I am already seriously planning a long treatment of primary and secondary process theory following the model you set with that very impressive treatment of affect. That demonstrated quite clearly the value of the work you and David have done: it is clearly not just a pretty intellectual exercise, but a powerful new tool.

[. . .]160

The other thought I had about the assumptions is that they need to be gone over carefully to make sure that none of them is testable, for a testable proposition is certainly not a basic assumption. The adaptive assumptions particularly I thought might need careful scrutiny from this point of view.

It's much harder to decide whether a set of assumptions is comprehensive. Fisher raised the question whether the temporal sequence that Freud described in the 7th chapter as being the essence of the distinction between the topographical systems (I am quoting very inexactly) ought to be in as a basic assumption. I don't think it should, partly because it seems pretty specific and also because it seems possibly testable. I wonder, though, if the postulate of universal psychic determinism has been adequately taken care of; it seems to me that some statement about it might be added to the dynamic point of view's assumptions.

I was a little disturbed about the fourth dynamic assumption. It seems to me that if one introduces this idea, it seriously reduces the possibility of ever measuring psychological forces, and I should think that it might create difficulties of a more far-reaching nature as well. I'd like to see a much closer consideration of the psychoanalytic propositions that seem to be inconsistent with the law of the independence of forces; that might cause a useful restatement of concepts in the purely psychoanalytic part of the theory.

[. . .]

---

160 Since much of the rest of the letter repeats points made in my letter of February 21, 1958, those parts of this letter have been replaced by ellipses.

I had hoped when I read the shorter paper that there would be considerable expansion of the discussion of the assumptions in the longer one, and was disappointed to find it missing. There is a great deal in that section of the longer paper that still seems to me extremely compressed. It takes a great deal for granted and assumes that the reader will immediately be able to see that various assumptions are contained in a variety of psychoanalytic propositions, which are alluded to in a way that leaves me at the post in many instances. That may be a tedious kind of job to do, but I think that it's necessary sooner or later. Incidentally, in his oral presentation David cleared up a number of points that are obscure in the papers, and I hope that he will insert some of them into the paper. What he had to say about the distinction between forces and energy and the need for both kinds of concepts was quite helpful.

I'm not very happy with the definition of psychological structure offered in the second assumption under the structural point of view; it seems to me to miss the main point.

[...]

I'm not too happy about the third and fourth genetic assumptions. I think that they imply a concept like that of memory trace, which perhaps needs to be explicitly introduced. Surely the "earlier forms of a psychological phenomenon" have contemporary existence and effects only through some contemporary reality such as a memory trace. And I don't really follow the point of the fourth assumption, nor am I convinced that it is necessary. If one holds to a strict determinist point of view, then isn't this assumption merely stating that memory traces, once laid down, don't simply vanish? As stated, it seems to claim much too much: that all of a person's history plays a determining role in all of his present behavior and psychological phenomena. The role of some past experiences (or "preceding forms") surely must be as vanishingly small as the gravitational effect on a distant star when I lift a finger. Or do you really mean to state something as general as the universal law of gravity? If so, I think there ought to be some discussion along with the assumption to point out the fact that it's taken for granted that the overwhelming preponderance of preceding experience has negligible effects on any particular current psychological phenomenon. The other way I think you may mean the reader to look at this assumption might be restated: everything that has happened to me has played some part in making me what I am today, and what I am at a given moment, together with what my environment is, determines any particular psychological phenomenon.

Of all the points of view, the genetic seems to me least basic and essential; we need it only because we have no other practical method of finding out about a person's current structure, forces and energies. As I say that, I'm struck by the fact that there is nothing in any of these assumptions about object relations. I know you wanted to keep specifically psychoanalytic propositions out, but I wonder if in a way objects aren't as basic as forces. They would have to be brought in under the adaptive point of view since of course they refer to aspects of the environment, but I don't have any very concrete ideas about how to do it.

I was very much impressed with the material in the long paper on the theory of affects, and think that it makes a truly effective demonstration of the power of what you've contributed.[161]

There are a few other minor points in my letters to David, but I think that covers the essential ones. After so many years of work, you probably are tired of this paper and want to get it published. I certainly wouldn't blame you, and it is surely publishable as it stands. But I think that its significance could be considerably increased by a careful reworking and expansion to monographic size—with perhaps the publication of a very brief version such as the one on which David's name was first, in one of the psychoanalytic journals.

Please let me know when you are going to be in New York next. I'd love to see you, and want you to meet my wife. We can put you up and would love an opportunity to do so.

---

[161] Today, I feel surprised that I found so much merit in the material about affects, which now seems of little value, being far removed from observations or other data.

I was thinking of writing [to you] about the problem of psychoanalytic training (or rather the question of whether or not I should apply for it), which is something much on my mind these days, but I think I'll defer that awhile.

My best to Charlotte—

        Cordially,

           Bob

Merton Gill to Holt—March 24, 1958

Dear Bob,

Just a note to thank you for your kind and thoughtful comments about the metapsychology paper. The only quick reaction I have is that the adaptive proposition about society <u>was</u> meant to cover object relations. Your point about separating out definitional aspects of assumptions is valuable but we felt that would be to enter a more empirical psychoanalytic realm. The assumptions take force and energy for granted. "Laws other than independence of forces" I do not take to mean nonmeasurability, but measurability by laws differing from those in the physical sciences. Without being able to specify how, determinism seems to me an order of a different level of abstraction—perhaps it is the total underlying assumption that we deal with lawful data. I'll have to think a good deal more about your structure point. Is oxidation the configuration or is it not the iron? By the genetic assumptions we <u>did</u> mean a general law—the specifics you suggest are again more empirical psychoanalytic, I think.

But I shall have to think it all thru a lot more. I wanted not to delay in expressing my appreciation.

As to publication, I'm sure you're right about a monograph and will talk with David about it in Los Angeles next month. But as you perhaps know, George K. has made an extensive criticism of the theoretical section of the hypnosis book [Gill & Brenman, 1969] and so again a major rewrite job, this time of something I thought was finished.

At the moment I'm doing little except routine work. Charlotte happily became pregnant again, then started to bleed—fortunately stopped now—but things have been very unsettled.

I have finished with Tim Leary a first statement of a psycho-therapy coding system [Leary & Gill, 1959] which I would like to get your opinion on and will send along fairly soon.

I don't think I have yet congratulated you on your marriage which I now enthusiastically do. No present plans for going to N.Y. but will let you know if & when.

Mert

Rapaport to Holt—June 20, 1958

[handwritten]

Dear Bob,

I just read your review in its final form. I like it and to my mind it will have a salutary effect.

Two things: (a) it is remarkable how independent it is from the points I made in our conversation. I don't mean that it didn't change since the first form, but it is organic continuation of what you wrote and all yours. This is somehow what I think our conversations should have as an effect. I believe (I hope it is true) that this is what happened to the System Paper in wake of our conversations. (b) Your listing me with Hartmann etc. seems to me strange. I do not think Jones knew any of those writings and mine do not deserve the listing. [It] May be that I did something in my teaching courses and conversations on those lines. Perhaps my unpublished or buried papers (Act[ivity]-Pass[ivity], System, Autonomy, and Cognition & Consciousness [Rapaport, 1953d, 1960a, 1958, 1957a, 1951d) did something. But that is qualitatively very different from what Hartmann and Erikson did. At any rate, I think it is a fine review.

We are awaiting you for a visit.

My best to both of you

David.

Rapaport to Holt—July 11, 1958

Dear Bob:

I have finally gotten around to reading your and Goldberger's paper. The subtitle of it is "Method and Group Results." It was only on the trip to Boston that I managed to get to it. These are rather hectic weeks and not much physical comfort.

I am under the impression that I read this paper before. So parts of it must have been different because they impressed me this time more strongly. By and large I should say that phenomenological description of what you have observed is very clearly and directly represented, more systematically so than in any of the other things I have seen.

The other thing that impresses me very much is on page 15 and following it, namely the direct statement that isolation in this whole thing was quite relative. I would think that a person who without overexaggeration maintained the frame of reference that he is not in an abandonment situation but in steady contact with you, should be characterized as a person who can provide himself with stable nutriment by this means. I would judge that those people, who had to call on you and who got angry with you, who thought of abandonment, were clinging to weakly working such structures [i.e., of that kind].

I would also suggest that the people who afterwards were sticky and would not leave the post-isolation interview must have belonged to the people who did not have such a strong and solid nourishing frame of reference. It would seem to me to be very interesting to try to sort your subjects this way. In fact, I think all the facts that you state in this section which goes from page 15 to 16 would be well worth to check against the general frame of reference of the person in regard to the experiment as a maintained contact with the experimenter or a situation of lost contact, social isolation.

When I say that the frame of reference provides nutriment, I mean to designate by the frame of reference some kind of a structure, of which the phenomena indicating maintained contact are manifestations, and which structure should provide safe-guards against far-reaching primitivizations. I realize that the small subject number will not allow decisions in this matter, but it will be well worth checking, in order to generate further hypotheses for future experiments.* Naturally this would not be the only kind of structure that provides such safe-guards. Maintained ability (or relatively better maintained) to carry on ordered thinking might be a different one or might be another manifestation of the same frame of reference. Another such structure or other manifestation of the same structure may be those memorial performances like singing, like poetry recall, etc. I think that you probably have thought all this through but still it may be worth while to mention these to you.

On page 17, at the end of the section, the phrase "summoned up all the energy" seems to be a very relevant comment. I think that it is pertinent to the point you made about the contrast between digit span and arithmetic on the one hand and tasks which require sustained performance such as logical reasoning. This point occurred to me in a conversation with Paul, who commented that his fragmentation scores on the same subjects correlated highly with the post-isolation Babcock score, but correlated very low with the preisolation one. I think this finding, if it could be made a hypothesis for future explorations, could be a very fruitful one.

---

* At this point your experiment merges—to my mind—on the experiments of Ach and on personal style problems like leveling. [Footnote in original.]

Namely, we do assume (I do anyway) that the synthetic function of the ego which "re-members," "re-collects" pieces of meaningful memory is always working at the brink of its capacity and requires sustained performance and even that way it is always limited. Thus it is that fragmentations and importations occur. Now the high correlation between this and the immediate recall in the post-isolation situation of the Babcock story is highly suggestive for a relative decrease of synthetic functions. I gather from second hand that this might be in conformity with your Rorschach findings also as to the people who are more prone to primitivization in such an isolation situation.

I was also very interested in the way you presented the Hoffman-Vernon findings. This is not really relevant to your study, but when I read the paper in <u>Science</u>, I did not quite realize its import for learning studies. We are engaged in such studies and I should take another look at it. It reminds one of the famous studies by Dallenbach, Van Ormer and Newman concerning sleep and its effect on memory. So this is just a side remark.

Now on the critical end I would have the following to say. On page 20, in the second half of the second paragraph, you write "We believe, therefore, that our method worked as well as it did because we used moderate levels of stimulation (rather than seeking the virtually unattainable complete reduction of stimulus level), and because we took pains to make the stimulation constant, unpatterned and homogeneous." Now I don't see the real cogency of this argument. I see where you draw your inference from, but I do not see the theory behind it. In so far as I see any theory here it seems to be one which lays the total burden of the difference on the final degree of "deprivation". Somehow this is rather difficult to square off with those points that one would draw from Riesen's studies and from Senden's studies. Here is a point I believe that has to be thought through theoretically.

While I was very interested in the kind of analysis you gave of the elements of what is called "hallucination", I am slightly doubtful of the weight and definitiveness you give to your conclusions there. You seem too be quite insistent that "reality testing" is not impaired. I am not so sure of this point. When one of the fellows "acts as though he would have heard your voice", does not he give expression to a "belief of reality" (I am using the expression Freud used in the "Metapsychological Supplement to the Theory of Dreams"). Now if you would argue that these sort of things are "illusions" rather than "hallucinations", I would certainly go along with you, because we do not have any evidence to the contrary. But illusions are also momentary "beliefs of reality" attached to intensely cathected memory or imagery.

More generally I would say that, though I realize that you promise in this paper to give theoretical treatment in other papers, I regret that there is hardly any theoretical statement here as to the significance of this issue. At least I regret that you decided to publish (if you did?) in such a fashion that part of the publication does not carry theoretical statement. I felt very disappointed when I read Luborsky's and Chevrin's Pötzl experiment which had quite a few interesting points, for the same reason. Experiments are being done all around without the theoretical views motivating them being expounded.

Just the same in general I enjoyed the paper, its unasked and direct phenomenological approach is salutary to my mind. It is a food for thought (much more so than the others which are very fragmentary) and thus it helps us all. I hope there will be enough opportunity to discuss this and also opportunity to see the other two papers which you refer to. Please give my best regards and compliments to your co-author and affectionate greetings to your wife.

Yours,

David

P.S. I do not know whether we will see each other or exchange letters before you go. We are looking forward to see you two when you get back. Good voyage and rest! And if you run into some interesting stamps—do remember me.

D.

Holt to Rapaport—July 21, 1958

Dear David,

I still feel a little sad that the weekend of the 20th has come and gone and we didn't make it up to Stockbridge. [. . .]

Let me first thank you for your long letter of July 11, which is concerned with Leo's and my paper that is to appear in the Journal of Nervous and Mental Disease. We are checking the suggestions you made about further analysis of the data. And in fact we'll write at least one more paper on further analyses of our data.

You had of course read an earlier draft of this paper, and this revision was based in large part on your suggestions; I'm glad it seemed more acceptable to you. I'm amused by your comment about the lack of theory, because the first draft of the paper had a brief summary of our theoretical position, which you criticized as being insufficient, and said that we should either have a more fully elaborated statement or none at all—so we took the latter course.

I'm interested in your comments on nutriment,[162] because this seems to me one of the most interesting aspects of the whole thing and one that we want to pursue further in our experiments. We tried to indicate briefly that much of the subjects' reactions could be understood as various types of attempts to provide nutriment. Leo recently made the interesting suggestion that the preoccupation of a number of subjects with their bodily pain,

---

[162] See comment following this letter.

with the unpleasantness of the situation and their desire to get out, which seems so curious on the face of it since it seems so maladaptive, is in fact a kind of nutriment and is in a way like the self-stimulation: they concentrate on a concrete and more or less realistic aspect of the situation, albeit an unpleasant one, and an actual input of stimulation, to maintain some stability and prevent anchorless drifting and the emergence of the primary process. Certainly your suggestion that the contacts with the experimenter served this purpose is very much to the point, and was neglected by us in this write-up.

We are now in the process of planning further work, which is going to be supported by the Air Force. One of the foci of future experimentation will be the nutriment issue. I thought it would be interesting to see if we could teach people ways of providing themselves with nutriment and see if such instructions wouldn't result in better ability to stand the situation, longer staying, less unpleasant affect, etc. We would plan to have several groups, one of which would be instructed to provide themselves with as much proprioceptive stimulation as possible, as well as self-produced auditory stimulation through humming, whistling, and singing, etc. Another group would be instructed in various time-passing games, making use of the overlearned frameworks of the number series, the alphabet, etc. Still another group would be given tasks to perform, in response to the regularly introduced stimuli like taps on the microphone; at one tap, the subject would have to respond by, let's say, sitting up, whereas at two taps he would be instructed to respond by clapping his cardboard cuffs together. I would predict, mostly on the basis of a hunch, that these instructions would be increasingly effective in the order given.

One of the other foci of our present plans is a more systematic exploration of functions that are impaired and functions that are unimpaired or even improved. We are devising a number of multi-stage problems which require sustained attention and concentration, not merely the brief performance of an overlearned act, and we are also going to have the "creative" task of telling TAT stories in response to pictures that are described. This last will be used both to measure imaginativeness, which we hope may increase, and also capacity to synthesize and maintain unity in a complex task stretching over a period of time—especially when the given materials include a number of figures in a complicated relationship, all of which are to be brought into the story.

In relation to your side remark on learning, you might be interested in looking at a paper I just finished reading, "The effects of sleep deprivation on performance in a simulated communication task," by Edgar Schein, in J. appl. Psychol., 1957, page 247. He reports the interesting finding that during a period of 72 hours without sleep, subjects did increasingly worse on a task borrowed from Alex Bavelas, but then when they were tested on the same function after sleeping, they did far better than they ever had before, reaching the same levels as the controls (or almost the same levels). This result, he points out, indicates that even though per-formance was undergoing successive decrements, learning was nevertheless taking place. It's one of the clearest demonstrations I know of showing operationally the difference between learning and performance. Certainly results like this create great difficulties for a stimulus-response approach to learning.

I can't take up your first criticism at any great length—the one having to do with a point about homogeneity of stimulation rather than its level. The situation is quite complicated, and I think that one has to draw on a psychoanalytic theory at times and a neurophysiological one at other times to encompass all of the data. From the standpoint of the psychoanalytic theory, at least as far as I understand it, I don't see why there should be any difference between darkness, let us say, and homogeneous light, yet experimental results seem to indicate pretty clearly that you need a great deal more isolation in darkness to get striking visual phenomena than you do when there is homogeneous stimulation. Apparently the continued steady visual input does furnish the visual centers with some kind of stimulus to autonomous activity.

I see that I didn't make myself wholly clear in the point about hallucinations and reality testing. What I tried to say is that a subject who "acts as though he would have heard your voice" does fail to test reality, in a certain literal sense, if he had not been spoken to. Yet the same subject after an even longer period of isolation and further decreases in secondary process efficiency, would <u>not</u> react to vivid but fantastic visual images as if they were real. It is the judgmental aspect of reality testing that is at issue here: the situation is one that puts a person in such a disadvantage that he pretty much has to rely on internal evidence to tell whether or not an image is produced by himself or arises from outside stimulation. If is seems plausible, if it could very well have really happened, and if he interprets it in that way, then I'm inclined to say that his reality testing has not suffered much. Do you see how the special nature of the situation complicates the usual criteria of reality testing? I don't think that it helps me particularly to use the term "illusion"; though I suppose that illusions differ from hallucinations in being somewhat more cognizant of existing reality. Thus, if I read: "Eisenhower calls summit meeting" when the newspaper headline clearly says in large type "Kruschev" I am guilty of an illusion, but the performance is more plausible than it would be if I made the whole thing up out of a non-existent newspaper. I think this issue of plausibility, of the extent to which the phenomenal production does actually correspond to the external reality—this should be the focus of our greatest concern in talking about reality testing. Obviously, we are dealing with a continuum phenomenon.

[. . .]

Bob

Comment

Elsewhere and many years later, I have commented on this concept, nutriment, as follows: "The interaction of reality with [psychic] structures appears as a issue in psychoanalytic theory primarily in Rapaport's (e.g., 1958) discussion of *nutriment*, which was his translation and adaptation of [Jean] Piaget's concept *aliment*. Rapaport's conception was, briefly, that structures require nutriment in order to be maintained, and that they get it primarily from environmental stimuli: "When such stimulus-nutriment is not available, the effectiveness of these structures in controlling id impulses may be impaired, and some of the ego's autonomy from the id may be surrendered" (1958, p. 728). In this conception, he did not distinguish clearly between two separate issues: First, structure building—undeniably, infants and children need contact with the rich world of stimuli for the growth of adequate structures; this seems to me to have been Piaget's meaning of *aliment*. Second, structure maintenance—that is, structures allegedly need constant nutriment lest they wither away; here I think Rapaport's formulation applies to some but not all structures" (Holt, 1989, p. 231). I went on to make a case for another concept to account for the same data from experiments on isolation/deprivation that concerned Rapaport.

Rapaport to Holt—July 29, 1958

[handwritten]

Dear Bob,

Thank you for your detailed letter and the many interesting points in it.

On those pertaining to your MS:

(a) thanks for the Schein reference, most interesting stuff!!!

(b) Looking forward to the additional analyses.

(c) Yes, I do contradict myself often, but in this case theory is most important!!

(d) Glad you're thinking in nutriment terms!

I'd like to discuss in person the rest of the points. I do not feel well physically and find it difficult to write more now. Will see you: please come as soon as you get back.

Superego: all your points are stimulating. This is a first draft and you do provide orientation points for redrafting.—I am glad you find it a worthwhile beginning. But there is only one simple idea in it which <u>might</u> have originated with me. [. . .][163]

Have a marvelous time and I hope Crusa will enjoy it all thoroughly. Then come and tell us all. There are a great many things I would like to talk to you about also . . . just gobs of it . . .

Affectionately

David

---

[163] Deleted paragraph concerning stamps for his collection we might be able to pick up in Europe.

Roy Schafer to Holt—October 9, 1958

This letter is included with the kind permission of Dr. Schafer.

Dear Bob,

I was glad to hear from you—and many thanks for your corrections.

On your major point about regression in the service of the ego in relation to dream work, my view as of the time I wrote that passage was this (following Freud): in the interest of sleep and of the psychic economy required in sleep, regressive forms of thought are allowed to attain conscious representation, with the potential being preserved to suspend the dream (as in [anxious] awakening or fluctuating depth of sleep) and with limits set on directness of representation. The setting and maintaining of limits, the potential to suspend the dream, and the primacy of the wish to sleep, all to me point up how active the ego is in dreaming. I meant to underscore this and not to minimize the ego-passive aspects of actualized dream thinking. My mistake on p. 85 was in saying "both are active <u>rather than</u> passive processes," for otherwise I say "do not <u>simply</u> submit to it" and "remain <u>largely</u> under the control of ego functions." I should have said "active <u>and</u> passive"—active in the respect of ego activity setting the stage for the play of primary processes and maintaining the censorship and setting the purpose of it in such dream thinking as then takes place.

I am not sure by the way that the Poetzl effect requires the explanation of <u>passive</u> appearance of stimuli in the dream; isn't the ego steadily engaged in meeting sensory impressions and binding their excitations, and may this not continue into dreaming, even recognizing the change brought about by these registrations becoming reinforced day-residues in the dream? For adaptive purposes we cannot adequately meet halfway and at the moment all impinging stimuli; we are thus left with unmastered reverberations (and reinforced ones) to deal with in sleep. (More on this in a moment.)

I did not take up unconscious fantasy because I wasn't ready to—and am not ready now. I am inclined to assume a series of levels here, each with its own censorship, as Freud said, with fantasies on some levels being like dreaming but with less awareness, and others like usual daydreams but too direct or raw and therefore censored perhaps between preconscious and conscious despite their formal closeness to the secondary process level. I think these unconscious fantasies <u>can be</u> more than hypothetical unities; interpretation can recover from amnesia a repressed fantasy and can also make it possible for an elusive, unverbalized fantasy to find a form and language in the preconscious and be born: wasn't it in a special sense in existence, as a daydream is, prior to its delivery by interpretation? The interpretation of body feelings, I think, often has just this result. I think of Loewald's [1960] paper on the Therapeutic action of psychoanalysis here (unpublished so far but available, I think) even though he does not center on unconscious fantasy as such.

Getting back to the dream work, etc.: I said "as of the time I wrote the passage" because I am no longer satisfied with the entire conceptualization. Something is missing, I feel. I can't express it yet. It has to do with levels of organization, with ego states on different levels, with the status of objects and self on these levels, with object-loss and self-loss and restitutive efforts, and I have no sense of synthesis or even of points of attack yet. I'm pregnant but not yet even bulging.

Roy

Holt to Rapaport—October 16, 1958

Dear David:

   I mentioned to you in passing that I had a number of thoughts about activity and passivity that I wanted to pass on to you, and in going through some of my files I came across the enclosed materials, which I am sending along in a relatively unedited form. I'm not sure whether I sent you the memorandum of December 6, 1955 before or not; it's poorly organized, but has some thoughts that might be of a little interest. My memo of October 29, 1957 is somewhat better focused, and may make the earlier one somewhat more intelligible.[164] I'd be very much interested to hear your reaction on the question whether this usage of activity and passivity is consistent with yours or not. I intended it to be so, but it is easy to slip into more traditional definitions, the distinction of which from yours is not always clear. All of which reminds me of a paper I just read in which active movement of the arm by the subject was compared to passive movement of the subject's arm by the experimenter, in a setup where the image of the arm was deflected by a prism, and the subject had the task of locating critical points on a design. The active subjects were significantly superior. It's not clear to me whether this is really relevant or not, but you might want to take a look at the paper: Held, Richard & Hein, A. V. Adaptation of disarranged hand-eye coordination contingent upon re-afferent stimulation. <u>Percept. Mot. Skills</u>, 1958, <u>8</u>, 87–90.

---

[164] These two memoranda were not preserved.

I also find some handwritten notes dating back about a year on dreams and passive impressions: perhaps the reason that dreams "have a preference for taking up unimportant details of waking life" is that they are the passively perceived or registered ones, without much attention cathexis, and thus are more suitable for the ego-passive type of return in dreams.

But certain dreams are filled with content that has been very much at the focus of awareness, and has had attention cathexis—particularly traumatic dreams. Attention cathexis cannot therefore be the important variable, unless it is a matter of whether attention has been passively captured or actively directed. It is notable that a traumatic experience has the effect of returning in dreams, probably, because of the ego's passivity—its inability to master the intense stimulus actively. Indeed, part of the problem of the involuntary repetition of such traumata may be in this basic phenomenon: when an experience has been received passively by the ego, it is difficult to bring it back actively and may be difficult to <u>prevent</u> its passive return. This suggests one way of understanding failure of treatment using the purely passive recall of hypnotic or drug experiments.

It now occurs to me, on looking over these old notes, that I was so struck by the apparent correlation—passive experience (subliminal or traumatic), recovery in dream—that I overlooked the fact that the traumatic experience usually returns in dreams without much change, whereas the tachistoscopically exposed picture almost never does. Moreover, it can hardly be contended that a percept has to be passively received in order to show up in dreams, for we do dream about things we have actively attended to; nor that every subliminal and incidental, unhypercathected stimulus finds its way into the dream. Can anything be salvaged of this general proposition? Perhaps, I think, if we remember that activity and passivity are a matter of degree, and if we modify the hypothesis to read: the more passively the ego receives a stimulus and the more it tends to be overwhelmed by the stimulus because of its highly meaningful or traumatic nature, the more the latter will recur in "passive recalls"—spontaneous waking imagery and in dreams, and the more untransformed it will be.

Maybe the puzzle can be further clarified if we remember that there are <u>other</u> determinants of just which aspects of waking experience are used in the manifest dream. It may be that an ordinary hypercathected and fully conscious experience does have a relative disadvantage as material for dream imagery, but that this disadvantage can be overcome if other conditions are right: if, for example, it forms a particularly good transference-substitute for a repressed wish (as in the example of the botanical monograph dream of Freud). This still leaves unexplained the difficult problem of the occasional dream that seems to contain on the manifest level material that one would expect to be found only in the latent dream thoughts—for example, direct incest dreams. Perhaps the point here is that the discussion has shifted to <u>themes</u> in place of imagery: if one has actually had an incestuous experience, it will in all likelihood have been traumatic and thus fall under the heading of traumatic repeated dreams; otherwise, it has the status of an infantile wish and if fulfilled in dreams must make use of imagery that is at least in part transformed.[165]

Of course, it may be that the whole attempt to apply the conception of activity and passivity to relations with external reality is mistaken; yet I'm sure that you are going to take it up from the standpoint of the adaptive point of view. I have assumed that conscious awareness and the "deliberate" or "willed" bestowal of attention are the hallmarks (though perhaps not sufficient conditions) of an <u>active</u> relation to reality. Of course, it may be that a literally active, manipulative dealing with and not simply perceiving of the world is the best criterion, though, I think, as soon as that thought suggests itself it is rejected because this proposition would get us into the problem of distinguishing between action and acting out and other passive though manipulative action. It's not simple!

---

[165] In the margin here there is a handwritten note by me which reads: "The more transformed the more activity."

I had made up a list of phenomena that I thought would be ordered and clarified by the concept of activity and passivity with reference to the external environment, but as I was going along I was struck with the fact that these were in large part the same things that had occurred to me in thinking about your last autonomy paper, and specifically autonomy from the environment. (Here is the list, anyway: latent learning; intent to learn; recognition vs. recall; all of the phenomena G. W. Allport [1945] cited in his paper on the psychology of participation; the relationship between set or intention and threshold, and perhaps many other set phenomena; conditioning and trial-error learning vs. "sensible" cognitive learning; pathological phenomena: arctic hysteria, echolalia and other instances of lost autonomy from the environment; the phenomena of surrender—fright paralysis; schizophrenic involuntary empathy; the empathy of babies for the mothering person; the passivity of brain-injured persons and their vulnerability to external influence; the apparent correlation of passive reaction to color and passivity with respect to drives.)

All of this raises the question in my mind, to what extent are the concepts of autonomy and those of activity and passivity the same, and how do they differ? I realize that they are not identical; obviously, one can make passive use of the apparatuses of primary autonomy, and perhaps of secondary autonomy, too. Yet it seems to me that every advance in autonomy is an increase in, or is achieved by virtue of, activity of the ego; and whenever autonomy is lost, we seem to be dealing with passivity. I'm sure you will have thought about these issues, and I look forward to getting clarification on them.

I wonder if you know about a phenomenon I read of some years ago in <u>Scientific American,</u> having to do with what happens when a person is struck by lightning? As I recall it, some people are able to withstand this tremendous external trauma, whereas others are killed; and the difference seems to be made by an attitude of active determination to master the trauma vs. passive, frightened submission.[166] I don't have a complete file, most of my issues before 1953 having been lost in transit to New York, so I haven't looked it up in the Cumulative Index.

A couple of more notes: it may be that dreams are so hard to remember in part because the experience of dreaming is a passive one, and is thus best suited to involuntary "arising" into consciousness rather than to voluntary search. I've certainly noticed that I can often recover a dream if I don't try but simply lie down and relax;* a number of other considerations suggest that there's a connection between the posture of reclining and passivity of the ego.

It is interesting that people differ a good deal in their ability to remember dreams; this may give clues to the kinds of people who can recapture, actively, memory traces that were passively laid down. It is possible that scanning (what used to be called focusing) is related to this: the "scanner" was more able to recall incidental percepts than the "focuser"; perhaps this was a memory phenomenon and not one of perception. If so, scanners should be able to remember more dreams than focusers [cf. Eagle, 1959; Fisher, 1960].

I'm also amused to note that I once made some notes to the effect that retroactive and proactive facilitation and inhibition might be ways to study passive memory—that is, the amount of learning that goes on when a subject receives a subliminal stimulus. I guess it's obvious what kind of design I had in mind.

I'm also enclosing a dittoed research proposal describing generally our next isolation experiment. As soon as detailed plans have been drawn up—we have begun them already—they will be sent along.

---

[166] It was not in the cumulative index, and no recent search has turned it up, so I now believe that there was no such article in that magazine. I have no idea where I may have gotten the notion, perhaps from a news article about a single instance which was not scientifically investigated.

* Curiously enough, this doesn't work for me recently, perhaps since I have become too self-conscious about it! [Handwritten footnote in original.]

Now about next year: I called the chief psychologist at the Psychiatric Institute; he said that he thought they would undoubtedly be very pleased to have you there, but that there was a great shortage of office space, and he was doubtful that it would be feasible. He's going to take it up with [Lawrence C.] Kolb [MD, Director] and will let me know. Meanwhile, I have also talked to George and to Stuart Cook about the possibility here. Stuart has authorized me to tell you that the Department would be delighted to be your host and that we can guarantee you space for yourself and for a secretary. Moreover, Stuart himself raised the question whether you might not want to be protected from visitors by having an office in another building near the Square, but not in 21 Washington Place. Of course, George and I would love to have you near us at the Research Center, but we can see that it might be better from your standpoint to have a little more seclusion. At any rate, however other possibilities may turn out, you can definitely count on a welcome at NYU.

        Yours,
            Bob

Rapaport to Holt—October 24, 1958

copy of this sent to Roy Schafer 10-29-58[167]

Dear Bob:

I now [have] read your memoranda and would like to comment on them in brief.[168]

Concerning your memorandum of October 29, 1957: I think that in view of my letter I do not have to say again that this memorandum seems to me very meaningful. I would like to suggest, however, that unless you have some very ingenious idea, instructions in regard to active or passive reception or active or passive recall are not going to do much good. It is the situation that you have to structure to achieve this. I think Behrick achieved it in his experiment. It might be interesting to see whether the Rock [1983] method[169] would or would not be a good one to use. If you are not familiar with it I will be glad to write to you about it. It is possible to use my digit experiment in a similar way also. I think that your idea about the Leo Postman[170] experiments might also be a very good one.

---

[167] Handwritten notation at top of letter.

[168] The two memoranda commented on here have not been found.

[169] I could not locate the Behrick reference, possibly an early publication by H. P. Behrick, who published research on memory some decades later. Irvin Rock, an influential American cognitive psychologist of the second half of the 20th century, showed in a series of ingenious laboratory experiments, that the perception of shape is indirect, affected by its orientation—not in the retinal image, but in the real environment.

[170] Postman, with whom George Klein had collaborated at Harvard, fits the same description. It is not clear from this context what idea I had borrowed from his work.

Altogether, these two memoranda both bring up many an issue which I have thought through only in connection with our recent experiments. I wish that you would reread your own memoranda in the light of what I told you about the hypotheses underlying the present experiments.

Concerning the memorandum of December 6, 1955: Your second paragraph deals with the "concept of [perceptual] identity as used by Hebb." I think you might with profit notice that the introduction to the part on concept formation in "Diagnostic Psychological Testing" has a discussion of "identifiability" which says in a sense the same thing as Hebb [1949] did, only does so five years before Hebb on the one hand, and on the other it spells out the connection to memory, concept formation, attention, anticipation, concentration. I think that at this point I should jump to the bottom paragraph on page three and point out to you that there you, in a way, misconceive concentration. It is quite possible that your misconception has a true core, namely that the concentration does involve certain kinds of motivations besides attention cathexis, but these motivations would be of the sort which we call "ego interests," that is to say, motivations very high up in the motivational hierarchy.

Concerning the big paragraph which goes from page 1 to page 2, many of your considerations are closely involved in the kinds of experiments Broadbent [1958] did as well as in those which others did in the Cambridge laboratories. The whole problem of vigilance, distraction and other such things comes in here. Rouse and I have thought quite a bit about these and have quite a bit of elaboration of the attention cathexis theory to these phenomena and to the experimental findings concerning them. Particularly interesting you may find our analysis of Skinner's pupil Homberg. His paper was published in one of the recent issues of <u>Science</u> about two months ago or so.[171] I think that Rouse has

---

[171] I have not been able to trace either Homberg or his paper. He published nothing in *Science* in 1957 or 1958.

detailed notes of our discussion of it and we can give you the reference to it also. I think that what you say on the top of page 2 about Koffka and his "trace aggregation" is probably correct. But the point you make about "perceptual identity" is to be handled carefully because, as I mentioned to you in my first letter which I dictated today, that is something which is connected with "primary process" functioning. Likewise, the paragraph which goes from page 2 to page 3 is connected with the kind of things I wrote earlier to you today about drive organization and conceptual organization of memories.

The idea [of studying] eidetic people is very good. I think that you will want to really find eidetic people. They never have been studied with an eye equipped with psychoanalytic theory and for that very reason itself it would be very interesting to study them.

In the third paragraph on page 3 you are discussing schizophrenics and it seems to me that your point is very relevant. In the fourth paragraph you raise the question whether schizophrenia has ever been studied from this point of view. Shakow's [1947] monograph (if you want I will send you a copy of it) deals with this problem. I must say, however, that "fluctuations" have never been properly studied because there was no real method available for it. I think we could design such methods and I would be glad to discuss it with you if you want to try to design one.

Now just one more comment for the last paragraph on page 4: I think that what one has to keep here in mind is that the pleasure principle really accounts for everything that people would call either death instinct, or nirvana principle, or repetition compulsion, etc. The pleasure principle itself is an ideal and not the representation of any actual condition. Freud said so in the seventh chapter of "The Interpretation of Dreams" about it and about the primary process in general. Why it must remain an ideal was not know[n] to Freud at the time. We, however, know why it must remain an ideal and can express it in a variety of ways. First of all, we can state that all energies exist only within structures, otherwise there is no sense of talking about them. Once there are such structures it is impossible to conceive of total discharge of energy, because that would amount to the destruction of the structures also since the structures will always have thresholds and anything that is below the threshold will not be able to be discharged.

We can express this, however, in a different way also, and that is where Bexton [et al., 1954] comes in. The fact is that the maintenance of structures itself requires steady "nutriment" and it is for this reason that stimulation as nutriment is steadily sought. The point is simply that the pleasure principle would obtain only for an ideal "autonomous" id, but it cannot obtain for an id coupled with an ego, which amounts to a structural connection. Then, Bexton found that intolerance for lack of stimulation is due to the fact that without such stimulation the structure is threatened with destruction from the id side also, and maybe is liable to an autonomous decay. There is much to be discussed further on this point also, but I can't go on further.

I hope you see how closely these memoranda are to my present preoccupations and I would be delighted to consider all these issues together with you further.

Sincerely yours,
David

Rapaport to Holt—October 25, 1958

Copy of this sent to Roy Schafer 10-29-58.[172]

Dear Bob:

[. . .]

I read your letter last night with a great deal of interest, though I have not yet gotten to your memoranda. I will react today to the letter and maybe tomorrow to the memoranda. Actually, I wish that we had the opportunity to sit down and talk rather than do it through letters, because you have touched on a series of questions which stand in the very focus of my interest. I will try to describe to you how I came upon the problems which you raised, because that will probably be the easiest way to show you how I would like to deal with them. I say "would like to" because the body of problems upon which you touch is one of the several which prevented me so far from publishing the paper [Rapaport, 1953d].

As I stated in the introduction of the last draft of the manuscript, my earliest experiences which served as sources and stimulations for the concept were connected with the conditions under which I and other people consider ourselves "creative." I mean that there are some people who feel that they have done something only when they suddenly get an idea without sweating for it, while others will feel that they have done something only if they worked their heads off. What is much less clear in the

---

[172] Handwritten notation at top of letter.

manuscript is that the second impetus for the whole theory formation is related to those passages in the 7th Chapter which speak about the secondary process and suggest that it is connected with a heightened potential. The peremptoriness of the primary process and the controlling and controllable "take it or leave it" character of the secondary process were actually the points where the conceptualization began.

Now, it is not just playing with words if I suggest that my own experience of the first of these points of departure which I mentioned was "passive" in regard to my conceiving of activity-passivity theoretically. This would not be correct to say, however, for the second point of departure, because there I actually fully actively pursued the problem. I did not just think it, I was reflectively aware of it. I am mentioning this for two reasons: partly to point out that the whole argument in "Cognitive Structures" [Rapaport, 1957a] concerning the various degrees of ability to reflect (awareness of awareness) belongs in this theoretical context; partly, however, I am mentioning it to indicate other things in dealing with which I also have been somehow deriving sources for the later forming of the concept of activity-passivity. These I shall discuss in a minute. For the moment I would like to point out only that the review of the literature which seems to be the real focus (together with the case illustration) of the manuscripts themselves, was totally deliberate effort. In this sense it was then fully active, even more so than my relation to the actual source from which the conceptualization issued, namely the passages in the 7th Chapter (and the paper "The Unconscious" [Freud, 1915]) to which I referred.

It will amuse you to notice that within the totally active orientation of the work of analyzing the literature there were also important passive phases, namely while I was determined by the time I started working this out to make something out of it, because I was convinced that I am relating myself to a real characteristic of phenomena, I nevertheless went to the literature with a suspended judgment and I think I did allow the material I collected to fall into whatever pattern it will. True, this pattern was within the force-field of my suspended active orientation, and that made a difference. What I mean to convey is that every active orientation has within itself also the possibility of suspending itself; the less active it is, the less possibility it has normally to suspend itself. In the terms Kris [1952] used, this would read: the less active an orientation is, the less regression in the service of the ego is possible from it.

I mentioned two of the sources for the conceptualization of activity and passivity above. In between these, however, there were other such major sources. The ones which stand out in relation to your letter were on the one hand the attitude of the patient, in the course of free association and the attitude of the therapist in "evenly hovering attention"; and on the other, one which closely interacted with this one was the attention-concentration business throughout our Diagnostic Psychological Testing [Rapaport, Gill, & Schafer, 1945–1946; Holt (ed.), 1968]. If you review the section on attention and concentration which introduces the part of Diagnostic Psychological Testing dealing with arithmetic and digit span, and the rationale sections of arithmetic and digit span, you will see that those considerations which you advance in your letter concerning "attention cathexis" and its relation to activity-passivity have been touched on there. In brief, one could say that under favorable conditions the automatic distribution of attention cathexis is passive, while in concentration it is active. The passivity condition obtains both when motivations or external stimuli are allowed to attract attention cathexis in the free competitive interplay that exists between motivations, between stimuli, and between both of these.

But not only under these conditions is such a passivity achieved; such a passivity is achieved also in "automatized performance." A further pursuit of this last point must lead back to Hartmann's [1939] big paper and particularly to the section on automatization, or preconscious automatisms. It should be kept in mind what he has to say there about what the French school called "automatic," which we would call the automatism of the id, and which is a passivity of a lower order than the one which we are talking about here. I am making this point partly to confirm what you had to say about the various layerings of activity and passivity. I am, however, implying also that there is not a smooth quantitative transition but qualitative differences obtain also for these various layers of activity and passivity. If this point is not entirely clear (though what I wrote above should illustrate in two or three places this point), ask me and I will be glad to dwell on it.

But it is not only in these sections on attention and concentration that activity-passivity issues are involved in <u>Diagnostic Psychological Testing</u>. I would like to enumerate a few others. At this moment it is not quite clear to me whether the text of the writing in the volumes itself reveals this directly. I know that I have taught it to the classes of the School of Clinical Psychology in this spirit. For instance, in the BRL,[173] when the subject is asked to say why a group of objects which were put together by the examiner belong together, you have by and large a passive position, while if the subject is asked to select out of all the objects those which belong with the object the examiner puts out, you have by and large an active condition. However, both the passive and the active condition can be transformed by the subject into its opposite. For instance, when the subject begins to actively analyze the commonalities of the objects put out and begins actively to analyze the difference between those objects which were not put out by the examiner and those which were put out by him, the passive condition is transformed into an active one. In turn, however, when the subject puts himself into a position of evenly hovering attention and thus scans all the objects and puts out all those which "seem to go" with the sample object, then he can achieve a great degree of passivity.

Even more important seems to be the relationship between

---

[173] An object-sorting test of conceptual thinking. Though it was created by Kurt Goldstein and Martin Scheerer, they did not publish about it until 1941. It came into wide use after Bolles, Rosen, and Landis (1938) wrote about their use of it with schizophrenics. So it became familiarly known by their initials instead of G&S.

digit span, information, and the Babcock story recall as well as the Babcock sentence recall [Babcock & Levy, 1930]. The rationale of the latter two should also contain some reference to the issues here discussed. If they do not, then my memory is misleading me and it mixes up what I taught about it with what we wrote about it. I imagine you know my considerations about the relationship between knowledge, information, and memory. Somewhere in Emotions and Memory [Rapaport, 1942a] these issues are discussed. But I imagine that I must have taken up something like this in one of the footnotes in Organization and Pathology of Thought [Rapaport, 1951] also. I can't for the moment take the time to put my finger on these. It suffices to say that memory, in contrast to much of perception, has a wealth of earmarks of subjective experience and context. It enriches the percept while it impoverishes it in some respects. This impoverishment is the one which is so commonly familiar, while the enrichment is partly the one to which I refer as "connotative enrichment" in "Cognitive Structures." [Rapaport, 1957a]

Now, as a memory is progressively transformed into information and then into knowledge, there is a continuous stripping away of the temporal, spatial, and personal earmarks of the origins of this information and knowledge. (I have discussed this issue also in connection with "identification" in some footnotes in Organization and Pathology of Thought.) With this relative impoverishment, however, an automatization in Hartmann's sense takes place. While this relative impoverishment makes information and knowledge less mobilizable by those motivations which attended their acquisition originally, it becomes (as a preconscious automatism) more readily available to mobilization by any high-order motivation and attention cathecting. This is the kind of thing to which Freud refers when he makes the distinction between identity of perception and identity of thought in the 7th Chapter of "The interpretation of Dreams." The reachability of information and knowledge items within the drive organization of memories (or, more correctly, from the side of the drive organization of memories) becomes more difficult, while it becomes more easy for experimentation in thought, that is to say through the network of thought relationships, through the conceptual organization of memories.

In general, information rises just as readily to consciousness in a passive way as does an easy digit series. But while digit span is transformed into concentration mainly by obsessional and compulsive people, all of us are capable, and constrained, to seek with a concentration for certain information items if the information questions get very difficult. However, we (all of us) know also that often this kind of search for information by concentration is unsuccessful. In such cases we say, "it will come to me if I do not think about it." In turn, however, sentence recall and story recall in the Babcock [test] are always to some extent concentration achievements and this is, as you will see in the rationale sections, connected also with "meaning" which always implies relationships which have to be sought out. I think that a little reflection will show you readily how our understanding at this time of these relationships obtaining between subtest[174] items was deeply influenced by the two basic rules of psychoanalysis, that pertaining to the patient and that pertaining to the therapist. I think that with these considerations I have laid the groundwork on which I can comment now on your letter.

First of all, I am very interested in the Held paper which you call attention to. I think it must be relevant. I would only say, before reading it, that I would expect some individual differences of significance in this kind of phenomenon. I am asking my secretary to get me this paper.

Concerning your second paragraph on the first page, I would like to say that the point is not so much that the dream prefers simply the items which are free of "attention cathexis," though

---

[174] In much of the preceding discussion, Rapaport was referring to subtests of David Wechsler's (1939) *Wechsler-Bellevue Adult Intelligence Scale*, revised and in current use as the *Wechsler Adult Intelligence Scale* (Wechsler, 1958).

this is the upshot; but rather that something which is attended by attention cathexis is thereby more strongly linked into the conceptual organization of memories (as I called it) and because of that it becomes either unavailable to the drive organization of memories (which is dominant in the dream) or else it becomes immediately repressed. If you take a look at "The Unconscious," you will see that you were right in some later comments you made in this letter that the derivative drive representations are always only those which are not solidly built into the secondary process (conceptual organization of memories). If by some quirk of circumstance an item becomes a drive derivative (displacement of drive energy takes place to it), it succumbs to repression.

Now to your sentence which goes from p. 1 to p. 2 of your letter. Again I think that you place too much emphasis on the fact of attention cathexis rather than on what it denotes. Don't forget please that a drive impulse, or drive derivative, can also become attention-cathected and does become if it reaches motility in a psychotic. (In the form of a slip of the tongue or other parapraxis it does not obtain attention cathexis.) I would also call attention to it that the emphasis is in this paragraph too much on "passively captured" rather than on the state of the ego which was so overwhelmed by the traumatic experience that it was not capable of activity. If you reinterpret [in] this sense what you wrote, I agree with it fully. Likewise I would agree that the last sentence of your paragraph represents correctly in the activity-passivity language (or at least it hints correctly at the possible expression in this language) a basic contribution of ego psychology to this problem of therapeutic technique. One could extend this point actually to the whole problem of "working through."

In the second paragraph of the second page of your letter, you ask "can anything be salvaged of this general proposition." I think that you again offer rich material for consideration. I think all of it is pertinent and therefore need not be salvaged. It is here where you talk about degrees of activity and passivity, and on that I have already commented that there are not only degrees but quantitative differences. There are various frames of reference within which something is active or passive. The same thing which is active in one way may be passive in another frame of reference. For instance, the ego's waiving activity within a certain function will result in passivity but only within <u>that</u> frame of reference and that will be a passivity which is still activity within another frame of reference. An example of this is what I described about myself in regard to my work on assembling the literature evidence in the activity-passivity manuscript. The fact that some passively received experiences are not [found in the content of dreams], and others are only in distorted form entering dreams is no contradiction to the theses. It would be a contradiction only if passivity could mean total exclusion of all activity. This is, however, never true. The passively received is favored by the dream because it is not integrated with the "conceptual organization of memory," that is to say with the secondary process. But active synthetic functions of the ego work on all levels of functioning (in this respect again I have to refer to "Cognitive Structures") and these synthetic functions may exclude or may reorganize and include material which was passively retained. As a matter of fact, it is going to do what is consonant with the possible synthesis in the given situation, and synthesis there always is, because there always must be. Nor is it a contradiction to this that the traumatic experience returns in the dream without much change. Regrettably, we do not know enough about the synthetic function which results in this effect, but we are safe in making the inference that it is a specific kind of synthetic function which produces it. How weak a synthetic function it is, is another question.

Your third paragraph on the second page does not really bring anything new except that it brings up the type of material which is usually latent dream thought and at times appears unchanged on the manifest level. I agree with you that here you shifted to a theme and did not stick to the material of the imagery. On the level of the theme this thing is relatively well understood, namely we conceive of such phenomena as defensive in relation to more repressed and even less available themes.

I am coming now to the paragraph which reaches from p. 2 to p. 3. I will have to catch up here with some historical reminiscences which I did not manage to put into the preamble of this letter. I would certainly deny that "to apply the conception of activity and passivity to relations with external reality is mistaken." Gill, [Allen] Wheelis, and I think Brenman too, have pointed out when I presented this paper in its early drafts at a staff seminar at Riggs, that I totally disregarded the problem of external reality and passivity in relation to it. It is a fact that at the time I did not know how to cope with this problem though as you can see, my original experiences which were the sources of the conceptualization necessarily implied it. I became then silent for a long while about this paper because I had to think it out. At this point I will have to make some comments which reach later parts of your letter also. Actually, I acted in the mss. both in regard to "autonomy" and in regard to "activity-passivity" as though I believed that the psychic apparatus is a closed system and a purely "intrapsychic" psychology could be formulated as a self-contained system. I did not at the time realize what you stress at the bottom of p. 2, namely that without the adaptive point of view no systematic psychology is possible. Maybe I am doing myself an injustice when I put it this way. Actually, I have been at the very same time full with the adaptive point of view and with studying it in relation to Hartmann, in relation to Erikson, and in relation to Piaget. It was particularly Piaget who, against the background of the other two, really triggered me to make something systematic out of it. I think that the attention focused on these three men's work prevented me from seeing the same thing in my own work. Only after the adaptation problem was metapsychologically becoming clear to me was I able to turn back to this.

Merton, in his early drafts of his chapter [of Gill & Brenman, 1959] on hypnotic regression, has actually undertaken the crucial step and without that crucial step I would not have been able to see Piaget the way I saw him, I couldn't have pitted him against the background of Hartmann and Erikson and I could not have made the step of linking all this to activity-passivity also. If you will read Merton's chapter and particularly early versions of it, you will see how it contains all the considerations which I later summarized in my recent "The Theory of Ego Autonomy: A Generalization" [Rapaport, 1958]. Now in that paper you will see for the first time that the adaptive point of view has been applied by me to the autonomy problem and that at the very end of the paper I even make a link between the autonomy problem and the activity-passivity problem. This also is in answer [to] a later point you have made about this relationship in this letter. Indeed it could be said that I was so blind at the time when I worked on the early drafts of the activity-passivity paper that without the criticisms and particularly without Merton's criticism, I might have seduced myself to publish the activity-passivity paper at the time. In the activity-passivity paper there is a point where in connection with a Freud reference I, by implication, take the stand that we are not interested in the activity-passivity relations in regard to the environment. But if this is the true record of the past, one could also say that the main reason I did not publish this paper as yet is that the adaptive problem, that is, the relation to the external environment and the passivity-activity implications of that, prevented me from publishing. I had to digest those first.

Nevertheless, I have to comment—particularly concerning the sentence which is transitional from p. 2 to p. 3—in a way, that sentence does not take account of it that within that very active relation which you are discussing, and which, from the [stand-]point of your attention cathexis, amounts to concentration, there is a place for a relative regression in the service of the ego which makes use of automatisms and allows automatic, intuitive, and free responding to the external world to be part of the relation to the external world. This is again that relationship between activity and passivity and the degrees of it which I have discussed above already. You are right: it is not simple, but the action and acting-out relationship is most relevant and there are many transitions and qualitatively different forms between the two ideal extremes, just as there are such between manipulation and passivity. There are activities which are not manipulations. Actually, we have been discussing such things particularly concerning acting out in my bull sessions [with patients at Riggs] for the last few weeks.

In the second paragraph on p. 3 you give a very striking long list of phenomena which to my mind are all very relevant to the problem we are discussing. May I point out to you that referring to "arctic hysteria" links this whole matter to stimulus deprivation. I think you will want to talk to Stuart Miller who is studying the whole literature of anecdotic material on stimulus deprivation. I would like to point out to you that the echolalia problem I touched on in the recent Ego Autonomy [paper]. Your very way of putting it seems to indicate that you are mindful of this. May I comment that the "passivity of brain-injured," the whole "concrete vs. abstract" issue comes in here, and links closely to those references I have made to the 7th Chapter of "The Interpretation of Dreams" in the very beginning of this paper. I would like to point out to you that to my mind all abstractions are built as higher-order structures by attention cathexes cathecting the concrete material. It is on a higher level of potential controlling a lot of lower-level potential investment in the concrete material. Actually, I think that in my discussions of schizophrenia in the footnotes in <u>Organization and Pathology of Thought</u> you will find this issue discussed. At least hinted at. I would add here that Shapiro's [1956] discussion of activity and passivity in his recent paper on color responses is relevant: you referred to it in the last lines of this paragraph. I would like also to add that "field dependence" [Gardner et al., 1959] is relevant also. But in the main what I would like to stress pertains also to the second paragraph on p. 4. There are two experiments by a fellow whose name is Burdick.[175] On these we have hit in connection with our present experiments. They are most significant and directly corroborative

---

[175] The only relevant reference I have been able to find was published a few years later: Schachter & Burdick (1955).

of the hypotheses and findings we have in our experiments. I am asking my secretary to get from Dr. [Richard] Rouse the references of these two papers. I think that all investigations concerning subliminal, or as George calls it "incidental," learning have to take these papers into account. If there is any question how these papers corroborate what we have been doing and thinking, let me have a chance to explain.

Concerning the third paragraph of your third page, I think I have already given the answer. In the main, I could like to refer you to the latter parts of my "The Theory of Ego Autonomy: A Generalization." If that will not clarify the issue sufficiently (and it was quite cryptically put there), I would like very much for you to write to me about it and I will spell out the point.

Concerning the fourth paragraph on your third page, I am ordering from Scientific American a reprint of that paper. You may want to ask Richter of Johns Hopkins to let you have either a manuscript or, if he has, a paper on his experiments with rats.[176] Wild rats, if thrown into the water and prevented by the shape of the vessel from freely swimming, give up and die. Domesticated rats will struggle and if left alone, die with exhaustion, while the wild rats will give up and die instantaneously. There is more to this, and the whole issue seems to be connected more or less in the way you connect the reaction of the people struck by lightning.

Concerning the last paragraph on your p. 3, I would feel again that you have put the emphasis too much on the "passive experience" of the dream. But this passive experience rather indicates the type of state of consciousness and state of ego which is in question. The problem is a very closely connected one to the paradox one finds in the 7th Chapter. On the one hand, Freud asserts

---

[176] Curt Paul Richter, a professor of psychobiology at Johns Hopkins Medical School, also held a domesticated rat tightly in one hand. Eventually, it stopped squirming as it realized its situation was hopeless. When he dropped the rat into a tank of water, it sank to the bottom of the tank making no effort to swim.

that it is distortion by censorship which is responsible for condensation, displacement, etc.; on the other hand, he asserts that these are part of "the function of the mental apparatus when freed of inhibition." I would express the whole issue by saying that there are different levels of mental functioning with different synthetic functions appropriate to them and the transition from one to the other is difficult and is what is then classified under the heading [of] censorship. This should shed some light also on why lying down and relaxing under certain conditions, but not under conditions of resistance in therapy, helps in recovering dreams. This has also a link to the point you made earlier in your letter that the somatic relaxation is passivity or is connected with passivity.

The first paragraph on your p. 4 tempts me to try to compare the scanners with people who allow in themselves an evenly hovering attention while the "focusers" are people who concentrate. I believe that this holds in these people to various degrees both in memory and in perception. The scanners should be able to remember dreams better than the focusers for this very reason then. Evenly hovering attention is something they are more capable of.

Concerning the last paragraph of your letter, I want to thank you for your interest and helpfulness. I do want you to remember, however, that I have asked you to wait with this matter because I have not yet gotten a chance to discuss it with Dr. Knight.

If Crusa wishes to, tell her to keep the Kant paper. I have other copies of it.

> Yours,
> David

Notes on Repression and
Subliminal Registration[177]

Robert R. Holt, April 1958

When the Poetzl [1917] experiment was first reported, some people thought that it was an experimental analogue of repression. Indeed, the fact that the device of subliminal registration implants an idea (a term used here to stand generally for images and other mental content) that could be shown to have effects, and yet which was not directly available to efforts at conscious memory, all strongly suggested repression.

Freud [1915] says that repression is a two-fold process: a) the withdrawal of attention-cathexis, plus b) counter-cathectic pushes downward (and possibly a third, downward pulling process also, as in the theory of primal repression and its later effects). One reason for the resemblance of subliminal registrations to repressions is that the former likewise lack attention-cathexis, but because it had never been bestowed. (How <u>does</u> attention-cathexis become attached to an idea that arises from within?)

We may see the difference by considering the problem of what happens when repression is lifted and what was formerly unconscious becomes conscious. When the counter-cathexis is removed, the force behind the idea (impulse, affect, and other instinctual de-

---

[177] Unpublished personal notes, mainly meant for discussions with Rapaport. Original sent to Rapaport on October 30, 1958.

rivatives) tends to project it into awareness, or endows it with enough cathexis so that it does not need additional attention-cathexis, or it puts it into a structural state where attention-cathexis is bestowed, or something—I don't think the process by which consciousness again accrues to what was repressed has been carefully worked out.

Note that there is a difference between two states of awareness: 1) Something is in consciousness and is recognized—it fits into a remembered context, it is not only understood but it bears a distinctive feeling that acts like a name-tag saying, "This is <u>my</u> idea." 2) Something is in consciousness without any such context and perhaps without the familiarity name-tag. (Some of the defenses akin to repression, especially isolation, may work by preventing the emergence of the context—keeping the idea separated from other things that give it its true significance for the person; while obsessional defense also splits it off and makes it seem ego-alien, so that it is not only not familiar, but lacks the personal tag.) A partial lifting of repression, then, may let an idea back into awareness but without part or all of its context. We see extreme examples of this in fugue states (see Rapaport's [1951d] paper on states of consciousness).

In the case of subliminally registered ideas, the fact that there was no conscious context to begin with, or rather no connection between what was going on consciously and the subliminal registration, produces an artificial isolation—an experimental analogue of the defense—and robs it of one of the usual aids to memory: associative links. When we try to remember something, we usually endeavor to reinstate in consciousness some kind of imagery of the most easily available aspects of the context (this is usually guided by the instruction to remember) and try to let the chains of association lead attention-cathexis to the missing idea. Since that possibility is not available in the case of a subliminally registered idea, and since we don't usually have direct access to our memory traces (something that is not feasible because they are so vast—some kind of scanning or search mechanism is necessary), the effort to remember produces nothing. My previous memo on two types of memory in relation to Rapaport's conception of activity and passivity contains ideas that should be brought in at this point: what has been <u>actively</u> received is available to active efforts at memory (as well as passive recurrences); what was <u>passively</u> received is available only or primarily to passive types of memory, especially if it was not consciously experienced, since consciousness involves at least a minimal activity of the ego. Such passive types of memory include imagery, fantasy, dreams, etc., in all of which the recovered images lack the hallmarks of recognition.

This formulation suggests that any device that would enable a repressed idea to remain ego-alien, or not be recognized as familiar and one's own, may enable it to come into consciousness without the lifting of the repression (that is, without the removal of the counter-cathectic barrier). Thus, passive forms of memory may succeed when active ones fail, with repressed as well as subliminally registered ideas. A good example would be the emergence in projective techniques of repressed ideas or their close derivatives (via displacement, symbolization, or other primary process mechanisms). Dreams and hysterical fantasies also provide excellent examples; compare also Aichhorn's[178] diagnostic device: "say 3 totally unconnected words" between which he was able to supply the missing connections due to his knowledge of the case or of delinquent children generally, and penetrate through the repressed idea. In children's play, likewise, what is repressed becomes conscious without recognition and thus without threat, so that the repression is bypassed but maintained.

Problem: Does being received in awareness give an idea more "identifiability"? making it more resistant to primary process modifications, less mobile?

---

[178] August Aichhorn (1878–1949), a Viennese school teacher turned psychoanalyst, was best known for his 1925 book, translated as *Wayward youth* (New York: Viking Press, 1935). As a training analyst, he analyzed several prominent American psychoanalysts.

Rapaport to Holt—November 3, 1958

Dear Bob:

Thank you for the exchange between Roy and you that you have sent me. I will respond to it here. I will send a copy of this to Roy and I would like to send along to him our exchange. By the way, I would like to send that exchange to several people of our circle. I hope you will not mind.

In general, I must say that I would take Roy's point of view on the major points of these exchanges. Except that I, just like you, would consider the activity-passivity issue more urgent in this context, in the sense I have expressed myself in our exchange. Also I feel that some of the problems Roy touches on in the second page of his letter of October 9 are somewhat clearer than they seem to him: some of them at least have been touched on in my "Cognitive Structures".

As for your letter of October 20, may I call your attention that the point you attribute to Erich Fromm is stated by Freud clearly in his last footnote in the 6th Chapter of "Interpretation of Dreams" and is taken up twice again in some detail in the 7th Chapter.

While I think that the Dement investigations are interesting, and the Dement-Fisher collaboration may bring very interesting new results, I seriously doubt whether at this stage of the game anything physiological learned about sleep or dreams will help us to unravel the problem of dreams.

Concerning the second paragraph of your second page: that dreams are actually "crowded junk shops to include everything."

May I call your attention particularly to the fact that the associative connections, which in the course of interpretation are discovered to link various parts of the dream, while they are not necessarily the actual path the dream formation took, show clearly where the "junk shop" character of the dream lies.

The main point, however, seems to me that George's conception of "incidental perception" replacing "subliminal perception" does link the whole dream problem to the memory problem at large. If you will take a look again at that old paper by Edwin Newman [1939] on forgetting in the sleep state vs. forgetting in the waking state, you will notice that it is the incidental and unimportant materials that are being lost during the sleeping state while the important material undergoes much less loss than it does in the waking state. If you link this up with Hebb's [1949] conception of how, through recruitment and fractioning, assemblies are formed and crystallized and broken up, you will see readily that the "autonomous" organization process leaves the important, that which has been structured already, untouched if no new important waking experiences interfere with this structuring. The incidental, that which in Hebb's terms is not steadily included in the firing pattern, becomes fractioned off or re-recruited to other connections.

I think this gives us grossly the backgrounds to what is happening during the sleep state. I would imagine that if the Dement results really pertain to dream formation then they will indicate to us only the real crystallization periods and not the steadily ongoing organization process which is steady. This conception, which I try to express here in Hebb's terms, can be demonstrated to be totally parallel with the Freudian conception in the 7th Chapter of "Interpretation of Dreams."

If we are lucky, our present investigations and our study of the literature will nail this stuff down at least on one point. I can't at this moment go further into this matter, but we can do so when we meet.

Yours,

David

P.S. As you can see I am under the impression that really there is much that we already know dimly and have to pull together. The points where we do not know enough are those where Roy touches on the hierarchic ordering of states of the ego or of consciousness, and where you—in your letter to me—touch on "the grease of activity and passivity." But even there we have a first entry on the issue.

cc. Dr. Roy Schafer

Comment

This letter seems to have been dictated and the transcript sent with only a hurried reading if any. It contains a good many obscure phrases, some of which I have attempted to clarify by punctuation, but I may have not succeeded in capturing Rapaport's intention. For example, in the P.S., the long second sentence reads as follows in the original: "The points where we do not know enough are those where Roy touches on the hierarchicly a ring [hierarchic ordering?] of states of the ego or of consciousness and where you touch on in your letter to me on "the grease of activity and passivity." I cannot find that final odd phrase in any of my letters to him, do not recognize it, but suspect it was the secretary's mishearing of a dictated phrase like "degrees of . . ."

Holt to Rapaport—November 11, 1958

Dear David:

It's neither orderly nor polite of me to leave your two long and thoughtful letters of recent date unanswered while I go on to raise new issues. When I read your letters, however, I realized that I needed to go back and re-read your paper on activity and passivity before I could answer them. And in the course of reading the paper, a number of new questions have arisen, which I'd like to pass on to you. At last, I may be able to come to comment on your letters.

Aside from occasional minor unclarities, I think the first eighteen pages of the paper go quite well. Your conception of activity and passivity grows understandably out of the clinical example, and many interesting points are made in these pages. I found the next big section, numbered III, a good deal harder to assimilate. It goes along clearly enough paragraph by paragraph, yet I think it fails to communicate in the large. I have the dissatisfied feeling that you never clearly show the relationship between Freud's usage of the terms activity and passivity and your own. I guess the point that I didn't get clearly in previous readings of the paper is that you actually reject Freud's usages by showing them to be internally inconsistent and to lead nowhere. I suppose it is difficult and in many ways undesirable to start the discussion by a bald statement that, although Freud frequently uses the terms activity and passivity and in several more or less related senses, he never clarifies these terms and when his usages are closely examined they prove to be confused and contradictory.

Or am I in some way caricaturing your critique? As I see it, you are saying that his discussions of the layering of defenses and the vicissitudes of instincts, in relation to activity and passivity, suggest essentially your concept of the latter. The difficulty for the reader, I think, is that these points get somewhat lost in the profusion of detailed and technical discussion of many theoretical points. This is a rather difficult and ticklish problem of organization in writing. I would help, I think, if somewhere you would state explicitly that there is no relationship between the concepts of masculinity-femininity and activity-passivity, as you see them.

Because of the structural difficulties in the paper, I didn't find the summary that starts on page 35 to be very convincing. When I read it this last time, I thought to myself that you hadn't really shown that the conceptions of activity and passivity you reject here in favor of your own are "not useful" though as I glance over the paper now and try to get a truly synoptic view, I think you probably did do so—just not in a clear-cut way. What jars me in this passage on page 35 is the repetition of the word "useful"— useful for what? In what context? By what criterion? My present impression is that you showed the other meanings of activity and passivity to be confused or internally contradictory, and of course this would make them "not useful" although only in an indirect and implicative way. My suggestion, in short, is that you make your stand not on the issue of usefulness but on formal methodological issues.

Somehow I found the brief section on regression in the service of the ego disappointing. Perhaps I expected too much from it; in any event, it seemed to me that you merely restated the issues in terms of activity and passivity.

In the next to the last paragraph of this section, on page 41, I found the final sentence unclear, partly because you introduce an undefined term, "ego integration." I translate this for myself as: "active organization work" but I'm not sure that that is exactly what you mean. Certainly the word <u>ego</u> in this context seems entirely redundant, for surely all integration is by definition an ego function. Then near the end of the sentence, your clause, "whether the process in question is one of activity or of passivity, as here defined" puzzles me. It seems to me that what you are saying is that in any creative product there is active organizing work, and therefore the process is essentially an active one even though the activity may not take place in awareness, so that the subjective <u>experience</u> may be either one of activity or of passivity. If I read you right, then, this last point could be taken care of by making the end of the sentence read: "whether the <u>experience</u> in question . . ."

Perhaps I am just repeating myself in an earlier letter when I note that I find the treatment of the relationship between activity-passivity and autonomy to be unsatisfactory in this draft. You indicate that there is some kind of relationship, but I still wonder whether the concept of activity-passivity adds anything essential that is not implicit in the concepts of primary and secondary autonomy.

Now when it comes to section V, where you take up the question of psychic structure in relation to activity-passivity, I have some more basic doubts. The section itself is greatly clarifying, I think, and I understood on re-reading it the problems of structure formation better than ever before—or so was my subjective impression.

Perhaps I can state my question best in terms of an issue that arose in a discussion I had with a student who is currently taking a reading course with me in the psychology of thinking. The question she asked, and which I was really unable to answer, is: If hypercathexis is used as countercathexis, and if defenses are structuralized countercathexes, <u>and</u> if the supply of hypercathexis available to a person is limited, how does it happen that as a person's defenses get built up he does not become progressively impoverished of hypercathexis? In this paper you come closer to answering these questions than I realized, and you seem very nearly to confront them head-on on page 45 in the footnoted sentence plus the note. If I understand your answer, it is that the hypercathectic energy is raised to a higher potential in the course of being structuralized, so that only a small part of it will do the work that a larger amount was originally required to do; and second, by the notion of a consolidated continuous defense line with token manning and a free reserve, you provide for the possibility that as defensive structure building proceeds, energies formerly locked in defensive struggle become freed.

These are ingenious, if to my taste somewhat too metaphoric answers; but I don't think they really dispose of the basic point. They only reduce to a minimum the amount of hypercathexis that has to remain tied up in defensive structures; I still see no way to account for the fact that people do not become progressively impoverished in hypercathexis as they develop increasingly elaborate structures. Your argument about the consolidation defensive line would seem to handle a limited range of phenomena, involved in the production of a generalized defensive strategy rather than many specific little defensive activities. I can see this argument as applied to the development of what I think you once called ego-narrowing as a result of the generalization of repression in hysteria.

However we term it, the fact that neutral information gets lost in a hysterical person who has a highly generalized strategy of repression would seem to call for this kind of model. The trouble is that, for me, the model fits the pathological over-extension of defense, not the mature, differentiated minimization of defensive interference with adaptation. A non-hysterical person who still represses certain selected impulses calls for a different kind of conceptualization, I think, than that of the continuous defense line. Any way I look at it, it seems to me that (1) maturity is a product of extensive structure-building and extensive differentiation of psychic structures; but (2) such a mature person with highly developed psychic structures has _more_ hypercathexis available freely to him for conflict free work than a person with simpler, more generalized psychic structure (e.g., the hysteric we've just been discussing).

Some way has to be found out of this dilemma. One way I know you have talked about elsewhere is the assumption that the energy of the impulse that is countercathected is somehow used in its own control—a possibility that goes so strongly against common sense that I find myself unable to entertain it seriously. I recall that somewhere in your book on the organization and pathology of thought you appealed to the analogy of a river that silts up its banks and directs itself into new channels; but I think that this analogy is really not a good one and that it won't hold up on close inspection. If you'd like me to, I'll criticize that in detail some time. I doubt that you need such a critique, however.

A second possibility would attack the problem through the assumption of a fixed reservoir or store of hypercathectic energy. This would be a little bit ad hoc in some respects, or would be if one simply assumed that whenever we notice an increase of available hypercathexis that can't be accounted for by the <u>partial</u> release of previously invested hypercathexis for defensive purposes, one simply assumes that new hypercathexis has been created somewhere. Rather, I think this notion of a fixed supply of libido (or of hypercathexis) needs to be attacked on quite different ground, as part of a thorough cleansing of psychoanalytic theory from the closed-system model that was clearly in Freud's mind and which is derived from the Bruecke-Helmholz school. They attempted to bring order into psychic phenomena by the strict application of principles borrowed directly from the physics of closed systems, with the accompanying thermodynamic laws. I think you agree that Bertalanffy [1950] has effectively argued against the application of such models to human psychology, and that I don't need to restate the arguments for the open system model.

Now I think this has very far-reaching implications for psychoanalytic theory, and I hope to see them clearly spelled out some day. Whether or not I can do the job myself I'm not sure at the moment. For a beginning, it seems to me that we still have a structural-functional model, or a structural-energetic model, but that energy is conceived of not in hydrodynamic terms nor in terms of economics[*] (so much money in the bank, which can be spent for this or for that); rather, I think we have to think of the human organism as an energy-using engine, with a <u>more or less constant</u> expenditure of energy, but with the possibility of having increases in both the input and output of energy.

In these terms, if structure building is conceived of as one result of the expenditure of hypercathectic energy, viewed as a continuously flowing stream or flame, then as long as the result of the structure building operation does not require the <u>continuous</u> expenditure of new inputs of hypercathectic energy for defense, there is a net saving and the problem is, I think, solved. Let me go back a step: in the acute phase of structure building, when there is an instinctual impulse threatening outbreak with the production of intolerable anxiety as a result, a considerable portion of the continuing income and outgo of hypercathectic energy has to be devoted to the continuous countercathecting of this instinctual derivative. Somehow (and this is a mighty big unclarity in my mind) a structure is then formed that does the job; the continuous flow of hypercathexis no longer needs to be diverted into this channel, and thus the person is left with his usual full supply.

Assuming that something along those lines takes care of that problem, let me next address the critical problem, how does hypercathectic energy become structure? I don't really see the applicability of the notion of a raise in potential here, and in fact it puzzles me why he appealed to this particular kind of physical energy transformation. Possibly the problem was that that was the only one he knew about. If one has to draw on physics for analogies, however, the one that seems to me a great deal more apposite is Einstein's formula, $E = Mc^2$. Here is the equation, which as I understand it shows in a precise way the equivalence of ener-

---

[*] I wonder if there isn't some implication of "scarcity economics"—the allocation of scarce resources—in Freud's use of an economic point of view in metapsychology. Perhaps that point of view needs to be re-named. [Footnote in original.]

gy and structure in the physical realm. It takes a tremendous amount of energy, measured by the square of the speed of light, to account for a unit of structure, or mass. As I read your argument, in psychology a similar equation might be written, but with the constant very different and working the other way around: apparently a small amount of energy goes into the formation of an appreciable amount of structure. Now if the physical analogy held, when structures break down there ought to be a release of energy, and it's possible that some of the pathological phenomena of decompensation could be coordinated to that notion.

This seems to me a very bold step to take in psychoanalytic theory—the postulation of a transformation of energy into the psychic equivalent of mass. But something has to be done to take the concept of psychic structure out of its present limbo. I can see one other possibility—no doubt there are many others. It would start from the observation that, in psychoanalytic theoretical terms, learning is structure building. What does this mean, when applied to school learning? Is it necessary, or even helpful, to assume some countercathectic structure corresponding to the proposition that $2 + 2 = 4$? I can follow your argument about countercathexis and abstraction in the last part of the paper, but I really don't see how the notion of countercathexis turning into structure helps us understand memorization.[179] Murphy has helped me see, with his concept of canalization, how trial and error learning or the learning of a skill is analogous to the development of controlled and precise motivational structures out of raw instinctual material: in both cases, it's possible to think of counter-cathectic organizations pushing the ongoing process into particular differentiated channels.

But where learning is more a matter of internalization than canalization, I think we need another model—or at least I don't understand how the old one fits. Much of learning, I am convinced, operates essentially through identification—through the internalization of persons or

---

[179] In the margin here there is a note which reads: "well, yes—maybe so."

partial objects (certain aspects or functions of persons). You have argued in the superego paper that this is an integral part of defensive structure formation, if I remember it properly. How do you see the hook-up to countercathectic conceptualization of structure building?

What I'm struggling to express is some kind of learning model for structure formation, which uses as the units of structure something other than energy: perhaps information or an ideational equivalent, perhaps even—and this is not really so alien to Freud's way of thinking—elements of the nervous system as the structural units! In your discussions of Hebb, you seem not too unfriendly to this last possibility, for Hebb's way of dealing with the nervous system is far more sophisticated than old-fashioned connectionism, and Hebb himself today admits that the model set forth in his book has been dealt a fatal blow—shown to over-simple—by Magoun and Lindsley.[180] This brings me back around to my attempts to link up the problems of attention-cathexis with the operation of the reticular system—an attempt that may be foolish if it disregards the different theoretical levels involved, but which might become fruitful if that problem of levels could be solved.

You will be even more vividly aware than I am of the many pitfalls and difficulties of embarking on a neurological model of structure, but I'm sure you are also sensible of its attractions.

I was interested in your footnote on page 51, bringing in a cybernetic model of analogy. But I don't think the analogy is satisfactory again: it by-passes the problem of structure.* Without structure, small amounts of energy cannot control large ones; the servomechanism is a structure as well as the application of a small amount of energy in a strategic way. Indeed, strategy itself in this sense is a matter of structure, and in the case of the servomechanism it is "structuralized"—

---

[180] G. Moruzzi and H. W. Magoun (1949) discovered the reticular formation critical to sleep vs. wakefulness and attention, work further elaborated by Donald B. Lindsley, Bowden & Magoun (1949).

* As does the idea of cathexis raised to a higher potential—for in physics, it takes a structural change in the system carrying or storing electricity, for there to be a rise in potential which is then the result, not cause, of structural change. [Footnote in original.]

embodied in a machine that carries out the strategy. In this machine, the energy operates through a structure the energic nature of which can only be dimly seen; in your sentence from which the footnote takes off, there is no such distinction between the energy as an operative force and as a structuralized analogue of material masses.

As still another anti-climatic footnote, I'd like to raise the question of whether the underlined word <u>bound</u> on page 45 refers to binding in the same sense as when we say that the energies of the secondary process are bound compared to the freely mobile energies of the primary process? It looks to me as if structuralization and binding in this other sense are quite different. I heard George quote a remark by Hartmann, an explanation of how binding is not identical with neutralization, which suggests to me that he was speaking of it in quite a different sense than structuralization. As I get it, he explained that in creative mathematical thought, for example, neutralized energies are used yet they are not bound because the thoughts are freely transformed and not held in rigid molds. If I understand this usage properly, it seems to me to be essentially a matter of what you call identifiability: binding would then be a matter of an idea's remaining reliably—or at the extreme, rigidly—itself, and not easily becoming fragmented or fused. Is that a correct understanding?

This letter is obviously too long already, so I'll not try to go on to take up your last one. I hope to do so soon, however, as well as your letter of November 3 commenting on my exchange with Roy.

I finally got in touch with Mary Bigelow, whose husband Julian Bigelow is one of the prominent people in the Institute for Advanced Study. She said that a few people are invited, but most people apply, and she would advise you to write to Dr. [Robert] Oppenheimer directly and ask him for application forms. I don't know what action you have taken about it; if I were you, I think I would talk with someone like [Solomon] Asch first and then probably make application.

       Best,

          Bob

cc: Dr. Roy Schafer

Comment

The final paragraph refers to exploration of the possibility that Rapaport might spend his "sabbatical" from Riggs at the Institute for Advanced Study in Princeton. As other letters indicate, he also inquired about some other locations before accepting our invitation to spend the year with me at the Research Center for Mental Health at NYU.

Rapaport to Holt—November 15, 1958

Dear Bob:

This is to answer your letter of October 30, and to respond to its enclosures. Once more, thanks for your efforts in connection with the New York Psychiatric as well as Princeton. Let us now wait and see how things develop.

I do not have George's "Consciousness" [Klein, 1959] paper in front of me. If he uses "modes of awareness" in the way you use it in the first paragraph of your memo[181] then he makes a mistake partly because we should consider the term "mode" preempted by Erik's concept and partly because I have persistently referred to these things as "varieties of conscious experience" and when we endeavor to bring a new thing into public consciousness it is a mistake to refer to it with varying terms, because it robs our efforts of their cumulative effects. Your third sentence in this paragraph surely is preemptory. I am not convinced at all that one concept cannot do both things, nor even that one can introduce structural concepts without directly linking them to attention cathexis. You may remember that in my "The Structure of Psychoanalytic Theory" I advocated dimensions in which process and structure can be simultaneously expressed. But, aside from such formal considerations it seems that structure building is, in psychoanalytic theory, con-

---

[181] Since the phrase does not occur in the memo "On Repression and Subliminal Registration," he was referring to the other one of the two I said I was enclosing, which has not survived.

ceived of somehow as something that occurs by means of cathexes. This is the kind of stuff at which my digit-series experiments as well as our present experiments are directed.[182]

My next comment pertains to the big parenthesis towards the bottom of page 1. It would seem that in this parenthesis you argue the same kind of thing that you disapprove of in the first paragraph. Nor is it correct that Freud argued this way. If you take page 146 (Coll. Pap. Vol. IV) in the "Metapsychological Supplement to the Theory of Dreams" then you will notice that his third sentence from the bottom of the page clearly questions an explanation purely in terms of "intensity." It is much more difficult to discover, as he progresses, what he considers the additional factor. But if you look at the end of the paragraph on page 147 and the one on the beginning of page 149, then it becomes clear that he considers the function of reality testing as this additional factor, that is to say he assumes some kind of functioning structure there. In other words, you actually could have used Freud's way or arguing as a support for the argument of the last sentence of your first paragraph. I would not have accepted that argument myself and would have indicated that though intensity alone doesn't do it we do not need to have a structural concept divorced from the cathectic conception. But all this is purely negative, and I would like rather to put in a positive way what I have in mind. For this purpose, I will have to advance two different considerations:

1) Please consider for a moment a memory image and compare it with a perceptual image and with something that I would call "pure image" or "an object imagined." Now it is clearly difficult at first to make the distinction between a "pure image" and a "memory image." But, with some practice I believe it becomes possible and then it becomes also quite clear that you can catch these two kinds of images when you encounter them in yourself spontaneously. I believe that on such spontaneous capture the

---

[182] It was never clear to me, then or since, how the experiments alluded to had or could have any direct relationship to the metapsychological concepts mentioned.

difference that you find between them is the following: though the "pure image" may be richer in perceptual content than the "memory image," it clearly is lacking many characteristics the "memory image" has. For instance, the memory image has a spatial-temporal earmark indicating when and where and how you acquired it. It usually also has some kind of affective characteristics and others besides which indicate the personal condition in which you experienced it. The remarkable thing about the perceptual image is that we usually experience it devoid of many of the spatial-temporal and personal earmarks while its internal articulation is usually richer than that of the "pure image" (except when the pure image is one of an eidetic person.)[183] I can't go now into the peculiar changes that occur when an eidetic person images something.

I think, however, that I can shed some light on the processes which occur in these three types of images if I call your attention to the relationship between memory, information, and knowledge.[184] You know that knowledge itself is as a rule devoid of spatial-temporal, etc., earmarks of its origin. Information may not be to that degree devoid of these, while memory, though it contains elements of knowledge has all these earmarks. I have used in my "Cognitive Structures" paper the term "connotative enrichment." I believe that in the course of transition from a percept to a memory, some process takes place which results in connotative enrichment, while in turn in the transformation of memory to knowledge there takes place a process of "stripping away." Concept formation, for instance, is such a "stripping away" process. I hope that the relationship to Hebb's recruitment and fractioning, and through these concepts also to what Irving Paul [1959] has been talking about, is here clear. I would like to stress that I do not

---

[183] A good many years later, I made an extensive study of the varieties and types of mental imagery (Holt, 1972). To some extent, Rapaport's typology was independently verified.

[184] It is unclear to me what distinction he was making between information and knowledge. I suspect that he was thinking about information in terms of the Wechsler subtest by that name, which caused him to make an unnecessary distinction.

by any means consider it necessary to sharply dichotomize the history
of the fate of a percept into a phase of connotative enrichment and into a phase of "stripping away." I do believe that both processes take
place simultaneously and we are dealing simply with various balances
between them at various points of the process in question. I do believe
also that the individual differences in regard to this balance are striking
and the styles Paul[185] talks about pertain to them. (For this reason I
would very much appreciate it if you would show Paul this letter as
soon as you can.)

2) I think that I have given in "Cognitive Structures" a genetic
picture of the processes I am discussing here. I believe what I tried
to show there was that there is a hierarchic layering of states of
consciousness and I tried to make it plausible how this hierarchy
is organized and what genetic connections explain this hierarchic
organization. I realize that I should have been much more specific
genetically in that paper, but I cannot even now try to make up
for those deficiencies.

I will try first to give a systematic statement of the conditions
and then add some minor genetic considerations. Assume that
there is a hierarchic layering of states of consciousness. Assume
also that most or all processes and with them most or all varieties
of conscious experience, which these processes produce in any
given state of consciousness [and] which constitute a low level in
the hierarchy of such states, are represented by some kind of
structures in any state of consciousness higher in the hierarchy.
Accordingly, varieties of conscious experience may occur either as
the functions of structures on [at] any given state of consciousness, or else as the effect of processes on a lower level of
consciousness (this latter naturally would imply always either re-

---

[185] I. H. Paul (1928–2006), a psychologist who was born and educated in Canada and in
1958 was a staff member at the Research Center for Mental Health, after a few years of
doing research under Rapaport's supervision, proposed a new cognitive style/control
variable, Importing. Its measure is the amount of new or extraneous material contained
in the subject's attempt to recall a standard brief story he has read with intent to remember it.

gression proper or regression in the service of the ego). Whenever it is a structure the function of which results in a given variety of conscious experience, what we call reality testing will be working in regard to it; whenever it is a process on a low level of the hierarchy (when therefore no "reflection" can take place in regard to it) no reality testing of the usual sort functions and whatever variety of the conscious experience it is, it may be blindly accepted as reality.

But it would be a mistake to assume that there is <u>no</u> reality testing on these lower levels. There is, but it is one of a different order than our usual waking one. There will be on each level also a hypercathectic pool—though of various degrees of neutralization. You notice that, even in this simplification, this kind of stuff appears as a three dimensional continuum. I have stressed in "Cognitive Structures" that the situation is much more complicated and we should not conceive of sharp dividing lines between various states of consciousness. Now I am coming to the supplementary genetic consideration I have been talking about. I believe that whenever processes take place so that consistent cathectic investment is made which follows a persistent pattern, structuralization will take place, which will make it unnecessary that the process ad hoc produces always again and again this pattern, and the pattern will be available as a ready made tool. Thus, it will emerge as a structure on a higher level of consciousness.

The relevance of this will become particularly clear if we shift at this point to the top of your page 3. What you suggest there as the distinction between "percepts and other modes of awareness" is the most primitive form of reality testing as described by Freud in the paragraph straddling the pages 148–149 <u>Collected Papers</u> IV.[186] Your pattern has also to do with what Freud described as "flight": the prototype of repression.

Let me elucidate this matter from another angle. I would say critically that if one would read only this passage on the top of

---

[186] Probably the last paragraph on p. 232 in *SE 14*.

page 3 and would not know your thinking, he might be ready to label you as a "naïve realist." The autonomy of percepts you speak about is limited, according to you, only by whether they move or do not move with a head movement. They do not have, however, that order of autonomy: we know that "percepts" are "concepts." We do not simply perceive them, we rather conceive them. The whole frame of reference of "apperception" indicates this. Piaget's findings showing how the constancy of objects, the constancy of volume, the constancy of mass etc. develops shows this very strikingly. In other words we are seeing things outside the way we see them because they are immediately integrated into "schemata" which are readily available, to which they are fully assimilated and which are fully accommodated to them. At this point you can already see that to my mind the "connotative enrichment" does not begin after perception but is already part of perception itself. I can't enlarge on this and I would like you to consider very seriously this point in connection with the points I made above about connotative enrichment.

I am coming to the second paragraph on your page 3. I do not see why the complex configurational relationship you talk [about] here about is "properly" called structural. I think that you should have given proof for that. Insofar as it is structural, as you must notice, I attempted to show that it is not structural in a very different sense than Freud's structural concepts of consciousness. Now concerning the third paragraph on this page, I believe it is a rather quickly thrown together paragraph the various ingredients of which are not on one level. I want to point out to you that particularly lines four and five of this paragraph should have taken into consideration Claparède's [1911] "Me-ness" concept as you find it in my Organization and Pathology of Thought.

I am coming to the first paragraph on page 4. I seriously doubt whether you have any right to generalize the way you do about the effect of trauma, drugs, and other organic influences upon the relations between conscious, preconscious, and unconscious. First of all it is not clear whether you are talking about these latter three as "qualities" or whether you use them as topographical systems. Furthermore, I think that any attempt to relegate something to physiology which is relevant to us is at this point a great mistake. The reticular formation and the findings about it are very interesting. The very complex subject matter that you and I are dealing with, however, already indicates that what we know now about the reticular formation cannot possibly account for it (if "attention" would be a simpler matter we might be tempted to account for it fully, but we see that it isn't a simple matter at all) and thus physiology will have to go very far before it can give us any contribution to our problems.

I am coming to the second paragraph on your page 4. I would like to recommend that you reread carefully the introduction to the section on digit span and arithmetic in Diagnostic Psychological Testing and the rationales of digit span and arithmetic. I would like to recommend that you reread my article in the "Samiksa" [Rapaport, 1947b] on related matters. I furthermore suggest that you reread what there is about this point in the rationale of the various memorial Babcock test items in the same volume [Rapaport et al., 1968]. You will realize that you are talking here about concentration rather than attention. Attention cathexis deployment plays a significant role in both attention and concentration.

I do agree, however, that the manner of attention cathexis deployment in attention as well as in concentration is subject to higher order organizations which could well be called cognitive styles, making for considerable individual differences. The exploration of this relationship seems to me indeed to be crucial. I think George has pointed repeatedly to this issue.

In the bottom paragraph on page 5 your argument seems to neglect that under such conditions for instance as wandering in darkness where the slightest shades may take on a very threatening impression, you have particular attention cathexis mobilizations which may be either of the "attention" or the "concentration" kind. I think you also neglected the fact that not only the external changes of sharp gradients but also "expectancies," that is to say anticipations, play a critical role here. In this respect just as in connection with "identifiability" you may want to reread the introduction to the chapter on concept-formation in <u>Diagnostic Psychological Testing</u>.

I hope that these comments will be of some use to you. Now I am going to turn to the memo on repression and subliminal registration.[187]

On the first page of this memo, the second paragraph has a parenthesis concerning downward pulling processes. This is simile made and used by Freud often and misleadingly. The fact is that the displacement of drive cathexes from any drive representation to any preconscious or conscious idea associatively connected with it results in the "censorship" exerting repressive efforts upon the latter idea. This appears to the onlookers as though something would pull it down. But, if you read carefully "The Unconscious" you will find there as well as in "Repression," discussions concerning the relation between cathectic intensity, distortion, and distance from the unconscious, which will clarify for you this issue: for instance, Collected Papers, Volume IV pages 88, 90.

In the third paragraph of the first page of this memo in the sixth line you use the expression "structural state," I do not know what that means and can understand it only in relation to those points which I have made in this regard in "Cognitive Structures."

On page 2, the second paragraph has a very interesting beginning idea. I would think, however, that this idea would gain considerable clarity if you would adopt following George the conception of "incidental registration" instead of subliminal registration. I think, in other words, that your conception that the Poetzl experiments and kindred experiments do not really represent repression is well taken, within certain limits. The chances are

---

[187] A reference to my "Notes on Repression and Subliminal Registration," which I had sent to Rapaport at the end of October.

that those things which are related to repressed things will be amongst those things which will be only "incidentally registered" instead of [having] direct conscious registration. Moreover, the artificial isolation that you speak about is due to the economics of attention cathexis distribution pertaining to focused vs. incidental registration. The isolation is not due to an elimination [of] associative links, but rather due to the fact that incidental registration allows all the associative links resulting in "connotative enrichments" to come to bear. This is not the case for social registration.[188]

I am turning now to the bottom of page 2, where you make the point that the actively perceived is available to the active efforts of memory and the passively perceived is not so available. Again a very interesting idea but it points [to, or posits] a too direct relationship between activity-passivity and memory. I think that the situation is far more complicated than that, and this is only a rule of thumb and cannot be held in any other sense. Yet it is an interesting idea which has to be further explored and can be explored if you keep in mind what I tried to say above about the difference between attention and concentration on the one hand and the difference between focal and incidental registration on the other. The same comments pertain to the end of the second paragraph on page 3.

Your last paragraph is also in need of clarification as to what "identifiability" means here. Diagnostic Psychological Testing clarifies at least the conceptual position of this term and maybe since other terms used here are also clarified there, the relationships between them can be approached.

I am aware that I am rather abrupt, but the many problems you raise in an interesting way constitute a big order.

Write to me again about these. I will show my reaction to this memo to Roy, Merton, George, and the people here who

---

[188] I don't recall his ever using this expression elsewhere. Presumably, it means the registration process at work during normal social life.

are interesting in this kind of stuff: Rouse, Schimek, and Miller. I would appreciate it if you could send me additional copies of your memos in the future so that I can send them along with my notes.

      Yours,

        David

Rapaport to Holt—November 19, 1958

Dear Bob:

I just sent off a long letter to you when I received your long letter of November 11.

I will react to this one and I think I can react to it somewhat more shortly than to the others. I agree rather completely with the first page of your letter. The Activity-Passivity paper is still simply a draft and you point out correctly that its purpose was to show the inconsistency of Freud's own usage, or rather the internal contradictions within it, and to demonstrate that the road from there leads to my conception. You are right in saying that this is not sharply put. In a sense, I might not like to put such a matter quite sharply and to let people think about it. But, then again, I might when I do the final drafting (it will be monograph if not book size, if I ever get to it)—decide to be as sharp as you want me to be. Anyway it helps that you point it out. About the last sentence concerning "no relationship between masculinity-femininity and activity-passivity," I would not be able to make such a blunt statement, because I am not at all sure but that the opposite is the case. I do not believe that this is something we know enough about. I do believe that Freud [1915a] is right ("Instincts and Their Vicissitudes") that somehow the fusion of these two pairs is the first to give psychological meaning to "masculinity-femininity." I do also think that there is a more basic and archaic connection also, but I am not sure of any of these details.

Concerning page 2: the first paragraph points out that I employ the word "useful" carelessly. I really meant "useless" in that broader sense which is not simply the opposite of "useful." Concerning the third paragraph: you are right, the relationship between activity-passivity and autonomy had not been worked out at that time, since this draft preceded my recent autonomy paper. That autonomy paper is really the prerequisite for working out that relationship. I gave at the end of that paper a tentative solution of the relationship. But I have not convinced myself about the nature of this relationship in a final way. It is, however, quite certain that activity-passivity has implications which reach far beyond autonomy. I am not in the position now to discuss this, except for pointing out, for instance, that activity-passivity has a far reaching hierarchic layering, and that which from one point of view (in relation to the lower layers) is active may be passive from the point of view of the higher layers. A similar statement could be made in converse concerning passivity. Now we know that with development the (always relative) autonomy increases. But this seems like a monotonous [monotonic] process, while the activity-passivity conception shows its "dialectics." I realize that I am not shedding sufficient light on this issue, but I am at least pointing to it.

With page 3, the misunderstandings and disagreements start. I would really suggest that you study through the Ego Psychology Seminar transcripts which contain the answers to many of the questions you raise. I believe that the transcript of the Elementary Metapsychology Seminar which is in preparation would be even more helpful, but it is not yet done. Your discussion on page 3 sounds as though you would consider structure building to be limited to the defensive and counter-cathectic form. If you remember our conversation concerning Dr. Rouse's present experiments you will realize that I consider all learning as structure building, using attention cathexes as the building material. Later on in the third paragraph on page 5 (to which I will come in due order) you suggest something like this as though it would be entirely new. But that is really irrelevant: the first sentence of that paragraph (omitting the reference to the nervous system) is really the way to solving this problem and I am glad that you imply that you think so too.

The rest of your argument is more difficult to meet because it leads into complexities. I will want first to agree with you partly and then go along with later points also and only then point out where you—to my mind—miss the boat. Let me comment here only that "ego narrowing" is not the correct expression, ego limitation is better, but Anna Freud who coined the term [i.e., concept] uses another term for it. Immediately under the line I just referred to is the phrase "neutral information gets lost in hysterics." This is, to my mind, an incorrect formulation. The neutral information is not lost. It is not acquired, or it is made into not-neutral material and therefore lost. This business, however, I think we discussed in Diagnostic Psychological Testing. It is a matter of styles developing on the foundation of repressive defensive structures: these determine the hysterical style of information poverty or unavailability. By the way, the emphasis is on unavailability, because part of it is not either lost, nor a failure to acquire, but a style which makes material unavailable.[189] In Freud's [1915b] paper "Repression" you will find quite a bit about this point.

Let me point out also to you that in the third paragraph you consider it clashing with common sense that the impulse should be used for its own control. As a matter of fact what it does not clash with is common sense: the defensive motivation always clearly reveals the nature of the motive defended against and therefore it would seem to suggest just precisely what Freud [1915c] suggested concerning it in "The Unconscious." The argument is weak, because on a similar basis the aggression character of resistances connected with defenses has suggested to Hartmann that all counter-cathecting is of aggressive energy. I think

---

[189] By this sentence in the margin is a handwritten note: "Cf. Cog. Style & Motive. Paper on how this can happen!" The script looks like Merton Gill's; I can't be sure.

that one can't choose between these two, they are both bad suggestions, but they both pose significant problems which the final solution will have to take care of. I would be glad to discuss with you the ins and outs of all this but again I can't dwell on it in detail.

Let me point out here only that the threshold heightening always occurs as the basis of defense structure building and it is accomplished by a counter-cathectic barrier. The simplest assumption would be that this counter-cathectic barrier derives from undifferentiated cathexes, or neutral cathexes which are at the disposal of the ego (even if it is a very primitive one at that point). If we assume that, for the beginning, then from there on there would be no difficulty whatsoever to build up the whole hierarchic theory. Let me finally comment that the second paragraph argument, that "ego narrowing" occurs only in pathological cases, is certainly not true. The fact is that as we grow up there is a process of "narrowing" going on steadily as we increasingly make renunciations and resignations from our original potentialities. I do not think, however, that this touches on the merit of the argument you are making—at all.

You are asking how is it possible that if cathexis is invested into building structure, cathexis remains still available afterwards. Please for the moment accept the assumption that we are dealing here with hypercathexes which are used for structure building. Assume also with me that once a structure has been built the cathexes used in building it are liberated in the main and only a small part of them are bound up in the structure. By the way, this is the only meaning of binding and you will find the background of it in Breuer's chapter in the Freud-Breuer book and in Freud's later varied references to it.[190] Neutralization pertains to the effect

---

[190] My attempt to follow his suggestion led to my own paper on binding, which demonstrated the untenability of what Rapaport said here (Holt, 1962a). In retrospect, this letter shows a basic problem with Rapaport's attempts to use metapsychology: He had elaborated Freud's (largely unsystematic) statements to such an extent that he had a

of structure building upon drives' cathexes and upon the character of the cathexes in the hypercathectic pool which is used both for attention cathexis and counter-cathexis.

Now you bring against this at the bottom of page 4 and the top of page 5 the argument that in physical science for mass formation you need to have a huge amount of energy. But this is the kind of analogy which I think we should avoid. (If you have to use such take the energy requirements and liberation in atomic fusion.) The much better analogy is the scaffolding and the concrete, or the putting on the mortar and the great amount of energy it requires to keep it on until it sets. But probably an even better analogy could be built if you consider that we are not dealing here with "matter" and energy but rather with "structure" and energy. When you put together an arch you have to support it and work fast. Once the "keystone" is in you are free to turn elsewhere and take your scaffolding away. What I am trying to show you is that the problem is a different one from the one you envisaged. I agree with you that all the analogies will just help us to think, but won't settle the issue. The issue is an empirical, experimental one, and it is the very one which Dr. Rouse's present experiments are trying to tackle. I could simply say about the whole argument you bring up in connection with Bertalanffy, that I agree with it. But actually, we do not need it. We never imagined that the psychological apparatus is divorced from the somatic apparatus. As a matter of fact our present experiments show that to conceive of a "static attention cathexis pool" is a mistake. I could show you that already in my lectures in Topeka on diagnostic psychological testing in general and on digit span in particular I have pointed that out. The very phenomena of "satiation" show us this point for which you want to invoke Bertalanffy[191] or might

---

solution to anything, granted enough complexity and freedom from the basic scientific requirement of testability. Even on that point, he mistakenly believed that the empirical work with Rouse was testing metapsychological propositions.

[191] Ludwig von Bertalanffy is considered one of the founders of General System Theory,

be inclined to invoke something physiological. We do not need either of them.

On page 5 in the second paragraph you discuss "internalization" in a sense in which I do not understand it at all. You seem to divorce it from "canalization," which I think is rather hopeless. But these are the very things we are trying to explore experimentally so one has to wait and see. It is true that I have tried to link identification with structure building in the Superego paper. But, I certainly did not (as your last sentence in this paragraph would suggest) identify structure building with counter-cathectic structure building.

On page 6 in the second paragraph you are touching on the issue of "binding" which I think I have discussed with you before in this letter.

I hope this will be of some use and I again want to indicate to you that I will show our exchange around to the people I mentioned in my last letter.

Yours,
David

---

to which he made a number of major contributions. His 1950 paper in *Science* made him famous, and led to his being invited to give a lecture in Topeka a few years later, which I attended. I was much taken with it, and took advantage of the opportunity to have some conversations with him. From then on, I gradually became immersed in systems theory, but could never interest Rapaport in it.

Discussion of "Further Observations on the Poetzl Phenomenon: A Study of Day Residues" by Charles Fisher

Remarks by Robert R. Holt
New York Psychoanalytic Society, November 25, 1958

Subliminal and other incidental stimuli, like the poor, have always been with us, however much the recent upsurge of research on such problems may have given them an aura of novelty. The very structure of man's perceptual apparatus guarantees that he is always being subliminally stimulated. We are, of course, constantly bathed in a flux of physical energies; all of our sense organs continually respond with at least low levels of discharge. At present each of us can easily notice, by turning attention to the various senses one after another, sensations of touch, warmth or cold, muscular strain, taste and smell, as well as a very wide range of auditory and visual sensations. Yet how difficult it is to be aware of them all simultaneously! And how confusing it would be if there were no dominant themes in this vast cacophonous symphony of sensation! Freud was very much aware of this point; he was almost unique among psychologists in pointing to the fact that the sensory apparatus has the dual function of making sensations available to us, and of protecting us from them. He offered the concept of the <u>Reizschutz</u>, or stimulus barrier, as the first line of defense against over-stimulation; we might translate it today into the general concept of <u>thresholds</u>. Stimulation has to be above a certain level before it can cause a conscious sensation, even though below that level the end-organs in the sensory surfaces do respond and send weak currents towards the brain. As Dr. Fisher's work [e.g., Fisher, 1954, 1956, 1960] has brilliantly shown, some such weak inputs do register somehow in the brain and may be recovered later [in part, I should have said] by their effects on subsequent dreams and images. Nevertheless, the thresholds serve the great function of screening out the many weak stimuli that might overwhelm us with their quantity if not their intensity.

Even so, a throng of inputs that are strong enough to be supraliminal comes in constantly, too many to be comprehended simultaneously. The function of attention is the second great protector: since there is just so much attention cathexis available at one time, one matter or at most a very few can be hypercathected, all the rest being relegated to various degrees of fringe awareness. Since the focus of attention is narrow but the scope of man's sensitivities is wide, most sensory inputs must go unnoticed. They comprise the great class of incidental stimuli, and include what is subliminal but still registers.

One of Dr. Fisher's great services is to have pointed insistently to the fact that so much stimulation that never receives the benefit of attention-cathexis is registered (that is, forms memory traces). Must we assume, therefore, such registration of every stimulus that is strong enough to activate the peripheral sense-organs? It is hard to credit even the amazing psychic apparatus that we have with the vast mnemonic storehouses that would be required to accommodate such a wealth of experiences and non-experiences. I doubt that all subliminal stimulation is registered.

Recently, neuro-anatomical and neuro-physiological workers such as Magoun [Moruzzi & Magoun, 1949], Hernandez-Peon and Jouvet [Hernandez-Peon, Scherrer, & Jouvet, 1956] have discovered brain mechanisms that do much of the job of protecting consciousness from inundation by stimuli. There are subcortical relay centers that screen and suppress unimportant inputs from the various senses, so that the cortex not continuously cluttered up with routine sensory information. Any <u>new</u> supraliminal signal gets through and may be attended to, but if it continues as a steady monotonous input, it quickly drops out of awareness as the suppressor mechanisms close the gates to the cortex. The thought occurs to me that this attenuation or exclusion of nerve currents may operate on subliminal inputs too. As long as they are unimportant, routine, weak signals, I suggest, subliminal and incidental stimuli are probably excluded from registering, and do not form traces.

What does register, then, of the mass of subliminal stimulation? We have little information from which to construct an answer; indeed, there is no way of establishing that a registration has taken place other than to show that it can be recovered as in the experiment we heard about this evening, or by somewhat similar techniques. From Dr. Fisher's work, as well as from logical and theoretical considerations, a few principles can be adduced, however.

First, the neurophysiological evidence just cited suggests that the novel, the unexpected or off-beat subliminal stimulus has a better chance of registering a memory trace than the routine, repetitive, or stereotyped.

Second, if the subject has been trying to catch a glimpse of something that occurs so briefly or goes by so quickly that it cannot be made out, this subliminal stimulus may have an advantage in registering and subsequently being recovered because of the tension of an incomplete task that attaches to it—an advantage, that is, over the great majority of subliminal impressions constantly raining on us. We know from the work of Kurt Lewin and his students [Zeigarnik, 1927] that the tension aroused by unfinished business can affect subsequent behavior in several ways, particularly by making the incomplete task easily remembered. Just so, the hypercathected stimuli surrounding the tachistoscopic flash and the intention of getting it may operate like an incomplete Gestalt, not only opening the doors to registration but motivating recovery.

The subliminal stimulus in a Poetzl[192] experiment meets these two criteria. Yet my experience with this kind of work, carried out in collaboration with Dr. George Klein at New York University, suggests that not every such input can be successfully recovered, and when it does occur, recovery may be partial and fragmentary. So we must look further.

Third, the principal motivational variable involved in determining what gets registered has already been pointed out by Dr. Fisher in previous communications: transference. If the subject knows that this particular bit of quasi-experience is very important to someone he admires and respects—whose love is important to him, in brief—he has an unusual incentive to open all channels for the tachistoscopic glimpse to register, and then the next day to bring the dream that is requested into which the hidden stimulus has found its way. In this context, the dream is a communication from the dreamer to someone important to him, just as it is in the context of psychoanalytic treatment; and the subject would have to be dull indeed to fail to pick up the fact that the experimenter expects a report, in some form, about what he presented in a hundredth of a second, or a rejoinder to his brief but heavily underlined communication.

Because this issue of transference is so important, it would be good to hear more about Dr. Fisher's relationships with the seven subjects reported on in tonight's paper, if discretion permits him to tell us more. The fact that three were "old subjects" tells us a little, but not enough. A psychological colleague of mine is convinced,

---

[192] In the 1919 edition of *The Interpretation of Dreams*, Freud (1900, footnote on pp. 181f.) called attention to the work of Otto Poetzl (1917), which had been presented at a meeting of the Vienna Psychoanalytic Society, "a paper which carries a wealth of implications." Fisher (1960) gives a persuasive explanation for its general neglect for over 20 years, but mentioning several researches stimulated by Poetzl's work. Fisher (1954) was the first to make the stimulating picture not consciously visible by use of a tachistoscope as Poetzl had done. It is an apparatus into which the subject looks at a precisely timed exposure of a picture, so brief that only "a flash" is reported. The subject is asked to return the next day bringing a report of any dreams he or she has experienced.

after seeing Dr. Fisher work with his subjects, that the reason he can get so much more dramatic results than most of us is that he arouses such a lot of positive transference in his subjects.

Fourth, my last selective principle is quite a familiar one. Freud told us that memories of indifferent events were particularly suited to become manifest dream-material when they met two criteria: they were not in themselves exciting or disturbing, and thus would not trouble sleep if admitted to the dream-consciousness, and they were suitable objects onto which to displace the cathexes of forbidden wishes. The more connections an indifferent image can be given to hot issues, the more it can serve as their innocent vicar, and receive (by displacement or condensation) their drive-cathexes, thereby being raised to the necessary sensory vividness. The implication is, therefore, that if an incidental and indifferent impression does not resonate with more important matters, it will be difficult to transfer enough mobile cathexis to it, and it will not get into the dream. Perhaps this argument can be pushed one step further: if a stimulus-pattern that was never hypercathected (that is, a subliminal input) does not have such resonances, it may well not register. I am suggesting here that it takes work of some kind to register a stimulus as a memory trace—work that is usually done by the hypercathexis that makes experience conscious, or by the more or less neutralized cathexis of a drive derivative, like an ego-interest, or by both. If the attention cathexis is not present, then, as in the case of a subliminal stimulus, it may be crucial for registration that contact is made with some motivational system, via the secondary-process associative connotations or the primary process symbolic resonances or the like, so that the incoming stimulus receives enough drive-cathexis to register. With his choice of a snake for the subliminal stimulus, Dr. Fisher has maximized the likelihood that his stimulus will have a wealth of drive-relevance.

There may seem to be a conflict between this last criterion for registrability and one of the points made in this paper. At the beginning of the discussion section, Dr. Fisher takes up the crucial point, how are we to understand conceptually the fact that the supraliminal, conscious part of the day-residue gave rise to derivatives in the dream by a process of rational, realistic association, whereas the subliminal part of it produced symbolic primary process transformations? His first approach to an answer is to cite Freud as having written that the dream prefers to take up recent and indifferent impressions "because such trivial elements have given no occasion for the formation of many associative ties and the factor of their recency has not given time for such formation." [Freud, 1900, p. 564] The point of difference, however, is that Freud is talking about the element's <u>conscious</u>, secondary-process associations, not its unconscious resonances. When I read over some of Freud's dreams and his associations to them, however, I feel that this point cannot be given a great deal of emphasis. Surely the associative links between his experiences of seeing a monograph on the genus cyclamen and the latent dream thoughts that followed were not all irrational or nonessential, for example; for the most part, they seem to follow the orderly associative principles of the secondary process. I would like to underscore Dr. Fisher's cautious statement, therefore, that there is no "hard and fast distinction between the ways in which the sub- and supraliminal stimuli are utilized by the dreamwork but only ... that there is a marked tendency in the direction indicated." Certainly Freud made it clear, in the context of disposing of Robert's theory of dreaming as psychic excretion of everything incidental and unfinished, that an indifferent impression "must have some attribute that makes it especially suitable for this purpose"—that is, suited to having the cathexis of repressed wishes transferred to it, if it is to be used in dreams (<u>Ibid.</u>, p. 178).

I'd like to turn now to the interesting question of how to conceptualize the central finding of this paper, which is supported by a study from our laboratory at the Research Center for Mental Health, the one by Dr. Fred Pine [1960] mentioned at the end: Why does the supraliminal stimulus (the vane) tend to give rise to dream-derivatives via rational, realistic associations, while the subliminal snake tends to elicit more symbolic transformations? Dr. Fisher suggests that this difference is due to the fact that the supraliminal stimulus has had time to get embedded in the context of secondary process associations, or as Rapaport puts it, it is taken into the conceptual organization of memory, while the subliminal registration is "free of secondary process involvement." But our speaker goes further; he says that "the greater availability of /subliminal/ registrations for primary process transformation lies not only in the fact of their freedom from secondary process elaboration but in the fact that the memory traces of such registrations appear to be highly unstable and to undergo condensations, displacement, fragmentations, etc." To paraphrase his next remarks about the subliminal registrations, again in Rapaport's words, they are taken into the drive organization of memories.[*]

For example, consider subject B: his dream image contained a much distorted transformation of the snake, yet in his images the successive trials produced pictures that were increasingly faithful to the original. To give rise to a variety of transformations and then a rather literal reproduction like the picture of the snake crawling through the ruptured vase, a trace must necessarily have been quite stable and at least as photographic as the final image.

Now for a few scattered critical comments. Dr. Fisher notes the frequency with which themes of dominance and submission appear in the dreams and images of this experiment, and seems to attribute them to the actual experience of having been an experimental subject. I wonder. Anyone who knows Dr. Fisher personally can hardly believe that he has suddenly become so domineering that the real experience of this group of subjects was of masochistic subjugation—something that seems not to have been experienced by subjects in his previous experiments on the Poetzl phenomenon. He spoke about the fact that the

---

[*] This would seem to follow from the assumption that their registration was accomplished with drive-cathexis, rather than the neutralized hypercathexis that registers a conscious percept. [Footnote in original.]

stimuli were sexual symbols, and mentioned that both snake and swastika have aggressive meanings. Yet he never quite focused on this latter fact when trying to account for the themes of dominance and submission, or for the finding that these two elements were frequently condensed. I think, however, that he would probably agree that the drive-meanings of the stimuli condensed with and caused a reinterpretation of the experimental situation in terms of sexual and aggressive, dominant-submissive relationships.

Concerning the suggestion that "the central point of sensory intensity is represented by the subliminal registration or its transformation"—again, I feel skeptical. Perhaps; but why should it? Is it not just as plausible to assume that if the data suggest this conclusion, the fact that the stimulus was a snake may be more relevant than the fact that it was subliminal? The symbol of the snake is well suited to touch off many wish-fulfillments, and might have done so even if the tables were turned and it was supraliminal, while the vase was subliminal. Dr. Fisher tells me that he is planning to test another series of subjects with just such a reversed slide. Tonight's paper has been presented with appropriate modesty as a pilot study; I hope that in the final experiment the point of maximum sensory intensity in each dream is established by asking the subject directly. It is too important and subjective a point to be left to the experimenter's judgment. It will also be necessary to set up procedures to measure, however crudely, the degree of primary process transformation to which an element of the stimulus has been subjected in the dream. The first approach to these matters has to be made by the clinical judgment of the exploratory researcher, but once the hypotheses have been formed they must be put to an objective test. Whoever judges the primary or secondary process nature of the relationship between dream elements and stimulus elements must not know whether the latter was exposed subliminally or supraliminally—otherwise, it is too easy to see in ambiguous qualitative data the answers one expects.

Even in these preliminary data there was only a tendency for the supraliminal parts of the stimulus to be less transformed by the primary process than was the subliminal part. Perhaps if attention were turned to the subjects and their personality structures it might be possible to obtain more clear-cut results. If in general it is true that when an impression is hypercathected, it is then registered in the conceptual organization of memory and is available mainly to the secondary process, we should expect that persons who have a capacity for regression in the service of the ego would be most likely to allow it to be transformed in dreams by the primary process. There are hints from an experiment by MacKinnon and Barron at the University of California [MacKinnon et al., 1958], that this variable may be highly relevant. They hypnotized a group of subjects that included some highly gifted creative artists and some ordinary, not noticeably creative people, tried to implant a specific conflict and told the subjects to dream about it. In the dreams that were brought the next day, the uncreative subjects reproduced parts of the implanted material with little or no distortion, whereas the creative subjects' dreams contained the material with imaginative transformations.

In closing, let me say that it is the great merit of Dr. Fisher's work that it always stimulates new theoretical speculation and further experimental ideas on basic problems. What more can we ask from a piece of exploratory research?

Rapaport to Holt—November 28, 1958

Dear Bob:

Thanks for the letter and your discussion of Dr. F[isher]'s paper. Don't feel embarrassed about not writing. As long as you give my notes as much of a reading as I give yours I am amply rewarded. Glad you are studying the transcripts: let me know how you find them.

J[uliet] is home and we expect to see H[annah] also either here or in Florida on vacation.

Let me see the new experimental plans with hypotheses etc. I'll be glad to come to discuss Activity-Passivity with your staff, but I can't now tell when. Maybe you ask me again in January.

As for your review [i.e., discussion of Fisher]: 1) The build up of your four points is to my mind very good. Not that I know whether or not these are the checkpoints, but there are such check points I am sure, and they do form a hierarchy. None of us spelled this out before you. Fine! 2) On p. 2, fourth line from bottom "un-important" and p. 3, third paragraph "off-beat," reveal a conception which in its absolute character I would reject. All this is far more relative than your phrasing suggests. 3) Third page top paragraph "probably excluded from registering" and p. 5 under-lined words reveal to me that you are asking and answering an unanswerable and irrelevant question. This question has a central role in your argument, as it becomes clear in the top paragraph of page 8, and in the one following.

I think it is necessary for us to conceive of traces in the way Hebb does. Everything impinging on the retina causes [a] process

447

once it provides a quantum of (light) energy. This process may have various fates: it may be extinguished by a "refractory phase" (Hebb) or it may form a part of an assembly, or it may be "fractioned (Hebb) by interacting assemblies or phase sequences." The argument about "stable" trace in paragraph 2 may be countered and replaced by one based on the assumption that each "fractioned" process may be "re-recruited" (Hebb) in propitious stimulation etc.

This will perhaps become more clear if I turn to 4) the second to last sentence on p. 5, "attention cathexis is not present": this is an all or none conception. I myself am inclined as in "Cognitive Structures" to assume that there are always a variety of cognitive levels with various degrees of neutralization of attention cathexes and various corresponding mechanisms of synthesis. Therefore it is not simply drive cathexis which causes primary process forms to emerge. I wrote to you about this before. Drive can do so, but lower level of organization can too: at this point the Hebb argument (and Werner's [1940] <u>Comparative Psychology</u>) become relevant. 5) Likewise at the end of the big paragraph on p. 7: the transition between the two kinds of memory organizations is correspondingly fluid.

I did not read the paper. From your discussion I should judge that you felt rather condescending to it. I have written to Fisher for a copy.

Yours,

David

Summary—Brief Letters from 1958

Two book reviews by Rapaport (Chapters 49 and 53 in Gill, 1967) had provoked a sharp rejoinder from George Miller, a prominent academic contributor to cognitive psychology. In a letter of January 15, Rapaport said that Miller had sent him a copy with a letter during his absence in December, and asked my advice about how he should respond to its inaccuracies. The critique was subsequently published as a letter to the editor in the March 1958 issue of Contemporary Psychology (vol. 3, p. 75f.), the journal of book reviews in which Rapaport's reviews had appeared. The enclosures (Miller's letter of transmittal, and drafts of possible answers) have not survived.

A January 16 letter from me apparently crossed his in the mail. Enclosed was a draft of my review of Jones's biography of Freud (Holt, 1958) for his reactions (see his letter of January 22), and a draft of Goldberger and Holt (1958; see his letter of January 29). After a brief report on my wedding to Crusa Adelman on December 27 and our new address, I said I was thinking about writing a more theoretical paper about the isolation experiment, using the concept of nutriment and his paper on ego autonomy (Rapaport, 1958), and a few others involving the latter and his one on activity/passivity.

I replied to his first letter on January 17, finding his reviews sharp but fair. As to Miller's comments, they were "one-sided and rather unfair [. . .] he didn't try nearly as hard as you did to grasp the point of view of the person he was criticizing." After some advice about his proposed points in rejoinder, I suggested that he:

add something like the following: "It is rarely helpful to respond to criticism one doesn't like by trying to psychologize the critic. Usually one is wrong, as you were in your attempts to discern my motives, and as I should undoubtedly be if I were to guess at yours. You would have served your friends' interests (as well as your own) much better by devoting the space that was spent on fruitless speculations to a more detailed statement of the merits you believe I neglected. It was of course decent of you to send me your letter, but it would have been even more so to have written me frankly to see if you could not get a better understanding of what I was about before writing to the journal. You could at least have saved yourself several factual errors which can only embarrass you. But I suppose that the tone of my reviews persuaded you that I was too prickly and irascible a person to make a direct approach worthwhile. You are an expert in the psychology of communication; let's have a little more direct communication and there will be less misunderstanding."

On March 1, Rapaport wrote about my review of the Jones biography that it was "excellent and clearly organized. [. . .] I can subscribe to all of it, except the last page, which [. . .] is <u>your personal evaluation</u> and mine would be different [. . .]" After a few minor points, he protested: "[. . .] if you <u>have to</u> name me, at least you could put Kris first—which would restore alphabetical order." He then asked me to order a score of reprints for him to distribute.

On March 4, I sent back a marked-up copy of his (and Gill's) "big paper on metapsychology," which was never published. I had hoped that the issues I had found obscure in the briefer version would have been clarified; I still found "much that is highly condensed and much that does not carry conviction in its own right; you demand a great deal of the reader [. . .]" Some detailed, mostly verbal, points of criticism followed, with some personal chit-chat.

A handwritten note from Rapaport dated April 22 reported on his recent visit to "SF & LA [where] the lectures went well. [. . .] CP [Contemporary Psychology] accepted my answer [to Miller], I spoke in LA on Superego for the first time." And more about our wives, who were getting on well with each other.

I responded with a letter of April 28, looking forward to the transcript on the superego. Much of it concerns personal news about my former wife, Louisa, and our children. I raised the possibility of my spending a soon-coming sabbatical in Stockbridge, hoping I might have time with him and with Erik Erikson, studying psychoanalytic theory and perhaps writing a monograph on the primary process.

His reply of May 1 was a somewhat cautious welcome. "It will be necessary for you and me to get quite clear in our minds what, how much and when we will work together." He offered to take Crusa on as a research assistant if she would be interested, or she could hone her clinical skills with David Shapiro.

A short letter from me on June 12 was almost entirely about weekends when Crusa and I might accept his invitation to come for a visit, with a brief reference to the work at the Research Center on the effects of LSD on various cognitive and emotional functions (much later published as Barr et al., 1972). It was followed by a handwritten note from Elvira inviting us to visit for a weekend. My response of July 26 explains why we couldn't accept—too busy before a planned European trip. Amid personal news, I reported that the Boston "conference on 'sensory deprivation' [...] was spotty but on the whole very stimulating. Leo Goldberger did a fine job of presenting our paper, which seemed to have been quite a hit." After conveying a few new findings, I added that the eagerly expected paper on the superego had arrived.

My letter of September 17 reporting our return from Europe asked for a date when we might have a Stockbridge weekend to convey all our personal news and talk about new research possibilities. I thanked him for his history of ego psychology (Rapaport, 1958b), and "for once have no critical remarks to make. It seemed clear and constructive, and I can say only that I would have liked more of the same." A note from him on September 23 proposed a date for the visit, adding that his secretary was sending six copies of his paper on activity and passivity, and asking that any recipients be warned to clear with him before quoting from it.

A letter from Gill, dated October 23, seems to be a reply to one from me, of which I have no copy. He enclosed a paper by him on empathy, which seems never to have been published as such. He confessed that he was not "close to" issues like activity/passivity and the experimental literature David and I had been discussing, and his subsequent scattered comments on our exchanges are difficult to summarize, but add little.

Rapaport sent me a copy of a letter he had written on October 28 in answer to a request from Nevitt Sanford for a reaction to his contribution, "Personality," to APA's Project A. After warning that it may have been a mistake to have asked for it, Rapaport wrote: "We are so different in temperament and we come from so different backgrounds that it is natural for me to have a quite negative view of the general approach you adopted. [. . .] What emerges is, by and large, the accepted views as to the differences" between Freud, Allport, and the "conditioning people." He respected what Sanford had done, but it was not what he had hoped for.

In my next letter (October 30), I enclosed two "drafts," Reflections stimulated by GSK's consciousness paper (Klein, 1959), and On repression and subliminal registration, dated April 1958. "There is nothing much new in them," I admitted; "they're mostly restatements for my own clarification." The rest of the letter deals with plans for his coming "sabbatical" year in New York.

On November 25, I acknowledged "three great letters of yours, still unanswered," but said that I felt first I must finish "slowly working my way through [transcripts of] your ego psychology seminars." I complained about busyness with "conferences on the LSD and isolation projects [. . .] and trying to get the plans for the building modifications in place"—modifications of a floor of an existing NYU building, a new and larger home for RCMH. The letter ends with discussion of both his and my sabbatical plans, on successive years.

My letter of December 19 continues the last topic, mentions my having begun theorizing about "isolation phenomena," and thanks him for having given me a subscription to I. F. Stone's periodical newsletter, then new to me.

The year ended with two brief letters from Rapaport. The one of December 19 notes with satisfaction that with the publication of our two volumes (Holt & Luborsky, 1958), Gill and Brenman's having their 1959 volume in press, and the near-completion of reports by Paul Bergman and Sybille Escalona of their respective projects, "we are about to wipe the slate of the old [Menninger Research] department clean by the end of next year." He wonders if many others have done as well, and why we succeeded. "The only thing I come to is the quality of responsibleness and ability of the people who gathered there." On Christmas eve, he sent thanks and said, "The plans still undecided." But he was counting on the backstop of our invitation to spend his sabbatical at NYU. Meanwhile, "between Rouse and me loads of thoughts about structure formation," recorded in notes which he is eager to show me and discuss if I can come up for a couple of days. "Health no good.—But children both home and loads of excitement and pleasure with them."

CHAPTER 9

Holt to Rapaport—February 11, 1959

Dear David:

Just a note to transmit some comments on a paper by Bob White [1963] of Harvard. I'm suggesting that he send you a copy, because I think it is worthy of careful study to see how the facts he adduces can be worked into a psychoanalytic theory. I'm convinced that they must be handled and that they have not been really adequately handled. I have no illusions that the simple suggestions I have made in this letter [an enclosure, not preserved] will really fill the bill, but perhaps they can stimulate some thought if you have not already worked on this problem.

I think White points up the fact that without some concept like the one he proposes, it is very difficult to explain Peter's [Wolff, 1966] observations on alert inactivity. If we assume that in the earliest years and perhaps even in the earliest days, only the primary model of thinking that you have described applies, I think there will be great difficulty in really explaining how reality contact and reality testing come about. I think he points to a development of the concepts of primary autonomy which may get us away from what is almost a "seething cauldron" conception of infantile reality contact. I think you will be interested in his paper also because of its relevance to the whole problem of activity and passivity in relation to the environment.

Best,

Bob

[Enclosure]

P.S. I also added a bit on the passage in <u>Ego psychology and the problem of adaptation</u> where Hartmann [1939] discusses the significance for the reality principle of the fact that there is a pleasure in the use of the apparatuses of primary autonomy.

Rapaport to Holt—March 4, 1959

Dear Bob:

Your review just arrived. In the meanwhile, I have read your very interesting letter to Bob White and to Roy Schafer. I can't comment on them. I am in a terrible stew with a hundred things. By April 10 I have to have an obituary for Leo Berman [1959] and a paper for the Bibring Memorial Meetings in addition to other things. Maybe just one point about each of these letters. The White paper I would like very much to have but White did not send it. Maybe you can send it to me. About the Schafer letter.[193] I can't help feeling that you overestimate the significance of the Dement [Dement & Kleitman, 1957a, 1957b] findings. I do not think we are so far as to be able to integrate physiological findings and their meanings. As for me they may mean a hundred different things.

Now to your review [of Hartmann, 1939; Holt, 1959]. I am returning it enclosed so that you can see my markings on it. I think Erikson should be mentioned already in the first paragraph. In the second paragraph the use of the term "everyday world" is peculiar. On the second page where you talk about the death instinct you should note that he repudiated it in the paper on aggression [Hartmann, 1948]. On the third page the undifferentiated phase should have a reference to the second volume of The Psychoanalytic Study of the Child. In the third paragraph on the third page you are neglecting

---

[193] Not preserved.

the fact that the internalization and the internal world arise not only in the way you speak about it but in the wake of conflicts also. On the fourth page in the last paragraph the phrase "though waveringly" is more applicable to Freud's <u>The Ego and the Id</u> [1923] than to <u>Inhibitions, Symptoms and Anxiety</u> [1926]. This does not do him justice. The last sentence on this page is quite weak and again does not really do justice to Freud himself. In the second paragraph of the fifth page, I think you are missing a very important opportunity. Because actually what Hartmann and Erikson have shown is that all those things which Horney, Fromm, and Sullivan are doing can be done without discarding psychoanalysis in the very framework of the psychoanalytic theory.

If I have any criticisms then they pertain to a slight rambling, or more precisely not tight enough structuring of this paper. When one is through with it one cannot see very sharply what one has actually read. The second thing would pertain to the first paragraph of the sixth page which I think is not sharp enough and not precise enough as a criticism of Hartmann. Most people won't even understand what you are talking about. I don't think that what you say in your second sentence on this page is really true. Those are not only "wise words" which he has about all those topics. They are many of them at least deep insights which are yet to be explicated. I would hate for it to appear this way. Hartmann certainly does not indulge in "wise words."

Maybe you would do the book a favor if you would indicate that my paper on autonomy is a simplification of some aspects of it and might well serve as an introduction to this rather complex paper. I certainly would think it would do more good to people than the word "brilliant" used in the text. If you do think that the commentaries are helpful to understand him say so, if not omit the adjective anyway.

This is, however, all I can do right now and I know that it is not very good and not very helpful.

My best to both of you,
David

Rapaport to Holt—April 6, 1959

Dear Bob:

Finally I got around tonight (April 3) to reading the memo "On Binding, Neutralization and Psychic Structure."[194] Today I sent off the third draft of my paper [1967a] for the Bibring memorial meeting to the discussant (Helene Deutsch) and to the gang. So you should see it soon. It was a rush job and involved many feelings. It was complicated by the fact that I was also writing the Berman obituary [1967b], which turned out to be a 12-page thing. It is only in its first draft of the third version and therefore I am not yet sending it around. The editor of the International Journal saw this version and accepted it.

So much for the delay.

I do not know really whether I should undertake to respond to your 18 pages. In a way I can't help doing it in spite of my hesitation. You write "I am looking forward to some of your characteristically vigorous criticism." Bob, there is a truth in that. I have been rather sharp in my criticism of your recent memoranda. It surprised me, because my feelings towards you have not changed. It is also a fact that you do take pains to put down your understanding and to try for clarification. This should work against any asperity and irritation, because it inspires respect. Yet there is something peculiar in these drafts which I find to be infallible in eliciting some irritation. This irritation is not really

---

[194] It was, in effect, a first draft of my later paper (Holt, 1962a).

important, and yet I think I should say that it exists. I am not sure of its source. It is quite possible that the source is something you also indicate in your letter. You write "If my reading were wider." It does seem to me that part of the irritation comes from the fact that you are apparently not sufficiently familiar with what was said by Freud, nor even with what was said by me. An example of this, for instance, is that I have taken some pains in "The Theory of Ego Autonomy: A Generalization" to clarify some of those issues connected with stimulus deprivation which you discuss at the tail end of your paper. Your discussion shows no evidence that you made an attempt to digest that.

Now it really is not necessary to know it or to digest it. But if you get into the issue without making any reference to it, some peculiar feeling is aroused in the other fellow who has been through this business. But I don't think that it is important to discuss this point further. I am reasonably sure that if we will find enough time to discuss these things together, then we will arrive at a common language and common understanding. I think that the irritation stems mainly from the fact that somehow the conditions are such that if we had a common language, much of this would be much simpler to discuss.

I think first of all it is correct to say that in most of those things which you are discussing in this paper there is no psychoanalytic literature extant except for what I myself have culled from Freud's writings, trying to make sense of them, and taking into consideration what Hartmann and Kris tried to make out of them. So this whole area is wide open, and any question is justified. Moreover, my own understanding of what Freud was after, as well as my own understanding of how one should, at this stage of the game, conceive of these things, has undergone considerable development and change over the years. Thus inconsistencies in my own writing are quite possible. I did not check the specific passages which you refer to, particularly not because it would have taken a study of the context. In some places I explain simply what Freud meant, in other places I explain how I see it. All of this results in considerable difficulties. For instance, before 1950, before the neutralization concept was propounded, I tried hard to get along with binding as the only concept. Some of this stayed with me in some of my writings even after 1950. So again you have many good reasons to have qualms. What surprises me is simply that you do not eliminate as many of these qualms as possible by simply studying the original and studying those of my writings which are aids in clarifying and reading the original. I would be very surprised if in the Ego Psychology Seminars and the Advanced Metapsychology Seminars there are not sufficient materials to clarify these points. I am sure, however, that in the Elementary Metapsychology Seminars, the transcript of which is now being prepared by Miller, there surely will be.

Let me once again state simply my own position.

1) Primary autonomous apparatuses are not physiological apparatuses but the psychological controlling organizations of these. I tried to make the necessity of this plain in the "System" paper. I would add that the fact that these can lose their autonomy and can become disorganized seems to suggest that we do not have to treat them differently from the secondary autonomous apparatuses. Thus any speculation of how they are built out of cathexes seems altogether unnecessary.

2) I believe that these apparatuses, particularly the threshold apparatuses, are the original templates on the pattern of which the earliest structures are formed. I believe that these earlier [presumably he meant to refer to the same "earliest" ones] structures consist of heightening or lowering these thresholds. The consequences of such threshold changes by means of the modification of the energy distributions both modifies the original drives and gives rise to some degree neutralized motivations. In this respect there seems to be no misunderstanding between us, nor in regard to the hierarchic layering that ensues in the long run.

3) Where the difficulties begin is the nature of these threshold alterations in particular and structures in general. The energy distributions modifying these thresholds are not themselves

structures from the beginning on. You too mention in one place or another that there are <u>ad hoc</u> such countercathecting energy distributions. In some fashion which we do not understand well, they turn into structures at which point they give off much of the cathexes used in building them, and remain nevertheless, or because of this, of a quasi-permanent character. As much of the cathectic energy that remained in these structures is bound in these structures. The rest which is given off is also energy which underwent a degree of neutralization. It differs from the earlier discussed motivations of some degree of neutralization in that [some?] of these energies I conceive as available for hypercathecting. In other words, there are hypercathectic pools (involving those cathexes also which we use for attention cathecting) on each hierarchic level, and of varying degrees of neutralization.

4) It is only in this sense that I propose to use the concept of binding and the concept of neutralization. If I have slipped up anywhere, the context should be able to show that the intent was still what I am stating here. I believe that the conception is harmonious with the basic Breuer-Freud conception, though Freud has often used the concept of binding in the sense in which you criticize me of having used it. One of the difficulties stems from the translation. The English translation of Brill used the terms "mobile" and "mobility" both for drive cathexis and for the displacements of attention cathexes. Freud used different terms in the German for each. Actually, there is easy displaceability of both, only in the former case it is that of the total cathexis, in the latter case it is that of small quantities. I think that I myself have been for a long while puzzled and confused by this. But no more in the last 5 or 6 years.

5) A distinction must be made between what we usually consider in psychoanalysis structures and the ideas which I too would treat as structures. I myself would make the distinction between macrostructures and microstructures. The ideas are microstructures. Their ecological niche in the psychological apparatus is

within what Hartmann calls the "inner world;" both the drive organization and the conceptual organization of memory pertain to
this. This inner world is in contrast to the "internal world" which
encompasses the whole psychic apparatus as against the external
world. The contents [presumably he meant ideas and memories,
but perhaps also percepts?] exist only in the "internal world."
They are supplying the base for our cognitive maps—if I may be
allowed for the moment to use such an expression—as well as indications of the processes and structures of the "internal world." I
think it is by far the simplest conceptualization to sharply separate the structures of the internal world from these
microstructures of the inner world.

I have repeatedly tried the idea that you bring up in a chiding
way as a reduction ad absurdum, namely, to get rid of this dichot-
omy and treat the ideas themselves as the elements of structure
formation and thus the stuff out of which identifications, defenses, controls, etc. are built up. One of my reasons for doing so was
that Glover [1939, probably] indeed considers memories the elements of structure formation. I found every time I tried this that it
leads to endless complications. It is possible, however, that one
could walk that path in a more parsimonious way, and I never
gave up on that.

But first we have to get a simpler solution, I think. I believe that
some of the difficulties you get into and you see are due to the fact
that you do not make such a separation [between structures and ideas
(or content?)]. I do believe that ideas are also structures (though microstructures) and that they too are built out of attention cathexis. Once
they are structured, however, they give off the attention cathexis. Why
is then attention cathexis not used up when endless numbers of ideas
are being created this way? The answer to that is that meanwhile attention cathexis is also created by the metabolism of the psychological
apparatus. What I mean by this metabolism is a complex thing, and
will be glad to explain it some day to you.

You raise the question whether or not motivational (you call
them drive) cathexes are those which build these idea or memory

structures. I think the question is a good question. We are wrestling with this problem in connection with our present experiments. Again, I have quite a few ideas and some empirical observations on this point. But to me it seems that this is a peripheral issue, that the major issues which I have been discussing are reasonably well established and have to be further scrutinized and clarified before we turn to these more complex problems. But again, I would be glad to discuss these more complex problems with you, but that requires quite a bit of clarification of how attention cathexes actually work.

Once we are on this topic, I want to call your attention to it that at the bottom of your page 2, you suddenly bring in learning as though that were something utterly independent from all that you are discussing and I have been speaking about. Now this again is a remarkable thing. You realize that this whole theory we are discussing ultimately hinges on the proposition that learning has to be explained by it. I told you in some detail how I am, with the help of Rouse and the present experiments, trying to explain learning this way. When you bring it in as a <u>deus ex machina</u>, then I can't help feeling irritated. If you want to take learning for granted, you must reject this whole theorizing. If you want to go into this theorizing, you must reject the idea that learning can be simply taken for granted.

Let me go through your paper now and indicate some of the points which are particularly confusing to me.[195] On p. 4, line 3, the term "subdivided" makes no sense to me. On the same page, in line 5, and many times after, you are discussing the "micro-developmental route." This is as if you were totally disregarding the autonomy issue, and assume that micro-development always takes place. This seems to me a most dangerous assumption. The second paragraph on this page talks about the difficulty which I

---

[195] This paragraph is particularly obscure without the text he was criticizing. But that was an early draft of what became my paper on binding, in which those ideas are not found.

explained above as a translation difficulty in the main. In the next paragraph you discuss the example of the girl. That can be explained much more simply. In the competition for attention cathexis, something else won out over the drive. Even the drive has to command attention cathexis in order to make its ideational representation conscious.

On page 5, in line 2, we run for the second time into the learning problem. We are obliged to explain how something "goes into storage as a trace." On the same page, in the next paragraph, you get into the role of drive cathexes in trace formation, and, as I tried to explain to you, that is certainly a doubtful assumption and, while it might find some place peripherally in the theory, there is sufficient evidence to reject making it central. In line 6 on page 6 and thereafter, you are arguing against the concept of "higher levels of potential." When you use an abstraction and handle that way many complex phenomena which you, without that abstraction, had to struggle with one by one, and when you notice that with one abstraction you can generate other abstractions without going down again the long road to the phenomena, then you can readily see that this is not so arbitrary. By the way, I discussed such issues in my review of Cybernetics [1950]. Further down on this page there are many things which I don't understand at all. The "stickiness issue" is dragged in here. I don't make any sense out of "neutralization dams up the drive energy."[196] If you look back above to my discussion, then you will see what I mean.

On page 7 the first two sentences attribute to me something which you see from what I wrote above I did not commit. At the bottom of this page 7, you are arguing about regression in a fashion which we have long overcome. The changed character of the state to which we regress is due partly to the fact that never do all

---

[196] Neither do I, today. It seems evident that I was still clinging to metapsychology despite my growing dissatisfaction, which finally became the insight that it needed to be replaced entirely.

the higher-order hierarchic levels get totally put out of function by regression; partly, however, it is due to the fact that in the course of development there is no simple eternally unchanging record, but the old records are to some extent influenced and integrated with the later ones.

On page 8, in the second paragraph, you speak about cathexis as if it existed only connected to ideas. This certainly isn't true, as is for instance the case in affects, and it isn't true either in many complex transactions within the psychological apparatus which never become conscious and when they are made by us conscious, they are made conscious by means either of their affect or idea indicators. In the 8th line from the bottom, I don't understand to what the "by its connections" refers.

On page 9, in the second paragraph, we have that microgenetic issue which I have mentioned already to you. It actually continues into the first paragraph on page 10.

The last paragraph on this page 10 restates the difficulty with binding and structures. If you look at what I have had to say about it, you will see that it is the neutralization that presupposes the structures, and it is the binding that creates the structures. To my mind, there is no difficulty there. But this same paragraph opens the discussion that goes on then on page 11 about "psychic energy turned into the psychic equivalent of mass." This is the kind of thing that gets me troubled. I have in some detail spelled to you in one of my memoranda that this whole business about your Einstein equation is not relevant. Now it recurs again as if I had said nothing about it. Now it is not necessary for you to accept what I said about it, because I myself am not sure about most of these things. But it is bothersome that the trouble I have taken over it is, as it were, disregarded.

The same thing, in a bit less direct way, obtains for what you have to say about structure in the beginning of the paragraph at the bottom of p. 10. Suddenly you try to define structures as "organization of parts in a dimensional manifold." I do not know where you get this definition, nor am I sure what it means. For all I know, it may be a most excellent definition. It so happens, however, that I tried to define it in the past, in something that you read, the only so-far discernible common meaning to all those things which are referred to as structures. I am referring to the point about "rate of change." Now it is perfectly all right for you to totally reject this proposed definition. Indeed, I am wondering much of the time whether I did not oversimplify things or whether I did not speak about this prematurely. But why should you disregard what I had to say about it? At any rate, if we are to exchange opinions, we have to have a common language. What I have tried to say about it is the basis of building a common language. Argue against it, reject it, but please do take cognizance of it. It is possible that the definition you propose is much better, but why do you not demonstrate that it is? Then you proceed to say that I consider bound cathexes the building-blocks of structure. I do consider bound cathexes the stuff which is structure. But that is, to me, something very different from "building-blocks."

But let me at this point turn to your equation. At the bottom of the page—p. 10—you argue the point that I have many times stressed; that there is not only no action of energy without structure, but we cannot talk about energy without structure because only structure establishes a system, and about energies we can talk only in relation to systems. But this is supposed to lead over to the discussion of the equation, and I do not see how you do that transition. Your discussion of the equation sounds as if you would equate—as you indeed did in the page previous—structure with mass. There is certainly no reason to make any such assumption.[197] Do we not have force fields in physics which are highly structured and yet carry no implication of mass? Does the electromagnetic field carry any connotation of mass?[198] I am repeating simply in essence a point which I probably in a different way have made in my earlier memo on this topic.

---

[197] Only that the physical structures that are easiest to understand are massive.
[198] It does, in fact.

The bottom paragraph of p. 11 I have already answered in my initial formulation.

Now we come to p. 12 which, first of all, equates primary apparatuses with physiological apparatuses, and I tried to explain this issue above. Again, I have tried to tell you in another memo also that dragging in physiological issues or neural issues to my mind obscures our behavioral theory at this moment. To my mind it will obscure it for a very long time. Our job is to keep ourselves free of such. Now it is perfectly all right to differ on this point, but why would you then not bring some new arguments to support your point, rather than stubbornly repeat the same point without new addition?

On p. 13 in the first paragraph, you discuss the memory trace as a prime unit for the formation of psychic structures. First of all there is, as I mentioned to you before, nothing new in this. Glover speaks about it this way. Moreover, I explained to you above some of the real difficulties in the way of this conception.

In the paragraph going from p. 13 to p. 14 and then going on to the rest of p. 14, you do what I tried to explain further above as a mistake of speaking about macrostructures and microstructures without realizing that they are within two different frames of reference. Moreover, you refer to my superego paper, but if you would reread the paper you would see that you disregarded that I already discussed there the issue of the "inner world." You would also have realized that the introject is not just a system of memory traces. On p. 15 it becomes further clear that this distinction which you disregard is coupled here, as it usually is, with a lack of distinction between content on the one hand and structure and process on the other.

As for p. 16, you start it by dragging in Bertalanffy by the hair. At the bottom of this page you make a very interesting suggestion about stimulation prompting the perceptual apparatuses to create hypercathexis. I think that this kind of thinking certainly should be tried out. You saddle it, however, with two difficulties. First of all, you mix in the perceptual apparatuses when one should talk about the primary autonomous apparatuses (a distinction which I tried to make above), and secondly, you go at using isolation studies to make this point plausible. But then concerning isolation studies, I have made a certain set of hypotheses explanatory of their effects in my "The Theory of Ego Autonomy: A Generalization." I referred to this in the beginning of this letter. So why not try out whether you could make an explanation which replaces my explanation, why just treat it as if mine didn't exist? Please believe me that I would simply be delighted if you showed that mine does not work and replace it with something which works and fits into all of those other things which—I think I have demonstrated—the explanatory conception of isolation studies must fit.

I realize that my way of writing must be even more irritating to you than some of the things you write are to me. But we ought to put these on the table so that we understand what prompts us to these mutually irritating things. To be blunt about it, I felt quite bothered by your letter concerning your review of the Hartmann book. You gave all kinds of explanations for your difficulties with the review. Some of them were such that they inevitably prompted me to ask, "So why did you agree to write it?" I am afraid I don't have the letter right now before me, but the crucial passage was something about your finding it difficult to decide what you should consider important about it. So why not wait until you become so acquainted with it that it comes natural for you to know what is important and what is unimportant about it? Bob, is it possible that you are doing too many things and these do not give you enough leisure to digest, to remember, to think through?

I hope you will take my writing this way in the spirit in which I am doing it.

Give my best to Crusa.

Yours,

David Rapaport

P.S. I am finishing this letter Saturday afternoon, and this morning the letter from Stuart Cook arrived. I know you must have been instrumental in it, and I appreciate it very much. I will answer him and send copies to you and George. Naturally I will gratefully accept the invitation. I would like to discuss with you and George what I will do to make returns.

Comment

There are many difficulties for the reader in this letter. First, there is the unfortunate fact that Rapaport speaks again and again about specific passages in the draft I had sent him, an evanescent document soon replaced by a series of later drafts culminating in my paper on binding (1962a). It is evident that in the manuscript I was struggling to work within both Rapaport's "common language" of metapsychology, and my growing sense that it needed somehow to be supplemented by a language about observable events in the real world, in which important discoveries were being made. My own struggle to reconcile incompatible points of view and to maintain my relationship with him while rebelling undoubtedly made for some confused writing in the draft.

Then, it is quite obvious that he was upset by my covert revolt, my failure to be satisfied with his explanations without boldly challenging them (though that might have disturbed him even more), and my repeated attempts to bring in concepts and points of view he considered unnecessary and diversionary. Indeed, on the first page he repeatedly spoke of an irritation he didn't fully understand. I would even venture the hypothesis that those emotions of his got in the way of clear verbal communication, complicating the reader's task.

For whatever reason, there are numerous passages in this letter that I do not feel confident that I understand. For example, in the first numbered paragraph on the second page, he says about the "apparatuses of primary autonomy" that "we do not have to treat them differently from the secondary autonomous apparatuses. Thus any speculation of how they are built out of cathexes seems altogether unnecessary." I can only presume that he considered that no speculation is needed because we already understand how that is done, though it still seems puzzling and indeed speculative.

Before leaving this paragraph, notice that the conception that the psychic structures of "apparatuses" which control the function of the physical sensory organs is a pretty clear instance of metaphysical interactionist dualism, a Cartesian position that few professional philosophers adhere to today.

I can recall no conversation in which Rapaport expressed any interest in or opinion about metaphysics. In his writings, he came closest to it in a paper he spoke about from time to time, occasionally urging a student to read it, but was never published until Gill decided to include it in the *Collected Papers*: Dynamic psychology and Kantian epistemology (Rapaport, 1947a).

A little later, the paragraph numbered 3) starts out with an admission that the exact nature of structures (in his usage) is not clear. Then he goes on to say that an energy distribution is not yet a structure, though not many pages later he protests that in physics, force fields without mass may be highly structured. Of course, he rejected my attempt to question his use of physicalistic concepts like force, energy, and structure without any necessity to respect their original relationships, because those corresponding concepts in physics were only analogies which we metapsychologists did not need to take seriously. I cannot resist the conclusion that he felt no compunction about using physical and other scientific disciplines opportunistically—using cross-disciplinary comparisons when they helped his argument, rejecting them at other times as mere analogies.

At this point, I interrupted writing by a re-reading of Rapaport's most philosophical paper, the one on Kant's epistemology, and the section on The Possibility of Knowledge (pp. 721–23) in the final synthetic chapter of *Organization and Pathology of Thought* (1951a). It is sad to report that though he gives lip service in the latter to Piaget's "organic adaptation-relationship of man to his environment" (p. 722), and in the Kantian paper to "the necessity for thinking in terms of a psychosomatic-environmental unity" (p. 296), his commitment to metapsychology prevented him from acting on the implications of those more systems-theoretical ideas. His metapsychology did accept the environment in the adaptive point of view; his deep admiration for and immersion in Erikson's work reminded him from time to time to consider culture and society. And yet, an attentive reader to these letters must have noticed that his was primarily a "one-person psychology" in today's terms, focusing most of the time on what was going on *inside* the psyche. Not even inside the *person* as a whole social organism!

Though he read and—admittedly, only partly—understood Wiener's (1948) *Cybernetics*, he never grasped the necessity of including the concept of information in his theories. Even memories were conceived of as structures of hypercathexes without a hint that these purely hypothetical energies could work only if they stored information (principally, meanings) by encoding it. In his defense, however, we should remember that he died long before the age of the personal computer, or even the big machines of pitifully small capacity that graced some university labs a relatively few years after the end of this correspondence. In 1959, the first UNIVAC Solid State Computer was only 4 years old and had a memory of under 10 kilobytes. *Information* is such a ubiquitous concept in contemporary scientific, even much popular literature that it may come as a shock to realize that Rapaport hardly ever used it (except in reference to the Wechsler subtest), certainly not in his most ambitious theoretical writing.

It happened that in the job from which Rapaport recruited me to learn diagnostic testing under his tutelage, I was taught and became immersed in the use of quantitative analysis of free verbal texts (interviews), a procedure that was held to high standards of reliability, in which the coding of information played a key part. I was thus spared the erroneous assumption of the advocates of hermeneutics, that just such types of data were beyond the reach of conventional scientific method. Unfortunately, after Rapaport's death, Merton Gill (1994) and several others of his students (e.g., Spence, 1982) fell prey to this misconception when they became disillusioned with metapsychology. Although George Klein (1976) also became disenchanted, until his untimely death he continued to believe that the clinical theory could be developed into full scientific status, applicable not only to the data of the psychoanalytic therapeutic encounter but to those of the laboratory.

Near the end of the first half of his letter, Rapaport made a statement that I find noteworthy about his modus operandi:

> When you use an abstraction and handle that way many complex phenomena which you, without that abstraction, had to struggle with one by one, and when you notice that with one abstraction you can generate other abstractions without going down again the long road to the phenomena, then you can readily see that this is not so arbitrary.

Here let me focus on the second half of this long sentence, his belief that having established one abstraction from phenomena, one can generate others without concern for links to observable data. Evidently, he believed that his theorizing was not detached from observation, merely liberated from slavery to maintaining it. Thereby, he thought that his continuous elaboration of abstractions remained faithful to basic scientific method.

Lurking in the background is Rapaport's not grasping how important it is for serious theory-building to ground it in a consistent stance on metaphysical issues, such as the mind-body problem. At the time, I was very far from such understanding also, with some resulting confusion in my own theoretical attempts. Years later, in attempting to understand a pattern of inconsistency in Freud's theories, I followed the generally useful path of looking into underlying assumptions. That led me to the irreducible ones we call metaphysical, with the result that I came to a deeper understanding of the internal contradictions in psychoanalytic theory (see Chapter 14 of Holt, 1989 and the papers referenced there). I want to acknowledge my great debt to the work of Stephen C. Pepper (1942, 1972) which provided me with an invaluable framework within which to study these difficult matters.

Holt to Rapaport—July 5, 1960

Dear David:

[. . .][199]

It is taking me longer than I had expected to find time to give the motivation paper [Rapaport, 1960c] as careful a reading as I want to. But I've been through the first half, so I think I'll write you now about my little points. They're mostly very minor stylistic suggestions.

[. . .]

Page 18, first sentence, lines 3 and 4: ". . . that is to say, for everything in behavior that cannot . . ." Incidentally, the last example seems very different from the other two. That is, the effects of social stimuli seem to be so different from those of poisons or physical accidents that I wonder at your bracketing them. If you fall or it you're poisoned, this has a kind of an effect on behavior that is direct, that by-passes the ego very largely, and is entirely ego alien. If, however, another person attacks you and you fight back, it's hard for me to see how this stimulus differs very much from any other kind of stimulus to which you react (for example, a painful surface from which you withdraw your hand, a bright light that causes you to close your eyes, or a beautiful painting that causes you to advance and look at it). I realize that in the last ex-

---

[199] This letter begins with four paragraphs of minor news and comments; the ellipsis indicates their omission. Much of the rest consists of minor editorial comments, the omission of which is similarly indicated.

amples I just gave, I started out with reflexes, which are perhaps worthy of being included as a separate class of examples, in which again the ego is hardly involved. But surely it is involved, and the behavior that ensues is not ego alien, when one responds to a social stimulus, or to any other stimulus that doesn't evoke a tropism or reflex. I realize also that my example of the painting gets us into the last section of the paper, and is not an example of responding in which a motivation is involved, but if we substitute a tempting looking delicacy in a shop window that arouses a latent desire and causes the person to go inside and buy it, we surely are getting into motivation—just as we do when a person responds to another person. In this last case, I don't see that it's a question of co-determination. That is, whenever there is a stimulus that is involved in behavior, you can always say that it is one of the determinants along with the motive that interacts with it; but that's a very different situation from the somatic and external physical determinants.

[. . .]

Page 22, second sentence: "For instance, the forces that manifest themselves as defenses against instinctual drives—are they motives? Should we consider as motives those forces that manifest themselves as 'reasons,' 'rule-following,' and 'will'—as Peters [1958] does?" [. . .]

Page 25, [. . .] End of the third paragraph, do you really mean to say that some motives are neither drives nor their derivatives? This surprised me considerably. [. . .]

Page 28, second paragraph from the end: in the last paragraph, you speak as if it's an unusual state of affairs for psychology not to have "a generally accepted definition" of a concept like emotional affect. But does psychology have any generally accepted definitions? How would you establish that it did? The commonest terms, like stimulus and response, are used in very different senses by different writers. I think the tone of this kind of complaint ought to be changed.

[. . .]

Page 30, first line: [. . .] This sentence, incidentally, sounds like a definition, and a very odd one. Rather, it's a partial one, I believe: one of the results of my thinking about binding and neutralization was to come to the conclusion that primary process really includes two kinds of phenomena: those coordinated to the concept of non-neutralized cathexis, and those coordinated to free-cathexis. It's only the former that are peremptory, in my view. At this point, it seems to me more reasonable to send you back the manuscript than to continue this tedious dictation of minor points. So I'm going to ask you to send me another copy, and will return this one herewith. There are still, however, a few points I want to mention.

On page 33, where you refer to Lindsley [1957], I think you might also mention Hebb's [1955] paper, Drives and the CNS (conceptual nervous system). In that, he renounces his earlier "inclination to equate drives with phase sequences."

On page 35, it sounds odd to my ear to say that we know only what we have postulated about something. That's a very special kind of knowing, and in the context would give rise to misunderstanding.

On page 43, you introduce your own special meaning of the term, concept. At least, you always speak as if everyone uses the term, concept, the same way that you do and so your usage of it doesn't need definition, but I believe that you're mistaken. There may very well be an important tradition that you are following, but certainly many psychologists are not aware of that. See, for example, the recent dictionary by English and English [1958]; it doesn't contain the meaning of concept that you are using.

On page 46, I've queried your attribution of the term, "equifinal," to Fritz Heider [1958]: I first saw it in Bertalanffy [1950], but of course he may have gotten it from Fritz.[200]

At the top of page 54, I was surprised by your saying that affect signals involve neutralized hypercathexes. Of course, they <u>involve</u>

---

[200] An implausible suggestion.

them, but you're making a distinction between primary and second-ary process, in a way that I don't follow. It seems to me that neutralized drive cathexis is not necessarily hypercathexis, and that it is the former and not the latter that you mean here. If the neutralized cathexis of a thought or an affect signal is joined by a hypercathexis, then we may become aware of the thought or signal, but don't we conceive that preconscious thoughts operate with neutralized drive cathexis and with little or no hypercathexis?

At the bottom of page 60, you're discussing anticathexes and their manifestation as forces. The example that you give seems to me unfortunately chosen: certainly the primary way in which anticathexes operate as forces is as restraining forces, poised counter to the drive forces. When a reaction formation is involved and an al-truistic motivation supervenes, new and derivative motivational forces my come about, but this is surely not the main meaning of what you had in mind when you said that anticathexis manifests it-self as a force. In any event, these new derivative forces are not (as I understand it) directed against the aggressive drive.

On page 62, your second paragraph struck my ear oddly. It seems to me that a reason can hardly be a structure, and that your expression is simply too condensed: what Peters is talking about may be behavior that is primarily to be attributed to the opera-tion of certain structures. But to pit structure against motivation seems to me unfortunate, since as you have pointed out earlier, structures give rise to motivations (or often do).[201]

When I have finished the second installment, I'll write again; or perhaps I'll bring it along with me. In any event, see you soon. With warmest regards to Elvira and yourself—

Bob

---

[201] Today, I cringe a little, reading my attempts to follow Rapaport into the maze of his convoluted metapsychology. I had to spend a lot of time and effort doing so before it gradually became evident to me that that intellectual system was worthless, because as clever an expert in it as Rapaport could always find a way around any objection—except the requirement that its prepositions be empirically testable, now, not someday.

Holt to Rapaport—October 20, 1960

Dear David,

This note is primarily to acknowledge receipt of a couple of communications from you. I am not likely to come up with any candidates for you and Rouse in this year (for research assistants), but I'll of course keep it in mind.

I had mixed reactions to getting the carbon of your letter to Don Spence. Of course, I am interested in his proposal and your critique of it, but I am a little troubled by the fact that you sent it to me (and perhaps to a number of others) without getting his permission or even notifying him. I just don't think that's very good manners, to be quite blunt about it; I'd be upset if you sent around critical reactions to my work in this way. (Of course, you did once suggest that we send copies of correspondence on theoretical matters to Mert, Roy and a few others—that's fine; and if you already have such an understanding with Don, please forgive me. But I have heard of other cases in which you did hurt feelings by doing it without such a prior arrangement.) Please forgive me for bringing this up; I do it with considerable discomfort, and only because I think that you may be inadvertently antagonizing some people by this practice.[202]

---

[202] The long exchange that this paragraph provoked, which will be recounted in a number of subsequent letters, and the comment by Ilse Javetz Wheelis and Rapaport's later response are included because they throw light on Rapaport's code of friendship, which cost him many close companions over the years.

By the way, I just reorganized the reprints I had brought and found the copy of your Wiener review. Please excuse me for not checking first.

I had a rather interesting experience in Princeton last week, attending an ETS [Educational Testing Service] conference—or did I already write to you about it? Sometimes I don't make carbons of letters I type myself, and get confused writing a number of people about the same topics! If I didn't send you copies of the paper I gave there [Holt, 1961b?] and also my recent one on ego psychology and testing [1960], please let me know and I'll make up the deficiency pronto.

Not long ago, I saw Allen and Ilse Wheelis in San Francisco. I have become quite fond of her after not terribly much contact— you know it was because of her that I got the house I'm living in with such pleasure. We spoke about many mutual friends, including you, and she said rather wistfully that you seem to have dropped her from your circle of friends. She understands why you no longer communicate with Allen, but wonders why you generalize to her. (Writing to you about it is, of course, my idea and not her request.)

I recently read the paper [Richard] Held presented last year at the APA symposium he organized (on sensory deprivation) [perhaps Held & Bossom, 1961]. Do you know it? Very impressive; and I think the model of perception that he offers looks extremely important. But I always have such trouble learning a new concept, like re-afferentation!

Yours,

Bob

Rapaport to Holt—October 27, 1960

Dear Bob:

Somehow from your note it is not absolutely clear whether all my letters have arrived to you or not. Did you receive the one in which I thanked you for the "Annotated Alice"? I did not read it all, but looking into it, it looks strikingly like <u>Organization and Pathology of Thought</u>. So I felt very amused though the joke was really on me.

It was no joking matter, however, that you sent me a scolding for having sent you a copy of my letter to Spence. I am afraid that I cannot agree with you. Letters I write contain my opinions. Anybody who shows me something, except if I agreed in advance that I will treat it as confidential material, exposes himself to my making comments about it, and these comments I may repeat in any quarters I see fit to repeat them in. Indeed the only limitation I see to this, and I practiced on this, is imposed by intimacy. To the degree I feel intimate with a person I usually refrain within limits from discussing matters which pertain to that range of intimacy with others. You have asked me to tell whenever I disagree. Here is one of these scarce occasions. I might as well add that I did not cherish your referring to this matter as "bad manners."

In regard to your comment concerning Wheelis and Jawetz, this is what I can say. Wheelis has put himself, as far as I am concerned, beyond the pale. If you want me to explain how this happened I will be glad to. Jawetz's allegiance is to be to her husband. Isn't it natural that I should avoid a situation which can lead only to tensions?

I am still not allowed to work full time: it is half time for me this week. I hope that, after close to a month, I can resume full work with the beginning of next week.

Would love to hear about your work. I have not received your manuscripts. Please send them.

Sincerely,

David

Holt to Rapaport—November 1, 1960

Dear David,

Yes, I believe I have received all your letters, including the one in which you thanked me for the "Annotated Alice." Of course I had the same association on looking into it at the Luborsky's this summer, which was why I could not resist sending it to you. The day after I mailed it off, I got a card from Basic Books telling that they were offering it as a kind of alternate selection, which made me feel a slight chagrin, such as I imagine that you might have felt if, after you had given me <u>Thousand Cranes</u> [it became] a Book of the Month selection. Ah me, what protean forms snobbery will take!

I am sorry that after your explanation, I still feel the same way about your practice of sending around carbon copies of your letters. I am perfectly aware of the grotesqueness of my presuming to scold you for bad manners, and you might perfectly well have replied in kind instead of with such patience and forbearance. Really the only thing in your position that I take exception to is the fact that you <u>assume</u> that everyone who shows you something knows that he exposes himself to your making comments about it that may be repeated in any quarters you see fit. If you do always make it clear that this is the case unless there is an explicit agreement to keep things confidential, then I am entirely out of order and offer my apologies.

I was sorry to learn about your illness, but hope very much that by the time you read these words you will be over it and back to work full time.

I had a delightful evening with Merton and Charlotte at the Lozoffs' Saturday night, and Merton told me about his recent visit to you. He and Charlotte were in their most coruscating form; I haven't had such an evening of hilarity in ages. I find the Lozoffs good, comfortable, warm, and solid friends with whom it is a pleasure to renew an acquaintance. Another old Topekan was there: Elsie Taboroff. You remember her husband, Leonard, who was a resident in one of the earliest groups? You know he died of a heart ailment shortly after he completed the residency; she is living in Palo Alto.

This Friday evening I am going in to hear Ken Colby at one of the meetings of the research group; I will pass on to you my reactions. I recently read a reprint he sent me from Behavioral Science [Colby, 1957] on his researches into association; I thought it an excellent piece of work, though the results were not exciting. It shows he has a sound grasp of research method in an extremely difficult field. He also sent me his little book on Psychoanalytic Research [Colby, 1960b], but I haven't had time to read it. I also just got Gardner Murphy's [1960] new book on William James and Psychical Research, which I have dipped into a little bit—an interesting thing. I hope very much that my papers and my dittoed letter have reached you by now; please let me know if they have not.

> Best,
>
> Bob

P.S. I see there are a couple of things in your letter of October 18 I haven't adequately responded to. I asked Merton about his manuscript that touches on the id [Gill, 1963], and he said that Sue [Annin] was editing it. I'd be grateful if you could help me get hold of any or all these three papers, which he tells me are to be in Psychological Issues. I hope to see Hanna sometime soon, but it's a long way to Berkeley, and I have a very absorbing social life here in Palo Alto. I am not sure I made it clear that the pictures I took are color slides. If you have a way of viewing or projecting them, let me know and I'll lend them to you.

Rapaport to Holt—November 15, 1960

Dear Bob:

A week passed since my last letter to you. The hope that I expressed, namely that over the last weekend I would be able to read your papers and react to them, was obviously a vain one. The amount of stuff I had to do simply to keep the most urgent correspondence going has occupied me over the whole weekend. This week was particularly bad: the two seminars which I condensed today into one 4¼ hour session were about "reality." It was a formidable, unsatisfactory and unsatisfying job, however much energy I invested into it.

In the meanwhile Wednesday we had here Donald Marquis.[203] We have invited him to go over our experiments with us. I discovered only after he arrived that he is now involved in psychology of management. But just the same he was very alert, very bright (so was his new wife) and it was rather gratifying to see how excited he got at some points with what we have. In general, he took a very positive attitude towards it, made a number of interesting though minor suggestions and felt that we have proven some things. He also would like to come back to keep in touch with it.

For us ourselves it was, quite aside from his comments and

---

[203] Donald G. Marquis (1908–1973) was at Yale from 1930 to 1945, getting his PhD there in 1932 and ending as chair of the department of psychology. He chaired the psychology department at the University of Michigan (1945–1958), being elected President of the American Psychological Association in 1948. He spent the rest of his career as Professor of Industrial Management at MIT. His best-known work, with Ernest Hilgard, was *Conditioning and Learning* (1940).

attitudes, a rather elating experience because we have surveyed some things in a way that we have not done before (it was always more piecemeal: Russell and Cofer[204] both went always into details and did not go over the all-over picture). It does make an interesting all-over picture and in a way it might well prove to be the preparation for the lecture you asked me to give at the APA next year. By the way I did not have the chance to thank you for this invitation. It took until now to overcome the ambivalence: at first I was not sure whether I am really grateful or not. By now I am.

But that day was also very exhausting. If you now add to this the notes and papers in preparation by [Fred] Schwartz,[205] the conferences with Rodrigue,[206] and with [John C.] Burnham,[207] and the preparatory readings for those, the conferences with [Arthur] Deikman (a young resident who is trying to do something [see Deikman, 1963]), my counselee [i.e., the woman he was counseling], bull session [informal meeting of Riggs staff and patients],[208]

---

[204] Charles C. Cofer (1916–1998) was a founder of the Group for a Study of Verbal Behavior at a time of behaviorist predominance when such work was considered "mentalistic" and thus unscientific. *Verbal Learning and Verbal Behavior* (1961), which he edited, had a great impact and he became prominent. W. A. Russell, who did similar work, made much less of a mark.

[205] Fred Schwartz (PhD 1959, U. Mass.) held a post-doctoral fellowship at the Austen Riggs Center from 1959 to 1961, continuing as a Research Investigator until 1968. His major work during those years was published in two monographs (Schwartz & Rouse, 1961; Schwartz & Schiller, 1970) as well as numerous papers referenced there. I am very grateful to Dr. Schwartz for supplying a great deal of information about the research group working with Rapaport during his final few years. See comment following this letter.

[206] Emilio M. Rodrigue (sometimes Rodrigué), then a fourth-year psychiatric resident at Riggs, had already been a practicing psychoanalytic clinician in Argentina and had published a paper (Rodrigue, 1956).

[207] Dr. Burnham writes (personal communication, March 2014), that after taking his PhD at Stanford, he received a three-year postdoctoral fellowship from the Foundations' Fund for Research in Psychiatry. He spent 1959 and 1960 at Riggs as a private pupil of Rapaport, remaining after the latter's death as a visiting staff member until the fall of 1961. See comment following this letter for further details he helpfully supplied.

[208] Arthur J. Deikman, MD (1929–2013) was already interested in altered states of consciousness and became well known for his work on them and mysticism.

staff conference, etc. then it simply adds up to a continuous bed-lam. Even though I am doing physically quite a bit better, I do get exhausted by all this.

So now to the papers. The Princeton paper [Holt, 1961] I find to be strikingly clear and straight-forward. The only point I really want to criticize on it is that my name should follow Hartmann's and Erik-son's (if at all) rather than to precede them. Maybe there is another phrase which I am not so sure of. This one is on page 3, line 6 where you write "but breadth requires eclecticism." I am not at all sure that using objective testing methods needs to be eclecticism and I cer-tainly would doubt that "breadth" does requite eclecticism. This, however, is a broad issue and I wish one day we would have the time to discuss the issues involved. To put it in the positive way: I felt that your ten points had real sweep and that you made them stick one af-ter the other. I was not sure that on page 8 in the first line of the second paragraph the "theoretical issues" was entirely clear. Just preceding it, you talk about very practical considerations and the theoretical issue to which you refer goes somewhat further back. I think that one gets a bit stuck there. I also enjoyed your quiet humor which was more apparent in this paper than in several recent ones. One of the major virtues of your paper was that it did not go any deeper into any of the issues than 19 pages permit and yet filled the 19 pages (without cramming them) with as rich a fare of problems and relationships as one possibly could. I hope that you will publish this and soon. I am tempted to say, and I yield to it, that in a funny way I realized while reading your paper that somehow I myself never pursued "personology." I think not even when I tested. This surely must sound like a cockeyed and peculiar, indeed even improbable statement. Yet, if you consider it, it will become somehow plausible that I was always concerned with thinking, thought processes—somehow schematic things rather than personology proper.

Funnily enough this may be related to the point that I myself never have been bothered with the question: What goes on in the other person? In an arrogant way I have usually assumed that somehow I know it. In turn, however—and this again may sound paradoxical—I was always puzzled how thinking works. I am under the impression that already when very young I had the idea that adults "think," that is to say, do something different than I have been doing who had only "things occur to him," "ideas come to his mind." I think somehow throughout my life I have tried to force myself into some sort of imagined position which I thought was that of the adults, namely that they "thought," that is to say pursued something which I didn't and I had only very vague idea of. I think I am doing just that very thing right now, so forgive me.

And now to your paper "Recent Developments in Psychoanalytic Ego Psychology and Their Implications for Diagnostic Testing" [Holt, 1960]. I am not a very good judge of the second half of it. In a way I regret that some of Marty Mayman's points and some of Roy's points do not come into the second half of it more extensively. But as far as the first half, I can say that these seven pages are the only good survey we have of this whole area. Reading them it suddenly becomes clear how Merton in his paper stuck to only the tallest peaks and how the papers of the rest of us have been always so close to one or the other of the issues (and this holds for the "structure" paper of mine particularly strikingly) that a total survey was never gained by us. I feel that you have given a real sense of what had happened. Peculiarly enough I was never sure that such a survey is possible and felt now for the first time convinced of it, though at times I did not want to believe my eyes.

As I came toward the end of it I wish you would have had just a little bit more space (not much more) and then my thoughts wandered, whether or not you will undertake a more extensive statement of this sort for the Psychological Bulletin. At any rate: it is going to be the first intimation to the majority of clinical psychologists just what was going on, and I do not believe that without very hard and back-breaking study they could have found out about it. As you can see I am really delighted with it and appreciate it.

This, however, must be all for today. I will write to you about your third paper maybe tomorrow, but maybe only in another week. I am dead tired after this morning's performance and still I must attend tonight to a series of letters which do not tolerate delay. Next week comes my last seminar and it is on the superego and you can well imagine how much I have to prepare for that one.

You might be interested to know that in this seminar group too, there was one man who really had a firm grasp on the material: it was George Mahl of Yale.[209] I was delighted to find today in a brief conversation I had with him that he would like to continue his studies on this and therefore he would also like to teach it. This will be then a new teacher in this whole field. I gather also that both he and a Dr. Pilot[210] who is doing some psychophysiological studies with Dr. [Theodore] Lidz of Yale and who was in this course would like to try to see how they could shift the emphasis of their studies so that while they have in the past not been directly related to any kind of theory and certainly not to psychoanalysis, that they could turn them into psychoanalytically relevant investigations. This all is very elating. The only thing depressing about it is that I should really have all the energy I used to have ten years ago and then I could really be helpful to them as they are turning to me for advice in just these matters. But God knows: "we have to do what we can," and that I will.

Please do not let my frequency of letters urge you to write to me when you should be doing something else. This is your sabbatical year and while I am extremely eager to hear what you are doing and what kind of thoughts you are turning around in your head and what kind of people you meet, I have first of all respect for it that this is your sabbatical and secondly, I wish for you that you would immerse yourself in whatever you are doing and not be pulled back by other considerations.

        Yours,

          David

---

[209] George H. Mahl, PhD (1917–2006) was best known for his research on the relationship between transitory anxiety and disruptions in speech (dysfluencies). See also Janis et al. (1969).

[210] I have been unable to trace Pilot.

Comment

The following description of the research group assembled by Rapaport on his return to Riggs after his year at NYU is based largely on information kindly furnished me by Fred Schwartz and John Burnham (personal communications).

After getting his PhD from the University of Massachusetts in 1959, Schwartz went directly to work with Rapaport, supported by a postdoctoral fellowship from NIMH. In addition to Rodrigue, Burnham, and Deikman, mentioned above, Schwartz recalls that there was a "kid who was in graduate school in Israel and joined us for the summer I started my post-doc with DR. This young student had the temerity to heckle DR until DR agreed to put his thoughts about attention cathexis into writing . . . [He was] Danny Kahneman." The draft on attention [Rapaport, 1959] was included in the *Collected Papers* by Merton Gill. Here is how "the kid" describes the experience in his autobiography (Kahneman, 2002):

> My most significant intellectual experience during those years did not occur in graduate school. In the summer of 1958 [actually, 1960], my wife and I drove across the United States to spend a few months at the Austen Riggs Clinic in Stockbridge, Massachusetts, where I studied with the well-known psychoanalytic theorist David Rapaport, who had befriended me on a visit to Jerusalem a few years earlier. Rapaport believed that psychoanalysis contained the elements of a valid theory of memory and thought. The core ideas of that theory, he argued, were laid out in the seventh chapter of Freud's "Interpretation of Dreams," which sketches a model of mental energy (cathexis). With the other young people in Rapaport's circle, I studied that chapter like a Talmudic text, and tried to derive from it experimental predictions about short-term memory. This was a wonderful experience, and I would have gone back if Rapaport had not died suddenly later that year. I had enormous respect for his fierce mind. Fifteen years after that summer, I published a book entitled "Attention and Effort,"

[Kahneman, 1973] which contained a theory of attention as a limited resource. I realized only while writing the acknowledgments for the book that I had revisited the terrain to which Rapaport had first led me.

Kahneman became widely known at the time of his collaborative work with Amos Tversky on other aspects of cognitive psychology, notably shortcuts of reasoning and problem-solving they termed heuristics. The work for which he won a Nobel Prize in economics (the only psychologist ever to win that honor, shared with V. L. Smith) was for research on judgment and decision-making under uncertainty.

Schwartz recalls a total of five other members of Rapaport's group (besides himself and, briefly, Kahneman): "three psychoanalysts as 4th year residents—Rodrigue from Argentina, Lofgren from Sweden, and Tieko from Finland. Emilio [Rodrigue] was a very lively man . . . DR liked Emilio. Dick Rouse was my technical mentor, but we had minimal contact." Rouse, an Associate Professor at nearby Williams College, started meeting with Rapaport in 1956 and taught him the basics of academic learning theory. "The monograph [Schwartz & Rouse, 1961] was my idea (from Chapter VII), and I did all the work." I have been unable to find further information about Rouse.

A word about the three foreign psychoanalysts: John Burnham (in a personal communication, March 2014) reports that they "turned out to be leaders in psychoanalysis or psychoanalytic psychiatry in Finland, Sweden, and Turkey." But since Rapaport does not mention any contact with Lofgren and Tieko, it is likely that they were getting research training from other Riggs staff. Even without them, we know that Rapaport did interact in a presumably advisory/supervisory way with a total of seven students during his hectic final months. Thanks to a personal communication from Roy Schafer (April 3, 2014), I can add that Lofgren joined the clinical staff at Riggs. About his subsequent career, I know nothing.

Writing about himself in the third person, Burnham recalls that "At Austen Riggs, he held classes for patients, audited the classes offered to the resident physicians and psychologists, and attended case conferences. The intention was that he have firsthand experience in the diagnosis and care of mental patients, which in fact has given him insight and authority in his historical writing. Rapaport was quite open that he wanted to leave a historical record that would do justice to Freud and to the ego psychologists and others of whom Rapaport approved. He thought having a well trained historian to tell the story would benefit future scientists and intellectuals. He sent Burnham all over the country to interview various psychologists, psychiatrists, and of course psychoanalysts who had left significant contributions or been influential." Wryly, Burnham adds: "Little came directly out of those interviews."

On leaving Riggs in the fall of 1961, he spent two years at San Francisco State University as Assistant Professor of History. In 1963, he joined the faculty at Ohio State University, where he remained the rest of his career except for two Fulbright appointments and two invited honorary visiting professorship years at Bowdoin and Cambridge. He retired in 2002 as Research Professor of History emeritus. In 1990–1992, he was president of the American Association for the History of Medicine. His dozen or so books include works on Edward Kempf, an influential psychoanalytically inclined psychiatrist, and Smith Ely Jelliffe, a major pioneer of psychoanalysis in the United States. His most recent book (Burnham, ed., 2012) celebrates the centennial of Freud's 1909 visit to America. It won the Courage to Dream book prize of the American Psychoanalytic Association in 2014. His next project is a book tentatively entitled "Understanding the Historical Impact of Sigmund Freud." With it, he hopes finally to fulfill the role that David Rapaport envisioned for him.

The other member of Rapaport's group, Peter H. Schiller, then a graduate student at Clark University, spent summers at Riggs from 1953 through 1960. Schwartz recalls that "DR took Peter under his wing when Peter came to this country. Some of the best individual studies in our monograph [Schwartz & Schiller, 1970] were done by Peter. A great guy to work with."

The two monographs by Schwartz and collaborators are the best (perhaps the only) published collection of experiments that realized Rapaport's often-expressed wish to test his theoretical ideas in the laboratory. Would that he could have lived to see them as well as the manuscript on which Burnham (1967) had begun working (for a few months; he was then supervised by Roy Schafer).

Schiller and Schwartz worked well and productively together. Their monograph (Schwartz & Schiller, 1970) contains 13 separate studies by the two of them. Since George Klein also spent his summers in Stockbridge, it is not surprising that he and Schiller became acquainted. They started working together on the development of visual interference in children, using the Stroop test of color-word interference. I believe that they kept in good communication for several years while they did similar research on visual masking and metacontrast, George working at the Research Center for Mental Health (e.g., Klein, Holt, Spence, & Gourevich, 1958).

Starting with a postdoctoral research appointment, Schiller has spent the rest of his career at the Massachusetts Institute of Technology, where he has held the Dorothy Pointras Chair for Medical Physiology since 1986. In his lab there, Schiller has done important neuropsychological research combining behavioral and brain sciences, largely on vision. In 2007, he was honored by the National Academy of Sciences and the American Academy of Arts and Sciences.

"Rapaport was a powerful figure at Riggs, even alongside Erik Erikson and Robert Knight and many others," Burnham comments. "He once told me he took on an institutional role that did not involve administration directly but rather stimulated institutional awareness, reality testing, and creativity. 'I am the witch of this place,' he said." An odd self-assessment, but when one looks back on his truly extraordinary gifts—for surrounding himself with young assistants and co-workers who later would become outstanding contributors, and for exerting a pervasive influence in any institution where he worked even if his job title did not suggest it—it is tempting to think in terms of the uncanny.

Holt to Rapaport—November 15, 1960

Dear David,

   [. . .] I hasten to enclose the pictures: after you two, some landscapes near Stockbridge; the Schafers (it would be nice if they could see these pictures while the latter [the slides] are east), then the Luborskys and my girls, taken on our southern jaunt in August. No great hurry about sending them back.

   [. . .] I have been making a little poll here, as I said I would [. . .]: A couple of times at coffee, I've raised the general question about the letter-sending issue, naming no names. There have been a couple of interesting discussions, but everyone agrees with me. [Dorwin] Cartwright asks, how would you feel if a correspondent quoted your <u>praise</u> of his work in a letter to someone else (where it might do him some good) without your knowledge? The case isn't parallel, but it's an interesting question. It seems that in England, and here too some generations ago, there was the custom that if someone didn't want any public use to be made of a correspondence, he explicitly asked that it be kept private. Someone else suggested that if a person wanted to send around carbons of his letters, he should have postcards mimeographed saying that he'd be glad to answer a letter (or request to read a paper, etc.) <u>if</u> the sender wouldn't mind his distributing copies of the reply to persons of his own choosing.

   [. . .] So much for today. My best to Elvira.

               Yours,

                    Bob

Rapaport to Holt—November 16, 1960

Dear Bob:

I am hastening to write in answer to your letter of November 1. I want you to know that the papers arrived. I hope that before this weekend passes I will have read them and I can react to them. Then I will attach here a second letter. But since I can't be absolutely sure of this, I want this note at least to go.

The situation with me is that I had to resume the Western New England Psychoanalytic Institute seminars. I planned them for twelve sessions, two of them I gave before I got sick. One they skipped for Anna Freud's visit. So after I was half way on my feet I had five weekends left in which to do the job of ten. So now I am mostly lecturing the same material, condensing two three-and-a-half- hour sessions into one each time. Today I taught from 9 until 1:15 and now I am back trying to catch up with what I neglected, while having spent most of my time since Wednesday morning in preparation. So there is much to catch up with and I hope I do get nevertheless to your papers.[211]

I am very glad that the "Annotated Alice" will be widely available. But if you would not have told me I would have never heard that it is. Likewise I felt no chagrin about the book of the month adopting Thousand Cranes as a selection, because I had no idea

---

[211] A good example of the way Rapaport drove himself, despite his chronically ailing heart and various intercurrent illnesses, in his final years. Surely it was "conscientiousness to a fault" plus a strong dose of perfectionism.

494

that they did. You may be right, however, and this innocence may be just another one of the protean forms of snobbery.

I am afraid you do not owe me any apologies on the carbon copies of letters. Like I do not have with you, I have also with nobody else any explicit agreement that my letters to them will not be sent in copy to others. I am assuming that my friends will trust me that I will not give away thereby any confidences and as far as strangers are concerned, my opinions of them, whether in the form in which I told it to them or whether in a form I choose to tell it to others, is definitely my business and not theirs. If they choose to expose themselves or even to solicit my opinion, it is by definition that they have exposed themselves to it that I will not make a secret of my opinion. Those people who range all the way between friends and strangers are from this point of view between two poles.

We seem to be at odds on this matter. I am trying to spell out my view. I do not yet quite see why you are so exercised. Honestly, I would like to know what principle you hold. It might be a very different business if you would protest about my sending around copies of somebody else's letter. This I rarely do, but I certainly couldn't say that I never do so. At times it simplifies my job, at times it helps in other ways. But there is no doubt, the writer definitely has legal rights, and certain moral rights also. I should be very interesting to explore what these moral rights really are. I do not think that I ever quite precisely defined that to myself.

I hear both from you and from my Hanna about marvelous times with Merton and Charlotte. My reaction is first of all to be delighted, but a slight tinge of envy does come into it: I can't deny that. I cannot image what Merton could have said about his visit because I was altogether so befuddled with weakness and embarrassment and impatience in the hospital, that besides his warmth I have hardly any memory left of it.

I will try to get Colby's paper in the Behavioral Science and I will order his book Psychoanalytic Research. I find him bright, but too ready to jump into print, too little inclined to discipline himself to get mastery of things [see Rapaport, 1957c]. So ultimately I consider him not very helpful. I did not see Gardner's new book. I am myself reading Bruno Bettelheim's new book The Understanding Heart [*The Informed Heart*, 1960]. A book that raises very important questions throughout, but is too ostentatious, lacks a knowledge of other things that happened which could give what he has to say a perspective. I found him nagging on psychoanalysis and on other things. In other words, terribly bright, very sharp but trying to appear even more bright and more sharp and somehow not learned enough to make an integrative contribution and not deep enough to make a single-handed contribution. Very useful and instructive in what he forces you to do, but he himself does not do enough.

I am asking my secretary to send you the only manuscript of the three which I have here in a prefinal form: that's the first one of the series [probably either his 1960a or 1960b]. Of the others I do not have here even a first draft: Merton has all of them. By the way, I will be sending Merton tapes of my present seminars. In them a number of ideas which are Merton's and some of them which are mine are expressed for the first time. You may be interested to borrow them from him and to listen to them. But I will need them back because we will need both of them for the transcription.

As for the pictures: I would love to see them and we do have here projectors which I could borrow for this purpose.

Let me hear from you.

Yours,

David

Holt to Rapaport—November 18, 1960

Dear David,

    If this answer to your letter of November 8, dictated the day it arrived, gets to you after the lapse of some little time, take that as a measure of the general increase of productivity of the six other Fellows with whom I share one secretary!

    I am glad that you have my papers, and hope that you won't feel that you owe it to me in any way to drop other things to read them. But I do look forward to your reactions as always. I was sorry to learn that the seminars were piled on top of your illness—a heavy load.

    It is really hardly worth my continuing the conversation, on what was after all only a poor joke, but I do want to clear up one point: Book-of-the-Month-Club did not adopt Thousand Cranes; I mentioned that only as a hypothetical situation for purposes of comparison. And the snobbery is all mine.

    On the question of the carbon copies, etc., it seems that we are getting into a rather interesting and—so far as I know— uncodified area of the mores. Surely I have never seen anything in print on this matter, and I have discussed it with very few people. My curiosity has been aroused, however, and I think I will raise the question over the coffee cups here at the Center, particularly with some of the sociologists and anthropologists.

    I suppose I have been following a kind of naïve projection of my own feelings in what I have said about manners, etc., but to make those feelings a little more explicit, I might say that I have always assumed that the private letter is a kind of privileged communication. Thus, on the few occasions that I have heard of someone's writing a letter to somebody else and simultaneously publishing it in the newspaper, it has seemed to me a violation of something or other. I suppose that "something or other" is the right of the party addressed to carry on a conversation without eavesdroppers unchosen by himself. The association of wire-tapping comes to mind, though that is of course a far more extreme instance of the same general type of thing.

When collections of personal letters[212] are published, it is my understanding that the persons addressed give their permission (if they are living; otherwise, their heirs are usually consulted, I believe) as well as the person who wrote the letter, of course. I recall a letter you wrote to me about five years ago concerning the historical chapter of the selection book, a letter that contained the sharpest criticism you have ever made of anything I wrote, to my memory. Though I came to realize that your criticism was nothing more than justified, I was momentarily hurt, and I would have been outraged if you had shown the letter to anyone else. Why? Because I think I always assume that in a private correspondence, things may be said between friends in utter candor without the necessity for face-saving that arises when more than the correspondents themselves are concerned.

You see, I think the situation is different with a published paper or book and one that is unpublished. If I send you a reprint of a paper that has appeared in a journal and ask for your opinion, I think I should be ready to receive criticism and to expect it to be known to others as in the case with a book review. When I send you an unpublished manuscript, I think the situation is different: there I am turning to you as a trusted friend, who will have the charity to overlook remediable faults, or rather to call them to my

---

[212] Such as this one! The search for Rapaport's heirs (all of whom gave their enthusiastic permission) led me to make e-mail friends with some remarkable, interesting people, his grandchildren. They have my heart-felt thanks.

attention so that I can correct them <u>without</u> their being known generally. Even in the case of something that is printed, however, I personally feel that some of these same considerations apply.

Doubtless the difference between us stems partly from our different backgrounds. I know that you come from a tradition of open scientific controversy, of published polemic and rebuttal, as a standard part of intellectual life. Polemical writing is surely not unknown in America, but I believe it is less prominent and less common than it has been in Europe.

I am inclined to agree with your evaluation of Colby, especially after having heard him last Friday night. He is devoting his very considerable talents to the rather chimerical project of designing a computer programmed in such a way that it will respond to interpretations in the way that a patient does. He has become so fascinated with computers and the simulation of various forms of intellectual activity that he is proposing the idea of such a setup (or artifact, as he calls it) as a kind of experimental animal for psychoanalysis. It may well be that something useful will come out of this endeavor, but so far it looks like little more than a stunt.

I am delighted to learn that you are sending one of Merton's manuscripts; I look forward to seeing it with considerable eagerness. I am going to be spending Thanksgiving with the Gills, and at that time will speak to Merton about the tapes you mentioned. I hope I will be able to arrange to listen to them.

Under separate cover, I am sending some slides—I only wish they were better!

I think I mentioned to you that I have been writing a paper [Holt, 1962b] attacking the concept of an idiographic science of personality. In the course of doing so, I have been doing a little more reading and think I see the problems in little more perspective. There is a brilliant Polish sociologist here named Szczepanski with whom I discussed the matter, and he has directed me to [Karl] Popper, who apparently has disposed of the distinction between Geisteswissenschaft and Naturwissenschaft on logical-positivistic grounds. Do you know Popper's [1934 (1959)] book,

The Logic of Scientific Discovery? I am not sure that that is the relevant work; Szczepanski thought that it was not his critique of historicism [Popper, 1957], but I haven't yet located any of the books. I am not yet convinced that I am not wasting my time; I keep myself going by the argument that, despite the methodological writings of the past fifty years, there are still plenty of psychologists who still talk gravely about idiographic science. I have so much of the arrogance of the reformer in me!

I hope to see Hanna on or before Thanksgiving. Meanwhile, I hope you mend as rapidly as possible. Please give Elvira my affectionate greetings.

Yours,

Bob

Rapaport to Holt—November 21, 1960

[handwritten]

Dear Bob,

Your good long letter just arrived. Yesterday we had much fun with the slides: the two of Elvira are the best pictures we have seen of her in years. Thanks. We will send them on in a few days to the Schaf's [Schafers].

The seminars are over as of last Saturday. Now I try to catch up so that I can turn to <u>Freud's Influence</u> [Shakow & Rapaport, 1964]. But this is not easy. Rouse and his assistant (good girl), Schwarz, Schiller keep me jumping with much interesting stuff.

The question of carbons: I am afraid I cannot agree with any of the arguments. Moreover it bothers me that you forget one factor: I send such letters to my <u>friends</u> only. I am quite selective with making friends. Also I exercise my discretion what letters I send <u>even</u> to my friends. Private matters, matters that would be embarrassing I do not send as a rule. It is my views that I communicate this way and not something particular about the other individual.

What you write about Colby makes me sick . . .

Yes I have the Popper. Very exciting book—judging by 1/3 I read . . . I do not remember <u>specific</u> treatment of idiography. Will be curious to read your views on it.

[. . .]

> My best
> David

Summary—Brief Letters from 1959–1960

This final period of the correspondence is unique in several ways. It coincided with sabbaticals for both of us: for Rapaport, the academic year
1959–1960, which he spent in New York; for me, the following one,
which I spent primarily in California, at the Center for Advanced Study
in the Behavioral Sciences. The 1959 letters, consequently, are from the
first half of the year and many were devoted to one or another aspect of
moving the Rapaport family to New York. During the many months
when David was not only in the same city, but occupied the office immediately adjacent to mine, there obviously was no need to write letters.
We had many conversations, continuing on the topics previously raised,
but no one recorded them in any way. Then, when it came my turn to
leave my home site for a year without administrative or teaching duties,
I was on the other side of the continent, to some degree preoccupied
with making new friends, and getting all the intellectual stimulation I
needed with some remarkable scholars with whom I shared the year in
Palo Alto.

That freedom made it possible for me to fly back to Stockbridge in
December 1960, as soon as I got the news that my dear friend David had
died, and to spend a few months there giving what emotional support I
could to Elvira (less to the girls, with whom I had had much less contact
and interaction). I also worked closely with his secretary (and personal
assistant), Suzette Annin, going over his extensive files and making tentative decisions about what should be published, what should go into
archives, and what could be discarded (like multiple copies of many
drafts of papers). In the end, of course, it was Elvira who made the final

decisions about what should go to the Library of Congress archives, and Merton Gill who decided what still-unpublished as well as published items to include in the Collected Papers.

Let us begin, however, as in others of these summaries of minor letters, at January 1959 and proceed in chronological order. The letters almost always had minor news about our respective families, omitted here.

On January 30, 1959, I asked Rapaport for an unpublished paper of mine on brain-washing (to be Holt, 1964), of which I seemed to have sent him my only copy. On February 16, I sent Elvira the name and address of a physician I knew and thought highly of, for David to consult about a medical problem. A week later, a handwritten note from him conveyed thanks for the referral. He said he was "swamped with things subsequent to [Leo] Berman's and [Edward] Bibring's passing in an effort to counteract my bereftness."

On February 24, I sent a draft of my review (Holt, 1959) of the Hartmann (1939) monograph for "corrections or suggestions" and reported that all was well "with the Center and at home too." On March 2, I sent the preliminary draft about binding, neutralization, and psychic structure. It had been stimulated by the theoretical chapter of the doctoral dissertation of a student, Anthony Philip. I added that I had had a good visit with Paul (presumably, Bergman), about whose "new theory" I was ambivalent. In a penned postscript, I said I was dissatisfied with my draft, "and have started all over again by going to the original Freudian sources to work over the usages of <u>binding</u> in detail. It's an exciting undertaking."

On March 11, I wrote that I was well into it, "a straight historical account of Freud's use of the concept. It's probably too exegetical and detailed, but I have been having a lot of fun" with it. So, I added, felt no obligation to send comments about the draft sent the previous month. I thanked him for the helpful comments on my review of Hartmann's book, and sent a copy of an unspecified paper by Robert W. White (perhaps White 1959).

There followed, beginning with a March 17 memo from me to Stuart W. Cook, my departmental chairman, a series of communications dealing with one or another aspect of plans for Rapaport's sabbatical in New York. Part of it was getting him an academic appointment of some kind at NYU; Cook came through quickly with a welcoming letter to Rapaport offering a Visiting Professorship, with various privileges and aids (supplies, graduate assistants, facilities) though no salary.

A note from Rapaport on March 25 conveyed a recommendation for a girls' summer camp, which I had requested for a daughter.

Virtually all of the next eight items pertained to one or another aspect of plans for the sabbatical year, when Rapaport was to be accompanied by his invaluable secretary, Sue Annin. NYU people found them apartments expeditiously. The Research Center provided a Research Assistant, Phebe Scott (later Cramer, who became a distinguished psychologist). With the help of the director of the graduate program in clinical psychology, Bernie Kalinkowitz, a manageable number of students was selected to attend the seminar Rapaport offered as his way of repaying NYU's hospitality. (It dealt with the seventh chapter of the *Interpretation of Dreams*. I had attended just such a seminar in Topeka; now I was to participate again, astonished to see how much more he had been able to do with that seminal text.)

In a brief note dated May 15, Rapaport responded to what seems to have been a memo describing one of a series of informal seminars held in my apartment where Bill Dement (1960) was giving the first accounts of the research on dream deprivation he was doing in Chuck Fisher's "lab" at Mt. Sinai Hospital. David said that he read it with great interest and would like to see "the forthcoming ones. Fisher may be right in his appraisal, but we have to wait and see. [. . .] I'd like to take advantage of your invitation to attend these when in NY, but I will have to discipline myself."

He commented on the dissertation proposal by Helene Kafka (1963), which if clarified might become "very worthwhile." Finally, after saying he was preparing some lectures to be given May 22–23 at the William Alanson White Institute, he asked if Phebe Scott might see him then for an hour to discuss plans, and if George Klein, Bernie Kalinkowitz, and I might also use the chance get together.

My response on the 18th reported Phebe's agreement, George's inability because he would be at a conference, and an invitation from Crusa and me. I apologetically complained about having been too busy to correspond about the issues we had been taking up.

On June 29, I told about my week at a conference and a visit to Wright-Patterson Air Force Base with Leo Goldberger, where we "nailed down prospects for a new research contract to continue our isolation work." Most of the rest was about how to limit the number of students eager to be in his seminar.

One reason I had little time that late spring was that Crusa and I were planning a European trip for our summer vacation. I sent David a note on August 20 from overseas asking him to talk to the graduate students' Colloquium in October, which I had forgotten to do in the rush of leaving. Only three days later, I sent an anguished brief report of Crusa's death in an auto accident which had left me unscathed, bodily.

I returned a few weeks later to find him already in the office next to mine, which George had vacated for his own sabbatical. There are, accordingly, no letters of substance during the academic year September 1959–June 1960.

The next item in the file is a 15-page report to friends, dated July 6, about the four weeks he and Elvira had just spent in Budapest. Very politico-economic; not a word about psychoanalysis or other topics of these letters.

Rapaport's personal note of July 12 was about my upcoming visit to Stockbridge, as was mine of the next day. Our agenda included discussing "the Bibring material, about Juliet, about work here" (DR) and "my binding paper [. . .] in final form [. . .] the second half of [his] motivation paper with annotations and questions" (RH). My letter of thanks for that visit, dated July 28, revealed that I was about to leave for my sabbatical year in California.

His letter of September 25, which greeted me on arrival in California, reported his news:

1. W[estern] N[ew] E[ngland] Psa. Inst. seminar going on—most exhausting, but interesting and it is being recorded. 2. While preparing for it I re-read [. . .] <u>Beyond P. P.</u> [Freud, 1920] and I have a new idea of what he means there by binding. When is your paper

coming out? Where? 3. [He cancelled a speaking trip.] 4. News from H[annah] and J[uliet] good [. . .] 5. Mert's paper (the first) finished and I think it is excellent. Burnham at work on his [historical] monograph. [. . .] 6. The factor analysis study (not yet finished, but the table of correlations done) seems to bear out what we predicted. Now comes the job of showing that it does not mean something else and more trivial. [. . .] [Three final points dealt with less substantive matters.]

My reply, dated September 29, told briefly about my trip to California and some pleasant features of life at the Center for Advanced Study in the Behavioral Sciences. I replied to his questions: the paper on binding had gone to JAPA; no reply yet. I expressed hope of seeing Mert Gill soon and getting his new paper; I reported on Russian novels I had been reading; and I confessed to accepting an invitation to an ETS conference in Princeton with "a stimulating group." I had completed a draft of the paper I would present (Holt, 1962c). I was starting to read about cybernetics and asked for a copy of his review of Wiener, and I tentatively broached the idea of a critical study of the Id concept (abandoned).

On October 18, he wrote a note, short because

I am still recuperating from a virus, with a touch of pneumonia and a week in a hospital. It may sound funny, but I can assure you that a hospital is really no place for a person who is sick. I needn't say that the debilitation and the dislocation of all plans certainly wreaks havoc with one's self-respect and the fervent hope which keeps me alive that some day I might manage to catch up with all I am obligated to and all I desire to.

He asked for copies of the papers I had mentioned, and would be interested to know what I make of cybernetics (his review on the way). "Here we have some data and maybe [will produce] some paper on [the] magic seven [Miller, 1956], information load, bits, chunks. But it will take time before we will have it in order." Before tackling the Id, I should read Merton's new monograph (Gill, 1963). He was hoping to be back at "full work. Elvira isn't well either. Age? Bad luck? Who knows?"

He wrote again on October 29, thanking me for my "travel letter" about my cross-continental drive. "Still half time, but I have given 2 Institute advanced Ego and Metaps.[ychology] seminars already. Very tiring. But it is recorded and maybe something will come out of it— maybe there are a few new things in it."

A formal note of November 3 to me as chair of the Program Committee of the APA division of clinical psychology read (in part): "I am honored by your invitation of October 28. I would like to accept it in the hope that no difficulties with my health would prevent me from making good on it."

The last of these brief letters was my November 21 response to a now-vanished one from him: "Thanks so much for your generous comments on my papers—I was particularly delighted that you liked the ego psychology [Holt, 1960]. I now have, and have started the exciting job of reading, Mert's [Gill, 1963] paper on the topographic point of view."

A month later, he died in Stockbridge of a sudden fibrillation, while visiting with Marty Mayman.

Appendix

Persons Mentioned

This is a list of people whose names recur in the letters, or who play a prominent part for a short time. It does not include those who are mentioned only as authors, who are mentioned a single time in a way that indicates their unimportance to the correspondents, or who will already be familiar to readers. I have tried to supply information about each listed person that will indicate his or her importance to Rapaport and me at the time, mostly omitting their achievements after 1960.

Aichhorn, August (1978–1949). Viennese school teacher turned psychoanalyst, best known for his 1925 book, translated as *Wayward Youth* (New York: Viking Press, 1935). As a training analyst, he analyzed several prominent American psychoanalysts.

Allport, Gordon (1897–1967). One of the most famous and honored psychologists of his time, Gordon had been mentor to my own first mentor, Hadley Cantril, who sent me to Harvard to study with him. Sadly, neither of us took to the other; but I learned a lot from him anyway.

Asch, S. E. (1907–1996). A major spokesman for the Gestalt outlook when I was a graduate student, which appealed to me though I hardly knew him as a person.

Bach, Sheldon (b. 1925). Psychologist and psychoanalyst living in New York City. Educated at the Sorbonne. He joined the Research Center for Mental Health at NYU in 1956, where he worked with George S. Klein and Leo Goldberger. He is currently Adjunct Clinical Professor of Psychology at the NYU Postdoctoral Program in Psychotherapy and Psychoanalysis and a Fellow of the International Psychoanalytical Association.

Baldwin, Alfred L. (1914–1998). A friend of mine from graduate student days at Harvard. Baldwin was Professor of Psychology at the University of Kansas from 1949 to 1953 and Chairman of the Department from 1950 to 1953. Later he was a Professor at Cornell and NYU.

Bergman, Paul. A Jewish refugee from Austria, with a PhD in literature though a fully trained psychoanalyst, he was a member of the Research Department when I arrived. I assisted his informal research on psychotherapy by doing before-and-after testing of a few of his patients. Discovering our mutual interest in Lieder, we spent many enjoyable hours reading through books of songs by Schubert, Schumann, and others, which he had hand bound.

Berman, Leo (1912–1958). Psychoanalyst known for work on the application of psychoanalytic group psychology to the disciplines of education, psychiatry, social work, mental health, and preventive medicine. Because of his interest in developing some scientifically controlled research, I served as a consultant to him for a few years. Rapaport and I had received a specific proposal from him which is briefly outlined in the letter dated November 15, 1956.

Bertalanffy, Ludwig von (1901–1972). One of the founders of General System Theory, to which he made a number of major contributions. His 1950 paper in *Science* made him famous and led to his being invited to give a lecture in Topeka a few years later, which I attended. I was much taken with it, and took advantage of the opportunity to have some conversations with him. From then on, I gradually became immersed in systems theory, but could never interest Rapaport in it.

Bibring, Edward (1894–1959). Analyst of Louisa Holt among many others.

Binswanger, Ludwig (1881–1966). Prominent Swiss psychiatrist and lifelong friend of Freud's. He contributed to a *Festschrift* in honor of Freud's 80th birthday (Binswanger, 1936).

Blitzten, N. Lionel (1893–1952). Analyzed in Vienna by Otto Rank and later in Berlin by Franz Alexander, before emigrating to the United States. As a Chicago psychiatrist-psychoanalyst he promoted Rank's ideas.

Boris, Bessie (1917–1993). George Klein's wife and a painter of landscapes and portraits known for their rich colors and expressive distortions. She studied at the Art Students League in the early 1930s and worked for the Works Progress Administration, teaching classes in a settlement house. Although she spent most of her life in New York City and Massachusetts, she had her first solo exhibition in 1949 at Washburn University in Topeka, Kansas.

Brenman Gibson, Margaret (1914–2008). One of Rapaport's first recruits to the psychological staff, she was its head when I arrived in Topeka. Early in her work at Menninger's, she completed research for her PhD and began the program of studying hypnosis and hypnotherapy, in which she was soon joined by Merton Gill. She was the first US psychologist accepted for full psychoanalytic training, at the Topeka Institute. Her husband, William Gibson, poet and playwright, became important to Rapaport.

Brožek, Josef (1914–2004). Responsible for psychological studies during the Starvation Study, including the psychomotor tests, anthropometric measurements, and statistical analysis of the results. Brožek had emigrated to the US from Prague in 1937 and joined the Laboratory of Physiological Hygiene at the University of Minnesota. His research in the Laboratory of Physiological Hygiene concerned malnutrition and behavior, visual illumination and performance, and aging.

Colby, Kenneth M. (1920–2001). Psychiatrist and psychoanalyst best known for his application of computer science and artificial intelligence to psychiatry. In particular, his computer program PARRY simulated a paranoid schizophrenic who could carry on limited "conversations" with others.

Deutsch, Albert (1905–1961). Published exposés of America's public psychiatric hospitals in the newspaper *PM* in the 1940s and in a 1948 book. He also wrote a less sensational history and edited an encyclopedia on mental illness in the United States.

Deutsch, Felix (1884–1964). Famous as Freud's physician, Deutsch later became an analyst. He was my first important personal psychotherapist. I had high regard for him; he helped me a lot.

Deutsch, Helene (1884–1982). Felix's wife, more famous than he, with whom I had little contact.

Eberhart, John C. (1907–1990). An elder statesman of psychology. From 1961 to 1981, he managed the research complex at the National Institute of Mental Health, where he promoted an environment of scientific freedom of inquiry in clinical psychiatry, psychology, and other disciplines. He was an organizer of the Boulder conference (1949), resulting in the scientist-practitioner model of clinical psychology. For years a member of its Policy and Planning Board, he represented the APA on the National Research Council.

Erikson, Erik H. (1902–1994). Though no reader needs to be told who he was, it may be helpful to learn that Erik had been a staff member at Menninger's for a short while before my time, where he and Rapaport learned to like and respect one another. Perhaps in 1947, when he came back to give a lecture, Rapaport introduced us and we remained friends for the rest of his life.

Escalona, Sibylle ("Bille") Korsch (1915–1996). I believe that she did her doctoral work with Kurt Lewin. Only recently I learned that she and I did our dissertations on the same topic (the level of aspiration experiment as a tool for the study of personality); somehow the matter never came up! One of my teachers in clinical psychology, she spent most of her time on a longitudinal infancy research project with Mary Leitch, MD. Rapaport and I thought very highly of her as a researcher, administrator, and person of integrity and warmth.

Fellows, Ralph M. Superintendent of the Osawatomie State Hospital, Kansas.

Feibel, Charlotte (1901–1973). A lay analyst who lived and practiced in New York City.

Fisher, Charles (1908–1988). A warm friend with whom I worked closely, in mutual respect and affection. A solid member of the psychoanalytic establishment, he was much more impressed with Rapaport than they were.

Gibson, William (1914–2008). Bill had published little besides a small book of fine poems by the time he and Margaret moved to Stockbridge, but he began writing the plays that were to make him widely famous (e.g., *Two for the Seesaw, The Miracle Worker*) and Rapaport turned to him first to clean up the English in his principal publications.

Gill, Merton Max (1914–1994). After his medical training, Gill did his residency in psychiatry at the Menninger Foundation, where he was retained a staff member. He soon showed aptitude for research, teaming with Brenman in studies of hypnosis and hypnotherapy that brought them fame. At the Austen Riggs Center, he became more interested in theory as well as research on psychotherapy, and worked closely with Rapaport.

Goldberger, Leo (b. 1930). Professor emeritus of psychology at NYU and a former director of its Research Center for Mental Health. He and I had done a series of sensory-deprivation studies (Goldberger & Holt, 1958, 1961a, b,; Holt & Goldberger, 1959, 1960, 1961) at the Research Center, starting with his dissertation. In each, volunteer participants rested on a bed in a sound-proof room with halved ping pong balls over their eyes for up to eight hours.

Goldstein, Kurt (1878–1965). German neurologist and psychiatrist who created a holistic theory of the organism based on Gestalt theory. His most important book, *Der Aufbau des Organismus* (1934) was recently republished in English as *The Organism* (1995), with an introduction by Oliver Sacks. Co-editor of the *Journal of Humanistic Psychology* and the first neurologist to determine the cause of Alien Hand Syndrome.

Hacker, F. J. (1914–1989). Vienna-born psychiatrist and psychoanalyst and an expert on aggression and terrorism. Founder of the Hacker Psychiatric Clinic in California. Worked on numerous high-profile cases.

Hanfmann, Eugenia (1905–1983). Russian-born psychologist and researcher. Because of her work with Kurt Koffka, David Jacob Kasanin, she was well known and respected by Rapaport, who regularly used the Hanfmann-Kasanin Test of concept formation.

Hartmann, Heinz (1894–1970). A gray eminence of the establishment, the senior member of "Hartmann, Kris, and Loewenstein," who collectively had enormous prestige among psychoanalysts as theorists, often considered rivals to Rapaport.

Hawkins, Mary O'Neil (1897–1983). A training analyst at the Topeka Psychoanalytic Institute and at one-time vice president of the American Psychoanalytic Association.

Heider, Fritz (1896–1988). Austrian-born psychologist. He and his wife Grace lived in Lawrence, where he was a professor in the KU Department of Psychology. A good friend of both Rapaport and me.

Hiss, Alger (1904–1996). American government official accused of being a Soviet spy in 1948 and convicted of perjury in connection with this charge in 1950. We were neighbors in New York and knew each other slightly. That disposed me to give him the benefit of doubt.

Holzman, Philip (1922–2004). Preeminent figure in the world of schizophrenia research. He trained at the Menninger Foundation School of Clinical Psychology, the Winter VA Hospital, and Topeka Institute for Psychoanalysis in Kansas.

Holt, Louisa (1915–1998). My first wife. We met as graduate students at Harvard. Louisa was a member of Rapaport's Research Department at Menninger.

Klein, George S. (1917–1971). See "Note on George Klein and His Contributions."

Klopfer, Bruno (1900–1971). In his prime generally considered the principal teacher and promoter of the Rorschach in America. His principles of interpretation were largely ad hoc and empirical, hence distasteful to Rapaport.

Knight, Robert P. (1902–1966). When Rapaport joined the Menninger staff, Bob (or RPK, as he was known) was already a principal psychiatrist and psychoanalyst. When he accepted the directorship of the Austen Riggs Center, he was a universally respected training analyst and chief of staff, with an active interest in research and fully supportive of it. He built Riggs into one of the foremost psychoanalytically oriented psychiatric centers in the world.

Kolb, Lawrence C. (1911–2006). Psychiatrist who played a prominent role in mental health administration, research, and community mental health.

Kubie, Lawrence (1896–1973). Psychiatrist, psychoanalyst, and theorist.

Leary, Timothy (1920–1996). A psychologist whom I knew and liked when he was working with Mert Gill, before he went off the deep end with drugs.

Lidz, Theodore (1910–2001). Psychiatrist best known for his work on the causes and treatment of schizophrenia.

Lifton, Robert J. (b. 1926). Psychiatrist and prolific author, known for his work on Nazi doctors and war. Founder, along with Erik Erikson, of the Wellfleet Psychohistory Group.

Lilly, John C. (1915–2001). Was at NIMH in 1954 and devised an isolation tank of warm salt water for some of the earliest studies on sensory deprivation.

Lozoff, Milton (1914–2006). A psychiatrist Rapaport met and worked with at Osawatomie, then brought to Menninger's. Milt and his wife Marge were genial people who became my good friends. Milt retained an interest in research though his work in Topeka was almost entirely clinical.

Luborsky, Lester B. (1920–2009). After getting his PhD in psychology from Duke, Les was an instructor at the University of Illinois for two years. An early proponent of scientific research in psychotherapy. He devoted most of his subsequent career on the faculty at the University of Pennsylvania, where he went after spending eleven years at the Menninger Foundation. In 1973–1974, he was president of the Society for Psychotherapy Research. His contributions to psychoanalysis were acknowledged by two major tributes from the American Psychoanalytic Association, the Sigourney award and one for Distinguished Psychoanalytic Theory and Research.

Marquis, Donald G. (1908–1973). An outstanding experimental psychologist. He became President of the American Psychological Association in 1948.

Mayman, Martin (1924–1998). Marty was brought to Topeka by Rapaport after getting his MA in psychology at NYU in 1947, and earned his PhD from the University of Kansas in 1953. For 15 years after Rapaport left, Mayman directed psychological training at the Menninger Foundation, where he completed psychoanalytic training. In 1966, he went to the University of Michigan, where he spent the rest of his career as Professor of Psychology.

Mayzner, Mark. Received his PhD in Industrial Psychology at NYU in the 1960s, but was interested in clinical issues, and sent some letters to Rapaport, which are in the Stockbridge archive.

Meier, Norman R. F. (1900–1977). A psychologist who came to national fame by an experiment: he produced "neurotic" behavior and convulsions in rats by giving them impossible problems.

Menninger, Karl A. (1893–1990) and **Menninger,** William C. (1899–1966). Brothers "Dr. Karl" and "Dr. Will" were psychiatrists and cofounders of the Menninger Foundation and the Menninger Clinic in Topeka, Kansas. Dr. Will was chief of Army psychiatry during World War II and returned to Topeka during my time there.

Miller, James G. (1916–2002). I knew him first as a fellow member of Harry Murray's research team from 1940 to 1943 at the Harvard Psychological Clinic. His first post-military job was as director of clinical psychology at the VA. He chaired the Psychology Department, University of Chicago (1948–1955) and then the Mental Health Research Institute at the University of Michigan. For a decade he had a distinguished career in systems science, notably publishing *Living Systems* (1978). It was he who introduced the term "behavioral science."

Morrow, William R. (b. 1919). Bill came to our Selection Project team in 1948 from the Berkeley research group that produced The Authoritarian Personality (Adorno et al., 1950) and contributed in several ways to the design and execution of the Selection Project research. He and Rapaport had hardly any contact.

Murphy, Gardner (1895–1979). Among the world's outstanding psychologists of his time, he was one of the first to recognize Rapaport's gifts and sent him students, notably Schafer and Mayman. He was also a productive researcher and theorist of personality, a lifelong contributor to parapsychology, a person of great wisdom and catholicity as well as humor and warmth. Most of his career was at Columbia but he came to Topeka from the City College of New York.

Murphy, Lois Barclay (1902–2003). Gardner's wife and frequent collaborator, Lois was a world authority on child psychology. Like him a dear, warm friend, she was much more focused on empirical research. Before going to Topeka, she taught and did research for many years at Sarah Lawrence College.

Murray, Henry A. (1893–1988). Distinguished head of the Harvard Psychology Clinic who trained me and many other researchers.

Pious, William L. A Menninger psychiatrist, somewhat later my analyst.

Paul, Irving H. (1928–2006). A psychologist who was born and educated in Canada and in 1958 was a staff member at the Research Center for Mental Health. After a few years of doing research under Rapaport's supervision, he proposed a new cognitive style/control variable, "Importing."

Piaget, Jean (1896–1980). Major contributor to phasic theory of cognitive development.

Postman, Leo (1918–2004). Collaborated with George Klein at Harvard. "New look" theorist. Conducted major research and theoretical work on forgetting.

Riesman, David (1909–2002). His book, *The Lonely Crowd* (1950), was among the most widely read works of social criticism of the mid-Twentieth Century. He postulated the existence of *inner-* and *other-directed* types.

Rock, Irvin (1922–1995). One of the first psychologists to show that higher-level processes affect perception.

Rubinstein, Benjamin "Beni" B. (1905–1989). The best catch from Rapaport's international search for research trainees. When he arrived in

1947, Rapaport assigned him to me to guide his research on an interesting idea, which proved infeasible. Nevertheless, he and his lovely wife Dinah became lifelong friends of mine. As a fully trained analyst, his clinical services were in demand, but he worked actively with the psychotherapy research group until he left for New York shortly before I did. He also composed Lieder, which Dinah and I sang. For more about him and his important work, see Holt (ed.) (1997).

Rubinstein, Dinah (1910–1987). The lovely and gifted wife of Benjamin B. Rubinstein and, like him, a Finnish Jew. Multitalented, she tried out several occupations in Topeka, where we became good friends, and later in New York, including that of interior decorator. She had a good soprano voice; she and I learned several Lieder written by Beni, performed them at parties, and even recorded a few. Later, she found her true calling as a photographer; the Museum of Modern Art has some of her prints. She was known professionally as Dena.

Sargent, Helen D. (d. 1959). Though wheelchair bound and always looking rather frail, Helen soon showed herself a person of remarkable ability when she came to Topeka in 1948, just after Rapaport's departure. In a series of administrative positions at the VA hospital and at Menninger's, and then in the Psychotherapy Research Project, she was a good leader with us.

Schachtel, Ernst G. (1903–1975). My first real teacher about the Rorschach in a course at the Washington School of Psychiatry, about 1942. Most remembered for his 1959 book, *Metamorphosis*, he wrote a series of influential papers on the theory of Rorschach responding, which were later collected in a book (Schachtel, 1966).

Schafer, Roy (b. 1922). Gardner Murphy, his mentor at Columbia University, sent Roy to Menninger's for the clinical training he sought. Roy had begun some research before getting his BA. Rapaport, immediately recognizing his great talents, trained him intensively in diagnostic testing, and used his research know- how as a member of the team that produced the manuals and then hefty books on *Diagnostic Psychological Testing*. He had been called to military service when I first came, returning a year later, long enough for us to become good friends. Knight recruited him to Riggs to become chief psychologist. He then became Chief psychologist in the Yale Medical School Department of Psychiatry (1953–1961).

Schur, Max (1897–1969). Freud's personal physician in Vienna and a prominent psychoanalyst.

Shakow, David (1901–1981). Close friend of and collaborator with Rapaport. Shakow developed the Scientist-Practitioner Model of graduate training for clinical psychologists.

Schlesinger, Herbert J. (b. 1921). Student of George Klein and major contributor to cognitive-style theory and research. Currently Professor of Clinical Psychology at the Center for Psychoanalytic Training and Research at Columbia.

Shapiro, David. Starting as Roy's trainee at Riggs, Dave took over his job when Roy went to Yale, and remained in it throughout the period of these letters. He produced not only some major Rorschach papers but two widely read books on character disorders. Currently on the faculty of the New School for Social Research.

Schiller, Peter H. (b. 1931). Schiller, a graduate student from Clark University, spent summers at Riggs from 1953 through 1960. Fred Schwartz recalls that "DR took Peter under his wing when Peter came to this country. Some of the best individual studies in our monograph [Schwartz & Schiller, 1970] were done by Peter. A great guy to work with." Schiller and Schwartz worked well and productively together. Their monograph (Schwartz & Schiller, 1970) contains 13 separate studies by the two of them. Schiller went on to have a wonderful career at MIT.

Schilder, Paul (1886–1940). A student of Freud, known for work on *The Image and Appearance of the Human Body*.

Sherrington, Sir Charles Scott (1857–1952). Nobel laureate recognized for his pioneering neuron theory.

Sullivan, Herbert ("Harry") Stack (1892–1949). The founder of interpersonal psychoanalysis, considered superficial by Rapaport.

Van Lennep, David. A Dutch psychologist, author of the Four Picture Test, an original projective technique. A man of great originality and charm.

Watterson, Donald J. (d. 2000) A British psychiatrist-psychoanalyst, Don and his family became good friends to Louisa and me. Though the letters tell of his increasing involvement in research on psychotherapy, he published very little, and after leaving Topeka settled into private practice in Vancouver.

Wheelis, Allen. (1915–2007). Allen was one of the best residents of the first group at the Menninger School of Psychiatry, and retained as a staff member and candidate at the Topeka Institute for Psychoanalysis. I believe that he was in analysis with Knight at the time they went to Stockbridge. It was only after leaving for California that he began publishing the papers and books that brought him fame, and he was never close to Rapaport.

White, Robert W. (1904–2001). Murray's second and his successor at the Harvard Psychology Clinic. He taught me how to interpret the TAT.

Whitehorn, John C. (1894–1973). A major figure in American psychiatry.

Whipple, Babette ("Babbie") Samelson (1918–2009). A minor follower of Murray and White.

Williams, Robin M. (1914–2006). A leading sociologist of the century.

Witkin, Herman A. (1916–1979). Known for his conceptual work on field dependence/independence and on personality and perception. Good friend of George Klein.

Wolff, Peter. Rapaport trainee responsible for major theoretical work and research on cognitive development.

Zachry, Caroline B. Did work on personality adjustments of school children.

About the Authors

David Rapaport was born in Budapest, Hungary in 1911 in an urban middle class Jewish family. He attended the Royal Hungarian Petrus Pazmany University in Budapest where he obtained Bachelor of Science degrees in math and experimental physics (1935) and a PhD in psychology and philosophy in (1938), as well as a Montessori teaching degree.

Rapaport came to the United States in 1938 and was assisted by the American Psychoanalytic Association's Emergency Committee on Relief and Immigration, mainly by Lawrence Kubie. He first got a temporary job as a psychologist at Mount Sinai Hospital, and then accepted a similar position at the Osawatomie State Hospital in Kansas. Karl Menninger found Rapaport in the Osawatomie State Hospital and brought him to the Menninger Foundation. From 1940 to 1948 Rapaport rose through the staff, helping to build the research departments of first the Menninger Clinic and then the Foundation, where he became the chief psychologist and research director. Robert Knight took Rapaport from Topeka to Stockbridge in 1939 and nurtured his research efforts at the Austen Riggs Center. Rapaport remained at Riggs as a senior staff member for the remainder of his life. In *The Collected Papers of David Rapaport*, Merton Gill (Ed., 1967) brings together 65 of Rapaport's most salient works. In these we see Rapaport's deep investment in psychoanalysis and psychology. In both fields he was an advocate, politician, teacher, psychometrician, and clinician, always searching for the answer to a single question: "how man can know of, and act in accordance with, his environment when his thoughts and actions are determined by the laws of his own nature"?[213]

Rapaport died from a heart attack on December 14, 1960, at age forty-nine, while on sabbatical at the Research Center for Mental Health at New York University.

Robert R. Holt is Professor Emeritus of Psychology at New York University. He was born in 1917 in Jacksonville, Florida. At Princeton University he was inducted into Phi Beta Kappa (1938) and earned a BA in psychology with highest honors (1939). Working with H. A. Murray and G. W. Allport at Harvard, he got his PhD in psychology in 1944. After two years in public-opinion survey work in Washington, he was brought to Topeka by David Rapaport, who trained him in diagnostic testing, then made him co-head (with Lester Luborsky) of the research on selecting physicians for psychiatric training. He received psychoanalytic training at the Topeka Institute for Psychoanalysis as well as the Washington School of Psychiatry. When he left for New York in 1953, he was Director of the Psychological Staff and Acting Head, Research Department, of the Menninger Foundation, and on the faculty of the Topeka Psychoanalytic Institute.

With George S. Klein, Holt founded and co-directed the Research Center for Mental Health at New York University from 1953 to 1969. From 1962 to 1988 he held a Research Career Award from the National Institute of Mental Health. Additional awards included the Great Man Award (Society for Projective Techniques and Personality Assessment, 1969), the Psychologist of the Year Award (New York Society of Clinical Psychologists, 1973), and the Award for Distinguished Contributions to Clinical Psychology (APA Division of Clinical Psychology, 1974), and the Great Teacher Award (NYU, 1985). He founded the NYU Program on Peace and Global Policy Studies, which he directed from 1985 until his retirement in 1989. His nearly 300 publications include more than a dozen books, among them *Freud Reappraised: A Fresh Look at Psychoanalytic Theory* (1989) and *Primary Process Thinking: Theory, Measurement,*

---

[213] Cited in Gill, 1967, p. 9; Rapaport, 1959a, p. 57.

and Research (2009). He has served on the editorial boards of seventeen journals and the *Freud Encyclopedia*. He has been active in professional and scientific societies and served as president of the APA's Division of Clinical Psychology (Division 12).

Since 1990, Holt and his wife, Joan, have lived in Truro, MA, where he has served on numerous town committees. He has four children, three grandchildren, and one great-grandson.

Arthur A. Lynch is the President of the Board of Directors, Senior Faculty member, Training and Supervising Analyst at the American Institute for Psychoanalysis (AIP). He is an Adjunct Professor at Columbia University School of Social Work and a Visiting Professor and head of training for the Chinese American Psychoanalysis continuous training program at the Wuhan Hospital for Psychotherapy affiliated with Tongji Medical School, Huazhong University of Science and Technology, Wuhan, China. Lynch is also the director of training at the Horneyan Guangzhou Psychodynamic Psychotherapy Training Program, an affiliate of AIP in Guangzhou, China. He has authored and co-authored numerous articles on psychoanalysis and is co-editor of *Encounters with Loneliness: Only the Lonely* (with Arlene Kramer Richards and Lucille Spira, 2013) and editor of *Psychoanalysis: Critical Conversations: Selected Papers by Arnold D. Richards, Volume 1* (2015). Lynch is in private practice in New York City.

References

Ackoff, R. L. & Churchman, C. W. (1950). *Methods of inquiry: An introduction to philosophy and scientific method.* St. Louis: Educational Publishers.

Adorno, T. W., Frenkel-Brunswik, E., Levinson, D. J., Sanford, R. N. (1950). *The authoritarian personality.* New York: Harper Brothers.

Allport, G. W. (1937). *Personality: A psychological interpretation.* New York: Holt, Rinehart, & Winston.

———(1945). The psychology of participation. *Psychological Review, 52,* 117–132.

———(1946). The psychology of participation. *Occupational Psychology, 20,* 54–62, March.

Angyal, A. (1941). *Foundations for a science of personality.* New York: Commonwealth Fund (244).

Asch S. E. (1952). *Social psychology.* Englewood Cliffs, NJ: Prentice-Hall.

———(1952). Group forces in the modification and distortion of judgments. [cited in McLeod, S. A. (2008)]. Asch Experiment. Retrieved from www.simplypsychology.org/asch-conformity.html

Babcock, H. (1930). An experiment in the measurement of mental deterioration. *Archives of Psychology, 18*(117), 1–68.

Barr, H. L., Langs, R. J., Holt, R. R., Goldberger, L., & Klein, G. S. (1972). *LSD: Personality and experience.* New York: Wiley-Interscience.

Barron, F. (1952). Some personality correlates of independence of judgment. *Journal of Personality, 21,* 287–297.

Bergmann, M. S. (1993), Reflections on the history of psychoanalysis. *Journal of American Psychoanalytic Association, 41,* 929–955.

Bertalanffy, L., von (1950). The theory of open systems in physics and psychology. *Science, 111,* 23–29.

Bettelheim, B. (1950). *Love is not enough: The treatment of emotionally disturbed children.* New York: Free Press.

———(1957). Book review: The life and work of Sigmund Freud. Vol. I: 1856–1900. Vol. II: 1901–1909 by Ernest Jones. *American Journal of Sociology, 62,* 418.

———(1960). *The informed heart: Autonomy in a mass age.* Glencoe, IL: Free Press.

Bexton, W. H., Heron, W. & Scott, T. H. (1954). Effects of decreased variation in the sensory environment. *Canadian Journal of Psychology, 8,* 70–76.

Birch, L. C. (1951). Concept of nature. *American Science, 39,* 294–302.

Binswanger, L. (1936). Freuds Auffassung des Menschen im Lichte der Anthropologie [Freud's conception of man in the light of anthropology]. In *Erweiterter Festvortrag gehalten zur Feier des 80. Geburtstags von Sigmund Freud [Festschrift to celebrate the 80th birthday of Sigmund Freud].* Vienna: Akademische Verein für medizinische Psychologie.

Bolles, M. M., Rosen, G. P., & Landis, C. (1938). Psychological performance tests as prognostic agencies for the efficacy of insulin therapy in schizophrenia. *Psychiatric Quarterly, 12,* 733–737.

Bonomi, C. (2008). Interview with Robert R. Holt by Carlo Bonomi. *International Forum of Psychoanalysis, 17,* 249–253.

Boring, E. G. , Langsfeld, H. S., & Weld, H. P. (1939). *Introduction to psychology.* New York: John W. Wiley & Son.

Brenman, M. (1942). Experiments in the hypnotic production of anti-social and self-injurious behavior. *Psychiatry, 5,* 49–61.

———& Gill, M. M. (1947). *Hypnotherapy: A survey of the literature.* New York: International Universities Press.

———,———, & Hacker, F. J. (1947). Alterations in the state of the ego in hypnosis. *Bulletin of the Menninger Clinic, 11,* 60–66.

———& Knight, R. P. (1943). Hypnotherapy for mental illness in the aged: Case report of hysterical psychosis in a 71-year-old woman. *Bulletin of the Menninger Clinic, 7,* 188–198.

————&————(1945). Self-starvation and compulsive shopping with paradoxical reaction to hypnosis. *American Journal of Orthopsychiatry, 15,* 65–75.

————& Reichard, S. (1943). Use of the Rorschach test in the prediction of hypnotizability. *Bulletin of the Menninger Clinic, 7,* 163–171.

Broadbent, D. (1958). *Perception and communication.* New York: Pergamon Press.

Brown, J. F. (1936). *Psychology and the social order.* New York: McGraw-Hill.

————& Rapaport, D. (1941). The role of the psychologist in the psychiatric clinic. *Bulletin of the Menninger Clinic, 5,* 75–84.

————&————Dubin, S., & Tillman, C. G. (1941). Analysis of scatter in a battery of tests. Paper presented at the meeting of Midwestern Psychological Association, Athens, OH.

Bruner, J. S. (1948). Perceptual theory and the Rorschach test. *Journal of Personality, 17,* 158–168.

————& Goodman, C. C. (1947). Value and need as organizing factors in perception. *Journal of Abnormal and Social Psychology, 42,* 33–44.

————& Postman, L. (1948). Symbolic value as an organizing factor in perception. *Journal of Social Psychology, 27,* 203–208.

————, Goodnow, J. J., & Austin, G. A. (1956). *A study of thinking.* New York: Wiley.

Burnham, J. C. (1968). Psychoanalysis and American medicine, 1894–1918: Medicine, science and culture: *Psychological Issues,* vol. 5, no. 4. Monograph 20. New York: International Universities Press.

————(1983). *Jelliffe: American psychoanalyst and physician and his correspondence with Sigmund Freud and C. G. Jung,* ed. McGuire, W. Chicago: University of Chicago Press, 1983.

————(Ed.) (2012). *After Freud left: A century of psychoanalysis in America.* Chicago: University of Chicago Press.

Capshew, J. H. (1999). *Psychologists on the march: Science, practice, and professional identity in America, 1929–1969.* Cambridge: Cambridge University Press.

Cassirer, E. (1950). *The problem of knowledge: Philosophy, science, and history since Hegel.* New Haven: Yale University Press.

Cattell, R. B. (1946). *Description and measurement of personality.* New York: World Book.

Chidester, L. (1934). Therapeutic results with mentally retarded children. *American Journal of Orthopsychiatry, 4*(4), October, 464–472.

———& Menninger, K. A. (1936). The application of psychoanalytic methods to the study of mental retardation. *American Journal of Orthopsychiatry, 6*(4), 616–625.

Claparède, E. (1911). Recognition et moiïté. *Archives de Psychologie, 11*, 79–90. Also in Rapaport (1951), pp. 58–75, with footnotes and commentary by Rapaport.

Cofer, C. C. (1963). *Verbal behavior & learning: Problems & processes.* New York: McGraw Hill.

Cohen, M. R., & Nagel, E. (1934). *An introduction to logic and scientific method.* New York: Harcourt, Brace.

Colby, K. M. (1955). *Energy and structure in psychoanalysis.* New York: Ronald Press.

———(1960a). Experiment on the effects of an observer's presence on the imago system during psychoanalytic free-association. *Behavioral Science, 5*, 216–232.

———(1960b). *An Introduction to Psychoanalytic Research.* New York: Basic Books.

Crutchfield, R. (1955). Conformity and character. *American Psychologist, 10*, 191–198.

Deikman, A. J. (1963). Experimental meditation. *Journal of Nervous and Mental Disease, 136*, 329–343.

Dement, W. (1960). The effect of dream deprivation, *Science, 131*(3415), 1705–1707.

———& Kleitman, N. (1957a). The relation of eye movements during sleep to dream activity: An objective method for the study of dreaming. *Journal of Experimental Psychology, 53*, 339–46.

———&———(1957b). Cyclic variations in EEG during sleep and their relation to eye movements, bodily motility, and dreaming. *EEG and Clinical Neurophysiology, 9*, 673–690.

Eagle, M. (1959). Some personality correlates of responsiveness to unperceived cues. *American Psychologist, 14*, 359 (abstract).

Einstein, A. & Infeld, L. (1938). *The evolution of physics*. New York: Simon & Schuster, 1965.

English, H. B., & English, A. C. (1958). *A comprehensive dictionary of psychological and psychoanalytical terms*. New York: David McKay.

Erikson, E. H. (1950). *Childhood and society*. New York: Norton.

———(1954). The dream specimen of psychoanalysis. *Journal of the American Psychoanalytic Association, 2,* 5–56.

———(1956). The problem of ego identity. *Journal of the American Psychoanalytic Association, 4,* 56–121. Also in *Psychological Issues,* 1959, Monograph 1, 101–164.

Erikson, K. T. (1957). Patient role and social uncertainty: A dilemma of the mentally ill. *Psychiatry: Journal for the Study of Interpersonal Processes, 20*(3), 263.

Fenichel, O. (1941). On the psychology of boredom. In Fenichel, H. & Rapaport, D. (Eds.), *The collected papers of Otto Fenichel*. New York: W.W. Norton. (Original published, in German, in *Imago,* 1934, *20,* 270–281. Also included as Chapter 18 in Rapaport (1951), with notes and commentary.)

Fenichel, H. & Rapaport, D. (Eds.) (1953). *The collected papers of Otto Fenichel*. New York: Norton.

Feshbach, S. (1954). The function of aggression and the regulation of aggressive drive. *Psychological Review, 71,* 257–272.

———(1955): The drive-reducing function of fantasy behaviour. *Journal of Abnormal and Social Psychology, 50,* 3–11.

Fisher, C. (1954). Dreams and perception. *Journal of the American Psychoanalytic Association, 3,* 380–445.

———(1956). Dreams, images, and perception: A study of unconscious-preconscious relationships. *Journal of the American Psychoanalytic Association, 4,* 5–48.

———(1956). The concept of primary process. Paper presented at the Annual Meeting of the American Psychoanalytic Association. (Summarized in Panel Report: The psychoanalytic theory of thinking. *Journal of the American Psychoanalytic Association,* 1958, 6, 143–153.)

———(1960). Introduction to O. Potzl, R. Allers and J. Teler. Preconscious stimulation in dreams, associations, and images. *Psychological*

Issues, 2(3), Monograph 7, pp. 1–40.

———(1988). Further observations on the Poetzl phenomenon: The effects of subliminal visual stimulation on dreams, images, and hallucinations. *Psychoanalysis and Contemporary Thought, 11,* 3–56. (Originally published, in French trans. by Dr. I. F. Foncin, in *L'évolution Psychiatrique,* 1959, 4, 541–566.)

Flesch, R. (1949). *The art of readable writing.* New York: Collins Reference; 50th Anniversary edition, May 24, 1996.

Frenkel-Brunswik, E. (1954). Psychoanalysis and the unity of science. *Proceedings of the American Academy of Arts and Sciences, 80,* 271–347.

Freud, S. (1900). The interpretation of dreams. In J. Strachey (Ed. and Trans.), *The standard edition of the complete psychological works of Sigmund Freud* (Vols. 4 & 5, pp. 1–622). London: Hogarth Press (Original work published 1923).

———(1905). Three essays on the theory of sexuality. In J. Strachey (Ed. and Trans.), *The standard edition of the complete psychological works of Sigmund Freud* (Vol. 7, pp. 130–243). London: Hogarth Press (Original work published 1923).

———(1908). Creative writers and day-dreaming. In J. Strachey (Ed. and Trans.), *The standard edition of the complete psychological works of Sigmund Freud* (Vol. 9, pp. 141–154). London: Hogarth Press (Original work published 1923).

———(1915a). Instincts and their vicissitudes. In J. Strachey (Ed. and Trans.), *The standard edition of the complete psychological works of Sigmund Freud* (Vol. 14, pp. 117–140). London: Hogarth Press (Original work published 1923).

———(1915b). Repression. In J. Strachey (Ed. and Trans.), *The standard edition of the complete psychological works of Sigmund Freud* (Vol. 14, pp. 146–158). London: Hogarth Press (Original work published 1923).

———(1915c). The unconscious. In J. Strachey (Ed. and Trans.), *The standard edition of the complete psychological works of Sigmund Freud* (Vol. 14, pp. 166–215). London: Hogarth Press (Original work published 1923).

———(1917 [1915]). A metapsychological supplement to the theory of dreams. In J. Strachey (Ed. and Trans.), *The standard edition of the complete psychological works of Sigmund Freud* (Vol. 14, pp. 222–235). London: Hogarth Press (Original work published 1923).

———(1920). Beyond the pleasure principle. In J. Strachey (Ed. and Trans.), *The standard edition of the complete psychological works of Sigmund Freud* (Vol. 18, pp. 7–64). London: Hogarth Press (Original work published 1923).

———(1923). The ego and the id. In J. Strachey (Ed. and Trans.), *The standard edition of the complete psychological works of Sigmund Freud* (Vol. 19, pp. 12–66). London: Hogarth Press (Original work published 1923).

———(1926). Inhibitions, symptoms and anxiety. In J. Strachey (Ed. and Trans.), *The standard edition of the complete psychological works of Sigmund Freud* (Vol. 20, pp. 87–172). London: Hogarth Press (Original work published 1923).

———(1950). *The origins of psychoanalysis. Letters to Wilhelm Fliess, drafts and notes: 1887–1902.* (M. Bonaparte, A. Freud, & E. Kris, Eds.) (E. Mosbacher & J. Strachey, Trans.). New York: Basic Books.

Gardener, R. W., Holzman, P. S., Klein, G. S., Linton, H. B., & Spence, D. P. (1959). Cognitive control: A study of individual consistencies in cognitive behavior. *Psychological Issues*, Monograph 4. New York: International Universities Press.

Gill, M. M. (1963). Topography and systems in psychoanalytic theory. *Psychological Issues* Monograph 10, New York: International Universities Press.

———(Ed.). (1967). *The collected papers of David Rapaport.* New York: Basic Books.

———(1976). Metapsychology is not psychology. In Gill & Holzman (Eds.) (1976).

———(1994). *Psychoanalysis in transition: A personal view.* Hillsdale, NJ: Analytic Press.

———& Brenman, M. (1943). Treatment of a case of anxiety hysteria by an hypnotic technique employing psychoanalytic principles. *Bulletin of the Menninger Clinic, 7,* 163–171.

———&———(1959). *Hypnosis and related states: Psychoanalytic studies in regression.* New York: International Universities Press.

———& Holzman, P. S. (Eds.) (1976). Psychology versus metapsychology: Psychoanalytic essays in memory of George S. Klein. *Psychological Issues,* Monograph 36. New York: International Universities Press.

Glover, E. (1939). The psycho-analysis of affects. *International Journal of Psycho-Analysis, 20,* pp. 299–307.

Goldberger, L. (1961). Reactions to perceptual isolation and Rorschach manifestations of the primary process. *Journal of Projective Techniques, 25,* 287–302.

———& Holt, R. R. (1958). Experimental interference with reality contact (perceptual isolation): Method and group results. *Journal of Nervous and Mental Disease, 127,* 99–112.

———&———(1961a). Studies on the effects of perceptual alteration (USAF ASD Technical Report No. 62–416). Wright-Patterson Air Force Base, OH: Aerospace Medical Laboratory: Aeronautical Systems Division.

———&———(1961b). Experimental interferences with reality contact (perceptual isolation): Individual differences. In P. Solomon et al. (Eds.) *Sensory deprivation* (pp. 130–142). Cambridge, MA: Harvard University Press.

Goldstein, K., & Scheerer, M. (1941). Abstract and concrete behavior; An experimental study with special tests. *Psychological Monographs, 53*(2).

Hacker, F. J. (1955). Scientific facts, religious values, and the psychoanalytic experience. *Bulletin of the Menninger Clinic, 19,* 229–239.

Hanfmann, E. (1956). The non-projective aspects of the Rorschach experiment: III. The point of view of the research clinician. *Journal of Social Psychology, 44,* 199–202.

———(1939). *Ego psychology and the problem of adaptation,* trans. Rapaport, D. New York: International Universities Press, 1958.

———Kris, E., & Loewenstein, R. M. (1946). Comments on the formation of psychic structure. In Papers on psychoanalytic psychology. *Psychological Issues,* 4 Monograph 14, 27–55. New York: International Universities Press.

Hartmann, H. (1939). *Ego psychology and the problem of adaptation.* (D. Rapaport, Trans.). New York: International Universities Press, 1958.

———(1948). Comments on the psychoanalytic theory of instinctual drives. *Psychoanalytic Quarterly, 17,* 368–388.

———(1950). Comments on the psychoanalytic theory of the ego. *Psychoanalytic Study of the Child, 5,* 74–96.

———, Kris, E., & Loewenstein, R. M. (1949). Notes on the theory of aggression. *Psychoanalytic Study of the Child, 3,* 9–36.

Hebb, D. O. (1949). *The organization of behavior: A neuropsychological theory.* New York: Wiley.

———(1955). Drives and the C.N.S. (Conceptual Nervous System). *Psychological Review, 62,* 243–254.

Held, R. (1961). Exposure-history as a factor in maintaining stability of perception and coordination. *Journal of Nervous and Mental Disease, 132,* 26–32.

———& Hein, A. V (1958). Adaptation of disarranged hand-eye coordination contingent upon re-afferent stimulation. *Perceptual and Motor Skills, 8,* 87–90.

Heider, F. (1958). *The psychology of interpersonal relations.* New York: Wiley.

Held, R., & Bossom, J. (1961). Neonatal deprivation and adult rearrangement: Complementary techniques for analyzing plastic sensory-motor coordination. *Journal of Comparative and Physiological Psychology, 21,* 33–37.

Hernandez-Peon R., Scherrer, H., & Jouvet, M. (1956) Modification of electric activity in cochlear nucleus during "attention" in unanesthetized cats. *Science, 123*(3191), 331–332.

Hilgard, E. R. & Marquis, D. G. (1940). *Conditioning and learning.* (In the Century Psychology Series, Richard M. Elliott Editor). New York: Appleton-Century.

———Kubie, L. S., & Pumpian-Mindlin, E. (1952). *Psychoanalysis as science.* Stanford: Stanford University Press.

Hiss, A. (1957). *In the court of public opinion.* New York: Knopf.

Hoffman, J., & Vernon, J. (1956). Sensory deprivation. *Science, 123,* 1074–1075.

Hofstadter, D. R. (1979). *Gödel, Escher, Bach: An eternal golden braid.* New York: Basic Books.

Holt, R. R. (1950). [Review of *Varieties of delinquent youth*, by William H. Sheldon.] *Journal of Abnormal and Social Psychology, 45,* 790–795.

———(1951a). The Thematic Apperception Test. In H. H. & G. L. Anderson (Eds.), *An introduction to projective techniques* (pp. 181–229). New York: Prentice-Hall.

———(1951b). Chapter 10 [An analysis of TAT and MAPS test.] In E. Shneidman et al., *Thematic test analysis* (pp. 101–118). New York: Grune & Stratton.

———(1951c). Our fears and what they do to us. *Menninger Quarterly, 6,* 9–16.

———(1951d). [Review of *Varieties of delinquent youth*, by William H. Sheldon.] *Bulletin of the Menninger Clinic, 15,* 72–73.

———(1951e). [Review of *Childhood and society*, by Erik H. Erikson.] *Journal of Personality, 21,* 149–153.

———(1952a). The case of Jay: Interpretation of Jay's Thematic Apperception Test. *Journal of Projective Techniques, 16,* 457–461.

———(1952b). [Review of *Personality*, by David McClelland.] *Journal of Abnormal and Social Psychology, 47,* 276–278.

———(1953). [Review of *Psychoanalysis as science*, by Ernest R. Hilgard, Lawrence S. Kubie, & E. Pumpian-Mindlin.] *Journal of Abnormal and Social Psychology, 48,* 607–608.

———(1954). Implications of some contemporary personality theories for Rorschach rationale. In B. Klopfer, M. D. Ainsworth, W. G. Klopfer, & R. R. Holt, *Developments in the Rorschach technique, vol. I. Technique and theory* (pp. 501–560). New York: World Book Co.

———(1955). [Review of *The origins of psycho-analysis. Letters of Wilhelm Fliess, Drafts and Notes: 1887–1902 by Sigmund Freud. M. Bonaparte, A. Freud, and E. Kris* (Eds.) Trans. by E. Mosbacher and J. Strachey.] *Scientific Monthly, 81,* 95–96.

———(1956a). Rejoinder to Mayzner's review of Schafer's "Psychoanalytic interpretation in Rorschach testing." *Psychology Newsletter, 7,* 47–50.

———(1956b). Metapsychology—1956 model. [Review of *Energy and structure in psychoanalysis*, by Kenneth M. Colby.] *Contemporary Psychology*, 1, 227–229.

———(1958). No depth analysis for Freud. [Review of *The life and work of Sigmund Freud. Vol. III. The last phase, 1919–1939*, by Ernest Jones.] *Contemporary Psychology*, 3, 145–148.

———(1959). Psychoanalysis finds reality. [Review of *ego psychology and the problem of adaptation*, by Heinz Hartmann.] *Contemporary Psychology*, 4, 332–333.

———(1960). Recent developments in psychoanalytic ego psychology and their implications for diagnostic testing. *Journal of Projective Techniques*, 24, 254–266.

———(1961). Clinical judgment as a disciplined inquiry. *Journal of Nervous and Mental Disease*, 133, 369–382.

———(1962a). A critical examination of Freud's concept of bound vs. free cathexis. *Journal of the American Psychoanalytic Association*, 10, 475–525.

———(1962b). Individuality and generalization in the psychology of personality. *Journal of Personality*, 30, 377–404. Revised edition (1998) with an introduction by Paolo Migone and a new preface available at http://www.pol-it.org/ital/documig6.htm.

———A clinical-experimental strategy for research in personality. In S. Messick & J. Ross (Eds.), *Measurement in personality and cognition* (pp. 269–283). New York: Wiley.

———(1964). Forcible indoctrination and personality change. In P. Worchel & D. Byrne (Eds.), *Personality change* (pp. 289–318.). New York: Wiley.

———(1967). David Rapaport: A memoir (September 30, 1911– December 14, 1960). In R R. Holt (Ed.), *Motives and thought: Psychoanalytic essays in memory of David Rapaport* (pp. 7–17). New York: International Universities Press. Also in *Psychological Issues*, Monograph 18/19.

———(Ed.) (1968). Revised edition of Rapaport, D., Gill, M. M., & Schafer, R. *Diagnostic psychological testing*. New York: International Universities Press.

———(1972). On the nature and generality of mental imagery. In P. E. Sheehan (Ed.), *The function and nature of imagery* (pp. 3–33). New York: Academic Press.

———(1983). The manifest and latent meanings of metapsychology. *The Annual of Psychoanalysis, 10*, 233–255.

———(1984). Freud, the free will controversy, and prediction in personology. In R. A. Zucker, J. Aronoff, & A. I. Rabin (Eds.), *Personality and the prediction of behavior* (pp. 179–208). New York: Academic Press.

———(1989). *Freud reappraised: A fresh look at psychoanalytic theory.* New York: Guilford.

———(1993). An exploratory study of life: Progress report. In C. E. Walker (Ed.), *A history of clinical psychology in autobiography* (Vol. 2, pp. 159–229). Pacific Grove, CA: Brooks/Cole.

———(Ed.) (1997). *Psychoanalysis and the philosophy of science: The collected papers of Benjamin B. Rubinstein.* Madison, CT: International Universities Press. Also in *Psychological Issues,* Monograph No. 62/63. (With preface, Editor's introduction, and notes by R. R. Holt.)

———(1998) Loevinger's conception of ego development and General Systems Theory. In P. M. Westenberg, A. Blasi, & L. D. Cohn (Eds.), *Personality development: Theoretical, empirical, and clinical investigations of Loevinger's conception of ego development* (pp. 71–86). Mahwah, NJ: Lawrence Erlbaum.

———(2009). *Primary process thinking: Theory, assessment, and empirical research* (2 vols.). *Psychological Issues* Monograph. Madison, CT: International Universities Press.

———(2012). On our golden anniversary: A letter to the members of the Rapaport-Klein Study Group. http://www.psychomedia.it/rapaport-klein/june2012–Pictures.pdf

———(2013). History of the Research Center for Mental Health, N.Y.U. *Psychoanalytic Psychology, 30,* 75–91.

———& Goldberger, L. (1959) Personological correlates of reactions to perceptual isolation. *USAF WADC Technical Reports,* No. 59-735, 46 pp.

————&————(1960). Research on the effects of isolation on cognitive functioning. *USAF WADC Technical Reports*, No. 60-260, 22 pp.

————&————(1961). Assessment of individual resistance to sensory alteration. In B. E. Flaherty (Ed.), *Psychophysiological aspects of space flight* (pp. 248–262). New York: Columbia University Press.

————, with Mayman, M., & Eagle, C. J. (2009). *Primary process thinking: Theory, measurement, and research* (2 vols.) *Psychological Issues*, Monograph 65–66.

————& Havel, J. (1960). A method for assessing primary and secondary process in the Rorschach. In M. A. Rickers-Ovsiankina (Ed.), *Rorschach psychology* (pp. 263–315). New York: Wiley.

————& Luborsky, L. (1958). *Personality patterns of psychiatrists* (2 vols.). New York: Basic Books.

Holzman, P. S. (1954). The relation of assimilation tendencies in visual, auditory, and kinesthetic time-error to cognitive attitudes of Leveling and Sharpening. *Journal of Personality, 22,* 375–394.

————& Klein, G. S. (1954). Cognitive system principles of leveling and sharpening: Progress report for 1953–54. *Bulletin of the Menninger Clinic, 18,* 260–266.

Horney, K. (1939). *New ways in psychoanalysis.* New York: Norton.

Jacobson, E. (1954). Contribution to the metapsychology of psychotic identifications. *Journal of the American Psychoanalytic Association, 2,* 239–262.

Janis, I. L., Mahl, G. F., Kagan, J., & Holt, R. R. (1969). *Personality: Dynamics, development, and assessment.* New York: Harcourt, Brace & World.

Jenkins, J. M., & Dallenbach, K. M. (1924). Obliviscence during sleep and waking. *American Journal of Psychology, 35,* 605–612.

Jones, E. (1953–1957). *The life and work of Sigmund Freud* (3 vols.). New York: Basic Books.

Kafka, H. (1963). The use of color in projective tests and dreams in relation to the theory of ego autonomy. Unpublished doctoral dissertation, New York University.

Kahneman, D. (1973). *Attention and effort.* Englewood Cliffs, NJ: Prentice-Hall.

———(2002). Biography. In Nobelprize.org, The Sveriges Riksbank Prize in Economic Sciences in Memory of Alfred Nobel 2002, Daniel Kahneman, Vernon L. Smith. Accessed at http://www.nobelprize.org/nobel_prizes/economic-sciences/laureates/2002/kahneman-bio.html, on March 25, 2014.

Kant, I. (1783). *Prolegomena to any future metaphysics.* (Trans. Paul Carus, 1903). [available on line at http://philosophy.eserver.org/kant-prolegomena.txt].

Kaplan, B., & Wapner, S. (Eds.) (1960). *Perspectives in psychological theory: Essays in honor of Heinz Werner.* New York: International Universities Press.

Katona, G. (1940). *Organizing and memorizing: Studies in the psychology of learning and teaching.* New York: Columbia University Press.

Kaufman, L., & Rock, I. (1962). The moon illusion I., *Science, 136,* 953–61.

Kelly, E. L., & Fiske, D. W. (1951). *The prediction of performance in clinical psychology.* Ann Arbor: University of Michigan Press.

Kenyon, V. B., Rapaport, D., & Lozoff, M. (1941). Note on metrazol in general paresis. *Psychiatry,* 4, 165–176.

Keys, A., Brožek, J., Henschel, A., Mickelsen, O., & Taylor, H. L. (1950) *The biology of human starvation* (2 vols.), Minneapolis: University of Minnesota Press.

Kernberg, O. F., Burstein, E. D., Coyne, L., Appelbaum A., Horowitz, L., & Voth, H. (1972). Psychotherapy and psychoanalysis: Final report of the Menninger Foundation's Psychotherapy Research Project. *Bulletin of the Menninger Clinic,* 36, Nos. 1 & 2.

Klein, G. S. (1949). Adaptive properties of sensory functioning. *Bulletin of the Menninger Clinic, 13,* 16–23.

———(1954). Need and regulation. In M. R. Jones (Ed.), *Nebraska symposium on motivation: 1954* (pp. 224–274). Lincoln: University of Nebraska Press.

———(1959). Consciousness in psychoanalytic theory: Some implications for current research in perception. *Journal of the American Psychoanalytic Association, 7,* 5–34. Also in Klein, G. S. (1970). *Perception, motives, and personality* (pp. 235–263). New York: Knopf.

———(1969). Freud's two theories of sexuality. In L. Breger (Ed.), *Clinical-cognitive psychology: Models and integrations* (pp. 136–181). Englewood Cliffs, NJ: Prentice-Hall.

———(1970). *Perception, motives, and personality.* New York: Knopf.

———(1975). *Psychoanalytic theory: An exploration of essentials.* New York: International Universities Press.

———& Holzman, P. S. (1950). The "schematizing process": Perceptual attitudes and personality qualities in sensitivity to change. *American Psychologist, 5,* 312 (Abstract).

———Spence, D., Holt, R. R., & Gourevitch, S. (1958). Cognition without awareness: Subliminal influences upon conscious thought. *Journal of Abnormal and Social Psychology, 57,* 255–256.

Knight, R. P. (1961). David Rapaport—1911–1960. *Psychoanalytic Quarterly, 30,* 262–264.

Koch, S. (Ed.) (1959). *Psychology: A study of a science* (Vol. 2). New York: McGraw-Hill.

Koffka, K. (1935). *Principles of gestalt psychology.* New York: Harcourt, Brace.

Krech, D., & Klein, G. S. (Eds.) (1952). *Theoretical models in psychology.* Durham, NC: Duke University Press.

Kris, E. (1952). *Psychoanalytic explorations in art.* New York: International Universities Press.

Koch, S. (1959). *Psychology a study of a science, volume II.* New York: McGraw-Hill.

Leary, T., & Gill, M. M. (1959). The dimensions and a measure of the process of psychotherapy: A system for the analysis of the content of clinical evaluations and patient-therapist verbalizations. In E. A. Rubinstein & M. B. Parloff (Eds.), *Research in psychotherapy* (pp. 62–95). Washington, DC: American Psychological Association.

Levitt, M. (Ed.) (1959). *Readings in psychoanalytic psychology.* New York: Appleton-Century-Crofts.

Lewin, K. (1951). *Field theory in social science: Selected theoretical papers.* (D. Cartwright, Ed.). New York: Harper & Row.

Lifton, R. J. (1961). *Thought reform and the psychology of totalism: A study of "brainwashing" in China.* New York: Norton.

Lindsley, D. B. (1957). Psychophysiology and motivation. In M. R. Jones (Ed.), *Nebraska symposium on motivation, 1957* (pp. 44–104). Lincoln: University of Nebraska Press.

———, Bowden, J. W., & Magoun, H. W. (1949). Effect upon the EEG of acute injury to the brain stem activating system. *EEG & Clinical Neurophysiology, 1,* 415–486.

Loewald, H. W. (1960). On the therapeutic action of psycho-analysis. *International Journal of Psychoanalysis, 41,* 16–33.

Luborsky, L., Crits-Christoph, P., Mintz, J., & Auerbach, A. (1988). *Who will benefit from psychotherapy?* New York: Basic Books.

———& Holt, R. R. (1957). The selection of candidates for psychoanalytic training: Implications from research on the selection of psychiatric residents. *Journal of Clinical and Experimental Psychopathology, 18,* 166–176.

MacCorquodale, K., & Meehl, P. E. (1948). On a distinction between hypothetical constructs and intervening variables. *Psychological Review, 55,* 95–107.

MacKinnon, D. W., Crutchfield, R. W., Barron, F., Block, J., Gough, H. G., & Harris, R. E. (1958). An assessment study of Air Force officers, part 1: Design of the study and description of the variables. *Technical Report* WADC-TR-58-91 (1) ASTIA Document No. AD 151-040. Lackland Air Force Base, TX: Personnel Laboratory, Wright Air Development Center.

Marx , M. H. (Ed.) (1951). *Psychological theory, contemporary readings.* Oxford (UK) & New York: Macmillan.

Mayman, M., & Faris, M. (1960). Early memories as expressions of relationship paradigms. *American Journal of Orthopsychiatry, 30,* 507–520.

McKelvey, R. K., & Marx, M. H. (1951). Effects of infantile food and water deprivation on adult hoarding in the rat. *Journal of Comprehensive Physiological Psychology,* 44, 423–430.

McClelland, D. C. (1951). *Personality.* New York: Sloane.

Meehl, P. E. (1954). *Clinical vs. statistical prediction.* Minneapolis: University of Minnesota Press.

Meyer, K. (2012). Another remembered present. *Science, 335*(6067), 415–416.

Miller, G. A. (1956). The magical number seven, plus or minus two: Some limits on our capacity for processing information. *Psychological Review, 63*, 81–97.

Miller, J. G. (1975). *Living systems.* New York: McGraw-Hill.

Miller, S. C. (1962). Ego autonomy in sensory deprivation, isolation, and stress. *International Journal of Psycho-Analysis, 43*, 1–20.

Moruzzi, G., & Magoun, H. (1949). Brain stem reticular formation and activation of the EEG. *EEG & Clinical Neurophysiology, 1*, 455–473.

Murphy, G. & Ballou, R. O. (Eds.) (1960). *William James on psychical research.* New York: Viking Press.

Murray, H. A. et al. (1938). *Explorations in personality.* New York: Oxford University Press.

Newman, E. B. (1939). Forgetting of meaningful material during sleep and waking. *American Journal of Psychology, 52*, 65–71.

Orbison, W. D. (1939). Shape as a function of the vector-field. *The American Journal of Psychology,* Vol. 52, No. 1, Jan., 1939 (pp. 31–45). DOI: 10.2307/1416658.

Orwell, G. (1949). *Nineteen eighty-four.* London, England: Secker and Warburg.

Patterson, C. H. (1953). *The Wechsler-Bellevue scales: A guide for counselors.* Springfield, IL: Charles C. Thomas.

Paul, I. H. (1959). Studies in remembering: The reproduction of connected and extended verbal material. *Psychological Issues,* Monograph 2.

Pepper, S. C. (1942). *World hypotheses: A study in evidence.* Berkeley: University of California Press.

———(1972). Systems philosophy as a world hypothesis. *Philosophy and Phenomenological Research, 32*, 548–553.

Peters, R. S. (1958). *The conception of motivation.* New York: Humanities Press.

Pine, F. (1960). Incidental stimulation: A study of preconscious transformations. *Journal of Abnormal and Social Psychology, 60*, 68–75.

Poetzl, O. (1917). Experimentell erregte Traumbilder in ihren Beziehungen zum indirekten Sehen. *Zeitschrift für Neurologie und Psychiatrie, 37*, 278–349. Also trans. as The relationship between experimentally induced dream images and indirect vision. *Psychological Issues* (1960), Monograph 7, 41–120.

Popper, K. R. (1934). *The logic of scientific discovery.* New York: Basic Books. (Original publisher London: Routledge).

———(1957). *The poverty of historicism.* Boston: Beacon Press.

Rapaport, D. (1941). The Szondi test. *Bulletin of the Menninger Clinic, 5*, 33–39.

———(1942a). *Emotions and memory.* Baltimore: Williams & Wilkins.

———(1942b). Principles underlying projective techniques. In M. M. Gill (Ed.), *The collected papers of David Rapaport* (pp. 91–97). New York: Basic Books, 1967.

———(1942c). The history of the awakening of insight. In M. M. Gill (Ed.), *The collected papers of David Rapaport* (pp. 100–112). New York: Basic Books, 1967.

———(1944). The psychologist in the private mental hospital. In M. M. Gill (Ed.), *The collected papers of David Rapaport* (pp. 160–164). New York: Basic Books, 1967.

———(1946). Principles underlying nonprojective tests of personality. In M. M. Gill (Ed.), *The collected papers of David Rapaport* (pp. 221–229). New York: Basic Books, 1967.

———(1947a). Dynamic psychology and Kantian epistemology. In M. M. Gill (Ed.), *The collected papers of David Rapaport* (pp. 289–298). New York: Basic Books, 1967.

———(1947b). Psychological testing: Its practical and its heuristic significance. *Samiksa, 1*, 245–262. Also in M. M. Gill (Ed.). *The collected papers of David Rapaport* (pp. 261–275). New York: Basic Books, 1967.

———(1949). [Review of Personality in nature, society, and culture, by Clyde Kluckhohn & Henry A. Murray (Eds.)] In M. M. Gill (Ed.), *The collected papers of David Rapaport* (pp. 309–312). New York: Basic Books, 1967.

———(1950a). On the psychoanalytic theory of thinking. In M. M. Gill (Ed.). *The collected papers of David Rapaport* (pp. 313–328). New York: Basic Books, 1967.

———(1950b). [Review of *Cybernetics, or control and communication in the animal and the machine,* by Norbert Wiener]. In M. M. Gill (Ed.).

The collected papers of David Rapaport (pp. 329–333). New York: Basic Books, 1967.

———(1950c). The theoretical implications of diagnostic testing procedures. In M. M. Gill (Ed.). *The collected papers of David Rapaport* (pp. 334–356). New York: Basic Books, 1967.

———(1951a). *Organization and pathology of thought.* New York: Columbia University Press.

———(1951b). The autonomy of the ego. In M. M. Gill (Ed.), *The collected papers of David Rapaport* (pp. 357–367). New York: Basic Books, 1967.

———(1951c). Paul Schilder's contribution to the psychology of thought processes. In M. M. Gill (Ed.), *The collected papers of David Rapaport* (pp. 368–384). New York: Basic Books, 1967.

———(1951d). States of consciousness: A psychopathological and psychodynamic view. In M. M. Gill (Ed.), *The collected papers of David Rapaport* (pp. 385–404). New York: Basic Books, 1967.

———(1951e). The conceptual model of psychoanalysis. In M. M. Gill (Ed.), *The collected papers of David Rapaport* (pp. 405–431). New York: Basic Books, 1967.

———(1951f). Interpersonal relationships, communication, and psychodynamics. In M. M. Gill (Ed.), *The collected papers of David Rapaport* (pp. 440–449). New York: Basic Books, 1967.

———(1952a). [Review of *Learning theory and personality dynamics,* by O. Hobart Mowrer]. In M. M. Gill (Ed.) *The collected papers of David Rapaport* (pp. 450–460). New York: Basic Books, 1967.

———(1952b). Projective techniques and the theory of thinking. In M. M. Gill (Ed.), *The collected papers of David Rapaport* (pp. 461–469). New York: Basic Books, 1967.

———(1953a). On the psychoanalytic theory of affects. In M. M. Gill (Ed.), *The collected papers of David Rapaport* (pp. 476–512). New York: Basic Books, 1967.

———(1953b). Discussion at mass communications seminar. In M. M. Gill (Ed.), *The collected papers of David Rapaport* (pp. 513–522). New York: Basic Books, 1967.

———(1953d). Some metapsychological considerations concerning activity and passivity. In M. M. Gill (Ed.), *The collected papers of*

David Rapaport (pp. 530–535). New York: Basic Books, 1967.

———(1956). [Review of *The psychology of thought and judgment, by* Donald M. Johnson]. In M. M. Gill (Ed.) *The collected papers of David Rapaport* (pp. 624–630). New York: Basic Books, 1967.

———(1957a). Cognitive structures. In M. M. Gill (Ed.) *The collected papers of David Rapaport* (pp. 631–664). New York: Basic Books, 1967.

———(1957b). A theoretical analysis of the superego concept. In M. M. Gill (Ed.) *The collected papers of David Rapaport* (pp. 685–709). New York: Basic Books, 1967.

———(1957c). [Review of *Energy and structure in psychoanalysis*, by Kenneth Mark Colby]. In M. M. Gill (Ed.) *The collected papers of David Rapaport* (pp. 670–673). New York: Basic Books, 1967.

———(1957d). [Review of *A study of thinking*, by Jerome S. Bruner, Jacqueline J. Goodnow, and George A. Austin]. In M. M. Gill (Ed.) *The collected papers of David Rapaport* (pp. 674–681). New York: Basic Books, 1967.

———(1958a). The theory of ego autonomy: A generalization. In M. M. Gill (Ed.) *The collected papers of David Rapaport* (pp. 722–744). New York: Basic Books, 1967.

———(1958b). A historical survey of psychoanalytic ego psychology. In M. M. Gill (Ed.) *The collected papers of David Rapaport* (pp. 745–757). New York: Basic Books, 1967.

———(1959). The theory of attention cathexis. In M. M. Gill (Ed.) *The collected papers of David Rapaport* (pp. 778–794). New York: Basic Books, 1967.

———(1960a). The structure of psychoanalytic theory: A systematizing attempt. *Psychological Issues*, Monograph 6. First published in S. Koch (Ed.) (1959), *Psychology: A study of a science* (Vol. 1). New York: McGraw-Hill.

———(1960b). Psychoanalysis as a developmental psychology. In M. M. Gill (Ed.), *The collected papers of David Rapaport* (pp. 820–852). New York: Basic Books, 1967.

———(1960c). On the psychoanalytic theory of motivation. In M. M. Gill (Ed.) *The collected papers of David Rapaport* (pp. 853–915). New York: Basic Books, 1967.

———(1967a). Edward Bibring's theory of depression. In M. M. Gill (Ed.) *The collected papers of David Rapaport* (pp. 758–773). New York: Basic Books, 1967.

———(1967b). Obituary: Leo Berman, M.D., April 13, 1913—December 27, 1958. In M. M. Gill (Ed.) *The collected papers of David Rapaport* (pp. 812–819). New York: Basic Books, 1967.

———& Gill M. M. (1959). The points of view and assumptions of metapsychology. *International Journal of Psychoanalysis*, 40, 153–62. Also in M. M. Gill (Ed.), *The collected papers of David Rapaport* (pp. 795–811). New York: Basic Books, 1967.

———& Schafer, R. (1946). The psychological internship training program of the Menninger Clinic. In M. M. Gill (Ed.), *The collected papers of David Rapaport* (pp. 230–236). New York: Basic Books, 1967.

———, Gill M. M., & Schafer, R. (1945–46). *Diagnostic psychological testing,* (Vols. 1–2). Chicago: Yearbook Publishers.

———, Schafer, R., & Gill, M. M. (1944–1946). *Manual of diagnostic psychological testing* (Vols. 1–2). New York: Josiah Macy, Jr., Foundation.

———& Gill M. M. (1959). The points of view and assumptions of metapsychology. *International Journal of Psychoanalysis*, 40, 153–62. Also in M. M. Gill (Ed.). *The collected papers of David Rapaport* (pp. 795–811). New York: Basic Books, 1967.

———,———, & Schafer, R. (1968). *Diagnostic psychological testing* (rev. ed. by R. R. Holt). New York: International Universities Press.

Richards, A. D. (2015). Extenders, modifiers and heretics, In A. A. Lynch (Ed.), *Psychoanalysis: Critical conversations, the selected papers of Arnold D. Richards,* Vol. 1. New York: IPBooks.

Richter, C. P. (1953). Experimentally produced behavior reactions to food poisoning in wild and domesticated rats. *Annual of New York Academy of Science*, 556, 225–39.

———(1957). Phenomenon of sudden death in animals and man. *Psychosomatic Medicine*, 19, 191–98.

———(1959). Rats, man and the welfare state. *American Psychology*, 14, 18–28.

Riesen, A. H., & Clark, G. (1973). Chimpanzees reared in darkness. *American Anthropologist, 75,* 2027–2028.

Riesman, D. Glazer, N., & Denney, R. (1950). *The lonely crowd: A study of the changing American character.* New Haven: Yale University Press, 2001. (Reprint).

Rock, I. (1983). *The logic of perception.* Cambridge, MA: MIT Press/Bradford Books.

———& Kaufman, L. (1962). The moon illusion II, *Science, 136,* 1023–1031.

Rodrigue, E. M. (1956). Notes on menstruation. *International Journal of Psychoanalysis, 37,* 328–334.

Rubinstein, B. B. (1952). On the psychoanalytic concept of sexuality. In R. R. Holt (Ed.), *Psychoanalysis and the philosophy of science, collected papers of Benjamin B. Rubinstein, M.D.* Madison, CT: International Universities Press, 1997. Also *Psychological Issues,* Monograph 62/63.

Ruff, G. E. (1956). A critique of Kenneth Mark Colby's *Energy and structure in psychoanalysis. Behavioral Science,* 1.2 (Apr 1, 1956), 143.

Schachtel, E. G. (1959). *Metamorphosis: On the development of affect, perception, attention, and memory.* New York: Basic Books.

———(1966). *Experiential foundations of Rorschach's test.* New York: Basic Books.

Schachter, S., & Burdick, H. (1955). A field experiment on rumor transmission. *Journal of Abnormal and Social Psychology, 3,* 363–371.

Schafer, R. (1954). *Psychoanalytic interpretation in Rorschach testing.* New York: Grune & Stratton.

Schein, E. (1957). The effects of sleep deprivation on performance in a simulated communication task. *Journal of Applied Psychology, 41,* 247–252.

Schilder, P. (1930). Studies concerning the psychology and symptomatology of general paresis. In D. Rapaport (Ed. & Trans.), *Organization and pathology of thought* (pp. 519–580). New York: Columbia University Press, 1951.

———(1953). *Medical psychology* (D. Rapaport, Trans.). New York: International Universities Press. (Original work published 1924)

Schimek, J. G., & Wachtel, P. L. (1969). An exploration of the effects of distraction, competing tasks, and cognitive style on attention deployment. *Perceptual and Motor Skills, 28,* 567–574.

Schlesinger, H. J. (1954). Cognitive attitudes in relation to susceptibility to interference. *Journal of Personality, 22,* 354–374.

Schwartz, F., & Rouse, R. O. (1961). The activation and recovery of associations. *Psychological Issues,* Monograph 9. New York: International Universities Press.

———& Schiller, P. H. (1970). A psychoanalytic model of attention and learning. *Psychological Issues,* Monograph 23. New York: International Universities Press.

Sears, R. R., Maccoby, E. E., & Levin, H. (1957). *Patterns of child rearing.* Evanston, IL: Row, Peterson & Company.

Shakow, D. (1947). *The nature of deterioration in schizophrenic conditions.* New York: Nervous and Mental Disease Publications.

———& Rapaport, D. (1964). *The influence of Freud on American psychology.* New York: International Universities Press. Also in *Psychological Issues,* Monograph 13.

Shapiro, D. (1956). Color-response and perceptual passivity. *Journal of Projective Techniques, 20,* 52–69.

Sheldon, W. H. (1949). Varieties of delinquent youth. *Journal of Abnormal and Social Psychology, 45,* 790–795.

Shneidman, E. S. (1952). D. J. van Lennep. *TAT Newsletter, 6,* 1.

Skinner, B. F. (1953). *Science and human behavior.* New York: Macmillan.

Spence, D. (1982). *Narrative truth and historical truth: Meaning and interpretation in psychoanalysis.* New York: Norton.

Stein, M. I. (1949). Personality factors involved in the temporal development of Rorschach responses. *Rorschach Research Exchange and Journal of Projective Techniques,* Dec. 13 (4), 355–414.

Syrkin, M. (1948). *Blessed is the match: The story of Jewish resistance.* London: Victor Gollancz.

Thurber, J. (1950). *The thirteen clocks.* New York: New York Review of Books Publishers.

Tresselt, M. E., & Mayzner, M. S. (1954). A further experiment in the recognition of ego-involved materials. *The Journal of Psychology:*

Interdisciplinary and Applied, Jan, 1954.

Van Ormer, E. B. (1933). Sleep and retention. *Psychological Bulletin, 30,* 415–439.

Vernon, J., & Hoffman, J. (1956). Effect of sensory deprivation on learning rate in human beings. *Science,* 123, 1074.

Wachtel, P. L. (1969). Psychology, metapsychology, and psychoanalysis. *Journal of Abnormal Psychology,* 74, 651–660.

Wallerstein, R. A. *(1986) Forty-two lives in treatment: A study of psychoanalysis and psychotherapy.* New York: Guilford.

———(1988). Assessment of structural change in psychoanalytic therapy and research. *Journal of the American Psychoanalytic Association* 36 (Suppl.), 241–261.

———(1997). Merton Gill, psychotherapy, and psychoanalysis: A personal dialogue. *Journal of the American Psychoanalytic Association,* 45:230–256.

Weber, A. O., & Rapaport, D. (1941). Teleology and the emotions. *Philosophy of Science,* 8, 69–82. In M. M. Gill (Ed.) *The collected papers of David Rapaport* (pp. 80–90). New York: Basic Books, 1967.

Wechsler, D. (1939). *Wechsler-Bellevue intelligence scale.* New York: Psychological Corporation.

———(1955). *Wechsler adult intelligence scale.* New York: Psychological Corporation.

Werner, H. (1940). *Comparative psychology of mental development.* New York: Harper.

White, R. W. (September 1959). Motivation reconsidered: The concept of competence. *Psychological Review,* 66(5): 297–333.

———(1963). Ego and reality in psychoanalytic theory: A proposal regarding independent ego energies. *Psychological Issues,* Monograph 11.

Whitehead, A. N. (1925). *Science and the modern world.* New York: Free Press.

Wiener, N. (1948). *Cybernetics, or control and communication in the animal and the machine.* New York: Wiley.

Witkin, H. A., & Goodenough, D. R. (1977). Field dependence and interpersonal behavior. *Psychological Bulletin,* 84, 661–689.

Wolff, P. H. (1966). The causes, controls, and organization of behavior in the neonate. *Psychological Issues*, Monograph 17.

Zeigarnik, B. (1927). Das Behalten von erledigten und unerledigten Handlungen. In K. Lewin (Ed.), Untersuchungen zur Handlungs und Affektpsychologie. *Psychologische Forschung*, *9*, 1–85.

www.ingramcontent.com/pod-product-compliance
Lightning Source LLC
Chambersburg PA
CBHW060302030426
42336CB00011B/907